HOW ACCOUNTING WORKS

A Guide for the Perplexed

James Don Edwards, Ph.D., C.P.A.
J. M. Tull Professor of Accounting
The University of Georgia

Roger H. Hermanson, Ph.D., C.P.A.
Research Professor of Accounting
Georgia State University

R. F. Salmonson, Ph.D., C.P.A.
Professor of Accounting
Michigan State University

Peter R. Kensicki, D.B.A., CPCU, CLU
Director of Producer Education
American Institute for Property
and Liability Underwriters, Inc.

DOW JONES-IRWIN
Homewood, Illinois   60430

ISBN 0-87094-394-4

Library of Congress Catalog Card No. 82–73625

Printed in the United States of America

2 3 4 5 6 7 8 9 0 MP 0 9 8 7 6 5 4

Preface

There are three purposes of this book:

1. To *present* the essential subject matter of accounting to nonaccountants in simple language.
2. To enable you to *understand* the concepts presented as they apply to you.
3. To enable you to use your understanding to *communicate* with accountants.

This book is designed for use in the following situations:

Self-study by persons desiring an understanding of the essentials of accounting.

Company in-house training programs to familiarize nonaccounting managers and executives with accounting concepts and terminology.

College and university continuing education programs for nonaccountants designed to give participants an introductory understanding of accounting.

Certain short courses offered to students for credit by business colleges and junior colleges or to nonbusiness students in a college or university.

Both financial accounting and managerial accounting topics are covered. Financial accounting is concerned with the preparation of financial statements to be used by persons outside the company for decision making. Managerial accounting is concerned with in-house accounting reports and analyses to be used by persons inside the company (managers) for internal decision making.

The subject matter is presented in three major parts consisting of 12 chapters. The main parts and chapter titles are:

Part I   Basic Concepts
     Chapter 1   Introduction to Accounting Concepts
     Chapter 2   The Process of Accumulating Financial Information

Part II   Income Measurement and Balance Sheet
     Chapter 3   Income Measurement in Merchandising Companies
     Chapter 4   Noncurrent Assets
     Chapter 5   Stockholders' Equity and Long-Term Liabilities
     Chapter 6   Analysis and Interpretation of Financial Statements; the Statement of Changes in Financial Position

These topics have been selected because experience indicates they are the most interesting and relevant to the nonaccountant. Each chapter begins with chapter goals so that you clearly know what you should be able to do with the material presented. The corporate form of organization is used throughout to illustrate the accounting concepts. While the concepts also pertain to the sole proprietor and partnership forms, most readers will have need for understanding the corporate form and its accounting features.

At the end of each chapter there are *questions, exercises,* and *business decision problems* relating to the subject material in the chapter. These are included to give you a chance to apply the material to real-life situations and to develop the skills necessary to use accounting in your day-to-day activities (the answers to these are at the end of each chapter). It normally takes about one hour to read a chapter. Depending on how many of the questions, exercises, and business decision problems you choose to answer, another one to two hours may be spent working on the end-of-chapter items.

We envision the use of the book in various situations. For example, this book could be used in a 12-week in-house training program in a company; a short course offered in a business college or junior college; or a quarter-length course for nonbusiness students. Each class session would cover one chapter per week. The class sessions would discuss the questions, exercises, and business decision problems in the book.

This book could also be used in a three-day in-house company training program or a continuing education program in a college or university. In such a situation, each day would be spent discussing four chapters. A few of the questions, exercises, and business decision problems could be assigned and discussed during the day.

Various other arrangements for using these materials may develop. Adjustments of the plans can be made to accommodate these situations. In-house company training programs of shorter duration could be conducted by eliminating certain chapters, depending on the emphasis given to the course. For example, a merchandising company might eliminate Chapters 7, 8, and 12, while a manufacturing company might eliminate Chapter 3 and any others not suiting its situation. Alternatively, all of the chapters could be covered but less time spent on each one.

The materials might also be used for a conference lasting less than three days. For instance, Chapters 7 and 8 could be covered for a one-day conference on manufacturing accounting. In fact, these materials have been used in such a presentation to a large computer company. This company had developed a software package for use by manufacturing companies in their accounting and production control functions. Chapters 7 and 8 served to provide the accounting background necessary to understand what the software package was designed to accomplish.

Other possibilities for short conferences also exist:

Chapters 1 and 2 could be used to convey a basic understanding of bookkeeping and the accounting cycle.

Chapter 3 could be used to illustrate accounting problems encountered in a merchandising company.

Chapters 4, 5, and 12 could be used in discussing long-term assets and the long-term financing of those assets.

Chapter 6 could be used in a session on understanding financial statements and their usefulness in evaluating a company's financial situation. If more background were needed, Chapters 1, 2, and possibly 3 could also be covered.

Chapters 9–12 could be used in a conference on planning and performance evaluation.

Again, these are merely suggestive of the many ways in which the materials in this book may be used. We have designed those materials to fit many needs and would be interested in knowing precisely how you used them and how well your program worked out.

The materials in this book have been used for many years in a variety of practical learning situations. In that sense, they have been thoroughly tested for their accuracy and effectiveness. But no materials are ever perfect. If you have suggestions for improvement, please send them to one of the authors in care of the publisher.

We wish you the best of success in achieving an understanding of accounting so that you can communicate with accountants. Thank you for using our book.

James Don Edwards
Roger H. Hermanson
R. F. Salmonson
Peter R. Kensicki

Contents

PART ONE

Basic Concepts

1

Introduction to Accounting Concepts

Chapter Goals

When you have completed Chapter 1, you should be able to:

1. Define accounting and identify the major classes of users of accounting information and the types of decisions they use accounting information to make.
2. Describe the content and use of the balance sheet and income statement.
3. Identify the types of financial information included in the balance sheet and income statement.
4. Identify transactions, analyze them, and incorporate their effects into the basic accounting equation.

Many executives not trained in accounting often find it difficult to understand and solve a problem they face. The reason may be that the problem is stated in accounting terms and requires the use of accounting information for its solution. The problem may also involve direct contact with accountants who, it seems, speak a language understandable only to other accountants. This book is directed toward executives and others who seek to understand accounting and the ways that it can be useful in solving problems or making decisions in a business setting.

Accountants and the statements they generate are a primary source of information on economic and business activity. Because economic activity includes the production, exchange, and consumption of scarce goods, accounting information is found everywhere in our society. Thus, wherever economic resources are used, an accounting is likely to be required to show what was accomplished at what cost or sacrifice. This is true whether the resources are used by individuals, business firms, units of government, churches, or hospitals.

ACCOUNTING DEFINED

Accounting is a process that measures and reports financial information about businesses and other economic entities to interested parties. Most accounting information is stated in monetary terms and is designed to be useful in making economic decisions. These decisions are made by persons both within and outside the firm.

Internal Users and Their Decisions

In most companies, accounting information is used by managers who make decisions. These decisions can be classified into four major types:

1. Financing decisions—deciding what amounts of capital are needed and whether the capital is to be obtained from owners or creditors.
2. Resource allocation decisions—deciding how the total capital of a firm is to be invested, such as the amount invested in a computer.
3. Production decisions—deciding what products are to be produced, by what means, and when.
4. Marketing decisions—such as setting selling prices and advertising budgets or determining where a firm's markets are and how they are to be reached.

Managerial accounting provides the information for these decisions. The information generated must be useful for its purpose and cost no more to generate than it is worth. In form, managerial accounting information may be general (for use in long-range planning) or detailed (for use in cost control). The uses of managerial accounting information are varied:

Decision making by managers charged with successful operations of the specific division to which the information relates.

Motivational communications to indicate targets for operations and benchmarks of success.

Measuring success of management, managers, divisions within the company, individual products, and so forth.

Planning in both the long and short range.

For internal use by management, managerial accounting information generally is narrow in focus. It usually relates to a part of the company's operation, such as single account (Accounts Receivable), product line (brake linings), plant or retail location (Appliance Motor Division in De Kalb, Illinois), or department (employee benefits).

External Users and Their Decisions

The external users of accounting information and the types of questions for which they seek answers can be classified as:

1. Stockholders, prospective stockholders in a corporation, and their advisers—financial analysts and investment counselors. Should an ownership interest be acquired in this firm? Or, if one is now held, should it be increased, decreased, or retained at its present level? Has the firm earned satisfactory profits?
2. Creditors and lenders. Should a loan be granted to the firm? Will the firm be able to pay its debts as they become due?
3. Employees and their unions. Does the firm have the ability to pay increased wages? Is the firm financially able to provide permanent employment?
4. Customers. Is this firm offering desirable goods and services at reasonable prices? Will the firm survive to honor its product warranties?
5. Governmental units. Is a public utility earning a fair rate of return on its capital investment? Can a firm install costly pollution control equipment and remain profitable?

Financial statements provide information on a firm's financial condition (or position), on changes in this position, and on the results of operations (profitability). Many companies publish these statements in an *annual report*. This report contains the auditor's opinion as to the fairness of the financial statements, as well as other information about a company's activities, products, profits by major segments or divisions, and plans.

Financial accounting information generally relates to the firm as a whole, since outsiders can make decisions only on matters pertaining to the firm in its entirety, such as whether to extend credit to it. Such information, usually historical, is a report upon what has happened. Because interfirm comparisons are often made, the information supplied must conform to certain standards, called generally accepted accounting principles (GAAP).

FINANCIAL REPORTING BY BUSINESS ENTERPRISES

The three most common financial statements are the *balance sheet,* the *income statement,* and the *statement of changes in financial position.*

The Balance Sheet

The balance sheet (often called the statement of financial position) presents measures of the assets and equities (also called liabilities and owners' equity) in a business firm as of a specific moment in time. *Assets* are things of value; they constitute the *resources* of the firm. They have value to the firm because of the uses to which they can be put or the things that can be acquired by exchanging them. In Illustration 1.1, the assets of the Mills

Illustration 1.1

MILLS COMPANY
Balance Sheet
July 31, 19x2

Assets			Liabilities and Stockholders' Equity		
Current assets:			Current liabilities:		
Cash................	$12,470		Accounts payable.....	$ 600	
Accounts receivable...	700		Notes payable........	3,000	
		$13,170			$ 3,600
Property, plant, and			Stockholders' equity:		
equipment:			Capital stock.........	$30,000	
Delivery equipment....	$20,000		Retained earnings	2,070	
Office equipment	2,500				$32,070
		22,500	Total liabilities and		
Total assets...........		$35,670	stockholders' equity...		$35,670

Company amount to $35,670. They consist of *current assets* of cash and accounts receivable (amounts due from customers) and *property, plant, and equipment* consisting of delivery equipment and office equipment. *Current assets* consist of cash and other short-lived assets reasonably expected to be converted into cash or to be consumed or used up in the operations of the business within a short period, usually one year.[1] *Property, plant, and equip-*

---

[1] Technically speaking, the time period is one operating cycle or one year, whichever is longer. An operating cycle is the length of time that it takes cash spent for inventory to come back to the selling company in the form of cash collections from customers. Thus, in some industries (distilling and life insurance, for example) the operating cycle extends for a number of years.

ment refers to relatively long-lived assets that are to be used in the production or sale of other assets or services rather than being sold.

Liabilities are the debts owed by a firm. Typically, they must be paid at certain known moments in time. The liabilities of the Mills Company are both relatively short-lived *current liabilities*. They consist of accounts payable (amounts owed to suppliers) and notes payable (written promises to pay) totaling $3,600. Other firms may have *long-term liabilities* on their balance sheets. Such long-term liabilities could include mortgages or bonds due in periods beyond one year.

The Mills Company is a corporation. It is customary to refer to the owners' interest in a corporation as *stockholders' equity*.[2] The Mills Company's stockholders' equity consists of $30,000 paid in for shares of capital stock and retained earnings (earnings not paid out to stockholders) of $2,070. All of these items will be discussed later in the text. At this point, simply note that thé balance sheet heading includes the name of the organization, the title of the statement, and the date of the statement. Also note that the claims upon or interests in assets equal the assets—an equality explained later in this chapter.

The Income Statement

The purpose of the *income statement* (sometimes called an earnings statement) is to report upon the profitability of a business organization for a stated period of time. In accounting, *profitability* is measured by comparing the *revenues generated* in a period with the *expenses incurred* to produce those revenues.

Revenue is defined as the inflow of assets resulting from the delivery of products or the rendering of services to customers. As discussed in Chapter 3, many firms earn their revenues by selling their customers tangible products, such as automobiles, office equipment, cameras, or paint. Others, called service firms or businesses, earn their revenues in the form of fees or commissions by rendering various types of services to customers, such as the fees for the professional services rendered by accountants, architects, lawyers, or physicians or commissions from the sale of life, property, and casualty insurance or real estate. Other types of services generate revenues for other firms—the interest earned by banks and small loan companies, the premiums received by insurance companies, the admissions charged by theaters, or the rents collected by firms owning apartment buildings. The reve-

---

[2] The other two types of business entities found in our society are the single or sole proprietorship (an unincorporated business owned by one individual) and the partnership (a business owned jointly by two or more individuals). In the former, the owner's interest would be reported as "Jim Mills, Capital." In the partnership, the owners' interest would be identified as "Partners' Capital," if there were many partners. If there were only a few partners, each partner's ownership interest could be stated separately.

nues earned are measured by the value of the assets customers are willing to surrender for the products or services received.

Expense is defined as the sacrifice made or the cost incurred to generate revenues. The expenses incurred can be classified into a number of categories that differ among firms. Common expense categories are wages and salaries, utilities (gas, oil, electricity, telephone, and water), insurance, taxes (both on property and on income or earnings), supplies used, advertising, and interest. Expense is measured by the cost of the assets surrendered or consumed in serving customers.

The process of comparing the revenues earned with the expenses incurred is referred to as *matching*. Expenses are matched against revenues to determine net income. If revenues exceed expenses, net income results. If the reverse is true, the business is operating at a loss. Illustration 1.2 contains

Illustration 1.2

MILLS COMPANY
Income Statement
For the Month of July 19x2

Service revenues		$5,700
Expenses:		
Wages	$2,600	
Gas and oil	400	
Rent.	300	
Advertising	200	
Utilities.	100	
Interest.	30	3,630
Net income		$2,070

The heading of an income statement always states the time period covered by the statement.

the statement of the Mills Company for the month of July 19x2. It shows that revenues in the amount of $5,700 were generated by serving customers. Expenses for the month amounted to $3,630, resulting in net income before taxes for the month of $2,070.

The Statement of Changes in Financial Position

Information on the *financing and investing activities* of a business may be helpful in appraising its continued profitability and solvency. Typically, a business needs cash to conduct its daily operations (pay for its expenses), to pay debts that become due, and to expand and invest. The needed cash is usually secured from owner investment, from borrowing, or from operation of the business. The statement that reports on the financing and investing activities of a business is called the *statement of changes in financial position*. Such a statement must be presented whenever an income statement and a balance sheet are published. The statement of changes in financial position is discussed and illustrated in Chapter 6.

THE FINANCIAL ACCOUNTING PROCESS

Now that the three principal financial statements have been briefly introduced, attention is directed to the process underlying such statements.

The Accounting Equation

In the balance sheet presented in Illustration 1.1, the total assets of the Mills Company are equal to its equities (liabilities and stockholders' equity). This equality follows from the basic assumption in accounting that the assets of a business are equal to the equities in those assets; that is, Assets = Equities. Assets have already been defined simply as things of value. In a more sophisticated sense, the accountant designates and records as assets all those economic resources owned by a business which can be measured. All desired things, except those available in unlimited quantity without cost or effort, are economic resources.

Equities are interests in, or claims upon, assets. For example, assume that you purchased a new automobile for $9,000 by withdrawing $900 from your savings account and borrowing $8,100 from your credit union. Your equity in the automobile is $900 and that of your credit union is $8,100. The $8,100 can be further described as a liability. Your $900 equity is often described as the owner's equity or the residual equity or interest in the asset. Since, in the case of a corporation, the owners are the stockholders, the basic equation becomes:

$$\text{Assets} = \text{Liabilities} + \text{Stockholders' equity}$$

This equation must always be in balance. The sum of the interests in assets must always be equal to the assets themselves. It is intuitively logical to hold that everything of value belongs to someone or to some organization.

The right side of the equation shows the sources of the existing stock of assets. Thus, liabilities are not only claims to assets but also sources of assets. In a corporation, all of the assets are provided by either creditors (liability holders) or owners (stockholders).

As a business engages in economic activity, the dollar amounts and the composition of its assets, liabilities, and stockholders' equity change, but the equality of the basic equation always holds.

Transaction Analysis

Our society is characterized by exchange. That is, most of the goods and services produced are exchanged rather than consumed by their producers.

Thus, much of the economic activity of society can be observed from the exchanges that take place. In accounting, these exchanges (as well as other changes) are called *transactions*. They provide much of the raw data entered in the accounting system. There are two major reasons why this is so. First, an exchange is a readily observable event providing good evidence that activity has occurred. Second, an exchange usually takes place at an agreed-upon price, and this price provides a highly objective measure of the economic activity that has transpired. Thus, the analysis of transactions is an important part of the accounting process.

To illustrate the analysis of transactions and their effects upon the basic accounting equation, the activities of the Mills Company that led to the statements in Illustrations 1.1 and 1.2 are discussed. Assume that the Mills Company was organized as a corporation on July 1, 19x2, and that in its first transaction it issued, for $30,000 cash, shares of capital stock to Jim Mills, his wife, and their son. Analyzed, the transaction increased the assets (cash) of the Mills Company by $30,000 and increased its equities (the capital stock element of stockholders' equity) by $30,000. Consequently, the transaction yields a basic accounting equation containing the following:

$$\underset{\text{(Cash, \$30,000)}}{\text{Assets}} \quad = \text{Liabilities} + \quad \underset{\text{(Capital stock, \$30,000)}}{\text{Stockholders' equity}}$$

A balance sheet could be prepared, if needed, at this time. If prepared, it would report one current asset—Cash in the amount of $30,000—and one stockholders' equity item—Capital Stock in the amount of $30,000. There are two points to emphasize: (1) financial statements can be prepared at any time, if needed; and (2) every transaction has two effects which can be recorded solely in balance sheet accounts, as they are called.

As its next transaction, the company borrowed $6,000 from Mrs. Mills' father, giving its written promise (called a note) to repay the amount in one year. As a result, the assets are increased by $6,000 and, since the written promise to repay is a liability, the liabilities are increased by $6,000, yielding a basic equation of:

$$\underset{\text{(Cash, \$36,000)}}{\text{Assets}} \quad = \quad \underset{\text{(Notes payable, \$6,000)}}{\text{Liabilities}} \quad + \quad \underset{\text{(Capital stock, \$30,000)}}{\text{Stockholders' equity}}$$

As its third transaction, the Mills Company purchases three delivery trucks for $20,000 and some office equipment for $1,500. In this transaction, the company received the trucks priced at $20,000 and office equipment priced at $1,500 and gave up cash of $21,500. This transaction thus does not change the totals in the basic equation; it merely changes the composition of the assets. The equation becomes:

Assets		=	Liabilities	+	Stockholders' equity	
Cash...........	$14,500					
Delivery						
equipment	20,000		Notes payable ...	$6,000	Capital stock	$30,000
Office equipment	1,500					
	$36,000	=		$6,000 +		$30,000

Assume that, as transaction 4 in the month of July, the Mills Company purchased an additional $1,000 of office equipment, agreeing to pay for it within 10 days after receiving a bill from the supplier. This transaction increases assets, in the form of office equipment, by $1,000 and increases liabilities, in the form of accounts payable (which are amounts owed to creditors for items purchased from them), by $1,000. The items making up the totals in the accounting equation now appear as:

Assets		=	Liabilities	+	Stockholders' equity	
Cash	$14,500					
Delivery						
equipment.......	20,000		Accounts payable ...	$1,000	Capital stock.......	$30,000
Office equipment ...	2,500		Notes payable	6,000		
	$37,000	=		$7,000 +		$30,000

Revenue and Expense Transactions

Thus far the transactions have consisted of the acquisition or exchange of assets either by borrowing or by stockholder investment. But a business is not formed merely to acquire assets. Rather, it seeks to use those assets to earn income. This is accomplished by providing customers with goods or services, with the expectation that the value of the assets received from customers will exceed the cost of the assets consumed or surrendered in serving them. This total flow of assets for services rendered or goods delivered (as measured by assets received from customers) has been defined as *revenue*. The cost of serving customers is called *expense*. Expense is measured by the cost of the assets surrendered or consumed. If revenues exceed expenses, net income exists. If not, a loss has been suffered.

Assume that, as its fifth transaction in July, the Mills Company renders delivery services for some of its customers for $4,800 cash. Cash has increased by $4,800, but what other change has occurred which, if properly recorded, would reflect the appropriate analysis of this transaction? Note that there is no increase in liabilities brought about by the rendering of the services, nor were any assets parted with. This leaves an increase in stockholders' equity of $4,800 as the only possible answer. More important, the basic objective of a business corporation in providing customers with goods and services is to bring about an increase in stockholders' equity. More will be said about this later.

Incorporating the effects of the revenue transaction yields the following basic equation:

Assets		=	Liabilities		+	Stockholders' equity	
Cash	$19,300		Accounts			Capital	
Delivery equip-			payable	$1,000		stock	$30,000
ment.......	20,000		Notes			Retained	
Office equip-			payable	6,000		earnings	4,800 (Service
ment	2,500						revenue)
	$41,800	=		$7,000	+		$34,800

The increase in stockholders' equity brought about by the revenue transaction is recorded as a separate item, "Retained earnings." It is further identified as "Service revenue" to aid in preparing the income statement. It cannot be recorded as capital stock because no additional shares of stock were issued. The expectation is that revenue transactions will yield net income. If net income is not distributed to stockholders, it is in fact retained, and the title "retained earnings" is used. Subsequent chapters will show that, because of complexities in handling large numbers of transactions, revenues will be shown as affecting retained earnings only at the end of an accounting period. The procedure presented above is a shortcut used to explain why the accounting equation remains in balance.

Assume that, as its sixth transaction in July, the Mills Company performs services for a customer who agrees to pay $900 at a later date. The transaction consists of an exchange of services for a promise by the customer to pay later. It is similar to the preceding transaction in that stockholders' equity is increased because revenues have been earned. It differs because cash has not been received. If revenue earned is not recorded until cash is received, the *cash basis of accounting* is being used. Under this basis, which is generally not acceptable, revenues are recorded only when cash is received. The generally accepted *accrual basis of accounting* requires that transactions like this one be recorded as earned revenue. Under the accrual basis, revenues are recorded when a valid asset is received for services rendered. In this case, the asset received is the claim upon the customer, the right to collect the amount due at a later date. Technically, such claims are called *accounts receivable*. The accounting equation, including this item, is:

Assets		=	Liabilities		+	Stockholders' equity	
Cash	$19,300		Accounts			Capital	
Accounts			payable	$1,000		stock	$30,000
receivable ..	900		Notes			Retained	
Delivery equip-			payable	6,000		earnings	5,700 (Service
ment	20,000						revenue)
Office equip-							
ment.......	2,500						
	$42,700	=		$7,000	+		$35,700

To illustrate one more step (transaction 7) in regard to accounts receivable, assume that $200 is collected from the customer "on account," to use business terminology. The transaction consists of giving up a claim upon the customer in exchange for cash. The effects of the transaction are to increase cash to $19,500 and to decrease accounts receivable to $700. This transaction consists solely of a change in the composition of the assets, not of an increase in assets resulting from the generation of revenue.

Attention may now be directed to expenses. Suppose (transaction 8) that the Mills Company paid its employees $2,600 for services received in conducting business operations during the month of July. The transaction consists of an exchange of cash for employee services. The accountant treats the transaction as a decrease in both an asset and stockholders' equity.

Expenses are recorded here as reductions of stockholders' equity because they are matched with the increase recorded there from the earning of revenue. For any given period of time, the net effect from operations on stockholders' equity will be determined by which is larger—expenses or revenues.

Further assume (as transactions 9 and 10) that the Mills Company paid cash of $300 as rent for truck storage space and office space and that it paid its utilities bill for July in the amount of $100. The payments cause a decrease in the asset cash of $400 and a decrease in stockholders' equity of $400 because of the incurrence of rent expense of $300 and utilities expense of $100. Incorporating these two items and the wages of $2,600 into the accounting equation, it now reads:

Assets		=	Liabilities		+	Stockholders' equity			
Cash..........	$16,500		Accounts			Capital stock ..	$30,000		
Accounts			payable	$1,000		Retained			
receivable ...	700		Notes payable ..	6,000		earnings	2,700	Service	
Delivery								revenue	$5,700
equipment...	20,000							Less expenses:	
Office								Wages	2,600
equipment...	2,500							Rent........	300
	$39,700 =			$7,000 +			$32,700	Utilities	100

Because of their similar effects, transactions 11 and 12 of the Mills Company may be treated together. Assume the company received a bill for gasoline, oil, and other delivery equipment supplies consumed during the month in the amount of $400 and a bill for $200 for advertising in July. Both transactions would be treated as involving an increase in a liability, accounts payable, and a decrease in stockholders' equity because of the incurrence of an expense. These expenses are recorded even though they did not involve an immediate cash payment. To require a cash payment before recording an expense is to apply the cash basis of accounting. The accrual basis of accounting requires that expenses be recorded as incurred, whether or not there is a concurrent cash payment. The accrual basis leads to a better matching of expenses and revenues in the determination of net income. The accounting equation depicting the financial position of the Mills Company now reads:

Assets		=	Liabilities		+	Stockholders' equity				
Cash.........	$16,500		Accounts			Capital stock ..	$30,000	Service		
Accounts			payable	$1,600		Retained		revenue.....	$5,700
receivable ...	700		Notes payable ..	6,000		earnings	2,100	Less expenses:	
Delivery								Wages......	2,600
equipment...	20,000							Rent........	300
Office								Utilities	100
equipment...	2,500							Gas and oil ..	400
	$39,700 =			$7,600 +			$32,100	Advertising ..	200

Next (transaction 13), the Mills Company paid the $1,000 balance due on the purchase of the office equipment (transaction 4). This reduced cash by $1,000 and reduced the debt owed to the equipment supplier, recorded as an account payable, by $1,000.

Finally (transaction 14), in reviewing his needs for cash at the end of the month, Mr. Mills decided he would not need as much cash as he now held. So he paid $3,000 on the note owed to his father-in-law, plus interest of $30 for the month. This transaction decreased cash by the total amount paid out, $3,030. Of this amount, $3,000 was applied to reduce the principal amount owed on the notes payable and the remaining $30 consisted of the payment of interest expense—an element that reduces retained earnings. This transaction illustrates how a certain transaction may affect assets, liabilities, and stockholders' equity at the same time.

Summary of Transactions

The effects of all the transactions entered into by the Mills Company in the first month of its existence upon its assets, liabilities, and stockholders' equity are summarized in Illustration 1.3. The ending balances in each of the columns are the dollar amounts reported in the balance sheet in Illustration 1.1. The itemized data in the retained earnings column are the revenue and expense items reported in the income statement in Illustration 1.2. This summary shows how the basic equation of Assets = Equities is subdivided into the five major elements of financial accounting: assets, liabilities, stockholders' equity, revenues, and expenses. As revenues and expenses impact stockholders' equity, sometimes a statement called the statement of retained earnings is prepared.

The Statement of Retained Earnings

The purpose of the statement of retained earnings is to explain the changes in retained earnings that occurred between two balance sheet dates. Usually, these changes consist of the addition of net income (or the deduc-

Illustration 1.3

MILLS COMPANY
Summary of Transactions
Month of July 19x2

Trans-action	Explanation	Cash	+	Accts. rec.	+	Del. equip.	+	Office equip.	=	Notes paya-ble	+	Accts. paya-ble	+	Capital stock	+	Re-tained earn-ings	
	Beginning balances	$ 0		$ 0		$ 0		$ 0		$ 0		$ 0		$ 0		$ 0	
(1)	Issued stock for cash	+30,000												+30,000			
(2)	Borrowed money on note	+ 6,000								+6,000							
(3)	Purchased equipment for cash	−21,500				+20,000		+1,500									
(4)	Purchased equipment on account							+1,000				+1,000					
(5)	Earned service revenue for cash	+ 4,800														+4,800	(Service revenue)
(6)	Earned service revenue on account			+900												+ 900	(Service revenue)
(7)	Collected cash on account	+ 200		−200													
(8)	Paid wages	− 2,600														−2,600	(Wages expense)
(9)	Paid rent	− 300														− 300	(Rent expense)
(10)	Paid utilities bill	− 100														− 100	(Utilities expense)
(11)	Received bill for gas and oil used											+ 400				− 400	(Gas and oil expense)
(12)	Received bill for July advertising											+ 200				− 200	(Advertising expense)
(13)	Paid equipment bill	− 1,000										−1,000					
(14)	Paid note and interest	− 3,030								−3,000						− 30	(Interest expense)
	Ending balances	$12,470	+	$700	+	$20,000	+	$2,500	=	$3,000	+	$ 600	+	$30,000	+	$2,070	
		$35,670								$3,600					$32,070		

tion of net loss) and the deduction of dividends. Dividends are the means by which a corporation rewards its stockholders for providing it with capital.

The effects of a cash dividend transaction are to reduce cash and retained earnings by the amount paid out. In effect, the earnings are no longer retained but have been passed on to the stockholders; and this is one of the primary reasons why stockholders organize corporations.

The statement of retained earnings for the Mills Company for the month of of July 19x2 would be quite simple. Since the company was organized on July 1, there would be no beginning retained earnings balance. Net income of $2,070 would be added, and since no dividends were paid, this sum would also be the ending balance.

To provide a more effective illustration, assume that the Mills Company's net income for August was $1,500 (revenues of $5,600 less expenses of $4,100) and that it declared and paid dividends of $1,000. Its statement of retained earnings for August is shown in Illustration 1.4.

Illustration 1.4

MILLS COMPANY
Statement of Retained Earnings
For the Month Ended August 31, 19x2

Retained earnings, July 31	$2,070
Add: Net income for August	1,500
	$3,570
Less: Dividends.	1,000
Retained earnings, August 31.	$2,570

(The statement of retained earnings may be replaced by a statement of changes in stockholders' equity when many changes occur in a variety of stockholder equity accounts, such as when there are a number of classes of stock outstanding.)

SUMMARY

The basic format of financial accounting statements, the flow of information, and how the information was summarized for the Mills Company were illustrated in this chapter. For managerial accounting, similar flows are recorded and summarized, but the format of presentation will be different because of the different uses managers have for their data. The next chapter will discuss the process of accumulating accounting data.

Questions

1. What is the primary objective of accounting?
2. How does accounting information usually enter into your decision-making process?

3. Distinguish briefly between financial accounting and managerial accounting.
4. Define asset, liability, and stockholders' equity.
5. How do liabilities and stockholders' equity differ? How are they similar?
6. Define revenue. How is revenue measured?
7. Define expense. How is expense measured?
8. What is the basic equation in accounting? Why must it always balance?
9. Illustrate how and explain why revenues affect the basic balance sheet equation of assets equal liabilities plus stockholders' equity.
10. What is a balance sheet? This statement generally provides information on what aspect of a business?
11. What is an income statement? This statement generally provides information on what aspect of a business?
12. What information does a statement of changes in financial position provide?
13. What information does a statement of retained earnings provide? What two statements does it link or tie together?

Exercises

1. Given the following account balances at December 31, 19x3, what is the name of the missing account, and what apparently is its balance?

Accounts payable	$15,000
Accounts receivable	10,000
Capital stock	40,000
Cash	5,000
Equipment	30,000
Land	20,000

2. Give examples of transactions that would have the following effects upon the elements in a firm's accounting system:
   a. Increase cash; decrease some other asset.
   b. Decrease cash; increase some other asset.
   c. Increase an asset; increase a liability.
   d. Increase an expense; decrease an asset.
   e. Increase an asset other than cash; increase a revenue.
   f. Decrease an asset; decrease a liability.
   g. Decrease cash; decrease stockholders' equity.
3. Assume that retained earnings increased $26,000 during the year, expenses amounted to $60,000, and dividends paid were $5,000. Compute the revenue for the year. Compute the net income for the year.
4. On December 31, 19x2, R Company had total assets of $360,000, liabilities of $160,000, capital stock of $150,000, and retained earnings of $50,000. During 19x3 R earned revenues of $240,000, incurred expenses of $196,000, and paid dividends of $15,000. Compute the retained earnings as of December 31, 19x3.
5. For each of the happenings below, determine whether or not it has an effect upon the basic accounting equation. For those that do, present an analysis of the transaction showing its effects clearly.
   a. Purchased supplies for cash, $1,000. They will be used next year.
   b. Purchased a truck for $10,000, payment to be made next month.
   c. Paid $200 cash for the current month's telephone bill.

    d. Paid for the truck purchased in *b.*

    e. Employed Don Kettler as a vice president at a salary of $4,000 per month. He starts work next week.

    f. Signed an agreement with a bank whereby the bank will lend the company up to $200,000 at any time within the next two years.

6. Which of the following transactions results in an increase in an expense or in a revenue in the current period?

    a. Cash of $20,000 was paid to employees for services received during the current period.

    b. Cash of $1,000 was paid to a supplier in settlement of the promise to pay that was given when some advertising supplies were purchased.

    c. Services were rendered for customers in the current period for which they were billed $5,000.

    d. Of the $5,000 billed in *c*, $4,500 was collected.

    e. Paid $10,000 of principal, plus $400 of interest on a note payable.

    f. Paid $50 as a refundable deposit when an additional telephone was installed.

7. At the start of the year, a company had liabilities of $36,000, capital stock of $80,000, and retained earnings of $20,000. Net income for the year was $30,000, and cash dividends of $10,000 were paid. Compute the stockholders' equity at the end of the year and the total assets at the beginning of the year.

8. Selected data for the Mork Company for the year 19x3 are as follows (including all income statement data):

Revenue from services rendered on account	$ 55,000
Revenue from services rendered for cash	15,000
Cash collected from customers on account	42,000
Retained earnings, January 1, 19x3	90,000
Expenses incurred on account	30,000
Expenses incurred for cash	20,000
Dividends paid	5,000
Cash received for additional stock issued	10,000
Retained earnings, December 31, 19x3	105,000

    a. Compute the net income for 19x3.

    b. Compute the net income for 19x3 by analyzing the appropriate stockholders' equity account.

9. If, during 19x2, retained earnings increased by $12,000, expenses amounted to $34,500, and dividends declared and paid were $5,000, what were the revenues and net income for the year?

Business Decision Problem 1-1

Upon graduation from high school, Bill Loma was employed by a builder of houses and small apartment buildings. During the next six years, Bill earned a reputation as an excellent employee, able to handle almost any job requiring carpentry, plumbing, electrical, and masonry skills faced in the light construction industry.

At this time, Bill decided to go into business for himself under the name of Bill's Fix-It Shop. He invested cash, some power tools, and a used truck in his business. He completed many repair and remodeling jobs for both homeowners and apartment owners. He operated out of his garage which he had converted into a shop, adding several new machines. The demand for his services was so large that he had more work than he could handle.

Three years after going into business for himself, Bill is faced with a decision of whether to continue on his own or to accept a position as construction supervisor for a home builder. He has been offered an annual salary of $40,000 and a package of "fringe benefits" (medical and hospitalization insurance, pension contribution, vacation pay, and life insurance) worth approximately $8,000 per year. The offer is very attractive to Bill. But he dislikes giving up his business since he thoroughly enjoyed "being his own boss," even though this often led to an average workweek well in excess of 40 hours.

Bill now comes to you for assistance in gathering the information needed to help him make a decision. Adequate accounting records have been maintained for his business by an experienced accountant.

Required:

Indicate the nature of the information Bill needs to make an informed decision. Pay particular attention to the information likely to be found in the accounting records of his business. Does the information available enter directly into the decision? Explain. Would you expect that Bill could sell his business assets for more or less than their recorded amount? Why?

Business Decision Problem 1-2

Given below are the May 31, 19x3, balance sheets of the A Company and the B Company, both of which were organized five years ago:

	A Company	B Company
Assets		
Cash	$ 20,000	$ 10,000
Accounts receivable	40,000	20,000
Land	100,000	50,000
Building	100,000	150,000
Equipment	50,000	80,000
Total assets	$310,000	$310,000
Liabilities and Stockholders' Equity		
Accounts payable	$ 20,000	$ 40,000
Notes payable (due in 60 days)	10,000	20,000
Capital stock	300,000	200,000
Retained earnings (deficit)	(20,000)	50,000
Total liabilities and stockholders' equity	$310,000	$310,000

Required:

a. Assume that you are a banker and have been asked for a $20,000, three-month loan by each of the above companies. To which company would you prefer to grant a loan? Why?

b. Assume that as a rather wealthy investor you have been offered all the outstanding capital stock of either or both companies. For which company would you be willing to pay the higher price? Why? (Base your answer solely on the information given.) What additional information would you consider absolutely essential in making the final decision to buy either or both of the above companies?

Solutions to End-of-chapter Questions, Exercises, and Business Decision Problems

Answers to Questions

1. The primary objective of accounting is to provide financial information about an economic entity that will help interested parties make decisions about the entity. For the most part, accounting information serves as a historical base from which to make projections about the future.
2. Answers vary based on student interest.
3. Financial accounting is concerned largely with reporting upon the financial position of a firm and upon its profitability to outsiders. Managerial accounting is concerned largely with providing information for internal use by the management of a firm. Financial accounting deals largely with providing a historical record of what happened, while managerial accounting focuses more upon planning where a firm is going. Financial accounting applies certain standards and principles across entities. Managerial accounting seeks to provide information that is useful and less costly than the benefits provided.
4. Simply stated, an asset is a thing of value to its owner. More strictly, the accountant records as assets those factors possessing service potential which can be measured. A liability is a debt of an entity, usually arising from past events or transactions. Stockholders' equity is the claim or interest of the stockholders in the assets of a business and is the residual equity or interest in the entity.
5. Liabilities and stockholders' equity differ in that the former usually have a maturity date, while the latter does not. They are similar in that they are both sources of the assets of the entity.
6. Revenue is the inflow of assets (or the increase in net assets) resulting from delivery of goods or rendering of services for customers. It is measured by the amount of assets customers agree to pay for the goods or services.
7. Expense is the cost incurred or the sacrifice made to generate revenue or, more simply, the cost of operating the business. Expense is measured by the cost of the assets consumed or given up or used up.
8. The basic equation in accounting is: Assets = Equities, which can be stated with equities subdivided to read: Assets = Liabilities + Stockholders' equity. The equation must always balance because the interests in (or claims to) assets must always be equal to the assets themselves.
9. Revenues increase assets, such as when a cash sale is made (increases the cash balance) or when a credit sale is made (increases accounts receivable). To balance the equation, a corresponding equity *must* increase. In the two examples, the Retained Earnings account of stockholders' equity would increase in the amount of the sale.

10. A balance sheet contains a classified array of the firm's assets, liabilities, and stockholders' equity as of a specific time. Such information is used to appraise the solvency of the firm.

11. The income statement reports on the revenues, expenses, and net income of the firm. Such information is essentially a report on the profitability of the firm.

12. The statement of changes in financial position reports upon the financing and investing activities of the firm. Such a report is needed because such activity cannot be readily seen from the balance sheet or the income statement.

13. The statement of retained earnings reports the beginning balance of retained earnings, the net income for the period, the dividends for the period, and the ending balance of retained earnings. It is the link between the income statement and the balance sheet.

Solutions to Exercises

1. The assets consist of Cash, $5,000, Accounts Receivable, $10,000, Land, $20,000, and Equipment, $30,000, for a total of $65,000. The equities consist of Accounts Payable, $15,000, Capital Stock, $40,000, and the missing item—Retained Earnings of $10,000.

2. a. Received cash as a payment on account by a customer.
   b. Purchased office equipment for cash.
   c. Purchased supplies on account.
   d. Paid cash for services rendered by employees.
   e. Rendered services for customers on account.
   f. Paid for machinery previously purchased on account.
   g. Paid a cash dividend to stockholders.

3. Net income = $26,000 + $5,000 = $31,000. Revenue = $60,000 + $31,000 = $91,000.

4. Net income = $240,000 − $196,000 = $44,000. Ending retained earnings = $50,000 + $44,000 − $15,000 = $79,000.

5. a. Increase asset; decrease asset.
   b. Increase asset; increase liability.
   c. Increase expense; decrease asset.
   d. Decrease asset; decrease liability.
   e. No effect.
   f. No effect.

6. (a) $20,000 of expense; (c) $5,000 of revenue; (e) $400 of expense.

7. Stockholders' equity at end of year: $100,000 + $30,000 − $10,000 = $120,000. Total assets at beginning of year: $36,000 + $80,000 + $20,000 = $136,000.

8. a. Revenues of $55,000 + $15,000 less expenses of $30,000 + $20,000 = net income of $20,000.

   b.
Retained earnings, December 31, 19x3	$105,000
Add: Dividends	5,000
	$110,000
Less: Retained earnings, January 1, 19x3	90,000
Net income for the year	$ 20,000

9. Net income: $12,000 + $5,000 = $17,000. Revenues: $34,500 + $17,000 = $51,500.

Solution to Business Decision Problem 1–1

Information needed to make an informed decision:

1. Present earnings from Bill's Fix-it Shop versus the $48,000 per year which Bill could earn as a construction supervisor.
2. Prospective future earnings from Bill's business versus prospective future salary and fringe benefits from the construction supervisor position offered.
3. The amount Bill could obtain from selling his business assets.
4. The value he places on being "his own boss" versus working as an employee for someone else. Also his feelings about risk should be considered.
5. The reputation and financial stability of the company which offered him the job as construction supervisor.
6. Knowledge of the people with whom he would be working as construction supervisor.
7. Opinions of family, friends, and knowledgeable persons regarding the decision to be made.

Only the information in (1) above could be obtained from Bill's accounting records. The comparison with the $48,000 amount to be earned as an employee would be useful, especially if the difference were larger. Possibly some indication of (3) would also be gained from these records. Bill probably may have to sell his business assets for less than the recorded amounts unless the effects of inflation are substantial.

Solution to Business Decision Problem 1–2

a. A Company would seem to be the better risk in granting a three-month loan because it has the better short-term debt-paying ability. It has more cash on hand, more accounts receivable, and less claims to meet in the very near future.
b. A Company would probably command the higher price based solely on the information available because it has the larger amount of stockholders' equity relative to total assets and the better short-term financial position. B Company appears to be in need of additional financing, and very soon. The one disturbing factor in the A Company information is the fact that the company has a deficit. The significance of the deficit can be made clear if the earnings history of the two companies is available. No decision should be made until this is known. Basically, it is earning power that gives value to assets and to companies.

2

The Process of Accumulating Financial Information

Chapter Goals

When you have completed Chapter 2, you should be able to:

1. Identify the basic classifying and storage unit for accounting information.
2. Define the terms *debit* and *credit* and explain how the effects of business transactions must first be expressed in these terms before they can be entered into accounting records.
3. Explain the use of the journal as the original record in which the effects of a business transaction are recorded.
4. Explain the process of journalizing a transaction and of posting journal entries to the accounts in the ledger.
5. Explain the use of a trial balance as a partial means of testing the accuracy of journalizing and posting.
6. Make adjustments required to bring the accounts up to date prior to the preparation of financial statements.
7. Explain the use of closing entries to remove from the accounts all of the expense and revenue accounts which are established for one accounting period and which are reported in the income statement.
8. Differentiate between the cash and accrual bases of accounting and explain the limited circumstances in which the cash basis is accepted.

In Chapter 1, the effects of business transactions as increases or decreases in the elements of the basic accounting equation were shown. This is an easy way to learn some basic relationships. But, because of the many transactions even a small business enters into, it is too clumsy an approach to be used in practice.

The goal of this chapter is to indicate the basic parts of an accounting system and to show how it operates to gather information for preparation of the financial statements. Knowing how the system functions will aid in understanding the end products of the system—the statements generated for managerial or financial purposes.

THE ACCOUNTING SYSTEM

The Account

Because every business engages in hundreds of transactions, the effects of these transactions must be classified and summarized to become useful information. The accountant's task is made easier because many business transactions are repetitive. The effects of transactions are classified into groups according to common traits. For example, many transactions involve the receipt or payment of cash. As a result, a part of every transaction affecting cash will be recorded and summarized in a Cash account. An account is set up whenever the data to be recorded in it will yield useful information. Thus, every business will have a Cash account simply because knowledge of the amount of cash owned is useful information.

An account may take a variety of forms, from printed formats on which entries are handwritten to invisible encoding on magnetic tape. Although the exact format is not important, several types will be illustrated. What is required is that an account readily accept increases or decreases and allow the difference between the increases and the decreases—the balance of the account—to be easily determined.

The number of accounts in an accounting system will depend largely upon the information needs of those interested in the business. The primary requirement is that the account provide useful information. Thus, one account may be established for cash—the company's immediate spending power—rather than separate accounts for cash in the form of coins, cash in the form of currency, and cash in the form of deposits in banks, simply because the amount of cash is useful information, while the form of cash is not.

The T-account. A way to illustrate how an account functions is by use of a "T-account." It is used for illustrative purposes only (it is not a replica of a form of account generally used), and it gets its name because it looks like a capital letter T. The name of the item to be accounted for (such as cash) is written across the top of the T. Increases are recorded on one side and decreases on the other side of the vertical line of the T.

Recording changes in assets and equities. By common practice, *increases in assets are recorded on the left side of the account, decreases on the right side.* For reasons explained later, *the process is reversed for equities.* Thus, a corporation would record the receipt of $10,000 for shares of its capital stock as:

Cash		Capital Stock	
(1) 10,000			(1) 10,000

(The number in parentheses is used in this text to tie the two sides of the transaction together.) The transaction involves an increase in the asset (cash), which is recorded on the left side of the Cash account, and an increase in stockholders' equity in the form of capital stock, which is recorded on the right side of the Capital Stock account.

Because liabilities are a subset of equities, changes in them are recorded in the same manner as changes in stockholders' equity—increases on the right side, decreases on the left. Note the consistency between the placement of amounts for assets and equities in the accounts and their presentation in the balance sheet (see Illustration 1.1). Asset amounts are shown on the left side of the account and the left side of the balance sheet; equity amounts (liabilities and stockholders' equity) are shown on the right side of the account and the right side of the balance sheet. For easy recollection of these rules, remember that increases in assets are recorded on the left side of the account. Increases in equities are recorded on the right side of the account.

Recording changes in expenses and revenues. To understand the logic behind the recording of changes in expense and revenue accounts, it is necessary to recall that all expenses and revenues could be recorded directly in Retained Earnings. Thus, the receipt of $1,000 of cash from customers for services rendered (2) and the payment of $600 of cash to employees as wages (3) could be recorded as:

Cash		Retained Earnings	
(2) 1,000	(3) 600	(3) 600	(2) 1,000

But since their dollar amounts are likely to be significant information, separate accounts are used for the various types of revenues and expenses. The recording rules for these are:

1. Since revenues increase stockholders' equity (and increases in stockholders' equity are recorded on the right side), increases in revenues should be recorded on the right side, decreases on the left.
2. Similarly, since expenses decrease stockholders' equity (and decreases in stockholders' equity are recorded on the left side), increases in expenses are recorded on the left, decreases on the right.

Following these rules, the service revenue and the wages expense mentioned above are recorded in the following manner:

Cash			Service Revenues	
(2) 1,000	(3) 600		(2)	1,000

Wages Expense	
(3) 600	

Debits and credits. Before a graphic summary of the recording rules is presented, the accounting terms *debit* and *credit* must be introduced. The accountant uses the term *debit* in lieu of saying "place an entry on the left side of an account" and the term *credit* for "place an entry on the right side of an account." While the terms *debit* (abbreviated Dr.) and *credit* (abbreviated Cr.) did have special meanings in Latin, these have long been lost and no special significance should be attached to the terms. *Debit means simply left side; credit, right side.*

Since assets and expenses are increased by debits, these accounts normally have debit (or left side) balances. Conversely, liability, stockholders' equity, and revenue accounts are increased by credits and normally have credit (or right side) balances.

The balance of any account is obtained by summing the debits to the account, summing the credits to the account, and subtracting the smaller sum from the larger. If the sum of the debits exceeds the sum of the credits, the account has a debit balance. For example, the Cash account has a debit balance of $4,000, computed as total debits of $14,000 less total credits of $10,000, in the following T-account:

Cash			
(3)	5,000	(2)	2,000
(3)	9,000	(4)	8,000
Bal.	4,000		

Similarly, the Accounts Payable account has a credit balance of $3,000:

Accounts Payable			
(7)	10,000	(5)	7,000
		(6)	6,000
		Bal.	3,000

For the most part, the amounts entered into the various accounts are found in the transactions entered into by the business. Business transactions are first analyzed to determine the effects (increase or decrease) that they have upon the assets, liabilities, stockholders' equity, revenues, or expenses of the business. Then these increases or decreases are encoded into the special accounting terminology of debit and credit. This double-entry procedure keeps the accounting equation in balance.

The rules of debit and credit may be presented in T-account form:

Debits	Credits
1. Increase assets.	1. Decrease assets.
2. Decrease liabilities.	2. Increase liabilities.
3. Decrease stockholders' equity.	3. Increase stockholders' equity.
4. Decrease revenues.	4. Increase revenues.
5. Increase expenses.	5. Decrease expenses.

These rules may also be summarized graphically as shown below. Note that the treatment of expense accounts is as if they were subsets of the debit side of a stockholders' equity account, specifically the Retained Earnings account—increases in expenses do tend to reduce what would otherwise be a larger growth in Retained Earnings; and if expenses are reduced, Retained Earnings will increase. The reverse holds for revenues.

Assets		=	Liabilities		+	Stockholders' equity	
An Asset Account			A Liability Account			A Stockholders' Equity Account	
Debit	Credit		Debit	Credit		Debit	Credit
+ In- creases	− De- creases		− De- creases	+ In- creases		− Decreases	+ Increases

Expense Accounts		Revenue Accounts	
Debit	Credit	Debit	Credit
+ In- creases	− De- creases	− De- creases	+ In- creases

The ledger.   The accounts in an accounting system are customarily classified into two general groups: (1) the balance sheet accounts (assets, liabilities, and stockholders' equity) and (2) the income statement accounts (revenues and expenses). Whether maintained in a bound volume, handwritten in loose-leaf form, or magnetically encoded on plastic tape and visible only as a computer printout, the accounts in an accounting system are collectively referred to as the *ledger*.

The list of the names of the accounts in an accounting system is known as the *chart of accounts*. Each account typically has an identification number as well as a name. For example, assets might be numbered from 100 to 199, liabilities from 200 to 299, stockholders' equity from 300 to 399, revenues from 400 to 499, and expenses from 500 to 599. The accounts are then arranged in numerical sequence in the ledger.

The journal. Every business transaction, under double-entry accounting, is analyzed as having a dual effect on the companies involved. And with the rare exception of transactions such as an exchange of land for land, every recorded business transaction affects at least two ledger accounts. Since each ledger account shows only the increases and decreases in the item for which it is established, the entire effects of a single business transaction normally will not appear in any one account. For example, the Cash account contains only information with respect to changes in cash and does not show the exact accounts credited for sources of cash or the exact accounts debited for cash disbursements.

Therefore, if transactions are recorded directly in the accounts, it is difficult to ascertain the entire effects of any transaction on a business by looking at the accounts.[1] To remedy this deficiency, the accountant employs a book or a record known as a journal. A journal contains a chronological record of the transactions of a business. Because each transaction is initially recorded in a journal, a journal is often called a book of *original entry*. Here every business transaction is analyzed for its effects on the entity and these effects are expressed in terms of debit and credit—the inputs of the accounting system.

The general journal. The general journal is the simplest form of journal. As shown in Illustration 2.1, it contains columns for:

1. The date.
2. The name of the account to be debited and the name of the account to be credited (shown on the line following the debited account and indented to the right). Any necessary explanation of a transaction appears below the transaction, indented halfway between the debit and credit entry.
3. The posting reference column; this will be explained in the section below headed "Cross-indexing."
4. The debit column, in which the money amount of the debit is placed on the same line as the name of the account debited.
5. The credit column, in which the money amount of the credit is placed on the same line as the name of the account credited.

A blank line appears between entries for purposes of easy identification of a complete entry.

Journalizing

Journalizing is the act of entering a transaction in a journal. Information on the transactions to be journalized originates on a variety of source materi-

---

[1] This would be true in an actual accounting system, which is likely to contain scores of accounts, each on a separate page. But, if all of an entity's accounts can be represented by a group of T-accounts on a single page, the dual effects of a transaction can be easily observed. For this reason, T-accounts will be used here extensively.

Illustration 2.1

GENERAL JOURNAL   Page 1

Date		Accounts and Explanation	Post. Ref.	Debit	Credit
19x2 May	1	Cash	100	10,000	
		Capital Stock	300		10,000
		Cash invested in the business . .			
	2	Rent Expense	410	500	
		Cash	100		500
		Rent for May 19x2.			
	3	Equipment.	110	2,200	
		Account Payable	201		2,200
		Tables and chairs, Diller Company.			

GENERAL LEDGER

Cash   Account No. 100

Date		Explanation	Post. Ref.	Debit	Credit	Balance
19x2 May	1		J 1	10,000		10,000 Dr.
	2		J 1		500	9,500 Dr.

Equipment   Account No. 110

Date		Explanation	Post. Ref.	Debit	Credit	Balance
19x2 May	3		J 1	2,200		2,200 Dr.

Accounts Payable   Account No. 201

Date		Explanation	Post. Ref.	Debit	Credit	Balance
19x2 May	3	Diller Company	J 1		2,200	2,200 Cr.

Capital Stock   Account No. 300

Date		Explanation	Post. Ref.	Debit	Credit	Balance
19x2 May	1		J 1		10,000	10,000 Cr.

Rent Expense   Account No. 410

Date		Explanation	Post. Ref.	Debit	Credit	Balance
19x2 May	2		J 1	500		500 Dr.

als or documents, such as invoices, cash register tapes, time cards, and checks issued. The activity recorded on these documents is carefully analyzed to determine whether a recordable transaction has occurred. If so, the specific accounts affected, the dollar amounts of the changes, and their direction (increases or decreases) are determined. Then all of these changes are translated into terms of debit and credit.

Posting

In a sense, a journal entry is a set of instructions. It indicates that a certain dollar amount is a debit in a specific account. It also directs the accountant to enter a certain dollar amount as a credit in a specific account. Carrying out these instructions is a process known as posting. In Illustration 2.1, the first entry directs that $10,000 be posted as a debit to the Cash account and as a credit to the Capital Stock account. The three-column balance type of accounts shown in that illustration for Cash and Capital Stock shows that these instructions have been carried out. In other words, the entry has been posted.

After each entry has been posted to an account, the balance of that account is determined and entered in the column headed "Balance." The "Dr." indicates a debit balance and the "Cr." a credit balance. After the posting of journal entries is completed, the accounts contain the same information that would emerge if entered directly into T-accounts. But, with the use of three-column accounts, the account balances can be determined after every entry.

Cross-Indexing

The number of the ledger account to which the posting was made is placed in the posting reference column of the journal. The number of the journal page *from* which the entry was posted is placed in the posting reference column of the ledger account. Posting is always from the journal to the ledger account. Cross-indexing is the placing of the account number in the journal and the placing of the journal page number in the account, as shown in Illustration 2.1.

Cross-indexing aids the tracing of any recorded transaction, either from the journal to the ledger or from the ledger to the journal. Cross-reference numbers usually are not placed in the posting reference column of the journal until the entry is posted; thereafter, the cross-reference numbers indicate that the entry has been posted.

Compound Journal Entries

The analysis of a business transaction often shows that more than two accounts are directly affected. In such cases, the journal entry involves more than one debit or more than one credit, or both. A journal entry with more than one debit or credit is a compound journal entry. An entry with one debit and one credit is a simple journal entry.

As an illustration of a compound journal entry, assume that J. T. Stine purchases $8,000 of machinery from the Myers Company, paying $2,000 cash with the balance due on open account. The journal entry for Stine is:

```
Machinery ............................................  8,000
    Cash ...............................................        2,000
    Accounts Payable, Myers Company......................        6,000
    Machinery purchased from Myers Company, Invoice No. 42.
```

Control of the Recording Process

As noted, increases in assets (and expenses) are recorded as debits and increases in equities (and revenues) as credits. The accountant's objective is to develop two sets of accounts, those with debit balances and those with credit balances, in a recording process such that the total of the accounts with debit balances agrees with the total of the accounts with credit balances. This provides an automatic check upon the arithmetic accuracy of the recording process.

The double-entry system of accounting requires, and the above examples illustrate, that to record each transaction properly the debits must equal the credits. This equality of debits and credits for each transaction will always hold because both sides of the transaction are recorded. This does *not* mean that the increases must equal the decreases. A perfectly valid transaction could involve an increase in both an asset and an equity account (the borrowing of money) or a decrease in both an asset and an equity account (the repayment of a loan), as well as an increase in one account and a decrease in another. It is the equality of debits and credits, not of increases and decreases, that provides the important control device. If every transaction is recorded in terms of equal debits and credits, the total of the accounts with debit balances must equal the total of the accounts with credit balances.

The trial balance.   The proof of the arithmetic accuracy of the recording process is secured by preparing a list of the accounts and their debit or credit balances, called a *trial balance*. An example is found in Illustration 2.2, the trial balance for Olin's, Inc., which operates a dry cleaning business and ends its first year of operations on December 31, 19x2. The balances reported are those in the ledger accounts after all of its transactions have been journalized and posted.

If the totals of the debit and credit columns do not agree, an error has been made. But the equality of the two totals does not indicate that the accounting has been error-free. Indeed, serious errors may have been made, such as the complete omission of an important transaction or the recording of an entry in the wrong account, for example, the recording of an expense as an asset.

Illustration 2.2

OLIN'S, INC.
Trial Balance
December 31, 19x2

	Debits	Credits
Cash..............................	$ 7,000	
Supplies on hand....................	12,000	
Prepaid insurance	4,000	
Equipment.........................	40,000	
Fixtures...........................	20,000	
Accounts payable....................		$ 2,000
Notes payable......................		10,000
Capital stock.......................		30,000
Sales		145,000
Salaries expense	72,000	
Advertising expense.................	5,000	
Utilities expense....................	8,000	
Rent expense	12,000	
Payroll taxes expense	6,000	
Miscellaneous expense	1,000	
	$187,000	$187,000

Adjusting entries. A trial balance is usually taken before the preparation of formal financial statements. Before the information in a trial balance can be used in the income statement and the balance sheet, the accountant makes sure the accounts do indeed contain up-to-date information. An analysis of the accounts will usually reveal that some updating adjustments, called *adjusting entries,* are needed. Adjusting entries are needed because economic activity has taken place that is not evidenced by a transaction. Hence, it has not been recorded. Some examples of adjusting entries, based in part upon the data in the Olin's, Inc., trial balance in Illustration 2.2 are illustrated below.

Supplies. Whenever supplies were purchased during the year, their cost was debited to an asset account called Supplies on Hand. Some of these supplies were used during the year, but, because no exchange occurred, their use has not been recorded. An inventory, taken at year-end, shows supplies on hand with a cost of $3,000. This means that the accounts should show an asset, Supplies on Hand, of $3,000 and an expense, Supplies Expense, of $9,000 since the supplies purchased, but no longer on hand, were used during the year. The adjusting entry, coded with lower case letters, in this example (*a*), brings the accounts to these balances:

Supplies on Hand				Supplies Expense	
Bal.	12,000	(a)	9,000	(a)	9,000
Bal.	3,000				

Prepaid insurance. The $4,000 balance in the Prepaid Insurance account represents the premium paid for insurance coverage for the years 19x2 and

19x3. Since one half of the period covered by the premium paid has expired, one half of the premium paid should be transferred from the asset account, Prepaid Insurance (*b*), to an Insurance Expense account:

Prepaid Insurance				Insurance Expense	
Bal.	4,000	(*b*)	2,000	(*b*)	2,000
Bal.	2,000				

Equipment and fixtures.   The equipment and fixtures were acquired at the beginning of the year. Since they were used in generating revenue throughout the year, it is logical that some part of the cost of these assets be considered an expense for the year. This is true because these assets will eventually be scrapped due to "wear and tear." This wear and tear is called *depreciation expense*. Assuming that both the equipment and the fixtures have estimated useful lives of 10 years, the depreciation expense for the year for Olin's, Inc., is:

Depreciation Expense—Equipment: $40,000 ÷ 10 years = $4,000 per year
Depreciation Expense—Fixtures: $20,000 ÷ 10 years = $2,000 per year

Using T-accounts, these depreciation amounts would be recorded as:

Depreciation Expense—Equipment		Accumulated Depreciation—Equipment	
(*c*)	4,000	(*c*)	4,000

Depreciation Expense—Fixtures		Accumulated Depreciation—Fixtures	
(*d*)	2,000	(*d*)	2,000

The depreciation expense recorded could be credited directly in the asset accounts Equipment and Fixtures. But, in order to show what proportion of the asset was used up, accountants prefer to use separate accounts, which are reported in the balance sheet as deductions from the related asset accounts.

Accrued salaries payable.   An analysis of the payroll records supporting the Salaries Expense account reveals that there are $3,000 of unpaid salaries at the end of the year. To have proper balances in the accounts, the following entry must be made:

Salaries Expense		Accrued Salaries Payable	
Bal.	72,000	(*e*)	3,000
(*e*)	3,000		

Because salaries payable are a debt that will be paid in the near future, Accrued Salaries Payable is reported as a current liability. (Payroll taxes on this portion are ignored in this illustration.)

Accrued interest payable. No entry has been made to record the interest expense incurred and owed on the note payable. The note is dated January 2, 19x2, and bears interest at a rate of 10 percent per year. The required entry would debit Interest Expense and credit Accrued Interest Payable for $1,000 (0.10 × $10,000). The Interest Expense would be reported in the income statement and the Accrued Interest Payable would be reported as a current liability in the balance sheet since it is also a short-term debt.

Accrued federal income taxes payable. Olin's, Inc., is subject to federal taxation of its taxable income. Assuming that its taxes payable are $4,000, the entry to record the income tax expense and the liability for such taxes is:

Federal Income Tax Expense		Accrued Federal Income Taxes Payable	
(g)	4,000	(g)	4,000

The above examples are a few of the many adjusting entries that may be required. These entries update the accounts to make them more accurate reflections of the assets, liabilities, owners' equity, revenues, and expenses of the business. After the adjusting entries have been posted, the accounts are ready for use in preparing the financial statements. The income statement for Olin's, Inc., is shown in Illustration 2.3. Its balance sheet is in Illustration 2.4. (The statement of changes in financial position is deliberately omitted at this time.) A statement of retained earnings could be prepared, but it is also omitted here since it would show only the net income for the year of $16,000, and this would be the ending balance of retained earnings.

Illustration 2.3

OLIN'S, INC.
Income Statement
For the Year Ended December 31, 19x2

Sales...........................		$145,000
Expenses:		
Salaries.........................	$75,000	
Advertising......................	5,000	
Utilities	8,000	
Rent............................	12,000	
Payroll taxes expense..............	6,000	
Insurance	2,000	
Supplies	9,000	
Depreciation—equipment...........	4,000	
Depreciation—fixtures	2,000	
Interest	1,000	
Miscellaneous	1,000	
Federal income taxes	4,000	
Total expenses..................		129,000
Net income......................		$ 16,000

Illustration 2.4

OLIN'S, INC.
Balance Sheet
December 31, 19x2

Assets				Liabilities and Stockholders' Equity		
Current assets:				*Current liabilities:*		
Cash..................		$ 7,000		Accounts payable	$ 2,000	
Supplies on hand........		3,000		Note payable	10,000	
Prepaid				Accrued salaries		
insurance............		2,000	$12,000	payable	3,000	
				Federal income taxes		
Property, plant and				payable	4,000	
equipment:				Accrued interest		
Equipment.............	$40,000			payable	1,000	$20,000
Less: Accumulated.....						
depreciation.......	4,000	$36,000		*Stockholders' equity:*		
Fixtures	$20,000			Capital stock	$30,000	
Less: Accumulated				Retained earnings	16,000	46,000
depreciation.......	2,000	18,000	54,000	Total liabilities and		
Total assets.............			$66,000	stockholders'		
				equity...............		$66,000

Closing entries. One step remains in the accounting process—a step known as "closing the books." As illustrated, after adjusting entries have been prepared and posted, the accounts contain basically two types of information: (1) information relating to the activities for the period just ended (reported in the income statement) and (2) information on financial condition (reported in the balance sheet).

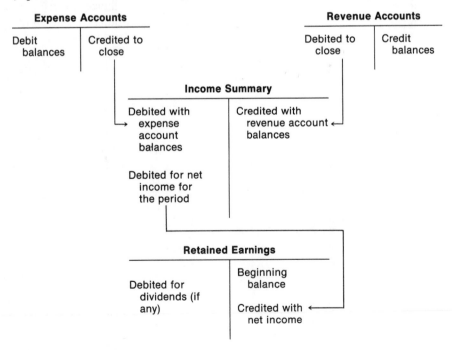

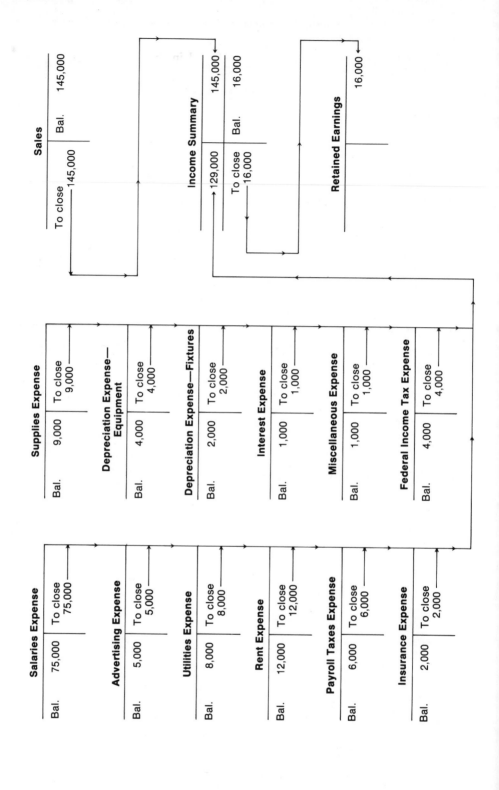

The first type of information is found in the expense and revenue accounts. These accounts are temporary subdivisions of the Retained Earnings accounts. They help the accountant fulfill an important task—the determination of periodic net income. After the financial statements for the period have been prepared, these temporary accounts have served their purpose. They are brought to a zero balance, or "closed," in accounting jargon. In this way, information pertaining to the next period can be gathered in them.

The balance in each expense and revenue account is transferred to an account called Income Summary. This is a *clearing* account used only at the end of the accounting period. It summarizes the expenses and revenues for the period, with the difference between these two being either net income or a net loss. Since revenue accounts have credit balances, they are debited and Income Summary credited. Conversely, expense accounts have debit balances, so they are credited and Income Summary debited. The Income Summary now contains either a debit (net loss) or a credit (net income) balance. It is then debited or credited to bring it to a zero balance. Retained Earnings is credited or debited to keep the entry in balance. With this last entry, the books are closed. Only the expense and revenue accounts and the Income Summary account are closed. If dividends are recorded by debiting Retained Earnings and crediting Cash, no closing entry is made. But, if dividends are recorded by debiting a separate Dividends account and crediting Cash, the Dividends account is credited and Retained Earnings debited as part of the closing process.

The closing process using T-accounts is as shown on page 35.

The balance in the Retained Earnings account after closing is correct as of the end of the period. It is reported in the balance sheet.

For Olin's, Inc., the accounts to be closed are all of the expense and revenue accounts shown in the income statement in Illustration 2.3. In T-account form, its closing entries would read as shown on page 36.

When the closing entries are posted, each of the company's expense and revenue accounts will be reduced to a zero balance and ready to accumulate data on the operations for the next year. Retained Earnings will have the same balance that it would have if all expenses and revenues had been entered directly in it. The use of expense and revenue accounts not only permits classification of these elements and makes them readily available for reporting in the income statement but also provides management with individual expense and revenue accounts to analyze internally.

The Financial Accounting Process Summarized

The steps involved in the operation of an accounting system are often referred to collectively as the accounting cycle. These steps include:

1. Journalizing transactions (and other events) in the journal.
2. Posting journal entries to ledger accounts.

3. Taking a trial balance of the accounts.
4. Journalizing the needed adjusting entries.
5. Posting the adjusting entries to the accounts.
6. Preparing the financial statements.
7. Journalizing the closing entries.
8. Posting the closing entries to the accounts.

THE CASH AND ACCRUAL BASES OF ACCOUNTING

In filing federal income tax returns, individuals and businesses in which inventories are not significant (movie theaters and insurance agencies, for example) may compute their taxable income under either the *cash basis* or the *accrual basis*. Under the cash basis, revenues are recorded *in the period in which cash is collected* from customers for services rendered. *Expenses are recorded in the period in which cash was paid* for them. Thus, the collection in 19x2 of $1,000 of cash for services rendered in 19x1 results in the recording of $1,000 of service revenue in 19x2. The payment of $6,000 of cash as the rent for the year 19x2 on December 28, 19x1, results in the recording of $6,000 of rent expense in 19x1. If the cash basis of accounting had been used in the example for Olin's, Inc., the only adjusting entry made would be for the depreciation on the equipment and the fixtures. The cash basis usually is not carried to the extreme of recording the entire price paid for a long-lived asset, such as office equipment, as an expense when paid. The supplies purchased and the insurance policy premium paid would, under the cash basis, have been charged to expense when paid for and thus would require no further adjustment.[2]

Under the accrual basis of accounting, *adjusting entries are required for accrued items* such as the accrued salaries and interest in the Olin's, Inc., example. In other instances, the recognition of the incurrence of a cost as an expense is said to be deferred. For example, the recording of the $6,000 rent expense would be deferred from the time of its payment in 19x1 until 19x2, the period for which it will be incurred. Similarly, the supplies on hand and the prepaid insurance in the Olin's, Inc., example are described as deferred items or prepaid expenses. Thus, under the accrual basis of accounting, *net income is determined by deducting from the revenues earned the expenses incurred* to generate those revenues. And this matching of expenses and revenues is carried out through a process of accrual and deferral, to use accounting jargon.

---

[2] Federal income tax regulations generally prohibit the deduction of more than one year's expense on the tax return for a year. Thus, a firm on the cash basis can deduct in, say, 19x2, only one year's premium of the three-year premium on an insurance policy paid in 19x2. The implication is clear: the strict application of the cash basis of accounting does not record revenues as earned or expenses as incurred, and it does not clearly reflect taxable income in all cases.

Questions

1. What is an account? What functions does it fulfill?
2. What are the two major components of an accounting system? What purpose does each fulfill?
3. Define *debit* and *credit*. Name the types of accounts that are increased by debits and decreased by credits and those that are increased by credits and decreased by debits.
4. Analyze the following transactions and indicate whether the accounts affected are debited or credited.
   a. Money is borrowed by the giving of a written promise to repay.
   b. Equipment is purchased on account.
   c. Services are rendered for customers who promise to pay later.
   d. Payments on account are received from customers.
   e. Cash is paid to employees for services rendered.
5. What are adjusting entries? In general, why must they be made?
6. What are closing entries? In general, why must they be made?
7. What is a trial balance? What purposes are served by its preparation?
8. What is a compound journal entry? Give an example.
9. List the steps taken to complete the accounting cycle.
10. What is meant by the balance of an account? How is it determined?
11. Why do asset accounts and expense accounts have debit balances when assets and expenses are so dramatically different?
12. What is the significance of the fact that a trial balance does indeed balance? What does this say about the accuracy of the accounting completed?
13. Why are expense and revenue accounts used when all revenues and expenses could be shown directly in the Retained Earnings account?
14. Which of the following cash payments would involve the recording of an expense under the accrual basis of accounting? Why?
    a. Paid vendors for office supplies previously purchased on account.
    b. Paid the current month's rent.
    c. Paid salaries for the last half of the current month.

Exercises

1. The payment of $18,000 as the premium for one year of insurance coverage beginning on July 1 was debited to a Prepaid Insurance account. What adjusting entry is needed on December 31, the end of the accounting year?
2. You note that a trial balance shows an account entitled Supplies on Hand in the amount of $2,700. An inventory shows $300 of supplies actually on hand. What adjusting entry would be needed if financial statements were to be prepared?
3. The ledger of a business firm contains an account entitled Accrued Salaries Payable in the amount of $1,900. Where would this amount appear in the financial statements? Why? Would it be closed in the closing of the books? Why or why not?
4. The accountant of the A Company forgot to make an entry for $800 of accrued wages at the end of 1982. What is the effect of this omission upon the reported $20,000 of net income for that year?

5. A firm borrows $10,000 on November 1 for 120 days with interest payable at the time of repayment of the loan at the rate of 9 percent per year. Interest is equal to $10,000 \times \dfrac{60}{360} \times \dfrac{9}{100} = \$150$. Prepare the adjusting entry needed on December 31.

6. Explain each of the sets of debits and credits shown in the T-accounts below. There are 10 transactions of the Walter White Company to be explained. Each set is identified by the small letters to the left of the amount. For example, the first transaction is the issuance of capital stock for cash and is identified by the letter (a).

Cash				Accounts Payable				Rent Expense	
(a)	70,000	(e)	50,000	(e)	50,000	(b)	50,000	(f)	200
(d)	600	(f)	200			(h)	400		
		(g)	1,200						
		(i)	10,000						

Accounts Receivable				Capital Stock				Repairs Expense	
(c)	600	(d)	600			(a)	70,000	(h)	400
(j)	4,700								

Delivery Equipment				Delivery Fee Revenue				Salaries Expense	
(b)	50,000					(c)	600	(g)	1,200
(i)	10,000					(j)	4,700		

7. Assume that the depreciation on the delivery equipment for the year ended December 31, 19x2, is $5,000. Prepare the income statement for 19x2 and the balance sheet as of the end of 19x2, assuming that the data given in Exercise 6 are for Walter White Company.

8. Given the following data with respect to wages earned by the Xcar Company employees:

Accrued wages payable, December 31, 19x3.	1,500
Payments to employees in 19x4.	104,000
Accrued wages payable, December 31, 19x4.	1,700

Compute wages expense for the Xcar Company for 19x4 under the accrual basis of accounting. Compute wages expense for the Xcar Company for 19x4 under the cash basis of accounting.

Business Decision Problem 2–1

Sammy West, husband of Dottie West, the president and sole stockholder of West Service Company, prepared the following income statement for the company's second month of operation, May 19x3:

Service revenue		$20,000
Wages	$11,200	
Oil and gasoline used	2,000	
Other	2,800	16,000
Net income		$ 4,000

In preparing the above income statement, Sammy merely looked at the checkbook and treated deposits of receipts from customers as revenue for the month and checks drawn in payment of expenses as expenses for the month. Further analysis shows that of the $20,000 collected from customers in May, $2,400 was for services rendered in April. Services were rendered in May for which customers were billed $2,800, none of which was paid by the end of May. The $11,200 of wages paid included wages of $3,200 earned by employees in April. Wages earned in May but not paid by the end of May amounted to $1,200. A $400 bill for gasoline and oil used in May remains unpaid at the end of May. The expenses shown above do not include depreciation on the equipment owned, which cost $120,000 and has an estimated useful life of 10 years.

At a business meeting, Dottie heard the president of another company talking about how much more accurately earnings are determined under the accrual basis of accounting as compared to the cash basis. She now asks you to review the above statement and additional data and prepare an income statement for May under the accrual basis. She also asks you to express your opinion as to which method is the better method for her company to use.

Business Decision Problem 2–2

A friend of yours, Sam White, is quite excited over a pending business deal. He expects to organize a corporation and invest $135,000 in its stock, and then the corporation would acquire the land, building, equipment, and several miscellaneous assets of the Strand Bowling Lanes for the $135,000. Sam tells you that the Strand's owner (who is retiring because of poor health) reports that his business earned a profit of $25,000 in 19x1 (last year). Sam believes that an annual profit of $25,000 on an investment of $135,000 is a really good deal. But, before completing the deal, he asks you to look it over. You agree to look it over and discover the following:

1. The owner has computed his annual profit for 19x1 as the sum of his cash withdrawals plus the increase in the Cash account—withdrawals of $15,000 plus increase in cash account of $10,000 = $25,000 profit.

2. Sam's corporation, as buyer of the business, will take over responsibility for the repayment of a $100,000 loan balance (plus interest) secured by the land, building, and equipment. These three assets were acquired seven years ago at costs of $10,000, $240,000, and $96,000, respectively. The building has a useful life of 40 years, while the equipment has an estimated useful life of 8 years. These two items are worth approximately their depreciated purchase price, while the land is worth $20,000.

3. An analysis of the Cash account shows the following for 19x1:

Rental revenues received......................		$140,000
Cash paid out in 19x1 for:		
Employee wages	$80,000	
Utilities	6,000	
Advertising	5,000	
Supplies purchased and used	8,000	
Interest paid on loan..........................	6,000	
Loan principal paid	10,000	
Owner withdrawals	15,000	130,000
Increase in cash balance for the year..............		$ 10,000

4. The first five items listed above for cash payments in 19x1 are properly includible in 19x1 expenses. But you discover that these expenses do not include the December utility bill of $1,000 or a $1,500 unpaid advertising bill for 19x1.

You are to prepare a written report for Sam giving your appraisal of the offer to sell the Strand Bowling Lanes. Comment on the owner's method of computing the annual "profit" of the business. Include in your report a statement of the assets expected to be employed in the business and an approximate income statement for 19x1 as the owner should have prepared it.

Solutions to End-of-Chapter Questions, Exercises, and Business Decision Problems

Answers to Questions

1. An account is a form designed to receive money measurements of the item accounted for. The primary functions of an account are to receive money measurements of changes and to permit the drawing up of a balance for that item.
2. The two components of an accounting system are the ledger of accounts and the journal. The ledger is the storeroom or data base, while the journal is the means of introducing changes into the stored information.
3. *Debit* means simply the left side of an account or to make an entry in the left side of an account. *Credit* means simply the right side of an account or to make an entry in the right side of an account. Assets and expenses are increased by debits and decreased by credits. Equities and revenues are increased by credits and decreased by debits.
4. *a.* Cash and liabilities both increase; debit Cash and credit Notes Payable.
    b. Equipment and accounts payable both increase; debit Equipment and credit Accounts Payable.
    c. Accounts receivable and service revenue both increase; debit Accounts Receivable and credit Service Revenue.
    d. Cash increases, accounts receivable decrease; debit Cash and credit Accounts Receivable.
    e. Cash decreases, wages expense increases; debit Wages Expense and credit Cash.
5. Adjusting entries are entries made at the end of an accounting period to update the accounts so that they reflect more completely the activities of the period and the financial position at the end of that period. They are made to include in the accounts changes which have occurred but which have not been recorded because the transaction which usually causes them to be recorded has not yet taken place.
6. Closing entries are entries also made at the end of an accounting period. They must be made in order to reduce all of the expense and revenue accounts to a zero balance and in this way prepare them to receive information on the activities of the next accounting period.
7. A trial balance is a list of the accounts in a ledger and the debit or credit balance of each account. The trial balance is prepared primarily as a proof of the arithmetic accuracy of the journalizing and posting the steps of the accounting

cycle. It also localizes the period in which errors, if any, have been made, and it may serve as a convenient listing of the accounts to be used in preparing financial statements.

8. A compound journal entry is a journal entry with more than one debit or credit, or both. Many examples could be given, such as the payment of a note and the interest on the principal of the note at maturity.

9. (1) Journalizing transactions, (2) posting the journal entries, (3) taking a trial balance, (4) journalizing needed adjusting entries, (5) posting the adjusting entries, (6) preparing financial statements, (7) journalizing the closing entries, and (8) posting the closing entries.

10. The balance of an account represents a measure of the item for which the account was established. For example, a $5,000 balance in the Accounts Receivable account indicates that the firm's customers owe the firm $5,000 for services rendered. The balance of an account is simply the excess of the additions to the account over the deductions entered in the account. An account will have either a debit or credit balance, depending upon whether the debits or credits to the account were larger.

11. Asset accounts have debit balances simply as a result of the practice of recording increases in asset accounts on the left or debit side of the account. Since accounts seldom have negative balances, assets typically have debit balances. Expense accounts have debit balances largely due to the fact that they are temporarily recorded reductions in retained earnings, and the retained earnings account (an equity account) is increased by credits (by agreement) and so must be reduced by debits.

12. The fact that a trial balance does indeed balance suggests that the more mechanical parts of the information process have been carried out correctly. It is a positive signal that things appear to be done correctly, since an out-of-balance trial balance always indicates the existence of an error. But even though a trial balance balances, significant errors may have been made, such as the recording of the receipt of cash for the shares of capital stock issued as a debit to Cash and a credit to a revenue account.

13. Expense and revenue accounts are used to make it easier to report the various kinds of expenses incurred and revenues generated in a period. Users of accounting information are believed to want to know more about net income than simply its amount for a period. Thus, the details of the income statement are believed to constitute useful information about the various revenues and expenses that lead to the net income reported.

14. Both *b* and *c* involve the initial recording of the receipt of services that will have expired by the end of the month. They can then be entered directly in expense accounts when paid for. Item *a* indicates that the item being paid for at this time is the bill for the supplies that has been previously recorded as a debit to Supplies Inventory and a credit to Accounts Payable. The supplies will be expensed as they are used.

Solutions to Exercises

1.

Prepaid Insurance	Insurance Expense
9,000	9,000

2.

Supplies Inventory	Supplies Expense
2,400	2,400

3. The account would appear as a current liability. It shows the amount of employee services received but not yet paid for by the company. It would not be closed; it is a balance sheet account, not an expense or revenue account.

4. The corrected net income for the year is $19,200. Because the adjusting entry for the $800 of accrued wages was omitted, the wages expense was understated by $800. This, in turn, overstated the net income.

5.

Accrued Interest Payable	Interest Expense
150	150

6. (b) Purchased delivery equipment on account, $50,000.
   (c) Rendered delivery services for customers on account, $600.
   (d) Collected cash from customers on account, $600.
   (e) Paid for equipment purchased, $50,000.
   (f) Paid rent expense, $200.
   (g) Paid salaries of employees, $1,200.
   (h) Repairs expense incurred on account, $400.
   (i) Purchased delivery equipment for cash, $10,000.
   (j) Rendered delivery services for customers on account, $4,700.

7.
WALTER WHITE COMPANY
Income Statement
For the Year Ended December 31, 19x2

Revenue from delivery services........................		$5,300
Expenses:		
Rent..	$ 200	
Repairs	400	
Salaries......................................	1,200	
Depreciation of delivery equipment.................	5,000	6,800
Net loss..		$1,500

WALTER WHITE COMPANY
Balance Sheet
December 31, 19x2

Assets

Current assets:		
Cash	$ 9,200	
Accounts receivable	4,700	
Total current assets.............................		$13,900
Property, plant, and equipment:		
Delivery equipment	$60,000	
Less: Accumulated depreciation.................	5,000	55,000
Total assets...................................		$68,900

Liabilities and Stockholders' Equity

Current liabilities:

Accounts payable. . . . . $ 400

Stockholders' equity:

Capital stock. $70,000

Retained earnings (deficit) . . . .   (1,500)   68,500

Total liabilities and stockholders' equity. $68,900

8.   Accrual Basis   Cash Basis

Payments to employees in 19x4 . . . . $104,000 $104,000

Wages of 19x3 paid . . . .   (1,500)   0

Wages of 19x4 unpaid at year-end.   1,700   0

Wages expense for the year 19x4. . . . . $104,200 $104,000

Solution to Business Decision Problem 2–1

WEST SERVICE COMPANY
Income Statement
For the Month Ended May 31, 19x3

Service revenue ($20,000 − $2,400 + $2,800). $20,400

Expenses

Wages ($11,200 − $3,200 + $1,200). $9,200

Oil and gasoline used ($2,000 + $400).   2,400

Other expenses.   2,800

Depreciation expense.   1,000   15,400

Net income . . . . $ 5,000

The accrual basis is to be preferred because it requires that expenses be recorded as incurred and that revenues be recorded as earned and realized. Such an accounting basis reflects more closely the actual underlying economic activity. In some instances, the results obtained under the cash basis may be misleading. If, for example, the cash basis method had been applied to the equipment owned, the entire cost of $120,000 would have been charged to expense in April and no expense would have been recognized from use of the equipment for the rest of its life. This does not yield a matching against revenue of the costs incurred to generate that revenue.

Solution to Business Decision Problem 2–2

Dear Sam:

I have analyzed the offer to sell the Strand Bowling Lanes to your wholly owned corporation for $135,000 plus the assumption of liability on a $100,000 loan, and have come to the following conclusions:

1.   The net income of the business for 19x1 was only $14,500 rather than $25,000. The owner's method of calculating annual profit was incorrect. He deducted as an expense the loan principal paid, which actually consists of the payment of a liability rather than the payment of an expense. He failed to deduct $1,000 of utility expense, an advertising expense item of $1,500, and depreciation expense of $6,000 on the building and $12,000 on the equipment. Exhibit B shows the calculation of the net income of the company under generally accepted accounting principles. Note that

46

the expenses shown in this exhibit do not include an item reflecting the services rendered to the business by its owner. If your corporation buys this business and you run it, you will undoubtedly draw a salary. The inclusion of any reasonable salary to you would most likely reduce the $14,500 of net income calculated in Exhibit B to a loss.

2.   The assets that you will be using in the business and their carrying values are computed in Exhibit A. Note that the equipment is almost fully depreciated. If the useful life of the equipment is eight years, it will have to be replaced next year. This means that you would have to invest at least $96,000 (or more because of inflation) or find other means to finance the replacement of the equipment.

3.   Your return on this investment would be approximately $14,500/$135,000, or 10.7 percent, using the purchase price and assuming that you draw no salary from the business. As noted above, if you draw a reasonable salary, the return on your investment will be negative.

4.   I recommend that you look elsewhere for a better investment.

Exhibit A

Statement of Assets Employed
At December 31, 19x1

Land.		$ 10,000
Building.	$240,000	
Less: Accumulated depreciation	42,000	198,000
Equipment.	$ 96,000	
Less: Accumulated depreciation	84,000	12,000
Other assets		15,000*
Assets employed at end of 19x1.		$235,000

* Price to be paid ($135,000) plus debt to be assumed ($100,000) equal total liabilities and stockholders' equity. Total assets must agree.

Exhibit B

Approximate Income Statement for 19x1

Rental revenue.		$140,000
Expenses:		
Wages	$80,000	
Utilities.	7,000	
Advertising	6,500	
Supplies.	8,000	
Interest on loan	6,000	
Depreciation:		
Building ($240,000 ÷ 40 years).	6,000	
Equipment ($96,000 ÷ 8 years).	12,000	125,500
Net income.		$ 14,500*

* Note: Does not include any deduction for salary for possible services rendered by Mr. White.

PART TWO

Income Measurement and Balance Sheet

3

Income Measurement in Merchandising Companies

Chapter Goals

When you have completed Chapter 3, you should be able to:

1. Explain the timing of recording sales and purchase transactions.
2. Explain the nature of, reasons for, accounting for, and reporting of sales or purchase returns and allowances and sales or purchase discounts.
3. Identify the characteristics, advantages, and disadvantages of perpetual and periodic inventory procedures.
4. Explain the nature of uncollectible accounts and the accounting for such accounts and for their recovery.
5. Illustrate the income statement usually prepared for a merchandising firm, explain the concept of gross margin, and compute gross margin.
6. Identify goods which should be included in inventory.
7. Explain the nature and importance of inventory in financial reporting and contrast the practical and theoretical considerations of the different methods of inventory measurement.
8. Explain the lower-of-cost-or-market rule and illustrate how it is applied.
9. Illustrate the gross margin and retail methods of estimating inventories and how they are applied.

One task of the accountant is to measure periodic net income by matching earned revenues and incurred expenses. This chapter discusses accounting for the major source of revenue for most business firms, sales of products, and a major element of expense, cost of the goods sold. The timing of the recognition of sales revenues and related items is discussed. On the expense side, attention is focused on the cost of the goods sold, not only because it is a relatively large portion of total expense but also because its magnitude may differ for the same accounting period and for the same firm, depending on the accounting method used.

Contra accounts are introduced and used extensively in this chapter. A *contra account* is an account that accumulates important information about another account and is then deducted from that other account on financial statements. For instance, a contra revenue account is deducted from a revenue account on the income statement. Thus, the Sales Discounts account (a contra revenue account) is deducted from the Sales account on the income statement. The use of contra accounts will be illustrated in this chapter.

ACCOUNTING FOR SALES REVENUE

The revenue of a merchandising company is recorded at the time of the sale (the sale is assumed to occur when the goods are delivered) and at the price agreed upon in the sales contract. Thus, a sale of a machine on account at a price of $3,000 is recorded when the machine is delivered:

Accounts Receivable		Sales	
(a)	3,000	(a)	3,000

Recording revenue at the time of sale is usually considered appropriate because (1) the revenue has been earned, that is, the seller has completed its part of the contract; (2) the revenue is readily measurable—the actual selling price is known; (3) legal title to the goods has passed to the buyer; and (4) the revenue has been realized—a valid asset has been received in an exchange with an outsider. As a practical matter, revenue from the sale of goods is usually recorded when the goods are delivered in a sales transaction. The cost of goods sold is deducted from sales revenues to determine the *gross margin*. The cost of goods sold is determined through use of either perpetual inventory or periodic inventory procedures.

COST OF GOODS SOLD—PERPETUAL PROCEDURE

Merchandising firms obtain revenue from the sale of goods on hand called merchandise inventory. To illustrate, a firm purchased three identical machines for resale on account at a price of $1,800 each. Using *perpetual inventory procedure,* the purchase is recorded in two balance sheet accounts as:

Merchandise Inventory		Accounts Payable	
(b)	5,400	(b)	5,400

Merchandise inventory is a current asset account, and accounts payable is a current liability. When a machine is sold on account for $3,000, Accounts Receivable is debited and Sales is credited for $3,000.

Accounts Receivable		Sales	
(a)	3,000	(c)	3,000

Under perpetual procedure, a second entry is required at the time of sale to record the *expense* incurred by transferring an asset, part of the inventory, to the customer:

Merchandise Inventory			Cost of Goods Sold	
(b)	5,400	(d)	1,800	(d)	1,800

The $1,800 in the entry is secured from supporting records called *stock cards* or *perpetual inventory cards*. These records show the dates, quantities, and prices of goods received and goods issued, and the quantities and prices of the goods on hand at any given time.

Assume that $500 of other expenses were incurred in the week of the sale and the sale was the company's only revenue. The income statement for the week would be:

Sales	$3,000
Cost of goods sold.................	1,800
Gross margin	$1,200
Other expenses	500
Net income	$ 700

The difference between sales and the cost of goods sold is called *gross margin* or *gross profit*. Gross margin is often expressed as a percentage of sales and called the *gross profit* or *gross margin rate*—40 percent in this instance ($1,200 ÷ $3,000).

Perpetual inventory procedure is widely used by companies that sell merchandise with high unit value, such as furs, jewelry, and autos. Because each unit has a high value, management finds it useful to know which merchandise is selling and which is not. Promotional activity and purchasing can be planned. Also, inventory shortages can be determined by comparing amounts shown on perpetual records with physical counts of the items on hand. Thus, the benefits derived from keeping detailed perpetual records are believed to exceed the cost of maintaining such records.

COST OF GOODS SOLD—PERIODIC PROCEDURE

Companies that sell goods with low unit values, such as greeting cards, nuts and bolts, and pencils, find it too costly to maintain perpetual records for their merchandise. Such companies use *periodic inventory procedure*. Under this procedure, the proper inventory balance is determined and recorded only after a physical count is taken of the goods on hand at the end of the accounting period. Such physical counts are usually taken once a year at a minimum. And the cost of goods sold is determined only after the physical inventory has been taken.

The Purchases Account

Under periodic procedure, merchandise acquisitions are recorded in a separate Purchases account. A purchase of $40,000 of goods on account is recorded as:

Purchases		Accounts Payable	
(b) 40,000		(b) 40,000	

The cost of the goods sold in any period is then determined:

> Merchandise inventory (at beginning of period)
> + Purchases for the period
> = Cost of goods available for sale
> − Ending inventory (goods on hand not sold)
> = Cost of goods sold (the expense for the period)

The computation of the cost of the goods sold can be included in the income statement, if desired, as shown in Illustration 3.1. Future examples will illustrate this periodic procedure only.

Illustration 3.1

X COMPANY
Partial Income Statement
For the Month Ended July 31, 19x2

Sales.		$50,000
Cost of goods sold:		
Inventory, July 1	$15,000	
Purchases	40,000	
Cost of goods available for sale	$55,000	
Less: Inventory, July 31	22,000	
Cost of goods sold		33,000
Gross margin.		$17,000

RETURNS AND ALLOWANCES

Whenever goods are sold, some may be returned to the seller for a variety of reasons. For example, assume that goods have been sold to a buyer on account for $5,000. This was recorded as a debit to Accounts Receivable and a credit to Sales of $5,000 by the seller, and as a debit to Purchases and a credit to Accounts Payable of $5,000 by the buyer. Now goods with a sales price of $400 are returned. The entry on the seller's books—entry (a)—would be:

Sales Returns		Accounts Receivable			
(a)	400	Bal.	5,000	(a)	400

The entry on the buyer's books—entry (b)—would be:

Purchase Returns		Accounts Payable			
	(b)	400	(b)	400	Bal.	5,000

The seller has credited the customer's account because the return has reduced the customer's obligation to pay. The customer (buyer) debited the vendor's account because the return reduced its obligation to the seller.

Occasionally, concessions are granted from the original price of merchandise because of blemishes, defects, or damage. Such price concessions are recorded in the same manner as returns, except that the accounts involved will be Sales Allowances and Purchase Allowances. Frequently, returns and allowances are recorded in combined Sales Returns and Allowances accounts and combined Purchase Returns and Allowances accounts. Because returns and allowances may represent or result from inefficiencies in operations, their amounts are likely to be significant information to management. Also, the handling of returns can be costly to both buyers and sellers (they amount to as much as 15 percent of sales in some businesses). Returns and allowances are, therefore, recorded in separate accounts (called contra accounts) and often are reported separately (as deductions from sales and purchases to arrive at net sales and net purchases) in the income statement (see Illustration 3.2).

CASH DISCOUNTS

Frequently, when goods are sold on credit, the buyer may pay an amount less than the full invoice price of the goods if payment is made within a stated period of time. For example, an invoice might state credit terms of "2/10, n/30" (read as 2/10, net 30), which means a 2 percent discount can be deducted from the total price of the goods if the invoice is paid within 10 days of the invoice date. Thus, the payment within the discount period of a

$1,000 invoice for merchandise sold under terms 2/10, n/30 and originally recorded at $1,000 is recorded as:

Seller's Books

Accounts Receivable			
(a)	1,000	(b)	1,000

Sales		
	(a)	1,000

Cash	
(b)	980

Sales Discounts	
(b)	20

Buyer's Books

Purchases	
(c)	1,000

Accounts Payable			
(d)	1,000	(c)	1,000

Cash			
Bal.	xxx	(d)	980

Purchase Discounts	
(d)	20

The Sales Discounts and Purchase Discounts accounts are contra accounts to the Sales and Purchases accounts. This treatment reflects the view that such discounts are adjustments of recorded revenue and cost.

An alternative accounting method consists of recording purchases at *net* invoice price (the sales price less the discount) and using a separate account for any discounts not taken. To illustrate, assume that a $1,000 invoice, terms 2/10, n/30, is recorded at net invoice price ($980) and is paid after the discount privilege period has expired. The required entries are:

Purchases	
(a)	980

Accounts Payable			
(b)	980	(a)	980

Cash			
Bal.	xxx	(b)	1,000

Purchase Discounts Lost	
(b)	20

This procedure applies the principle of management by exception by drawing attention to the exception rather than the routine, that is, to discounts *not* taken. Well-run businesses seldom fail to take all discounts offered simply because of the relative cost involved. For example, failure to take a 2 percent discount under credit terms of 2/10, n/30 is the equivalent of paying 2 percent for 20 days since the account is due 20 days after the discount period expires. Two percent for 20 days is roughly equal to an annual rate of interest of 36 percent figured:

$$\frac{(\text{Discount rate})(360)}{(\text{Day due} - \text{Discount period})} = \text{Annual interest rate}$$

Thus, in the above example:

$$\frac{(2\%)(360)}{30 - 10 \text{ days}} = \frac{720\%}{20 \text{ days}} = 36\% \text{ annual interest rate}$$

Transportation-In

The cost a buyer incurs to have merchandise delivered is part of the total cost of the goods. But because the total freight costs incurred may be significant information, the receipt of a freight bill usually results in an entry debiting Transportation-In and crediting Accounts Payable.

The partial income statement shown in Illustration 3.2 illustrates the financial reporting of returns, allowances, discounts, and transportation-in.

Illustration 3.2

FICTITIOUS COMPANY
Income Statement
For the Year Ended December 31, 19x2

Sales...		$100,000	
Less: Sales returns and allowances	$ 4,000		
Sales discounts	1,000	5,000	
Net sales..			$95,000
Cost of goods sold:			
Inventory, January 1		$ 28,000	
Purchases......................................	$60,000		
Less: Purchase returns and allowances $5,000			
Purchase discounts.................... 1,000	6,000		
Net purchases	$54,000		
Transportation-in	3,000	57,000	
Cost of goods available for sale		$ 85,000	
Less: Inventory, December 31		21,000	64,000
Gross margin			$31,000
Operating expenses:			
Administrative expenses.........................		$ 6,000	
Selling expenses		9,000	15,000
Net income.....................................			$16,000

ADJUSTING AND CLOSING ENTRIES

The data in Illustration 3.2 can be used to show the adjusting and closing entries required in the accounts of a merchandising firm. An entry is needed to accumulate in one account (Cost of Goods Sold) all costs relating to the goods available for sale. Adjusting and closing entries for a merchandising firm, such as in Illustration 3.2, follow a six-step process to determine net income. First, the existing balances in the inventory, transportation-in, and the purchase-related accounts are transferred to the Cost of Goods Sold account:

Inventory				Transportation-In				Purchases			
Bal.	28,000	To close		Bal.	3,000	To close		Bal.	60,000	To close	
		(a)	28,000			(b)	3,000			(c)	60,000

Cost of Goods Sold				Purchase Returns and Allowances				Purchase Discounts			
(a)	28,000	(d)	5,000	To close		Bal.	5,000	To close		Bal.	1,000
(b)	3,000	(e)	1,000	(d)	5,000			(e)	1,000		
(c)	60,000										
Bal.	85,000										

Second, the Cost of Goods Sold account (which started with a zero balance) now contains the cost of the goods *available for sale*. But not all of the goods have been sold. An inventory of $21,000 remains on hand. This must be set up as an *asset* and deducted from the balance in the Cost of Goods Sold account:

Cost of Goods Sold				Inventory			
Bal.	85,000	(f)	21,000	(f)	21,000		
Bal.	64,000						

Third, the revenue and revenue contra accounts (Sales Returns and Allowances or Discounts) are closed to the Income Summary account:

Sales				Sales Returns and Allowances			
To close		Bal.	100,000	Bal.	4,000	To close	
(g)	100,000					(h)	4,000

Income Summary				Sales Discounts			
(h)	4,000	(g)	100,000	Bal.	1,000	To close	
(i)	1,000					(i)	1,000
		Bal.	95,000				

Fourth, the Cost of Goods Sold account is closed in an entry involving a debit to the Income Summary account and a credit to Cost of Goods Sold:

Income Summary				Cost of Goods Sold			
(j)	64,000	Bal.	95,000	Bal.	64,000	To close	
		Bal.	31,000			(j)	64,000

Fifth, the operating expenses are closed in an entry involving a debit to the Income Summary and a credit to each of the appropriate expense accounts:

Income Summary				Administrative Expense				Selling Expense			
(k)	6,000	Bal.	31,000	Bal.	6,000	To close		Bal.	9,000	To close	
(l)	9,000					(k)	6,000			(l)	9,000
		Bal.	16,000								

Finally, the net income is closed to the Retained Earnings account:

Income Summary				Retained Earnings			
To close		Bal.	16,000			Bal.	xxx
(m)	16,000					(m)	16,000

BAD DEBTS

A seller doing business on a credit basis faces the virtual certainty that some customers' accounts will ultimately become uncollectible. For example, assume that, because of past experience, a seller expects to collect only $95,000 out of $100,000 of accounts receivable outstanding at year-end. Normally, this generates the following entry:

Bad Debts Expense			Allowance for Doubtful Accounts		
(a)	5,000			(a)	5,000

This entry serves two purposes: (1) uncollectible accounts are charged as an expense in the year of the sale; that is, a proper matching is secured when uncollectible accounts arising from credit sales made in 19x2 are charged as an expense in 19x2; (2) the accounts receivable at year-end are properly valued at their *net realizable value*—the amount of cash expected to be collected.

The Bad Debts Expense account is shown as an operating expense in the income statement (that is, it appears as an expense *after* the gross margin is determined). The Allowance for Doubtful Accounts is a contra asset account to Accounts Receivable and is credited rather than crediting Accounts Receivable directly because it is not known at this time which customers' accounts will actually prove uncollectible. A typical reporting of the

$100,000 of accounts receivable and the related allowance for doubtful accounts of $5,000 is to include the following in the current assets section of the balance sheet:

Accounts receivable (less estimated uncollectibles of $5,000)......... $95,000

Subsequent Write-Offs

Later, when a specific customer's account is determined to be uncollectible, an entry is made debiting the Allowance for Doubtful Accounts and crediting Accounts Receivable. This entry has no effect upon net income or upon the valuation of the accounts receivable. The expense and the reduced valuation for the asset were recognized when the adjusting entry for estimated uncollectibles was made. The write-off entry confirms an event anticipated when the allowance was established.

If, by chance, an error was made in writing off an individual customer's account (as shown by the subsequent collection of the account), an entry is made debiting Accounts Receivable and crediting the Allowance for Doubtful Accounts. Then the cash collection is recorded as a debit to Cash and a credit to Accounts Receivable.

INVENTORY MEASUREMENT

A crucial step in the determination of net income is the measurement of the ending inventory of the period. This is true not only because it affects net income but also because it affects measurements of current assets, total assets, gross margin, retained earnings, and total stockholders' equity. How this happens will be explained later.

The Basic Rule

Inventories are usually accounted for at cost. However, a departure from cost is required when the goods' utility is no longer as great as their cost. Thus, inventories are usually reported in the balance sheet at a dollar amount described as *cost or market, whichever is lower*.

In applying this basic rule, several problems exist, including:

1. Which costs should be included as part of the cost of the inventory?
2. What is the cost of the inventory when goods have been purchased at different unit costs?
3. What constitutes evidence of a decline in the utility of goods, and how is it measured?

Inventory Cost—Possible Inclusions

In principle, the cost of inventory includes all costs incurred, directly or indirectly, to acquire the goods and place them in position and condition for sale. Inventory cost includes the net invoice price of the goods less purchase allowances plus insurance in transit; transportation charges; and receiving, handling, and storage costs. But, as a practical matter, these related costs are often omitted from inventory cost because (1) they are not material in amount relative to the total cost of the goods purchased, or (2) there often is no easy way to allocate these costs to individual units of merchandise. Also, purchase discounts are, on occasion, not deducted from the invoice price because they are so small as to be immaterial.

Accounting for Inventory

In valuing inventory, accountants need to treat three different types of situations:

When prices of inventory vary from purchase to purchase, the valuation of inventory will depend on the costing method selected.

When the *value* of inventory is less than what was paid for it, the cost of the inventory must be written down to the lower value.

When estimates of inventory cost are needed (as when a physical inventory cannot be taken for practical reasons or when inventory has been stolen or destroyed), a method must be used to estimate the cost of inventory.

Inventory costing methods.   The cost of the goods available for sale (beginning inventory plus purchases) must be apportioned between ending inventory and cost of goods sold. For example, suppose that at the beginning of a month a retailer has three units of a product on hand, one acquired at $10, another at $11, and the third at $12. Suppose that during the month two units were sold. Was their cost $21, the cost of the first and second units? Or was it $22, the cost of the first and third units? Or was it $23, the cost of the second and third units? Or should it be $22, determined as two units at an average cost of $11? Four inventory costing methods have been developed for this type of problem: (1) specific identification, (2) first-in, first-out (FIFO), (3) last-in, first-out (LIFO), and (4) weighted average. Each of these methods may be used for income tax purposes as well as for financial accounting purposes.

The data in Illustration 3.3 are assumed for the beginning inventory, purchases, and sales of a given product in order to illustrate the application of these four inventory costing methods.

The total goods available for sale consisted of 80 units with a total cost of $854. Of the units available, 60 were sold, producing sales revenue of $940, and 20 units were on hand in inventory. The accountant's task is to apportion the $854 between cost of goods sold (an expense) and ending inventory (an asset).

Illustration 3.3
Inventory Purchase, and Sales Data: Product X, Model 12

Beginning Inventory and Purchases				Sales			
Date	Number of Units	Unit Cost	Total Cost	Date	Number of Units	Price	Total
1/1 inventory........	10	$10.00	$100.00	3/8..........	10	$15.00	$150.00
3/2	10	10.40	104.00	7/5..........	10	15.00	150.00
5/28	20	10.50	210.00	9/7..........	20	16.00	320.00
8/12	10	11.00	110.00	11/27.........	20	16.00	320.00
10/12	20	10.90	218.00				
12/21	10	11.20	112.00				
Total	80		$854.00		60		$940.00

Specific identification. Specific identification calls for the assignment of an actual cost to an identifiable unit of product. The specific product is usually identifiable through the use of a serial number plate or an identification tag. The method is appropriate when large, readily identifiable products, for example, automobiles, are purchased and sold.

To illustrate, assume that the 20 units of product on hand at the end of the year in Illustration 3.3 are definitely known to consist of 10 from the August 12 purchase and 10 from the December 21 purchase. The ending inventory then is shown in Illustration 3.4.

Illustration 3.4
Ending Inventory under Specific Identification

From Purchase of—	Number of Units	Cost Each	Total Cost
August 12	10	$11.00	$110.00
December 21....................	10	11.20	112.00
Total	20		$222.00

The cost of the ending inventory of $222 is deducted from the total cost of goods available for sale of $854 to get the cost of goods sold of $632.

The specific identification method results in the cost of goods sold and the inventory being stated in terms of the actual cost of the actual units sold and on hand. Thus, costs are precisely matched against revenues. The method is used most logically to account for "big-ticket" items, such as autos and trucks, because each unit tends to be unique. Also, the selling price of such items tends to be based on a markup over a specifically identified cost.

The method is criticized because it may result in two identical units of product being included in the inventory at different prices even though they have the same utility. But supporters contend this is entirely logical and consistent with the cost basis of asset measurement. The method is also criticized because net income may be manipulated when it is used. If higher earnings are desired, ship the units with the lower cost. If lower earnings are desired, ship the high-cost units. But the major problem with the specific identification method is that it is simply too costly and too time consuming to apply for most businesses. This is true where large quantities of many different types of products with low unit costs are purchased and sold.

First-in, first-out (FIFO).   Good merchandising policy usually calls for selling the oldest goods first, if at all possible. In reality, in most businesses, the actual physical flow of goods *is* first-in, first-out and has to be to avoid losses from spoilage, as in the case of dairy products and fresh produce. Conforming the flow of costs through the accounting system to the actual physical flow of goods is logical, and the first-in, first-out method of inventory measurement results.

The application of the FIFO method results in the latest costs being included in inventory, while the older costs are charged to cost of goods sold. The method may be applied even in those circumstances in which goods do not flow in a first-in, first-out manner.

FIFO applied under periodic procedure.   Since, in the data presented in Illustration 3.3, the inventory consists of 20 units, under the FIFO method these units would be priced as shown in Illustration 3.5.

Illustration 3.5
FIFO Cost of Ending Inventory under Periodic Procedure

From Purchase of—	Number of Units	Unit Price	Total Cost
December 21	10	$11.20	$112.00
October 12	10	10.90	109.00
Total	20		$221.00

Under FIFO the ending inventory includes the costs of the latest purchases, and the balance of the cost of the goods available for sale (consisting of older costs) is charged to cost of goods sold. The ending inventory is $221, which is deducted from the total cost of goods available for sale of $854 to get the cost of goods sold of $633.

Last-in, first-out (LIFO).   Under LIFO, the costs of the last goods purchased are charged against revenues as the cost of the goods sold, while the inventory is composed of the costs of the oldest goods acquired. Although the costs of the goods purchased are assumed to flow in a last-in, first-out manner, this does not necessarily mean that the goods physically flow in this manner.

In order to determine the cost of the ending inventory under LIFO, ac-

countants list the goods in the beginning inventory and continue listing subsequent purchases until enough units have been listed to equal the number in
the ending inventory. Illustration 3.6 shows the determination of the ending
inventory for the data listed in Illustration 3.3.

Illustration 3.6
LIFO Cost of Ending Inventory

From Purchase of—	Number of Units	Unit Cost	Total Cost
Beginning inventory	10	10.00	$100.00
March 2...........................	10	10.40	104.00
Total	20		$204.00

The cost of the ending inventory of $204 is deducted from the cost of the
goods available for sale of $854 to show cost of goods sold of $650. In this
example, the costs charged against revenues as the cost of the goods sold are
all fairly current or recent costs, while the inventory consists of a March 2
cost and the cost of the beginning inventory, which may actually have been
incurred many years ago.

FIFO and LIFO compared. Much has been written concerning the merits of FIFO and LIFO. LIFO's appeal can be tied directly to rising prices
experienced in this country since the early 1930s. Using recent (higher)
prices for cost of goods sold reduces net income *and* current income taxes.
An example will make this point clear.

Beginning with FIFO, suppose that Company A has one unit of a given
product on hand which cost $10. The unit is sold for $15; other expenses of
sale amount to $3.50; the tax rate is 40 percent; and the unit is replaced for
$11 prior to the end of the accounting period. Under FIFO accounting, net
income is computed as:

Net sales	$15.00
Cost of goods sold...............................	10.00
Gross margin	$ 5.00
Expenses.......................................	3.50
Net operating margin.............................	$ 1.50
Federal income taxes (40 percent rate)...............	0.60
Net income	$ 0.90

According to the above schedule, the company is selling this product at a
profit. But consider the following:

Cash secured from sale..	$15.00
Expenses and taxes paid ($3.50 + $0.60)	4.10
Cash available for replacement and for dividends..................	$10.90
Cost to replace...	11.00
Additional cash required to replace inventory	$ 0.10

Company A, which is reporting a profit, finds itself unable to replace its inventory without additional cash. But note what happens when Company A uses LIFO as the method of inventory pricing:

Net sales............................	$15.00
Cost of goods sold	11.00
Gross margin........................	$ 4.00
Expenses	3.50
Net operating margin	$ 0.50
Federal income taxes	0.20
Net income.........................	$ 0.30

The $0.30 of net income is the same as the increase in cash that is available for dividends or other purposes:

Cash secured from sale......................................	$15.00
Expenses and taxes ($3.50 + $0.20)...........................	3.70
Cash available for replacement and dividends..................	$11.30
Cash spent to replace unit sold	11.00
Cash available for dividends (or other uses)...................	$ 0.30

Because the unit sold was replaced before the end of the year, the effect of using LIFO increased cost of goods sold $1 ($11 − $10). This, in turn, reduced taxable income by $1 and, with a 40 percent tax rate, reduced federal incomes taxes by 40 cents. Some of LIFO's popularity thus is due to its ability to minimize current tax payments in periods of rising prices.

But LIFO is also supported on the ground that it tends to match costs and revenues on a more reasonable basis than FIFO. The income statement reports sales and the most recent costs of making those sales when LIFO is used. Thus, the income reported reflects operating results and does not include gains from holding inventory in periods of rising prices—"inventory profits," as they are called. The inventory profit in the above example was $1—the difference between the cost to replace the unit sold at the time of sale ($11) and its actual cost ($10). LIFO is also supported by accountants who believe that selling prices are most likely to be based on replacement cost and that LIFO cost approximates replacement cost.

On the other hand, LIFO matches the cost of *un*sold goods (because goods usually move in a first-in, first-out manner) against sales revenue. LIFO also tends to yield an inventory amount that, after a period of rising prices, is substantially below the inventory's current replacement cost. The net income reported under LIFO can also be manipulated to a certain extent by purchasing, or not purchasing, goods near the end of the accounting year when unit costs have changed. If smaller income is desired, increase the amount of purchases at current high costs, and, under LIFO, these high costs will be charged to cost of goods sold. If higher income is desired, delay making purchases and charge to cost of goods sold some of the older, lower costs in inventory.

Weighted-average method. Under the weighted-average method, the total number of units purchased plus those on hand at the beginning of the year is divided into the total cost of the purchases plus the cost of the beginning inventory to derive a weighted-average unit cost. This unit cost is then multiplied by the number of units in the ending inventory to arrive at the cost of the inventory. Illustration 3.7 shows the application of this procedure.

Illustration 3.7
Application of Weighted-Average Method

Purchase Date	Number of Units Purchased	Unit Cost	Total Cost
1/1 inventory	10	$10.00	$100.00
3/2	10	10.40	104.00
5/28	20	10.50	210.00
8/12	10	11.00	110.00
10/12	20	10.90	218.00
12/21	10	11.20	112.00
Total	80		$854.00

Weighted average unit cost is $854 ÷ 80, or $10.675.
Ending inventory, then, is $10.675 × 20 .... 213.50
Cost of goods sold $640.50

Differences in cost methods summarized. Illustration 3.8 summarizes the cost of goods sold, ending inventories, and gross margins which will result from the application to the same inventory data of the four basic cost methods of pricing ending inventory.

Illustration 3.8
Summary of Effects of Employing Different Inventory Methods with Same Basic Data

	Specific Identification	FIFO	LIFO	Weighted Average
Sales	$940.00	$940.00	$940.00	$940.00
Cost of goods sold:				
Beginning inventory	$100.00	$100.00	$100.00	$100.00
Purchases	754.00	754.00	754.00	754.00
Cost of goods available for sale	$854.00	$854.00	$854.00	$854.00
Ending inventory	222.00	221.00	204.00	213.50
Cost of goods sold	$632.00	$633.00	$650.00	$640.50
Gross margin	$308.00	$307.00	$290.00	$299.50

Each of the inventory costing methods produces a different inventory measurement and gross margin. As might be expected, since the trend of prices was upward during the period. LIFO shows the highest cost of goods sold and the lowest gross margin.

Which is the "correct" method? All of the methods are considered acceptable, and none is considered the only "correct" one. Each method is attractive in particular circumstances. The application of LIFO results in matching current cost with current revenue, and makes it more likely that any net income reported can be distributed as dividends without impairing the level of operations. LIFO is actually a partial answer to the problems encountered in accounting under inflationary conditions. Also, LIFO reduces the amount of taxes payable currently under these conditions.

On the other hand, LIFO often charges against revenues the cost of goods *not* sold. LIFO permits manipulation of income simply by changing the time at which additional purchases of merchandise are made. If precision in the matching of *actual historical cost* with revenue is desired; FIFO or specific identification is to be preferred. But income may also be manipulated under the specific identification method, as it may be under the simple weighted-average method. Under the weighted-average method, the purchase of a large amount of goods at a relatively high price after the last sale of the period will change the average unit cost of the goods charged to the Cost of Goods Sold account. Only under FIFO is the manipulation of income *not* possible. But because net income under FIFO, in periods of rising prices, may have to be reinvested in inventory in order to maintain a given level of sales volume, this income is considered fictitious by many accountants and dubbed "paper profits."

In practice, some companies change their method of inventory measurement because others in their business have changed. This allows outsiders, such as investors, to make easier comparisons among companies in an industry. Some companies even employ different costing methods for different items in their inventories.

Inventories at less than cost. The basic rule of inventory measurement requires a departure from the cost basis for inventories when the utility of the goods is less than their cost. Such loss of utility may be evidenced by damage, obsolescence, or a decline in the selling price of the goods.

Net realizable value. Damaged, obsolete, or shopworn goods are carried in inventory or reported in the financial statements at their net realizable value. Net realizable value is defined as estimated selling price less costs to complete and sell the goods. For example, assume an auto dealer has used one auto as a demonstrator. The auto was acquired at a cost of $7,200 and had an original sales price of $8,400. But, because it has been used and it is now late in the model year, the net realizable value of the auto is estimated at:

Estimated selling price.	$7,000
Estimated repairs and selling costs	600
Net realizable value	$6,400

The auto would be valued for inventory purposes at $6,400. In this way, the $800 reduction in value would be treated as an expense in the period in which the decline in utility took place. If net realizable value exceeds cost, the item is carried at cost because accountants generally frown upon recognizing profits before goods are sold.

Inventories at cost or market, whichever is lower. Pricing inventories at the lower of cost or current market price is based, in part, on the assumption that if the purchase price in the market in which the firm buys has fallen, its selling price has fallen or will fall. But this is not always a valid assumption.

The term *market* as used in this context generally means replacement cost in terms of the quantity usually purchased. In using the method, it is still necessary to determine cost (by either the specific identification, FIFO, LIFO, or average method).

The lower-of-cost-or-market method uses market values only when these values are less than cost. If the inventory at December 31, 19x2, has a cost of $20,000 and a market value of $21,000, this increase in market value is not recognized. To do so would be to recognize revenue prior to the time of sale.

On the other hand, if market value is $19,400, the inventory may be written down to market value from cost and a $600 loss recognized since the inventory has lost some of its revenue-generating ability. Thus, the entry made anticipates a reduced selling price when the goods are actually sold.

Application of the method. As shown in Illustration 3.9, the lower-of-cost-or-market method may be applied to each item in the inventory, to each class in the inventory, or to the total inventory. Each application is considered acceptable, although tax regulations require application to individual items whenever feasible.

The inventory in Illustration 3.9 could be reported at $4,210, $4,240, or $4,410, and each can be referred to as the lower of cost or market. When applied to each individual item, all possible losses are consistently anticipated. But this may be unduly conservative, as the inventory may be written down even though there has been an actual increase in its total market value.

Illustration 3.9
Application of Lower-of-Cost-or-Market Method

Item and Class	Quantity	Unit Cost	Unit Market	Total Cost	Total Market	Lower of Cost or Market	
						By Classes	By Units
Class A							
A1	100	$8.00	$6.90	$ 800	$ 690		$ 690
A2	200	5.00	4.25	1,000	850		850
				$1,800	$1,540	$1,540	
Class B							
B1	500	3.00	3.40	$1,500	$1,700		1,500
B2	300	4.00	3.90	1,200	1,170		1,170
				$2,700	$2,870	2,700	
				$4,500	$4,410	$4,240	$4,210

Methods of Estimating Inventory

The gross margin and retail methods are procedures for estimating the amount of an inventory which is used:

1. To obtain an inventory at the end of each month of a fiscal period except the last when it is not economically feasible to take a physical inventory. The inventory cost so computed is used in the interim external reporting that is required for many companies.
2. To compare with physical inventories to determine whether shortages exist.
3. As a method of estimating the cost of inventory destroyed or lost.

The gross margin method. The gross margin method is based on the assumption that the gross margin *rate* realized is stable from period to period; the method is satisfactory only if this assumption is correct.

To illustrate the gross margin method of computing the inventory, assume that the Sweet Company has for several years maintained a rate of gross margin on sales of 40 percent. From this fact and the data given below, the approximate inventory of December 31, 19x2, may be determined as shown in Illustration 3.10.

Inventory, January 1, 19x2.	$ 30,000
Purchases of merchandise in 19x2	390,000
Sales of merchandise in 19x2.	600,000

Illustration 3.10
Computation of the Inventory, December 31, 19x2

Inventory, January 1, 19x2.		$ 30,000
Purchases		390,000
Cost of merchandise available for sale		$420,000
Less estimated cost of sales:		
Sales.	$600,000	
Gross margin (40% of $600,000)	240,000	
Estimated cost of sales		360,000
Estimated inventory, December 31, 19x2		$ 60,000

Because the gross margin method is based on the assumption that the gross margin rate in the *current* period is the *same* as in prior periods, which may not be true, it is generally not accurate enough to be used for the year-end financial statements. One of the other methods described in this chapter should be used, preferably using a physical inventory.

The retail method. The retail method is used by companies which sell goods directly to the ultimate consumer. In such companies, each item of merchandise is usually marked or tagged with its retail or selling price. The result is that the goods are referred to and inventoried at their retail prices.

In skeletal form, the retail method consists first of determining the ending inventory at retail prices:

> Beginning inventory at retail prices
> + Purchases at retail prices
> = Goods available for sale at retail prices
> − Sales (which are at retail prices)
> = Ending inventory at retail prices

To convert the ending inventory at retail prices to cost, the relationship between cost and retail prices must be known. This requires that information on the beginning inventory and purchases be accumulated so that goods available for sale can be expressed in terms of *cost* and *retail prices*. Transportation-in is added to beginning inventory and net purchases in the cost column. A cost/retail price ratio is developed and applied to sales to determine cost of goods sold and to the ending inventory at retail to reduce it to cost. This procedure is shown in Illustration 3.11.

Illustration 3.11
Inventory Calculation Using the Retail Method

	Cost	Retail Price
Inventory, January 1, 19x2...............................	$ 12,000	$ 20,000
Purchases, net	115,000	200,000
Transportation-in	5,000	0
Cost/retail price ratio:		
$132,000/$220,000, or 60%............................	$132,000	$220,000
Cost of goods sold and sales (cost is 60% of retail)	111,600	186,000
Inventory, January 31, 19x2 (cost is 60% of retail)	$ 20,400	$ 34,000

The $186,000 on the line entitled "Cost of goods sold and sales" is the amount of sales in the department for the month of January and is taken from the accounting records. The $111,600 is the cost of goods sold during the month, found by applying the cost/retail price ratio of 60 percent to the sales of $186,000. Deducting these two amounts, $111,600 and $186,000, from the $132,000 and $220,000 amounts on the preceding line—goods available for sale at cost and at retail—gives the January 31, 19x2, inventory for the department at cost and at retail.

Conclusion on Inventory Costing

For a manager being evaluated on profits or for an outsider evaluating the income of a firm, knowing the method of costing inventory is important. There are occasions when inventory values must be reduced below cost to recognize loss of market, decreased market prices, or other declines in value. Also, if a company changes its costing methods, previous financial statements are not necessarily comparable to the current figures. To understand any changes in financial results and the impact of the changes on net income, both managers and outsiders must know the standards used.

Questions

1. State several of the advantages of recording revenue at the time a credit sale is made. State one disadvantage.
2. Explain how perpetual procedure results in control over inventory.
3. Give some examples of the types of decisions management might make using information obtained from perpetual inventory stock cards.
4. Explain the meaning of the phrase "to take a physical inventory."
5. Why does an understated ending inventory understate net income (before income taxes) by the same amount?
6. In what respects are a purchase return and a purchase allowance similar? How do they differ?
7. What kind of an account is Sales Returns? Why is such an account used?
8. What should the cost of inventory include?
9. What is the effect of a failure to include in inventory the cost of transportation, insurance in transit, and other handling and receiving costs?
10. Show how reported net income can be manipulated by a company using LIFO in pricing its inventory. Why is the same manipulation not possible under FIFO?
11. In what three ways can the lower-of-cost-or-market method of inventory measurement be applied?
12. Under what operating conditions will the gross margin method of computing an inventory produce approximately the correct amounts?
13. A financial manager is engaged in explaining a firm's policy to you and states, "Our firm is in a tight financial position. No one will lend us money to take advantage of our discounts. But even though we can't pay within the discount period, I do the next best thing. I pay each bill as soon thereafter as I can." Do you agree that this is the next best approach? Why?
14. How can it be argued that the net price procedure of accounting for merchandise acquisitions permits the application of the management by exception principle?
15. Why is it considered acceptable accounting practice to recognize a loss by writing down an item of merchandise in inventory to a lower market price but unacceptable to recognize a gain by writing up an item of merchandise in inventory?
16. How can the retail method be used to estimate the cost of the ending inventory?

Exercises

1. *a.* The Young Company purchased merchandise from the Metro Company on account, and before paying its account returned damaged merchandise with

an invoice price of $750. Assuming use of periodic inventory procedure, prepare entries on both firms' books to record the return.

b. Prepare the necessary entries, assuming that the Metro Company granted an allowance of $225 on the damaged goods instead of accepting the return.

2. The Drew Corporation purchased goods for $3,000 on June 14 under the following terms: 2/10, n/30. The bill for the freight amounted to $75 and was paid in cash on June 14. Assume that the invoice was paid within the discount period, and prepare all of the entries required on Drew's books.

3. The Grosse Company inventory records show:

```
Inventory:
  Jan. 1.....................  500 units at $6.00 = $3,000
Purchases:
  Feb. 14....................  300 units at $5.40 = $1,620
  Mar. 18....................  800 units at $5.25 = $4,200
  July 21 ...................  600 units at $5.70 = $3,420
  Sept. 27 ..................  600 units at $5.40 = $3,240
  Nov. 27....................  200 units at $5.85 = $1,170
  Dec. 31 inventory.............  800 units
```

a. Prepare a short schedule showing the measurement of the ending inventory using the LIFO method.

b. Repeat using the FIFO method.

4. The Miller Company's inventory of a certain product consisted of 8,000 units with a cost of $11 each on January 1, 19x2. During 19x2, numerous units of this product were purchased and sold. Also during 19x2, the purchase price to Miller of this product fell steadily until at year-end it was $9. The inventory at year-end consisted of 12,000 units. State which of the two methods of inventory measurement, LIFO or FIFO, would have resulted in the higher reported net income, and explain briefly.

5. The following inventory data are for the Davis Company for 19x2:

```
Jan. 1    Inventory, 100 units at $40 = $4,000.
Jan. 31   January sales were 20 units.
Feb. 28   February sales totaled 30 units.
Mar. 1    Purchased 50 units at $42.
Aug. 31   Sales for March through August were 40 units.
Sept. 1   Purchased 10 units at $48.
Dec. 31   September through December sales were 55 units.
```

Determine the cost of the December 31, 19x2, inventory and the cost of goods sold for 19x2, using the weighted-average method.

6. Jimmy's Furniture Store has a stereo on hand at year-end that cost $300 and that it expected to sell for $450. But, since the stereo has been used as a display model, the estimated selling price is now only $250. Estimated reconditioning costs and selling commission amount to $40. At what dollar amount should this set be included in the year-end inventory?

7. Your assistant prepared the following schedule to assist you in pricing the inventory under the lower-of-cost-or-market method applied on an item basis. What is the dollar amount of ending inventory?

Item	Count	Unit Cost	Unit Market	Total Cost	Total Market
A	200	$18.00	$17.00	$ 3,600	$ 3,400
B	200	8.00	9.00	1,600	1,800
C	600	6.00	6.00	3,600	3,600
D	1,000	10.20	10.40	10.200	10,400
				$19,000	$19,200

8. Richie Company follows the practice of taking a physical inventory at the end of each calendar-year accounting period to establish the ending inventory amount for financial statement purposes. Its financial statements for the past few years indicate a normal gross margin of 20 percent. On July 25, a fire destroyed the entire store building and contents. The records were in a fireproof vault and are intact. These records through July 24 show:

Merchandise inventory, January 1	$ 50,000
Merchandise purchases.....................	1,350,000
Purchase returns	15,000
Transportation-in	85,000
Sales	1,550,000
Sales returns..............................	50,000

The company was fully covered by insurance, and it asks you to determine the amount of its claim for loss of merchandise.

9. Determine the ending inventory at cost, using the retail inventory method, from the following:

	Cost	Selling Price
Beginning inventory	$105,000	$ 195,000
Purchases	954,000	1,584,000
Purchase returns	12,000	22,500
Sales.........................		1,224,000
Sales returns..................		6,000
Transportation-in	6,500	

10. A Company sold goods on account in 19x2 in the amount of $250,000 and collected $200,000 of these accounts by the end of the year. The company estimated that only $46,000 of the outstanding accounts were collectible and adjusted its accounts accordingly. Early in 19x3, the $200 account of Bill George, which arose from a sale made in 19x2, was written off as uncollectible.
    a. Give the journal entry needed on December 31, 19x2, for the estimated uncollectible accounts.
    b. Show how the accounts you used in part a would be reported in the financial statements for the year ending December 31, 19x2.
    c. Give the entry to write off the Bill George account as uncollectible.
    d. State the effect on net income for 19x3 of the entry made in part c.

Business Decision Problem 3–1

Don Clark taught physical education classes at Pine Valley High School for 20 years. In 19x0, Don's uncle died and left Don $100,000. Don quit his teaching job in December 19x0 and opened a hardware store in January 19x1. On January 2, 19x1, Don deposited $60,000 in a checking account opened in the store's name, Clark's Hardware Store. During the first week of January, Don rented a building and paid the first year's rent of $4,800 in advance. Also during that week, he purchased the following assets for cash:

Delivery truck costing $10,000.
Store equipment costing $5,000.
Office equipment costing $3,000.
Merchandise inventory costing $10,000.

During the remainder of the first six months of 19x1, Don received cash of $70,000 from customers and disbursed cash of $42,000 for merchandise purchases and $15,000 for operating expenses.

Don never had an accounting course, but he had heard the term *net income*. He decided to compute his net income for the first six months of 19x1 and prepared the following schedule:

Cash receipts		$ 70,000
Cash disbursements:		
Delivery truck	$10,000	
Store equipment.	5,000	
Office equipment	3,000	
Prepaid rent	4,800	
Merchandise purchases	52,000	
Operating expenses.	15,000	89,800
Net loss.		$(19,800)

Required:

Do you agree with Don Clark's statement that his hardware store suffered a net loss of $19,800 for the six months ended June 30, 19x1? If not, show how you would determine the net income (or net loss).

Assume that the annual depreciation rates are:

Delivery truck, 20%.
Store equipment, 10%.
Office equipment, 12.5%.

Also assume that you obtain the following information:

Clark owes $8,000 to creditors for merchandise purchases.
Customers owe Clark $10,000.
Merchandise costing $6,000 is on hand.

Business Decision Problem 3–2

The Griffin Company, which began operations on January 2, sells a single product, Product X. The following data relate to the purchases of Product X for the year:

January	2	....	500 @ $2.00
February	15	....	800 @ $2.00
April	8	....	1,000 @ $2.15
June	6	....	400 @ $2.25
August	19	....	800 @ $2.30
October	5	....	600 @ $2.50
November	22	....	400 @ $2.80

Periodic inventory procedure is used. On December 31, a physical inventory of Product X shows that 800 units are on hand.

Mr. Griffin is trying to decide which of the following inventory costing methods he should adopt: weighted average, FIFO, or LIFO. Since Mr. Griffin is short of cash, he wants to minimize the amount of income taxes payable.

Required:

In this case, which of the three inventory costing methods will minimize the amount of income taxes payable? What will be the cost of goods sold and the cost of ending inventory under this method?

Solutions to End-of-Chapter Questions, Exercises, and Business Decision Problems

Answers to Questions

1. Among the advantages of recording revenue at the time a credit sale is made are: (1) the revenue is realized—that is, a valid asset has been received in an exchange; (2) the revenue is earned—that is, the seller has completed its share of the transaction; (3) the title to the goods passes to the buyer; and (4) the amount of revenue is measurable. A disadvantage is that revenue may be recognized that is never realized in cash form because of uncollectible accounts.

2. A perpetual inventory system provides control over inventory by showing the number of units of a good that should be on hand and against which a physical count can be compared. Shortages can be immediately spotted, with the added possibility of determining responsibility for them.

3. After looking at perpetual inventory records, management may decide to increase the selling price of a good or to increase the size of the next order. Or it may decide to decrease the price and engage in a special promotional campaign to get rid of slow-moving merchandise.

4. To make an actual, physical count or other measurement of the goods on hand.

5. Cost of goods sold is an expense deducted from revenues in arriving at net income. Cost of goods sold is determined as follows: Beginning inventory + Purchases − Ending inventory = Cost of goods sold. It follows that if the ending inventory is understated, cost of goods sold is overstated. If cost of goods sold is overstated, net income is understated.

6. A purchase return and a purchase allowance are similar in that both result in cancellation of all or a part of a purchase. They differ in that a return involves actual return of the merchandise, whereas an allowance does not.

7. Sales Returns is a contra or deduction account to Sales. It is used to accumulate information on the total amount of returns in the expectation that this may be significant information to management.

8. The cost of inventory should include the net invoice price of the merchandise acquired less purchase allowances plus all costs specifically incurred to acquire the inventory and place it in condition for use or sale. Such costs include insurance in transit, transportation charges, unpacking, checking, other receiving costs, and, possibly, storage costs.

9. Ending inventory is understated, with the probable understatement of net income, depending upon whether the costs also were omitted from the beginning inventory and upon which batch of costs omitted was larger.

10. If a firm has 1,000 units with a cost of $1 each in the beginning inventory, purchases 2,000 units at $2 each, and has 1,000 units in its ending inventory, under LIFO its cost of goods sold would be $4,000 and its ending inventory would be $1,000. But, if it wished to show greater net income, it could delay purchasing, say, 500 units of inventory (thus, its purchases would be 1,500 units at $2 each, or $3,000); its ending inventory would then be $500, and its cost of goods sold would be $3,500. Net income would be larger because some of the old, lower-priced inventory was sold.

    Such manipulation is not possible under FIFO because the cost of goods sold is always made up of the cost of the oldest units on hand and cannot be changed merely by timing additional purchases.

11. The lower-of-cost-or-market method can be applied to individual units, to classes of goods, or to the total inventory (usually with different results in each application).

12. When the gross margin rate remains relatively stable from period to period.

13. No. The financial manager would be better off to let those bills run up to the date they become overdue. But, if at all possible, the bills should be paid within the discount period unless the firm has to pay more for borrowed money than the rate of interest implied in the discount terms. Assume that merchandise purchased under terms of 2/10, n/60 is paid for on the 20th day. You would be paying 2 percent for the use of the supplier's money for only 10 additional days. Stated in annual terms, the rate of interest is approximately: 360 days/10 days × 2% = 72%. If the financial manager had waited until the 60th day to pay, the annual rate of interest would have been approximately: 360 days/50 days × 2% = 14.4%.

14. Net price procedure permits application of the management by exception principle by drawing attention to what should be in any well-run firm an exception to standard policy, namely, the failure to take a discount. It does this by requiring that an entry be made in an account called Discounts Lost for all discounts not taken. During periods of high interest rates, it may be a wiser policy not to take the discounts offered and to pay an account when it becomes due.

15. If the market value of the inventory has declined, then a loss is believed to already exist, since a loss can exist before a sale is made. Since losses are not assets, the amount of the loss must be removed from the inventory. On the other hand, increases in market value are not recognized because doing so would mean recognizing revenue before the time of sale. Revenue is called unrealized until a sale has taken place.

16. Ending inventory is determined first at retail prices by subtracting sales from goods available for sale (Beginning inventory + Purchases) at *retail*. A cost/

retail price ratio is determined by relating cost of goods available for sale to the retail price of the goods available for sale. Then, the cost/retail price ratio is applied to the ending inventory at retail to determine ending inventory at cost.

Solutions to Exercises

1.

	Young Company				Metro Company

a.

Accounts Payable (Metro Co.)		Purchase Returns and Allowances		Sales Returns and Allowances		Accounts Receivable (Young Co.)
750			750	750		750

b.

Accounts Payable (Metro Co.)		Purchase Returns and Allowances		Sales Returns and Allowances		Accounts Receivable (Young Co.)
225			225	225		225

2. June 14—purchase and freight (*a*).
   June 24—payment on account with discount taken (*b*).

Purchases		Accounts Payable		Transportation-In	
(*a*) 3,000		(*b*) 3,000	(*a*) 3,000	(*a*) 75	

Cash			Purchase Discounts	
Bal. xxx	(*a*) 75			(*b*) 60
	(*b*) 2,940			

3. *a.* Inventory under LIFO is:

$$
\begin{array}{lll}
500 & @ \$6.00 = & \$3,000 \\
300 & @ \$5.40 = & \underline{1,620} \\
\overline{800} & & \$4,620
\end{array}
$$

   b. Inventory under FIFO is:

$$
\begin{array}{lll}
200 & @ \$5.85 = & \$1,170 \\
600 & @ \$5.40 = & \underline{3,240} \\
\overline{800} & & \$4,410
\end{array}
$$

4. The use of LIFO would have yielded the higher reported net income. Under LIFO, the ending inventory would have consisted largely of units with a cost of $11 each, while under FIFO, the ending inventory would have been priced largely at prices approximating $9 each. Thus, LIFO yields the greater inventory and consequently the lower cost of goods sold and the higher reported net income.

5.

Beginning inventory, 100 @ $40.00................		$4,000.00
Purchases:		
50 @ $42.00		2,100.00
10 @ $48.00		480.00
Goods available, 160 @ $41.13		$6,580.00
Inventory, 15 @ $41.13		616.95
Cost of goods sold		$5,963.05

6. The set should be included in inventory at its net realizable value, computed as follows:

Estimated selling price....................................	$250
Estimated reconditioning and selling costs.................	40
Net realizable value......................................	$210

7.

Item	Inventory Amount
A....................	$ 3,400
B....................	1,600
C....................	3,600
D....................	10,200
	$18,800

8. The loss is the entire inventory amount and is computed as follows:

Inventory, January 1		$ 50,000
Purchases.......................................	$1,350,000	
Less: Returns	15,000	1,335,000
Transportation-in.................................		85,000
Cost of goods available for sale....................		$1,470,000
Less estimated cost of goods sold:		
Sales..	$1,550,000	
Less: Sales returns.........................	50,000	
Net sales	$1,500,000	
Less: Gross margin ($1,500,000 × .20).........	300,000	
Estimated cost of goods sold		1,200,000
Estimated cost of inventory, July 14		$ 270,000

9.

	Cost	Selling Price
Beginning inventory	$ 105,000	$ 195,000
Purchases, net	942,000	1,561,500
Transportation-in.................................	6,500	
Goods available (cost/price ratio is $1,053,500/$1,756,500 = 60%)....................	$1,053,500	$1,756,500
Net sales..		1,218,000
Ending inventory at retail		$ 538,500
Ending inventory at cost ($538,500 × 0.6)	$ 323,100	

10. *a.*

Bad Debts Expense	Allowance for Doubtful Accounts
4,000	4,000

b. In income statement in Operating Expenses:

Bad debts expense $4,000

In balance sheet under Current Assets:

Accounts receivable less estimated uncollectible
    accounts of $4,000...................................... $46,000

c.

Allowance for Doubtful Accounts	Accounts Receivable
200	200

d. No effect on net income of 19x3. The $200 is part of the estimated expense of $4,000 for 19x2 in the entry in part *a.*

Solution to Business Decision Problem 3–1

No, I do not agree with Don Clark's statement. He did not actually compute net income or net loss. He just prepared a list of cash receipts and cash disbursements. Even in doing this, he showed cash disbursements for merchandise purchases at $52,000 instead of the correct amount of $42,000. Correcting for this, the excess of cash disbursements over cash receipts is $9,800 instead of $19,800. Net income is actually $7,162, computed as follows:

CLARK'S HARDWARE STORE
Income Statement
For the Six Months Ended June 30, 19x1

Revenues:		
Sales ($70,000 + $10,000)............................		$80,000
Cost of goods sold:		
Merchandise Inventory, January 1, 19x1...............	$10,000	
Purchases ($42,000 + $8,000).......................	50,000	
Cost of goods available for sale......................	$60,000	
Merchandise inventory, June 30, 19x1.................	6,000	
Cost of goods sold		54,000
Gross margin		$26,000
Operating expenses:		
Rent expense ($4,800 × 0.5)	$ 2,400	
Other cash operating expenses	15,000	
Depreciation on delivery truck	1,000	
Depreciation on store equipment.....................	250	
Depreciation on office equipment	188	
Total operating expenses		18,838
Net income		$ 7,162

Solution to Business Decision Problem 3–2

Since prices increased through the period, LIFO is the method that will minimize the amount of income taxes payable. Under LIFO, the cost of goods sold is $8,510 and the cost of ending inventory is $1,600, determined as follows:

Cost of goods available for sale:
  Purchases:

January	2	500 @ $2.00 =	$ 1,000
February	15	800 @ $2.00 =	1,600
April	8	1,000 @ $2.15 =	2,150
June	6	400 @ $2.25 =	900
August	19	800 @ $2.30 =	1,840
October	5	600 @ $2.50 =	1,500
November	22	400 @ $2.80 =	1,120
		4,500	$10,110

Inventory (800 units):

500 @ $2.00	$1,000	
300 @ $2.00	600	1,600
Cost of goods sold		$ 8,510

Under FIFO, cost of goods sold and ending inventory would be as follows:

Cost of goods available for sale....................		$10,110
Inventory (800 units):		
400 @ $2.80	$1,120	
400 @ $2.50	1,000	2,120
Cost of goods sold		$ 7,990

Under weighted average, it would be as follows:

Cost of goods available for sale...................	$10,110
Inventory (800 units @ $10,110/4,500).............	1,797
Cost of goods sold.............................	$ 8,313

4

Noncurrent Assets

Chapter Goals

When you have completed Chapter 4, you should be able to:

1. Explain the nature, general characteristics, and various types of plant and equipment.
2. Describe what is included in the cost of plant and equipment.
3. Explain the nature of depreciation.
4. Explain various methods of determining depreciation and their effects on net income and income taxes.
5. Differentiate between capital and revenue expenditures and the accounting treatment of each.
6. Explain the nature and accounting treatment of dispositions of plant assets.
7. Explain the various types of natural resources and the determination of, and accounting for, their depletion.
8. Define various types of intangible assets and record their amortization.
9. Distinguish between capital and operating leases and the accounting for both.

Business assets may be broadly classified as current assets, such as cash, marketable securities, accounts receivable, and inventory, or as noncurrent assets, depending on the amount of time expected to expire before they are consumed or used up in the operations of the business. For many firms, the noncurrent category consists largely of assets that will be used or consumed over a long period of time. Such assets may appear on financial statements as *property, plant, and equipment* (or *plant assets, fixed assets,* or *plant and equipment*), *natural resources,* and *intangible assets.*

PLANT AND EQUIPMENT

Plant and equipment refers to tangible long-lived assets (assets with useful lives in excess of one year) obtained for use in the firm's operations instead of for resale. Examples are land, buildings and other structures, machinery, delivery equipment, office equipment, and furniture and fixtures. These assets are viewed as consisting of "bundles of service potential" that will be used up over several accounting periods. A building, for example, may represent 40 years of housing service. To match revenues and the related expenses of a period, the part of the service potential of any asset that expired during a period, called depreciation, depletion, or amortization, must be measured and its cost assigned as an expense of that period.

Plant and equipment can be subdivided into land and depreciable property. Land, because it does not deteriorate through use or with age, is not depreciable. All other items of plant and equipment are depreciable; their usefulness is reduced through wear and tear and obsolescence.

The Cost of Plant and Equipment

Plant and equipment are initially recorded at cost because cost is an objective measure of their value at the time of acquisition. Cost includes all normal, reasonable, and necessary outlays to obtain the asset and place it in a condition ready for use.

Land and land improvements. The cost of land includes the purchase price; option cost, if any; real estate commissions; the cost of title search; fees for recording the title transfer; unpaid taxes assumed by the purchaser; local assessments for sidewalks, streets, sewers, and water mains; and the cost of grading. Since land improvements such as parking lots, fences, driveways, and sprinkler systems are depreciable, their cost should be recorded in a separate Land Improvements account.

Building. If a building is purchased, its cost includes the purchase price, the costs of repairing and remodeling it for use by its new owner, unpaid taxes assumed by the purchaser, legal costs, and broker's commissions. When land and buildings are purchased for a lump sum, the total cost is divided and separate accounts set up for land and for buildings. This division of cost is usually based on values set by an appraiser. Separation is needed so that depreciation of the building can be calculated and included in computing net income.

If a building is constructed, its cost may be more difficult to determine. But its cost usually includes payments to contractors, architect's fees, building permits, taxes, insurance and interest during construction, and the salaries of persons supervising the construction.

To illustrate, assume that the Carson Company purchased a farm near Topeka, Kansas, as a factory site. The company paid $300,000 to the owner of the property. In addition, Carson agreed to pay unpaid land assessed taxes (back taxes) of $12,000. Attorney's fees and other legal costs of the purchase amounted to $1,800. The old buildings on the farm were demolished at a net cost of $20,000 (the cost of removal less proceeds from sales of salvaged materials). A new building was constructed at a cost of $400,000, plus $30,000 of building permit fees and architect's fees. Finally, the company paid an assessment to the city of $12,000 for water mains, sewers, and street paving. The cost of the land and the factory building will be initially recorded as:

	Land	Building
Cost of factory site	$300,000	
Back taxes	12,000	
Attorney's fees and other legal costs	1,800	
Demolition	20,000	
Cost of factory building		$400,000
Building permits and architect's fees		30,000
City assessments	12,000	
	$345,800	$430,000

All costs of purchasing the farm and demolishing (razing) the old buildings are assigned to the land because none of the old buildings was used. The goal was to get the land, which was not available without the buildings. If one of the buildings was remodeled for use by the company, a part of the $333,800 ($345,800 − $12,000) would be allocated to the building on the basis of relative appraised values. The $12,000 of back taxes would not be allocated because it was assessed on the land only. If an appraiser placed a value on the land of three fourths of the total value, and one fourth on the building, $250,350 (0.75 × $333,800) of the $333,800 is allocated to the land and $83,450 (0.25 × $333,800) is allocated to the building.

Machinery and equipment.   If machinery and equipment are acquired by purchase, their cost includes the net invoice price, transportation charges, insurance in transit, cost of installation, costs of attachments and accessories, testing and break-in costs, and other costs incurred to acquire and place the assets in use. If a company builds a machine for its own use, the cost of the machine includes materials, labor, and an amount equal to the increase in factory costs caused by building the machine. No profit is recorded on the construction of a machine by a company for its own use. The cost basis of accounting requires that a machine constructed at a cost of $40,000 be recorded at $40,000 even though it could not have been purchased for less than $43,000.

Noncash acquisitions and gifts of plant and equipment. On rare occasions, plant assets are received in exchange for assets other than cash, for securities issued, or as gifts. Such assets are recorded at their fair market value. Fair market value is determined from the fair market value of what was given up or the fair market value of what was received, whichever is more clearly evident. For example, a machine received in exchange for 1,000 shares of the company's stock with a market value of $15 per share is recorded at $15,000 even though the machine has a list or catalog price of $16,000. In cases where there are no market values for either the asset received or the item given up, appraised values are sometimes used. If neither appraised values nor market values are available, the asset received is recorded at the book value of the asset given up, as will be discussed and illustrated in a later section of this chapter.

Depreciation of Plant and Equipment

In accounting, depreciation is an estimate, usually expressed in terms of cost, of the amount of an asset's service potential that expired in an accounting period. The major causes of depreciation are physical deterioration, inadequacy for future needs, and obsolescence. Wear and tear and the action of the elements cause physical deterioration. Even an excellent maintenance and repair policy cannot prevent an asset from eventually being discarded. A machine may simply be inadequate to meet a company's requirements, or a machine may be in excellent physical condition and yet also be obsolete because more efficient, more economical, and higher-quality machines are available. Both inadequacy and obsolescence, as well as possible physical deterioration, must be taken into consideration in depreciation accounting.

Depreciation accounting. Depreciation accounting distributes in a systematic and rational manner the cost of a depreciable asset, less its salvage value, over the assumed useful life of the asset. Depreciation is a process of allocating cost to the revenues the depreciable asset produces, not a valuation technique. It is recorded by debiting a Depreciation Expense account and crediting an Accumulated Depreciation (contra asset) account. The costs of providing and using the long-lived physical assets of a firm are reflected as depreciation expense in the income statement.

To estimate periodic depreciation, three factors are generally considered by accountants: (1) cost, (2) estimated salvage value, and (3) estimated useful life. The cost to be recorded for an asset was discussed. Estimated salvage value is the salvage or scrap value estimated to be recoverable at the end of the asset's useful life. The estimated useful life of an asset may be expressed in years, months, working hours, or units of output.

Depreciation methods.   Because it is not possible to measure the exact amount of depreciation to be allocated to each period of an asset's life, a number of methods of computing depreciation are permitted, including straight-line depreciation, the units-of-production method, and accelerated depreciation.

Straight-line depreciation.   Straight-line depreciation assigns the same amount of asset cost to each year of an asset's estimated useful life. The formula used is:

$$\text{Depreciation per period} = \frac{\text{Cost} - \text{Estimated salvage value}}{\text{Number of accounting periods in estimated life}}$$

On a machine that cost $10,000 with an estimated useful life of five years and a salvage value of $1,000, the annual straight-line depreciation charge is $1,800:

$$\text{Depreciation per period} = \frac{\$10,000 - \$1,000}{5 \text{ years}} = \$1,800 \text{ per year}$$

The $1,800 of depreciation per year is recorded by debiting Depreciation Expense—Machinery and crediting Accumulated Depreciation—Machinery. The Depreciation Expense—Machinery account is closed to the Income Summary account, while the Accumulated Depreciation—Machinery account appears in the balance sheet as a deduction from the amount shown for machinery. At the end of its first year of life, the machine is shown at its *net book value* (cost less accumulated depreciation) of $8,200 ($10,000 − $1,800). The same depreciation entry is made in the second year, and the net book value of the machine is $6,400 [$10,000 − 2($1,800)].

Use of the straight-line method is supported (1) where the asset will be used at a fairly constant rate and (2) where deterioration and obsolescence occur in direct proportion to elapsed time.

Units-of-production method.   If usage is the main factor causing the expiration of an asset, depreciation may be based on its physical output. The depreciation charge per unit of output is computed by dividing the asset's cost, less its estimated salvage value, if any, by the estimated number of units to be produced by the asset in its life. Periodic depreciation is obtained by multiplying the rate per unit by the actual number of units produced in the period.

To illustrate, assume that on April 1, 19x2, Lee Company purchased a machine at a total cost of $10,000. The machine is estimated to have a 10-year useful life and a $1,000 salvage value. It is further estimated that the machine will produce 900,000 units of product during its useful life. The depreciation charge per unit of output is $0.01:

$$\text{Depreciation per unit of product} = \frac{\text{Cost} - \text{Estimated salvage value}}{\text{Estimated units of production}}$$

$$= \frac{\$10,000 - \$1,000}{900,000} = \$0.01$$

If the machine produces 120,000 units in 19x2, the depreciation recorded on the machine for the year is $1,200 (120,000 × $0.01). Similarly, if 250,000 units are produced in 19x3, the depreciation charge is $2,500 (250,000 × $0.01).

This method is supported in situations in which usage is the primary factor leading to the demise of the asset. The method is not widely used because of the difficulty of estimating output and because it does not take into account the possible loss of service potential that might occur when the asset is idle.

Accelerated depreciation.   Companies may also use the double-declining-balance method or the sum-of-the-years'-digits method of computing depreciation. These methods, often called accelerated depreciation, permit larger amounts of depreciation to be recorded in the earlier years of an asset's life than in the later years. The accelerated methods seem appropriate when the service-rendering or revenue-producing ability of the asset declines with age, when the value of the asset declines more in the earlier years of its life than in the later years, and when repairs and maintenance costs increase over time.

Double-declining balance method.   Under this method, the straight-line depreciation rate is doubled, and the doubled rate is applied to the asset's net book value. Salvage value is not considered initially in the calculation, but serves as a base below which the asset is not depreciated. Illustration 4.1 contains an example of the application of the method to an asset having a cost of $10,000, an estimated useful life of five years, and an estimated

Illustration 4.1
Double-Declining-Balance Method Depreciation Schedule

End of Year	Depreciation Expense Dr.; Accumulated Depreciation Cr.	Total Accumulated	Net Book Value
			$10,000
1................	$4,000(40% of $10,000)	$4,000	6,000
2................	2,400(40% of $6,000)	6,400	3,600
3................	1,440(40% of $3,600)	7,840	2,160
4................	864(40% of $2,160)	8,704	1,296
5................	296*	9,000	1,000

* The depreciation recorded in year 5 is limited to an amount sufficient to reduce the asset to its salvage value of $1,000.

salvage value of $1,000. The 20 percent straight-line depreciation rate (100 percent ÷ 5 years) is doubled, resulting in a depreciation rate of 40 percent, which will be consistently applied to the asset's net book value until the net book value equals the salvage value.

Sum-of-the-years'-digits method.   This method also produces larger depreciation charges in the earlier years of an asset's life. The years of estimated asset life are added together and used as the denominator in a fraction. The number of years of life remaining at the beginning of the accounting year is the numerator. Cost, less estimated salvage value, is then multiplied by this fraction to compute the periodic depreciation. This method is illustrated below for an asset with a cost of $10,000, an estimated useful life of five years, and an expected salvage value of $1,000. The sum-of-the-years' digits for five years is 15 (1 + 2 + 3 + 4 + 5 = 15). The annual depreciation then is:

Year 1 (5/15 × $9,000)	$3,000
2 (4/15 × $9,000)	2,400
3 (3/15 × $9,000)	1,800
4 (2/15 × $9,000)	1,200
5 (1/15 × $9,000)	600
Total depreciation	$9,000

At the beginning of year 1, there are five years of life remaining; thus, the ratio used for year 1 is 5/15. At the beginning of year 2, there are four years of life remaining, so the ratio used is 4/15, and so on.

Depreciation on assets acquired or retired during an accounting period. When plant assets are acquired or retired during an accounting period, depreciation often is computed for the nearest full month. If an asset is purchased on or before the 15th of the month, it is treated as if acquired on the 1st day of the month of acquisition. An asset acquired after the 15th is treated as if purchased on the 1st day of the next month. Thus, $4,000 of depreciation is recorded in 19x2 under the straight-line method on an asset acquired on March 14, 19x2, at a cost of $52,000, which has an expected salvage value of $4,000 and an estimated useful life of 10 years [($52,000 − $4,000) × 0.1 × 10/12 = $4,000].

Revisions of life estimates.   When the estimated useful life is found to be incorrect, the annual depreciation charge is revised to allocate the net book value less salvage value of the asset over its remaining life. For example, assume that a machine with a $60,000 cost and an estimated $6,000 salvage value is being depreciated using the straight-line method over an estimated eight-year useful life. At the end of the fourth year, the accumulated depreciation on the machine is $27,000. In the fifth year, it is estimated that the asset will last six more years, while its salvage value remains at $6,000. The revised annual depreciation charge is $4,500 [($60,000 − $27,000 − $6,000) ÷ 6].

Depreciation in the financial statements. The depreciation expense account appears in the income statement as one of the expenses of generating revenue. In a highly condensed income statement, the amount of periodic depreciation may be disclosed in a footnote. The periodic depreciation amount debited as an expense is also credited to an accumulated depreciation account. The use of this account permits showing the original cost of the asset rather than directly reducing the balance of the asset account. The ratio of the accumulated depreciation account to the asset's cost may give a hint as to the age of the asset. The total cost and accumulated depreciation may be shown separately on the balance sheet:

Plant and equipment:		
Store equipment	$ 24,000	
Less: Accumulated depreciation	4,000	$ 20,000
Building	$200,000	
Less: Accumulated depreciation	40,000	160,000
Land		80,000
Total plant and equipment		$260,000

Some mistakenly assume that the amount of accumulated depreciation represents cash available for replacing old assets with new. But accumulated depreciation is simply a measure of the cost of the portion of the asset that has expired and has been charged to depreciation expense. Cash is required to replace assets, and the cash available is shown as a current asset on the balance sheet.

Capital and revenue expenditures. It is often necessary to make expenditures on plant assets at times other than their acquisition date. Such expenditures may be allocated by charging them to (1) an asset account, (2) an accumulated depreciation account, or (3) an expense account.

Expenditures added to the asset account or charged to (deducted from) the accumulated depreciation account are often called *capital expenditures*. They increase the net book value of the assets. On the other hand, expenditures recorded as expenses are called *revenue expenditures*. The differences between them are discussed below.

Expenditures capitalized in asset accounts. Expenditures for new or used assets, additions to existing assets, and betterments or improvements to existing assets are called capital expenditures. They are properly chargeable to asset accounts because they add to the service-rendering ability of the assets. For example, assume that a used press cost Lee Company $50,000 cash plus $900 in transportation costs, both of which were recorded in the company's Machinery account. The company immediately spent $7,900 to recondition the press. The $7,900 should be added to the Machinery account. It is part of the total cost incurred to obtain the services of the press throughout its entire life. It is a capital expenditure.

Betterments are increases in the *quality* of the services an asset provides.

For example, the air conditioner installed in a previously un-air-conditioned owned auto is a betterment, and its cost will be added to the asset's account.

Expenditures capitalized as charges to accumulated depreciation. Occasionally, expenditures are made on a plant asset which extend its life or increase the *quantity* of output expected but not the *quality* of the services it provides. Because these expenditures will benefit future periods, they are properly capitalized. But because there is no visible, tangible addition to or improvement of the assets, such expenditures are often charged to the accumulated depreciation account. The expenditures are viewed as canceling a part of the accumulated depreciation.

To illustrate, assume that after operating its press for four years, Lee Company spent $4,720 to recondition it. The effect of the reconditioning increased the total expected useful life of the press to 14 years from an original estimate of 10 years. The T-account to record the reconditioning is:

Accumulated Depreciation Machinery			Cash		
	Bal.	23,520	Bal.	xxxx	
4,720					4,720
	Bal.	18,800			

When it was acquired, the press had an expected useful life of 10 years with no expected salvage value. Under straight-line depreciation, the balance in the accumulated depreciation account at the end of four years is $23,520 [($58,800 ÷ 10) × 4]. After the $4,720 is subtracted from the previous balance in accumulated depreciation, the balances in the asset account and its related accumulated depreciation are:

Cost of press.	$58,800
Accumulated depreciation.	18,800
Net book value	$40,000

The remaining net book value of $40,000 is divided equally among the 10 remaining years—$4,000 per year. The effect of the expenditure, then, is to increase the net book value of the asset by reducing its contra account, Accumulated Depreciation.

Even expenditures for major repairs which do *not* extend the life of the asset are often charged (debited) to accumulated depreciation (which increases future depreciation charges). In this way, the cost of major repairs is spread over a number of years. This avoids a distortion of net income which might occur if such expenditures were expensed in the year incurred.

If the expenditure described above did not extend the life of the asset but, because of its size, was still charged to accumulated depreciation, the $40,000 would be spread over the remaining *six* years of life in equal annual amounts of $6,667.

Expenditures charged to expense. Recurring expenditures that neither add to the service-rendering abilities of the asset nor extend its life beyond the original estimate are treated as expenses. Thus, regular maintenance (lubrication) and ordinary repairs (replacing a broken fan belt) are expensed immediately as revenue expenditures. For example, if the Lee Company spends $58 to lubricate and adjust the press, the T-accounts would be:

Machinery Maintenance Expense		Cash		
58		Bal.	xxx	
				58

Company policy and expenditures on plant assets. In practice, it often is difficult to distinguish between capital and revenue expenditures. As a result, the accounting for expenditures on plant assets is often guided by the unit of property concept or the establishment of arbitrary minimums for capitalization.

Unit of property concept. Under this concept, an expenditure on a plant asset for anything less than a complete replacement of the unit of property is charged as an expense. For example, under this concept, the cost of replacing the motor of a truck would be charged as an expense if the truck were considered the unit of property.

Arbitrary minimums. As a matter of managerial policy, expenditures for plant assets, such as the $4.95 cost of a wastebasket, may be expensed immediately because the benefits which result from the application of depreciation accounting procedures to such items would not be worth the cost involved. Similarly, a firm may decide to capitalize all repair costs incurred on a specific asset in a single act of repair in excess of an arbitrary amount, such as $500, while expensing those of a lesser amount.

Disposal of Plant Assets

The disposal of a plant asset by sale, scrapping, theft, or destruction may require recognition of a gain or loss. Assume, for example, that a company sells for $5,000 cash a machine which cost $24,000 and on which $20,000 of depreciation has been accumulated (a gain of $1,000). The entry for the sale would be:

Cash			Machinery				Allowance for Depreciation			
(1)	5,000		Bal.	100,000	(1)	24,000	(1)	20,000	Bal.	40,000

Gain on Sale of Machinery		
	(1)	1,000

If less than $4,000 (in this case) is received, a loss account would be debited for the difference between $4,000 and the amount received. Gains or losses upon disposal of plant assets are reported in the income statement, frequently as elements of "other revenue" or "other expense."

NATURAL RESOURCES

Natural resources, such as mines, quarries, and timber stands, are originally recorded in the accounts at cost of acquisition plus cost of development. Natural resources are later carried in the accounts at total cost minus *depletion*. Depletion is a cost allocation brought about by removal of a physical quantity of the resource.

Depletion charges may be computed by dividing the total cost of acquisition and development by the estimated number of units—tons, barrels, or board feet—that can be economically obtained from the property. This is known as the unit method of computing depletion. To illustrate, assume that $1 million was paid for a mine estimated to contain 800,000 tons of ore which can be economically extracted. The unit (per ton) depletion charge is $1,000,000 ÷ 800,000 tons, or $1.25 per ton. If, in 19x8, 80,000 tons of ore were extracted, the depletion charge is 80,000 × $1.25, or $100,000. This $100,000 is recorded in a separate Depletion account and either as a direct credit to the Mineral Deposits account or in a separate Accumulated Depletion account. For example, the T-accounts appear as:

Depletion		Mineral Deposits	
100,000		Balance 1,000,000	100,000

The Depletion account contains the material cost of the ore mined. It is combined with labor and other mining costs to arrive at the total cost of the ore mined. This total cost is then divided between cost of goods sold and inventory.

To illustrate, assume that in addition to the depletion cost of $100,000, mining labor costs for 19x8 amounted to $210,000, while all other mining costs (depreciation, property taxes, supplies used, power, similar costs) amounted to $90,000. The total costs of mining 80,000 tons then are $400,000, and the cost per ton is $5. If 70,000 tons are sold, the income statement shows cost of ore sold at $350,000, and the balance sheet shows inventory of ore on hand at $50,000.

INTANGIBLE ASSETS

Intangible assets have no physical characteristics. They have value because they give business advantages and exclusive privileges or rights to their owners. Intangible assets arise from (1) superior management know-how or ability—*goodwill*; and (2) exclusive privileges granted by governmental authority or by contract—*patents, copyrights,* and *franchises.*

As a general rule, intangible assets are recorded at their acquisition cost. As a result, the balance sheets of some companies fail to show extremely valuable intangible assets simply because they were acquired at little or no cost.

Intangible assets are usually classified as assets that are (1) specifically identifiable and can be acquired individually or in groups, such as patents, trademarks, and franchises; or (2) not individually identifiable and can be acquired only as part of a group of assets, such as paying $1 million for a firm with assets of $750,000. Because the extra $250,000 cannot be identified with specific assets, it is often lumped and called goodwill.

All intangible assets are subject to amortization. *Amortization* is similar to depreciation and depletion. It is an estimate of the cost of the services or benefits received from an intangible asset in a given period. Amortization is recorded by debiting an amortization expense account and crediting the intangible asset account or an accumulated amortization account.

In general, intangible assets are amortized over the shorter of their expected useful life or their legal life. In any case, the amortization period cannot exceed 40 years. Straight-line amortization is used unless another method can be shown to be superior.

Patents

Patents are grants made by the federal government which give an inventor the sole right to make, use, or sell an invention for a period of 17 years. Patents are recorded at cost and are amortized over the shorter of their expected economic (useful) life or legal life. For example, assume that Curry Company purchased patent rights to a machine invented by Denton Company. The patent rights cost $30,000 and have a 10-year estimated economic life. The following entry would be made each year for 10 years to amortize the cost of the patent rights:

Amortization of Patents		Patents		
3,000		Bal.	xxx	3,000

The Patents account may also be debited for the costs of successful lawsuits brought in defense of a patent.

Copyrights

A copyright gives its owner an exclusive right protecting writings, designs, and literary productions from being illegally reproduced. A copyright has a legal life equal to the life of the creator plus 50 years. Since most publications have a limited economic life, the cost of a copyright is often expensed against the revenue from a first edition.

Franchises

A franchise is a contract, frequently between a governmental agency (such as a state public service commission) and a private company (such as a gas and electric utility). Or it may be a contract between two private parties (such as in a McDonald's franchise). A franchise gives the holder certain rights, ranging from rights of a nominal nature to the right of complete monopoly. It often places certain restrictions on the holder, such as the regulation of utility rates. If periodic payments are made to obtain the franchise, the payments are expensed when paid. If a lump-sum payment was made to obtain the franchise, the cost is amortized over the shorter of the useful life of the franchise or 40 years.

Goodwill

Goodwill is best viewed as an intangible value attached to an entity which results primarily from the skill of its management. A firm may be continuously generating goodwill. Such goodwill may be represented by a superior marketing organization, product reputation, marketing channels, technical know-how, and astute management. Such factors, though, are hard to identify and value. Thus, the value of goodwill is often described as the value of the entity over the sum of the fair values of its net discernible assets. It arises because management has the ability to use the resources of the entity to produce an above-average rate of earnings per dollar of investment. This means that the proof of the existence of goodwill is found in the ability to generate superior or above-average earnings.

A Goodwill account will appear in the records only if the goodwill has been purchased. Goodwill cannot be purchased separately; an entire business or a portion of it must be purchased.

To illustrate, assume that Company A purchases all the assets of Company B. The assets consist of the following *market* (not cost or book) values:

Accounts receivable	$100,000
Inventories	90,000
Land	150,000
Buildings	250,000
Equipment	200,000
Patents	35,000
Total assets	$825,000

Company A pays Company B $600,000 in cash and assumes responsibility for $300,000 of debts owed by Company B. The intangible (goodwill) value attached to Company B and purchased by Company A is $75,000:

Cash paid...	$600,000	
Liabilities assumed.....................................	300,000	$900,000
Less: Fair market value of identifiable assets		825,000
Goodwill		$ 75,000

The $75,000 of goodwill is recorded in a Goodwill account. It is treated in this way because it is difficult to identify specific reasons for its existence. The reasons might include a good reputation, product leadership, valuable human resources, and a good information system.

Under federal income tax regulations, goodwill amortization cannot be deducted from revenues to compute taxable income. But current accounting practice requires the amortization of goodwill over a period not to exceed 40 years. The reasoning behind this requirement is that the value of the purchased goodwill will eventually disappear. If Company A in the example decided that the goodwill attached to Company B would last 10 years, it would make annual adjusting entries debiting Goodwill Amortization Expense and crediting Goodwill for $7,500. Successive balance sheets would show a decreasing goodwill asset.

Research and Development Costs

Current accounting practice requires that all research and development costs be expensed in the period incurred. This position is taken even though it seems logical that such costs are expected to benefit future periods and that a better matching of expense and revenue might be obtained if such costs were capitalized and amortized. Immediate expensing is justified on the grounds that (1) the amount of costs applicable to the future cannot be measured, (2) doubt exists as to whether future benefits will be received, and (3) even if benefits are expected, they cannot be measured.

Leases and Leaseholds

A lease is a contract in which a party acquiring the lease (the renter or the lessee) makes payments to the party granting the lease (the lessor or the owner) in exchange for the right to use property for the amount of time stated in the lease. Depending on the circumstances, a lease may be a capital lease or an operating lease.

Capital leases. Certain contracts, although legally drawn as leases, are in substance purchases financed by the lessor. For example, accounting practice requires that an asset and a liability be recorded for a lease which (1) transfers ownership of the property to the lessee, or (2) contains a bargain purchase option (which permits the lessee to purchase the leased property at a nominal amount), or (3) runs for at least 75 percent of the life of the leased property, or (4) calls for lease payments that have a *present value* equal to or greater than 90 percent of the fair value of the leased property.

To illustrate, assume that Day Company leased a machine for three years at an annual rental of $10,000 payable at the beginning of each lease year. Assume that the economic life of the machine is three years, which according to (3) above qualifies the lease as a capital lease, and that the going rate of interest at the time of purchase is 10 percent.

To account for the lease as a capital lease (entry a), Day Company would record an asset, called Leased Machinery under Capital Leases, of $27,355 reflecting the *present value* of the three $10,000 payments at a discount rate of 10 percent (the rate of interest). It would record a liability, called Obligations under Capital Leases, of $17,355, representing the discounted value of the final two lease payments of $10,000 using a 10 percent interest rate.[1] Finally, cash would be reduced (credited) $10,000 to reflect the initial payment on the capital lease. The T-accounts would appear as:

Leased Machinery under Capital Leases		Obligations under Capital Leases		Cash	
(a) 27,355			(a) 17,355	Bal. xxx	(a) 10,000

The $27,355 cost of the machine is allocated (entry b) to each of the three years of useful life (equal to the lease term), using one of the depreciation methods discussed earlier in the chapter. An adjusting entry is also required to record the interest expense on the liability. The adjustment (entry c) records the interest expense and increases the liability by the amount— $1,736 in the first year and $909 in the second year. The liability is then decreased (debited) when the $10,000 lease payment is made (entry d). After the second $10,000 lease payment is made, the T-accounts would appear as:

Leased Machinery under Capital Leases		Obligations under Capital Leases		
(a) 27,355		(d) 10,000	(a) 17,355	
			(c) 1,736	
			Bal. 9,091	

---

[1] The asset's assumed cost is the present value of payments under the lease at the assumed rate of interest of:

Year 1.....................................	$10,000/1.00	= $10,000
2.....................................	$10,000/1.10	= 9,091
3.....................................	$10,000/(1.10)^2 =	8,264
Total present value...............................		$27,355

The logic of the values is that in the first year the payment is due now and is therefore worth its full value. The second payment is due in one year, and $9,091 invested at 10 percent will grow to $10,000 in one year. Similarly, $8,264 invested at 10 percent will grow to $10,000 in two years. The liability is $17,355 because only the second and third payments are owed, and their sum is $17,355.

94

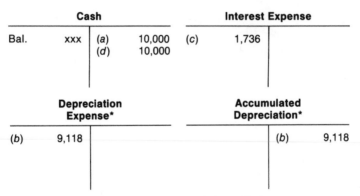

Cash				Interest Expense	
Bal.	xxx	(a)	10,000	(c)	1,736
		(d)	10,000		

Depreciation Expense*			Accumulated Depreciation*		
(b)	9,118			(b)	9,118

* Assumes use of the straight-line depreciation method.

Operating leases. If a lease does not qualify as a capital lease, it is an operating lease. An example of an operating lease is leasing an auto for 10 days from a rental agency such as Hertz. An operating lease is not shown on the lessee's balance sheet, except that any advance lump-sum payment made when the lease is signed, is recorded in a Leasehold account. The balance in the Leasehold account is amortized over the life of the lease by a debit to Rent Expense and a credit to Leasehold. Straight-line amortization is commonly used to reduce any advance payment on an operating lease.

Leasehold improvements. Often, a lessee will improve leased property by, for example, erecting a building on leased land or by making major changes remodeling a leased building. Normally, the cost of these improvements is recorded in a Leasehold Improvements account and amortized over the shorter term of the life of the lease or the useful life of the improvements. Straight-line amortization is common, although accelerated methods may be used to obtain a better matching of expense and revenue.

To illustrate, assume that a company leases a tract of land at an annual rental of $10,000 plus a $60,000 nonrefundable advance payment on the lease. The advance payment is called a leasehold and is amortized over the life of the lease. The company immediately erects a building at a cost of $150,000 on the leased property. The lease runs for 20 years, while the physical life of the building is estimated at 25 years. Assuming the company uses the straight-line amortization method, the total annual expense to be recognized on the lease and the leasehold improvement is $20,500:

Annual rental	$10,000
Amortization of advance payment ($60,000 ÷ 20 years).	3,000
Depreciation on the building ($150,000 ÷ 20 years)	7,500
	$20,500

In this case, the building is amortized over the life of the lease since it is less than the useful life of the building. The company will be able to use the services of the building only for the period of the lease.

Although a leasehold is an intangible asset, leaseholds and leasehold improvements are typically reported in the plant asset section of the statement of financial position.

Questions

1. Which of the following items are properly classifiable as plant and equipment in the balance sheet?
    a. The costs incurred to inform the public about new energy-saving programs at a manufacturing plant.
    b. The cost of a truck acquired by a manufacturing company to be used to deliver the company's products to wholesaler customers.
    c. The cost of an automobile owned by a company and used by one of its salespersons.
    d. The cost of several hand-held calculators acquired by an office supply company to be sold to customers.
    e. The cost of constructing and paving a driveway on leased land.
2. Why should depreciation, depletion, or amortization be recorded on virtually every plant or intangible asset or natural resource?
3. Should the cost of each item below be recorded as an expense, recorded as an asset, or charged to the Accumulated Depreciation account?
    a. Cost of new air-conditioning equipment installed in a leased building.
    b. The cost of a biennial painting of an owned factory building.
    c. The cost of installing a new battery in an owned automobile. The battery will last two to three years.
    d. The cost of replacing the roof on a 10-year-old building that was purchased new and has an estimated useful life of 40 years.
4. Distinguish between depreciation, depletion, and amortization and give two examples of assets subject to each of these.
5. Distinguish between plant and intangible assets. Classify the assets listed in your answer to Question 4 accordingly.
6. What is the primary task faced by accountants in accounting for noncash exchanges of assets? What is the general rule used to fulfill this task?
7. What four factors must be known in order to compute depreciation on a plant asset?
8. What does the balance in the Accumulated Depreciation account represent? Can this balance be used to replace the related plant asset?
9. Distinguish between: (a) leaseholds and leasehold improvements; (b) capital leases and operating leases.
10. Why does a business executive generally favor quick write-off of depreciable assets for tax purposes? Why might a business change from an accelerated method to the straight-line depreciation method of accounting?
11. What accounting treatment is generally required for research and development costs? Why?
12. A certain store enjoys a reputation for fair dealing with its customers, employees, and suppliers; is favorably located; seems to enjoy repeated visits from loyal customers; and sells high-quality merchandise. Does it follow that such a

store has goodwill? Explain. If the store does have goodwill, would the goodwill be recorded? Why or why not?

13. Distinguish between capital and revenue expenditures.
14. Briefly outline the accounting for an operating lease.
15. What is the measure of the gain or loss when a depreciable asset is sold?
16. What reasons are usually advanced in support of the accelerated depreciation methods?
17. How does one identify a capital lease? What is the significance of a determination that a certain lease is a capital lease?

Exercises

1. Babson Company recently purchased, for $200,000, a tract of land on which to construct a new warehouse. Legal fees related to the transaction amounted to $2,200. Babson Company also assumed liability for $8,000 of unpaid real estate back taxes. The old warehouse was razed at a cost of $9,000. Compute the cost of the land.
2. On January 2, 19x2, a new machine was acquired at a cost of $50,000. The machine has an estimated salvage value of $2,000 and an estimated useful life of 10 years. The machine is expected to produce 500,000 units of product during its useful life. Compute the depreciation for 19x2, and 19x3, using each of the following methods: (a) straight-line, (b) units-of-production (assuming that 30,000 units and 50,000 units were produced in 19x2 and 19x3, respectively), (c) double-declining-balance, and (d) sum-of-the-years'-digits.
3. Matte Company purchased a new machine on January 2, 19x2, at a cash cost of $60,000. The machine has an estimated useful life of five years and no expected salvage value. If federal income taxes are levied at a 50 percent rate on net income, how much would the income taxes payable for the years 19x2 and 19x3 be reduced if the company chose the double-declining-balance method of computing depreciation rather than the straight-line method?
4. Blake Company purchased a machine for $48,000 on January 2, 19x1, with an expected life of five years to be depreciated on a straight-line basis. No salvage value was expected. On December 31, 19x4, before recording depreciation for the year, Blake decided that the machine would last a total of eight years. Compute the depreciation to be recorded on the machine in 19x4.
5. Kemp Company paid $1,200,000 for the mineral rights, estimated at 6 million tons, in a certain tract of land. In the first year of operating the property, Kemp extracted 600,000 tons of ore, and sold 400,000 tons. Compute the amount of depletion that would be reported as an expense in this first year.
6. Carter Stores leased a tract of land and a building under an operating lease for a 20-year period beginning on January 1, 19x2, paying $80,000 in cash and agreeing to make annual payments equal to 1 percent of its first $1 million of sales and ½ percent of all sales in excess of $1 million. The minimum annual payment must be at least $12,500. Compute the rent expense for 19x2, assuming sales were $1,400,000.
7. Hatten Company purchased a patent on January 2, 19x0, at a total cost of $68,000. In January 19x7, the company successfully defended its patent against

an infringement suit at a cost of $15,000. If the useful life of the patent was 17 years on January 2, 19x0, compute the patent amortization expense for 19x7.

8. Bob Decker purchased a franchise from the U-Big-Burger company for $20,000. The contract also called for Decker to make annual payments equal to ½ percent of sales for the right to operate under the U-Big-Burger name. Decker can continue to hold the franchise as long as the annual payments are made and certain other operating conditions are met. Decker expects to meet these conditions as a routine matter. Decker's sales for 19x3 were $800,000. Compute the franchise expense for 19x3.

9. Lambden Company leased a computer on December 31, 19x2, for four years at an annual rental of $10,000, payable on each December 31, beginning in 19x2. Lambden could have purchased the computer, which has an expected useful life of four years, for $34,868. Thus, the lease payments include interest at 10 percent per year. Compute the depreciation expense (straight-line method) on the leased computer for 19x3. Also, compute the interest expense on the lease liability for 19x3.

Business Decision Problem 4–1

On January 2, 19x2, Crowley Company acquired new equipment costing $170,000. The equipment has an estimated salvage value of $5,000 and an estimated useful life of 10 years. It is further estimated that the equipment will produce 4 million units of product during its life. During 19x2, 360,000 units were produced. The company had income before depreciation and taxes of $100,000. Company officials are now trying to decide which depreciation method to use for accounting purposes. They ask you to prepare information showing the effects of the various methods of depreciation on income before income taxes and for your recommendation.

Required:

a. Compute the depreciation on the equipment for 19x2, using each of the following methods:
   1. Straight-line.
   2. Double-declining-balance.
   3. Sum-of-the-years'-digits.
   4. Units-of-production.
b. Prepare a schedule showing net income before taxes under each of the depreciation methods.
c. State your recommendation to management.

Business Decision Problem 4–2

Bill Redmond has just about decided to purchase all of the assets of the Hector Company, including its land, building, and equipment. He favors purchase of the Hector Company assets over purchase of the Victor Company assets even though the two companies have nearly identical assets, because Hector Company appears to be more profitable, as shown below:

Year	Net Income before Income Taxes	
	Hector Co.	Victor Co.
19x2	$84,000	$76,000
19x3	88,000	80,000

The two companies produce a nonpatented product which is rather standardized and which Bill expects to continue producing with the purchased assets. Both companies have been in operation two years and have virtually identical plant assets consisting of the following:

Plant Asset	Cost	Expected Salvage	Estimated Useful Life
Land	$ 80,000		
Buildings	200,000	0	40 years
Equipment	200,000	0	10 years

Bill feels that he is making the right decision. But he is bothered by some information which he does not understand. Hector Company reports that it uses the straight-line depreciation method for financial accounting purposes, while Victor Company reports that it uses the double-declining-balance method. Bill now comes to you for help.

Required:

a. Compute the amount of depreciation deducted by each company in arriving at income before income taxes.
b. Prepare a schedule showing the income before depreciation and income taxes to show which company is more profitable after the distorting effects of alternative depreciation methods are removed.
c. State your recommendation to Bill Redmond.

Solutions to End-of-Chapter Questions, Exercises, and Business Decision Problems

Answers to Questions

1. The items classifiable as plant and equipment are b, c, and e.
2. Since most plant assets and all intangible assets and natural resources eventually become worthless, periodic depreciation, amortization, or depletion must be recorded to spread their costs over those periods in which they render benefits. If not, the matching principle is violated.
3. a. Asset, because benefits will be received over a number of years in the future. The fact that the building is leased is irrelevant.
   b. Expense, because it is a normal, expected maintenance expenditure even though it is not incurred annually.

    c. Expense, since it is a minor repair. Also, the auto is undoubtedly the unit of property for depreciation accounting purposes. Under this concept, an expenditure to replace anything less than the unit of property is charged to expense.

    d. Expense, although another possibility is the Accumulated Depreciation account, simply as a means of spreading the cost of a major repair over a number of years.

4. Depreciation, depletion, and amortization are all means of allocating the cost of long-lived assets to the periods in their useful lives. Depreciation is related to all plant assets except land; depletion, to natural resources; and amortization, to intangible assets. Listed below are some typical long-lived assets that would fit these categories.

Depreciable Plant Assets	Depletable Natural Resources	Amortizable Intangible Assets
Buildings	Coal mines	Patents
Machinery	Oil reserves	Copyrights
Office equipment	Uranium deposits	Franchises
Delivery equipment	Timber stands	

5. Basically, tangible assets can be seen and touched; intangible assets cannot. The depreciable plant assets and the depletable natural resources listed in the preceding answer are all tangible assets; the other assets are intangible.

6. The task is to find the appropriate valuation to be used to record the exchange. The general rule is to use the fair market value of whatever was received or whatever was given up, whichever is the more clearly evident.

7. The four factors are: (1) cost, (2) estimated salvage value, (3) estimated useful life, and (4) depreciation method.

8. The balance in the Accumulated Depreciation account represents that part of the cost of the asset that has been charged to depreciation expense. It does not represent money available to replace the asset. Cash is required to replace the asset, and the Cash account shows the amount of cash on hand.

9. Leasehold is the title given to an account in which is recorded the down payment or advance deposit on a long-term operating lease. The cost of erecting structures on leased land or otherwise renovating leased property is recorded in a Leasehold Improvements account. (*b*) Capital leases are contracts that appear to be leases, legally, but are, in substance, contracts to purchase the asset, financed by the lessor. All leases other than capital leases are operating leases, and the intent here is to secure relatively short-term use of property owned by another.

10. Such a practice is favored for tax purposes if the increased deductions can be taken in arriving at taxable income so that current income taxes payable are reduced. In recent years, there have been several instances where firms have returned to straight-line depreciation for accounting purposes after using an accelerated method, primarily because of the adverse impact upon earnings and earnings per share of the heavy earlier depreciation charges under the accelerated methods.

11. Unless such costs are reimbursable, they are to be charged to expense in the period in which they are incurred. The reasons for such an accounting treatment are that the amount of the costs to be deferred cannot be easily measured, that there is doubt as to whether any benefits will be secured from the incurrence of the costs, and that even if benefits are expected, they cannot be easily measured.

12. Unless all of these factors combine to produce an above-average rate of earnings, there is no goodwill. The "proof of the pudding" as regards goodwill can be found only in the earnings (or expected earnings) of a firm. But even if the factors combined to yield above-average earnings, the goodwill would not be recorded. Only *purchased* goodwill is recorded because only purchased goodwill can be measured objectively.

13. Capital expenditures are expenditures that add to the stock of capital (long-lived) assets of the firm. Revenue expenditures are expenditures made to obtain current revenues and are treated as expenses.

14. Under an operating lease, rent expense is recorded in the period in which it is incurred. If it is paid in advance for a period, the amount paid is recorded as prepaid rent and amortized. If it is paid at the end of a period, it is expensed when paid. If not paid, it is accrued. If a lump-sum down payment is made, it is recorded in a Leasehold account and amortized.

15. The gain or loss recognized when a depreciable asset is sold is the difference between the net book value of the asset and the cash received. If the cash received is greater than the net book value, a gain is recorded; if less, a loss is recorded.

16. The methods are considered appropriate for accounting purposes where the revenue-producing ability of the asset declines with age, where maintenance costs increase with age, and where the value of the asset declines with age.

17. A lease that contains one or more of the following is a capital lease:
    a. It transfers title to the property to the lessee at the end of the lease.
    b. It permits the lessee to buy the property for a nominal sum (the bargain purchase option).
    c. The lease runs for 75 percent or more of the economic life of the asset.
    d. The present value of the minimum lease payments is equal to or more than 90 percent of the fair value of the leased property.

    A capital lease is recorded by the lessee as both an asset and a liability. No similar entry is made for an operating lease.

Solutions to Exercises

1. The cost of the land includes:

Cash purchase price	$200,000
Liability assumed for unpaid taxes	8,000
Legal fees	2,200
Cost to raze old warehouse	9,000
Total cost	$219,200

2. *a.* Straight-line:

19x2: [($50,000 − $2,000)/10]	$ 4,800
19x3: [($50,000 − $2,000)/10]	4,800

    b. Units-of-production:

        19x2: [($50,000 − $2,000)/500,000] × 30,000 2,880
        19x3: [($50,000 − $2,000)/500,000] × 50,000 4,800

    c. Double-declining-balance:

        19x2: ($50,000 × 0.2). 10,000
        19x3: [($50,000 − $10,000) × 0.2] 8,000

    d. Sum-of-the-years'-digits:

        19x2: [($50,000 − $2,000) × 10/55] 8,727
        19x3: [($50,000 − $2,000) × 9/55] 7,855

3. 19x2:
    Depreciation—double-declining-balance method:
      $60,000 × 0.4. . . . . $24,000
    Depreciation—straight-line method: $60,000 ÷ 5 years. 12,000
    Additional depreciation under double-declining-
      balance method. $12,000
    Tax rate 0.50
    Taxes levied for 19x2 would be lower by. . . . . $ 6,000

    19x3:
    Depreciation—double-declining balance method:
      ($60,000 − $24,000) × 0.4. . . . . $14,400
    Depreciation—straight-line method (as above). 12,000
    Additional depreciation under double-declining-
      balance method. . . . . $ 2,400
    Tax rate 0.50
    Taxes levied for 19x3 would be lower by. . . . . $ 1,200

4. Cost of machine $48,000
    Accumulated depreciation ($48,000 ÷ 5) × 3 28,800
    Net book value, December 31, 19x3. . . . . $19,200
    Estimated remaining life (in years). 5
    Annual depreciation (as revised). . . . . $ 3,840

5. Cost of mineral rights $1,200,000
    Estimated ore content (tons) 6,000,000
    Depletion cost per ton. $0.20
    Total depletion cost recorded (600,000 × $0.20). . . . . $ 120,000
    Depletion cost in cost of ore sold (400,000/600,000
      × $120,000). . . . . $ 80,000

6. Rent expense for 19x2:
    Amortized: ($80,000 ÷ 20). . . . . $ 4,000
    Accrued:
      $1,000,000 × 0.01 . . . . $10,000
      $400,000 × 0.005 2,000
      To meet minimum required. 500   12,500
        Total rent expense for 19x2. . . . . $16,500

7.	Cost of patent on January 2, 19x0	$68,000
	Less: Amortization for seven years ($68,000 ÷ 17) × 7	28,000
	Unamortized cost, December 31, 19x6..............................	$40,000
	Legal costs incurred to defend patent.............................	15,000
	Total..	$55,000
	Annual amortization expense ($55,000 ÷ 10)	$ 5,500

8.	Franchise expense for 19x3 is:	
	Amount paid currently: $800,000 × 0.005..........................	$ 4,000
	Amortize cost of franchise: $20,000 ÷ 40..........................	500
	Total franchise expense.....................................	$ 4,500

9.	Depreciation expense: (34,868 ÷ 4 years)	$ 8,717
	Interest expense: ($34,868 − $10,000) × 0.1	2,486.80

Solution to Business Decision Problem 4–1

a.	1.	Straight-line method: ($170,000 − $5,000) ÷ 10	$16,500
	2.	Double-declining-balance method: ($170,000 × 0.2)...............	34,000
	3.	Sum-of-the-years'-digits method: ($170,000 − $5,000) × 10/55	30,000
	4.	Units-of-production method: ($170,000 − $5,000) × 360,000/4,000,000	14,850

CROWLEY COMPANY
Schedule to Compute Net Income
For the Year Ended December 31, 19x2

	Straight-Line	Double-Declining-Balance	Sum-of-the-Years'-Digits	Units-of-Production
Earnings before depreciation and income taxes.......	$100,000	$100,000	$100,000	$100,000
Depreciation (see part a)...	16,500	34,000	30,000	14,850
Earnings before income taxes.................	$ 83,500	$ 66,000	$ 70,000	$ 85,150

c. If management desires to maximize income in 19x2, it should select the units-of-production method. If it wishes to minimize income, it should select the double-declining-balance method.

Solution to Business Decision Problem 4–2

a. Depreciation recorded.

	19x2	19x3
Hector Co.:		
Building ($200,000 × 0.025)	$ 5,000	$ 5,000
Equipment ($200,000 × 0.1)	20,000	20,000
Total	$25,000	$25,000
Victor Co.:		
Building ($200,000 × 0.05)	$10,000	
$200,000 − $10,000) × 0.05		$ 9,500
Equipment ($200,000 × 0.2)	40,000	
($200,000 − $40,000) × 0.2		32,000
Total	$50,000	$41,500

b. Income before depreciation and income taxes.

	19x2	19x3
Hector Co.:		
Income before income taxes	$ 84,000	$ 88,000
Depreciation (see part *a*).	25,000	25,000
Income before depreciation and income taxes	$109,000	$113,000
Victor Co.:		
Income before income taxes	$ 76,000	$ 80,000
Depreciation (see part *a*).	50,000	41,500
Income before depreciation and income taxes	$126,000	$121,500

c. As the schedule in part *b* shows, Hector Company is not more profitable than Victor Company when the distortive effects of different depreciation methods are removed from the comparison. The available information strongly indicates that Victor Company is the more profitable company, and purchase of its assets rather than those of the Hector Company is recommended.

5

Stockholders' Equity and Long-Term Liabilities

Chapter Goals

When you have completed Chapter 5, you should be able to:

1. Account for the issuance and retirement of both preferred and common stock.
2. Explain what treasury stock is, why it exists, and how it is accounted for and reported.
3. Identify and account for cash and stock dividends and stock splits.
4. Define and compute book value per share and explain its significance.
5. Explain how retained earnings and restrictions on retained earnings come into existence and are reported.
6. Explain why a corporation might use long-term debt to finance its capital needs.
7. Account for the issuance, recording of periodic interest expense on, and retirement of long-term notes and bonds payable.
8. Explain why bonds sell at a premium or a discount and account for the amortization of such premiums and discounts.
9. Illustrate how deferred income taxes payable arise.

This chapter deals with the two major sources of long-term or relatively permanent capital of a corporation—stockholders' equity and long-term liabilities.

STOCKHOLDERS' EQUITY

In terms of economic power, the corporation is the major form of business firm, largely because of its ability to raise capital by selling shares of its stock to the public. The owners' interest in a corporation usually is called stockholders' or shareholders' equity. Other advantages of the corporate form include the ease of transferring ownership interest by sale of the shares owned and the limited liability of the stockholders. This means, in most cases, stockholders are not liable for the debts of the corporation and, thus, can only lose the amount paid for the shares. Finally, the corporation has a life of its own, which may extend beyond that of its original shareholders.

The goal in accounting for stockholders' equity is to show the sources of equity capital. Equity capital may be obtained by retention of earnings as well as by owner investment. The corporation, a legal entity separate from its owners, is required by state law to maintain this distinction in its records.

The corporate charter, by which the state grants the corporation the right to exist and to conduct certain activities, typically states the maximum number of shares and the par value, if any, per share of each class of stock the corporation is *authorized* to issue. When authorized shares are issued which have not been reacquired by the issuer, the shares are referred to as *outstanding*. Control of the corporation resides in these shares since only outstanding shares carry the right to vote for the members of the board of directors and to receive dividends or other distributions.

Classes of Capital Stock

Common stock. Every business corporation will have common stock outstanding. The primary rights of the common stockholder may include the right (1) to share in earnings when dividends are declared; (2) to subscribe to additional shares of the same stock, when offered for sale, in proportion to the amount currently held, unless this right has been waived; (3) to share in assets upon liquidation; and (4) to share in the management through the election of the board of directors, which guides the broad policy decisions of the business. The ownership interest of the common stockholders is often called the residual equity of the corporation, meaning that all other claims rank ahead of the claims of the common stockholders. The primary rewards and risks of ownership accrue to the common stockholder.

Recording issuance of common stock. The exact manner of recording the issuance of stock for cash will depend upon whether the stock has a par value per share or is of no par value. If it has a par value, this amount will be stated in the corporate charter and printed on the stock certificates. Par value may be of any amount and serves two purposes. First, it is the amount that is recorded in the capital account for each share issued and outstanding. Second, the par value of the issued shares is often the legal or stated capital of the corporation. A corporation is forbidden by law from declaring dividends or acquiring its own stock if such action will reduce stockholders' equity below the legal capital of the corporation. When stock is first sold to owners, the sales price may be below par, at par, or above par. If stock is issued at a discount from par, the stockholders may be liable to the creditors up to the total discount from par value. The most common practice is to sell stock originally above par (at a premium). The entry to record the sale (issuance) of 10,000 shares of 20,000 authorized of $10 par value common stock for cash of $12 per share involves three accounts:

Cash		Common Stock		Paid-in Capital in Excess of Par Value	
Bal. xxx			Bal. xxx		Bal. xxx
120,000			100,000		20,000

Par value is not an indicator of the amount of stockholders' equity per share (book value per share as it is called) that is recorded in the accounting records of the corporation. Stockholders' equity consists of paid-in or contributed capital and retained earnings. Retained earnings are the undistributed profits (or losses) of the firm and, hence, may be positive or negative. Neither does par value give any clue to the market value of the stock, because market value is based largely upon investor expectations concerning future earnings, dividends, and general market prospects.

The balance sheet prepared immediately after the above transaction shows:

Stockholders' equity:
Common stock—$10 par value; authorized 20,000 shares; issued and out-
standing, 10,000 shares $100,000
Paid-in capital in excess of par value 20,000
Total stockholders' equity $120,000

In the illustration, the number of shares authorized (assumed to be 20,000), the number of shares issued and outstanding, the par value of the issued and outstanding shares in the common stock account, and the amount received in excess of par value in a separate account are all disclosed.

Assume that the shares in the illustration were of no par value and that no stated value was assigned or required by state law. Under such circumstances, the entry to record the issuance would be:

Cash		Common Stock	
Bal.	xxx	Bal.	xxx
	120,000		120,000

The balance sheet would show:

Stockholders' equity:
  Common stock—no par or stated value; authorized 20,000 shares; issued
    and outstanding, 10,000 shares $120,000

The entire $120,000 received for the shares generally is considered the stated or legal capital of the shares.

A corporation may be authorized to issue no par value stock. (Such stock came into use when states based franchise taxes on the par value of the shares outstanding.) In such cases, the stock may be assigned a stated value by the board of directors. If so, the accounting procedure is the same as for a par value stock, except for the use of "stated" value rather than "par" value in account titles.

Established corporations often issue stock through investment bankers (called stockbrokers or underwriters) who guarantee the corporation a fixed price per share and earn a commission by selling the stock to the public at a higher price. Only the proceeds received by the corporation are recorded on the books. To illustrate, assume a corporation is guaranteed a price of $21 per share for the $10 par value shares it issues through an underwriter. The price to the public is $22. The shares will be treated by the issuing corporation as issued at $21 per share. The underwriters' commission never appears in the accounts.

Preferred stock.   In seeking capital, a corporation may find it necessary to issue another type of capital stock called preferred stock. The features usually found in preferred stocks include:

  1.   A preference over the common stock as to dividends—a dividend of a certain amount or percentage of par must be declared on the preferred stock before a dividend can be declared on the common stock.

  2.   A preference over the common stock in case of liquidation. To illustrate, assume that a corporation has $100,000 par value of preferred stock and $200,000 par value of common stock outstanding and $240,000 of cash left to distribute to the stockholders in liquidation. The preferred is preferred as to assets in liquidation to the extent of par value. Therefore, the preferred stockholders receive the par value of their stock before the common stockholders receive anything. If, in this example, there are no dividends in arrears (discussed below), the preferred stockholders will receive $100,000 and the common stockholders will receive $140,000. If the preferred stock is not preferred as to assets, the preferred and common stockholders would each receive a pro rata share based on total values. Thus, the preferred

stockholders would receive one third of the cash and the common stockholders would receive two thirds of the cash.

3.   A cumulative right to receive dividends, which means that all preferred dividends, including dividends in arrears (dividends not paid—passed—in prior periods), must be declared before dividends can be declared on the common stock. Dividends in arrears are not shown as a liability until declared. But since the amount of dividends in arrears may be useful information for potential investors, it is disclosed in a footnote to the financial statements. A preferred stock on which the right to receive dividends does not accumulate if the dividends are not paid is called a noncumulative preferred. Such stocks hold little attraction to investors and are quite rare.

4.   A call price, which permits the issuing corporation to redeem the preferred stock at a specified price. For example, a corporation may issue a preferred stock that has a $6 annual dividend, a par value of $100, and a call price of $105 per share. If the corporation calls the preferred stock, it must pay the preferred stockholders $105 per share plus any dividends due.

Preferred stocks may contain some of the following features:

1.   A convertible provision that permits the holders of the preferred stock to convert preferred stock, at the preferred shareowners' option, into shares of the issuing company's common stock. This feature allows the preferred stockholders to participate in the increase in value of the common stock that often accompanies profitable operations.

2.   A participation feature that may lead to dividends being paid to the preferred stockholders in excess of the fixed, specified annual dividends. Participating preferred stocks are rare.

3.   A sinking fund provision that requires the periodic allocation of funds to retire the preferred stock (usually by calling the stock at the "call price" or by purchasing the stock in the open market).

Which features will be included in a preferred stock is determined largely by what is being offered in competing securities. Management will include those features necessary to sell the stock.

The entry for recording the issuance of 1,000 shares of 8 percent preferred stock having a par value of $100 for $103 is similar to the entry for recording the issuance of common stock above par value. Only the names of the accounts differ:

Cash		Preferred Stock		Paid-in Capital in Excess of Par—Preferred	
Bal. xxx			Bal. xxxx		Bal. xxx
103,000			100,000		3,000

The $3,000 in the above entry often is referred to as the premium on preferred stock.

The issuance of preferred stock may have other advantages to the corporation: (1) since preferred stocks may have no voting rights, their issuance will not weaken the control of the common stockholders; and (2) the return (dividend) is usually fixed, thus giving an additional return (through favorable financial leverage) to the common stockholders. Favorable financial leverage exists when the funds obtained from a sale of preferred stock or bonds earn a return in excess of the fixed payment promised.

The entry to record the calling of the above preferred stock at $105 and its retirement, assuming no dividends are due upon call and there is a call price of $105, is:

Preferred Stock		Paid-In Capital in Excess of Par—Preferred		Retained Earnings		Cash	
	Bal. xxx		Bal. xxx		Bal. xxx	Bal. xxx	
100,000		3,000		2,000			105,000

In the above entry, the $2,000 is looked upon as a dividend paid to retire the preferred stock. Retained Earnings was debited because the total call price ($105,000) exceeded the original issuance price ($103,000).

Treasury Stock

Treasury stock is capital stock, either preferred or common, that has been issued but reacquired by the issuing corporation. It has not been canceled, and it is available for reissuance. Because it has been issued, treasury stock is differentiated from unissued stock.

Treasury stock may be acquired in settlement of a debt owed the corporation. But it is more likely to be purchased in the open market for the following purposes:

1. To be reissued to employees as bonuses or in accordance with stock option or stock purchase plans.
2. To increase earnings per share by reducing the number of shares outstanding.
3. To be reissued in the acquisition of the stock or net assets of other corporations.

The corporation laws of most states consider treasury stock as issued but not outstanding. Treasury shares cannot be voted, and dividends are not paid on them. Dividends, in most states, are limited to the amount of retained earnings in excess of the cost of the treasury shares. The effect of these laws is to prevent a corporation from impairing (reducing) its legal or stated capital by declaring dividends or purchasing treasury stock, or both.

The accounting for, and financial reporting of, treasury stock is illustrated by the Hillside Company example. Hillside Company has stockholders' equity consisting of capital stock and retained earnings. The company purchased 2,000 shares of its capital stock for $70,000, which would be recorded in a Treasury Stock account at cost. Immediately after the purchase, the balance sheet shows:

Stockholders' equity:

Common stock—$10 par value; authorized and issued 40,000 shares, of which 2,000 shares are in the treasury.	$400,000
Retained earnings (including $70,000 restricted by acquisition of treasury stock)	500,000
Total	$900,000
Less: Treasury stock at cost, 2,000 shares	70,000
Total stockholders' equity	$830,000

The restriction upon retained earnings, and hence dividends, can be disclosed as shown or in a separate footnote. The reporting of treasury stock is as a deduction from total stockholders' equity. Like unissued shares, treasury stock represents a potential source of assets (or resources). Neither should be reported as assets on the balance sheet.

To show the accounting for treasury stock, the Hillside Company illustration continues. Two months after purchasing the treasury stock, the company reissued 800 shares (at a market value of $40 each) to several of its key employees as bonuses. A year later, when Hillside Company needed additional cash, the remaining shares were reissued for cash of $30 per share. The accounting entries in T-account format show (1) the original purchase of the treasury stock at $35 each, (2) the bonuses to employees, and (3) the reissue of treasury stock for cash.

Cash				Treasury Stock				Paid-in Capital—Treasury Stock Transactions			
Bal.	xxx	(1)	70,000	(1)	70,000	(2)	28,000	(3)	4,000	(2)	4,000
(3)	36,000					(3)	42,000				

Salaries and Bonuses Expense						Retained Earnings			
Bal.	xxx					(3)	2,000	Bal.	xxx
(2)	32,000								

The acquisition of the shares is recorded at cost ($70,000). The issuance of the 800 shares as bonuses requires a debit to the Salaries and Bonuses Expense account for the market value of the shares, a credit to Treasury Stock for the cost of the shares, and a credit to a paid-in capital account for the excess of the fair value of the shares over their cost. When the remaining shares are reissued, the deficiency of reissue price from cost is charged against Paid-In Capital—Treasury Stock Transactions *until the credit balance in the account is exhausted.* The remaining deficiency is then charged to Retained Earnings.

If at the end of the fiscal year the Paid-In Capital—Treasury Stock Transactions account contained a positive (credit) balance, it would be reported in the balance sheet below capital stock as Paid-In Capital in Excess of Par (or Stated) Value. The "gain" on the transaction represents an increase in invested capital, not a gain includible in net income.

Treasury shares may also be formally canceled, reducing the number of authorized shares.

Other Sources of Paid-In Capital

While the major source of capital is investment by stockholders, a corporation may on occasion receive *donated capital*. This is most likely to occur when property is given to a firm to induce it to begin or expand operations in a given area. The assets received should be recorded at their fair value and the total credited to Paid-In Capital—Donations. For example, Red Cedar Company received land and a building (fair values: $10,000 and $30,000) from the city of Lennox in exchange for a promise to locate a plant in the city. The entry needed is:

Land	Building	Paid-in Capital —Donations
Bal. xxx 10,000	Bal. xxx 30,000	Bal. xxx 40,000

Other sources of paid-in capital in excess of par value of the stock outstanding include: (1) transfers from retained earnings by issuance of stock dividends, (2) "gains" on treasury stock transactions (discussed above), and (3) paid-in capital from reduction of the par value of the outstanding shares and from assessments levied upon stockholders in periods of financial distress. Separate accounts are maintained for each source in the accounting system. But in highly condensed balance sheets, the total of such separate accounts is usually reported as a single sum called Paid-In Capital in Excess of Par Value.

Dividends

Dividends are distributions by a corporation to its stockholders. While the typical dividend is paid in cash, stock dividends are also common. Less common types of dividends (not discussed here) include those paid with other assets, such as marketable securities.

Cash dividends.   Because dividends are the means by which the owners of a corporation share in its earnings, most dividends are reductions in retained earnings and in cash, although state laws may permit the declaration of dividends that are debited to paid-in capital in excess of par value. The significant dates relating to a dividend are the *declaration date,* the *date of record,* and the *date of payment.* For example, a corporation declared a dividend of $1.50 per share on December 10, to stockholders of record on December 20, payable January 12. The required entries are, assuming 10,000 shares outstanding:

Retained Earnings		Dividends Payable	
	Bal. xxx		
(Dec. 10) 15,000			(Dec. 10) 15,000

The December 10 entry records the fact that the corporation has a legal liability to its stockholders (reported in the balance sheet as a current liability) to pay them $15,000. The date of record is used only to determine who gets the dividend, that is, who are the recorded owners of the corporation's stock on this date; therefore no accounting entry is made. The January 12 entry records the payment of the dividend liability.

Cash		Dividends Payable	
Bal. xxxx			Bal. 15,000
	(Jan. 12) 15,000	(Jan. 12) 15,000	

Stock Dividends

Stock dividends are pro rata distributions of a corporation's stock (usually common stock) to its stockholders (usually the common stockholders). They do not affect a stockholder's ownership interest in the corporation. If Judy Smith owns 1,000 of the 100,000 shares of common stock outstanding, she owns 1 percent of the shares outstanding. After a 10 percent stock dividend, she still owns 1 percent of the shares outstanding (1,100/110,000). Stock dividends do not affect assets or total stockholders' equity. And they do not constitute taxable income to the stockholders at receipt of the additional shares.

The only accounting question in dealing with stock dividends is the amount of retained earnings to be transferred to the capital accounts. The answer depends on the size of the stock dividend. A stock dividend of 25 percent or less is recorded at market value. Stock dividends of greater than 25 percent are recorded at an amount needed to meet legal requirements, namely, the par or stated value of the shares to be issued.

Assume that a corporation is authorized to issue 50,000 shares of $20 par value common stock, of which 30,000 shares are outstanding. Its stockholders' equity is:

Common stock—$20 par value; authorized 50,000 shares, of which 30,000 shares are issued and outstanding	$ 600,000
Retained earnings	500,000
Total stockholders' equity	$1,100,000

The entry to record a 10 percent stock dividend (3,000 shares) at the market price of $54 is:

Retained Earnings		Common Stock		Paid-in Capital —Stock Dividends	
	Bal. xxx		Bal. xxx		Bal. xxx
162,000			60,000		102,000

The entry to record a 50 percent, rather than a 10 percent, stock dividend (15,000 shares) would be different because the stock dividend exceeds 25 percent and is recorded at the par value of the shares issued (15,000 × $20):

Retained Earnings		Common Stock	
	Bal. xxx		Bal. xxx
300,000			300,000

Stock Splits (Split-Ups)

In a stock split, a corporation typically doubles (two-for-one split) or triples (three-for-one split) the number of shares outstanding at no cost to the shareholders. The par value is usually reduced accordingly so that the total par value of the stock outstanding does not change. A stock split does not change either assets or stockholders' equity; rather, it changes the number of shares outstanding and their par or stated value. Proportional ownership of the stock stays the same. For example, assume Company A has $400,000 (20,000 shares of $20 par value) of common stock outstanding. After a two-for-one stock split, 40,000 shares of $10 par value stock would be outstanding. The total par value remains at $400,000. A person who previously owned 200 shares, or 1 percent of the outstanding shares, would now own 400 shares, or the same 1 percent interest. No formal entries are required for a stock split. The typical action taken by the corporation would be to issue the additional shares and indicate that the par value per share of the outstanding shares has been changed to the new, lower amount. A stock split seeks to reduce the market price of the stock by increasing the number of shares outstanding. Stock selling for $100 per share will usually sell for about $50 per share after a two-for-one stock split.

Retained Earnings

Retained earnings is the term used to describe the increase in stockholders' equity resulting from profitable operation of the corporation. As such, it shows the source of assets received as earnings but not distributed to stockholders as dividends. Thus, the balance in the Retained Earnings account is the difference between (1) the net income of the corporation during its existence to date and (2) the sum of dividends declared during the same period.

When the Retained Earnings account has a negative (or debit) balance, a *deficit* exists. It is shown under that title as a negative amount in the stockholders' equity section of the balance sheet.

As noted, the purchase of treasury stock often restricts the amount of retained earnings available for cash dividends. Certain business contracts may do the same. For example, a loan agreement may restrict dividends to retained earnings in excess of some amount, say, $250,000, until the loan is repaid. The $250,000 is sometimes referred to as "frozen" or "appropriated" retained earnings. The balance in regular retained earnings is then called unappropriated retained earnings. The T-account entry to record appropriated retained earnings is:

Retained Earnings		Appropriation for Loan Repayment	
250,000	Bal.　　　　　xxx		250,000

On payment of the loan, the entry is reversed, as the loan restriction is no longer in effect. The confusion sometimes caused by such restrictions has established a trend in modern financial reporting to disclose the restrictions in a footnote rather than in a formal account. Such a footnote might read:

> The provisions in a loan agreement limit dividends to retained earnings in excess of $250,000 until a 9 percent loan due in 1995 is paid.

Book Value per Share

An amount often calculated in appraising the merits of a given common stock for investment purposes is *book value* per share of common stock. When only common stock is outstanding, book value per share is simply total stockholders' equity divided by the number of common shares outstanding. If preferred stock is outstanding, the computation is more complex. A portion of total stockholders' equity must be allocated to the preferred stock. There is general agreement that the amount allocated must include any cumulative dividends in arrears. But accountants disagree as to whether the par value, liquidating value, or call price should be used. The call price seems best because the most likely way to dispose of the preferred stock is to call and retire it.

As an illustration, assume the Cole Company's stockholders' equity is:

Preferred stock—$50 par value, 8%, cumulative, 8,000 shares	$　400,000
Common stock—$10 par value, 400,000 shares	4,000,000
Paid-in capital in excess of par value—preferred	40,000
Retained earnings	600,000
Total stockholders' equity	$5,040,000

Assume that the preferred stock has a call price of $52 per share and that dividends on the preferred stock have not been paid for the latest fiscal year. The book values of each class of stock are shown in Illustration 5.1.

Illustration 5.1

	Total	Book Value per Share
Total stockholders' equity	$5,040,000	
Book value of preferred stock, 8,000 shares:		
Call price ($52 × 8,000) $416,000		
Dividends in arrears (1 year at $32,000) 32,000	448,000	$56.00
Book value of common stock (400,000 shares) . .	$4,592,000	$11.48

Because book value is based on assets valued at historical cost and because its amount is affected by choice of accounting methods (FIFO versus LIFO, for example), book value may be a misleading indicator of the value of a share of stock. Therefore, it is not correct to automatically assume that a share of stock selling in the market at 25 percent of its book value must be a good buy.

LONG-TERM LIABILITIES

For several reasons, most business firms seek to obtain long-term capital by borrowing. First, borrowing may be the only source of funds available to the firm. Second, the existing owners need not dilute or surrender their control of the firm if funds can be borrowed rather than obtained by issuing additional shares of stock. Third, the use of borrowed funds may enhance the return to stockholders by earning more with the funds than the amount of interest paid (financial leverage). Lenders, on the other hand, may require that the loan agreement include certain restrictive covenants to ensure that the loan will be repaid. These often include (1) the maintenance of a certain level of working capital and (2) restrictions on dividends, treasury stock purchases, additional borrowings, and the acquisition of additional plant assets.

Mortgage Notes Payable

In addition to some or all of the above restrictions, a note may be secured by a mortgage on real property. If the borrower defaults (fails to live up to the terms of the loan agreement), the lender can seize the pledged assets, sell them, and use the funds received to retire the loan. To illustrate, assume a business acquires a small building. In addition to a down payment, the firm agrees to make constant lump-sum payments each month until the $100,000 mortgage loan is paid. The interest rate is 16 percent, and the loan runs for 20 years. A mortgage payment schedule book indicates that the monthly payment is $1,391.26 and that most of the early payments are for interest. Here is how the payments for the first two months and the last month are applied:

	Monthly Payment	Interest at 16 Percent on Principal Balance	Payment on Principal ($1391.26 less interest)	Principal Balance
Date of purchase..........				$100,000.00
1st month................	$1391.26	$1,333.33	$ 57.93	99,942.07
2d month	1391.26	1,332.56	58.70	99,883.37
240th month..............	1391.26	18.31	1,372.95	0

Interest is calculated on the latest principal balance. For instance, when the first $1391.26 payment is made, interest is calculated as follows:

$$\frac{\$100,000 \times 0.16}{12} = \$1,333.33$$

It is necessary to divide by 12 because the interest rate is 16 percent *per year* and the interest calculation is for *one month*. The excess of the payment over the interest is applied against the principal ($57.93 in the first payment). Thus, the principal balance decreases slowly (but more rapidly each month), so that the last payment, at the end of 20 years, pays interest ($18.31) on the remaining principal balance ($1,372.95) and then reduces the principal balance to zero.

As another example of long-term financing through use of a note, assume that Adams Company borrowed $600,000 on January 1, 19x3, pledging a tract of land and a building as security. Adams agreed to make annual December 31 payments of $200,000, plus interest on the unpaid balance at 10 percent, until the note was paid. The entries to record the first payment, on December 31, 19x3, are:

Mortgage Note Payable		Interest Expense		Cash	
200,000	Bal. 600,000	60,000		Bal. xxxx	260,000

The entries for the second payment are:

Mortgage Note Payable		Interest Expense		Cash	
200,000	Bal. 400,000	40,000		Bal. xxxx	240,000

The balance sheet prepared on December 31, 19x3, after one payment has been made, would show:

Current liabilities:
    Current portion of long-term note payable. $200,000
Long-term liabilities:
    Notes payable, 10%, due 19x5   200,000

Because it is due within one year, the $200,000 of principal maturing in 19x4 is classified as a current liability in the 19x3 balance sheet.

Bonds

A bond is a written, formal contract containing the promises of the issuing company to the bondholders (lenders). The major promises are to pay interest periodically at the rate stated on the face of the bonds and to repay the principal amount of the bonds at the maturity date, which could be any number of years from the issue date. The contract between the issuing company and the bondholders is called the *bond indenture*. A trustee is appointed to make sure that the issuer lives up to the promises contained in the indenture. Bonds are typically issued in $1,000 denominations of face value, maturity amount, or principal amount through an investment banker. The interest rate stated in the bond determines the size of the periodic interest payment and is called the coupon or nominal rate. The price of a bond is usually quoted in percentages—a bond quoted at 105 sells for $1,050 (105 percent of $1,000).

Many different types of bonds can be found today. *Debentures* are unsecured bonds backed only by the general credit of the issuer. *Mortgage bonds* may be first, second, or even third liens upon specific assets, typically real property. *Revenue bonds* are first claims upon the revenues of certain entities. Bonds scheduled to be retired in installments—specific bonds on specific dates—are called *serial bonds*. *Sinking-fund bonds* are, in essence, the same as serial bonds. And bonds that give their holders the right to exchange them for the capital stock of the issuing company are called *convertible bonds*. Despite their variety, the accounting for bonds is essentially the same.

Accounting for bonds issued at face value. Valley Company on December 31, 19x2, issued $100,000 face value of 12 percent, 10-year bonds (dated December 31, 19x2) for $100,000. Interest is payable semiannually on June 30 and December 31. The entries on Valley's books, if interest and principal are paid when due, are:
On December 31, 19x2—the date of issuance:

Cash		Bonds Payable	
Bal. xxx			
100,000			100,000

On each June 30 and December 31 for 10 years, beginning on June 30, 19x3:

Bond Interest Expense		Cash		
6,000		Bal.	xxx	
				6,000

On the December 31, 19x3, maturity date (10 years later):

Bonds Payable			Cash		
100,000	Bal.	100,000	Bal.	xxxx	
					100,000

The price received for a bond. The price a bond will bring when offered to investors often differs from its face or maturity value. Basically, a bond will sell at a premium (a price higher than face value) or at a discount (a price lower than face value) if the rate of interest in the bond is higher or lower than the rate that can be secured from similar bonds of other issuers. The effect of issuing a bond at a premium or a discount is to change the rate of interest offered by the bond to the effective rate desired by the investor. The method of computing the price an investor would be willing to pay for a bond is discussed in the Appendix to this chapter.

Bonds issued at a discount. Western Company issued $1 million face value of first-mortgage, 12 percent, 10-year bonds for $980,000—or at 98. The bonds, issued and dated July 1, 19x3, call for semiannual interest payments on January 1 and July 1 and mature on July 1, 19x3 (10 years later). At issuance, the required entry is:

Cash		Discount Bonds Payable		Bonds Payable	
Bal. xxxx					
980,000		20,000			1,000,000

The bonds are carried at face value on the issuer's books in one account, and the discount (or premium) is carried in another. It is customary to record liabilities at the amount expected to be paid at maturity, excluding interest unless interest has actually accrued.

To the issuer, bond discount is a cost of using borrowed funds just as it is additional interest earnings to the investor. Thus, the total cost of borrowing includes the interest currently payable in cash plus the total discount which is paid as a lump sum at maturity. In this case, the cost over the life of the bond is $1,220,000 [($1,000,000 × 0.12 × 10) + $20,000]. This amount must be allocated to the periods of life in the bond issue. One way to do this is to assign equal amounts of expense to each year (called the straight-line method). Under this method, the annual interest expense is $122,000 ($1,220,000 ÷ 10). For each six months' interest period, it is $61,000. Assuming a calendar-year accounting period, the entry needed on December 31, 19x3, is:

Bond Interest Expense		Discount on Bonds Payable		Accrued Interest Payable	
61,000		Bal. 20,000	1,000		60,000

Under the straight-line method, the semiannual expense can be computed as the interest payable currently of $60,000 ($1,000,000 × 0.12 × ½) plus the amortization of the discount of $1,000 ($20,000/20). The sum of these two amounts yields the semiannual expense previously computed of $61,000.

Financial reporting.   The above accounting yields the following items for the financial statements for 19x3:

Income statement (included in the expenses for the year):

Interest Expense .... $ 61,000

Balance sheet:

Current liabilities:
    Accrued interest payable .... $ 60,000
Long-term liabilities
    Bonds payable, 12%, due 19x3 .... $1,000,000
    Less: Unamortized discount................   19,000 $981,000*

   * An alternative would show bonds payable at $981,000, with the details provided in a footnote.

Entries in subsequent years.   The entries for the bonds in 19x4 are:

Accrued Interest Payable		Cash	
Jan. 1 60,000		Bal. xxx	Jan. 1 60,000

This entry eliminates the current liability reported on the December 31, 19x3, balance sheet. On June 30, 19x4, a new entry is required.

Bond Interest Expense		Discount on Bonds Payable		Cash	
61,000		Bal. 19,000	1,000	Bal. xxx	60,000

The pattern of entries established would be repeated every year through 19x3 if the cash payments promised by the bonds are actually made.

Bonds issued at a premium. To illustrate the accounting for bonds issued at a premium, assume that the 12 percent, 10-year Western Company bonds were issued on July 1, 19x3, for $1,020,000. The required entry to record issuance of bonds at 102 is:

Cash		Bonds Payable		Premium on Bonds Payable	
Bal. xxx 1,020,000			1,000,000		20,000

When the bonds are issued at a premium, the total interest cost of the borrowing is the sum of interest payable periodically ($1,200,000) *less* the premium received on issuance ($20,000), or $1,180,000. The bond interest expense amount per semiannual interest period is $59,000 and the first six months' interest is recorded on December 31, 19x3, as:

Bond Interest Expense		Premium on Bonds Payable		Accrued Interest Payable	
			Bal. 20,000		
59,000		1,000			60,000

The entry shows how the fact that the bonds were issued at a premium (thus reducing the total interest cost to an amount less than the interest payable currently) is reflected in each six months' interest expense. The $20,000 premium is amortized on a straight-line basis to interest expense at a rate of $1,000 per semiannual interest period.

The straight-line method of discount or premium amortization is widely used because it is easy to understand and to apply. But it is not the theoretically correct method (discussed in the Appendix to this chapter), and it may be used only where its use yields results that do not differ *materially* from those obtained under the alternative. Material differences in results seem unlikely in most instances. Thus, continued use of the straight-line method is expected.

Financial reporting. The income statement for Western Company for 19x3 would show interest expense of $59,000, while the balance sheet would report accrued interest payable of $60,000 as a current liability. The balance sheet would also report bonds payable of $1 million *plus* unamortized bond premium of $19,000 for a total long-term liability on the bonds of $1,019,000.

Entries in subsequent years. For bonds issued at a premium, the entry for January 1 would be the same as when the bonds were issued at a discount. The June 30, 19x3, entry would be:

Bond Interest Expense		Premium on Bonds Payable		Cash	
			Bal. 19,000	Bal. xxx	
59,000		1,000			60,000

The December 31, 19x4, entry would be the same as the one given above for December 31, 19x3. The pattern of entries given would be repeated until the bonds were redeemed.

Deferred Income Taxes Payable

An item described as deferred income taxes payable often appears among or just below the long-term liabilities on the balance sheets of most business corporations. It reappears every year, usually with a larger balance. It results from engaging in a process called *interperiod tax allocation,* which is required accounting when *timing differences* exist. Timing differences consist of those items that are included in both taxable income and accounting pretax income but cause these two to differ because the items are recognized in *different years*. For example, the most common timing difference is created by—accelerated depreciation.

A corporation subject to a 40 percent income tax rate has $200,000 of taxable income and pretax income before depreciation. Depreciation on the tax return is $100,000, but only $60,000 using the straight-line method for accounting purposes. The income tax expense shown on the income statement would be $56,000 [0.4($200,000 − $60,000)]. The income taxes payable, shown as a short-term liability, would be $40,000 [0.4($200,000 − $100,000)], generating a long-term liability called *deferred income taxes payable* of $16,000.

Income tax expense is recorded at an amount equal to the "normal" amount of taxes levied upon $140,000 of pretax income, while the *actual* taxes payable, $40,000, are recorded in the Income Taxes Payable account (a current liability). Income taxes are said to be deferred because more tax expense was recorded than the amount of taxes payable currently. Income taxes are not permanently reduced; they are only deferred. In later years, the timing difference will *reverse*. Then more taxes will be paid currently than are recorded as expenses. In the meantime, the corporation has the "interest-free" use of the deferred tax amounts, a tax advantage that must be significant or it would not be so widely used.

APPENDIX TO CHAPTER 5

This appendix discusses the concepts of future worth (or value) and present value, and illustrates application of these concepts in several situations, including the determination of the price of a bond. The effective rate (or yield) method of accounting for the periodic interest on bonds payable is also illustrated.

Future Worth

The *future worth* or *value* of any investment is the amount to which a sum of money invested today will grow in a stated time period at a specified interest rate. The interest involved may be simple interest or compound interest. *Simple interest* is interest on principal only. For example, $1,000 invested today for two years at 12 percent simple interest will grow to $1,240 since the interest is $120 per year. The principal of $1,000, plus 2 × $120, is equal to $1,240. *Compound interest* is interest on principal and on interest of prior periods. For example, $1,000 invested for two years at 12 percent compounded annually will grow to $1,254.40. Interest for the first year is $120 ($1,000 × 0.12). For the second year, interest is earned on the principal plus the interest of the previous year, $120. Thus, the interest for the second year is $134.40 ($1,120 × 0.12). Future value at the end of year 2 is $1,254.40. The $1,254.40 is found by adding the second year's interest ($134.40) to the value at the beginning of the second year ($1,120). This future worth problem is portrayed graphically in Illustration A.1.

Illustration A.1

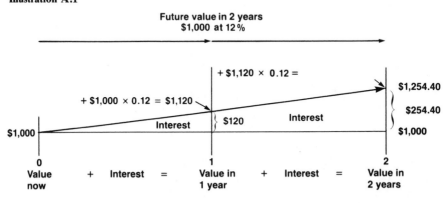

The illustration shows the growth of $1,000 to $1,254.40 when the interest rate is 12 percent compounded annually. The effect of compounding is $14.40—the interest in the second year based on the interest earned for the first year, or $120 × 0.12 = $14.40.

The task of computing the future worth for a stated period is aided by the use of interest tables. An example is Table 1, Appendix A, at the back of this book. To use the tables, first determine the number of compounding periods involved. The compounding period tells how frequently interest is computed and added to the base for future interest calculations. A compounding period may be any length of time, such as a day, a month, a quarter, a half year, or a year, but normally not more than a year. The number of compounding periods is equal to the number of years in the life of the investment times the number of compoundings in a year. Five years compounded annually is 5 periods; five years compounded quarterly is 20 periods; and so on.

Next, determine the interest rate per compounding period. Interest rates are usually quoted in annual terms. In fact, federal law requires statement of the interest rate in annual terms in certain situations. Divide the annual rate by the number of compounding periods per year to get the proper rate per period. Only with an annual compounding will the annual rate be the rate per period. All other cases involve a lower rate. For example, the rate per period will be 1 percent if the annual rate is 12 percent compounded monthly.

To use the table in a given situation, find the number of periods involved in the "Period" column. Move across the table to the right, stopping in the column headed by the interest rate per period, which yields a factor. The factor shows the amount to which an investment of $1 will grow for the periods and the rate involved. To compute future worth of the investment, multiply the number of dollars in the given situation by this factor. For example, suppose you invest $8,000 at 12 percent for four years. How much will you receive at the end of four years if the interest rate is 12 percent compounded annually? How much will you receive if the interest rate is 12 percent compounded quarterly?

The four-periods row in the 12 percent column of Table 1, Appendix A, yields the factor 1.57352. Multiply the factor by $8,000 to get $12,588.16 as the answer to the first question. Then look for 16 in the "Period" column and under 3 percent for the needed factor to answer the second question. The factor is 1.60471, and the value of your investment is $12,837.68. The more frequent compounding would add $249.52 ($12,837.68 − $12,588.16) to the value of your investment. The reason for this difference in amounts is that 12 percent compounded quarterly is a higher rate than 12 percent compounded annually.

Present Value

Present value is the current worth of a future cash receipt and is essentially the reverse of future worth. In future worth, a sum of money is possessed now and its future worth is sought. In present value, rights to future cash receipts are possessed and their current worth is sought. Future receipts are discounted to find their present value. To discount future receipts is to deduct interest from them. If the proper interest rate is used, it should not matter whether cash in an amount equal to its present value or the rights to the future receipts are possessed.

Assume that you have the right to receive $1,000 in one year. If the appropriate interest rate is 12 percent compounded annually, what is the present value of this $1,000 future cash receipt? You know that the present value is less than $1,000 because $1,000 due in one year is not worth $1,000 today. You also know that the $1,000 due in one year is equal to some amount, P, plus interest on P at 12 percent for one year. In other words, P + 0.12P = $1,000, and 1.12P = $1,000. Dividing $1,000 by 1.12 yields $892.86. Or, since dividing by 1.12 is the same as multiplying by $1/1.12$—which equals 0.89286—the $892.86 is computed by multiplying $1,000 × 0.89286. The interest that is deducted from the $1,000 to find its present value if due in one year is $107.14 ($1,000 − $892.86). If the $1,000 were due in two years, you would find its present value by dividing $892.86 by 1.12, or multiplying by $1/1.12$, which equals $797.20. Graphically portrayed in Illustration A.2,

Illustration A.2

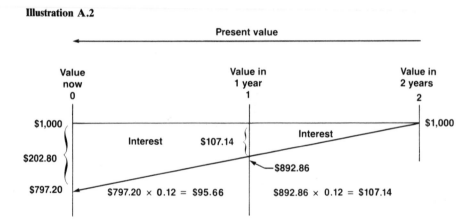

present value appears very similar to future worth, except, as the arrows show, that a future sum is known and its present value is sought.

Table 3, Appendix A, contains present value factors for a number of periods and interest rates. Table 3 is used in the same manner as Table 1. For example, compute the present value of $1,000 due in four years at 16 percent compounded annually. The factor sought is found on the four-periods line in the 16 percent column and is 0.55229. The present value is $1,000 times this amount, which equals $552.29.

As another example, suppose that you wish to have $4,000 in three years to pay for a vacation in Europe. If your investment will earn at a 20 percent rate compounded quarterly, how much should you invest now? Table 3,

Appendix A, 12-periods line, and a 5 percent rate yields the proper factor, 0.55684. The amount you should invest is $2,227.36. Bon voyage!

Present Value of an Annuity

An *annuity* may be defined as a series of equal cash flows (often called rents) spaced equally in time. The semiannual interest payments on a bond are a frequently encountered annuity. The approach to valuing an annuity can be illustrated by finding the present value, at 6 percent per semiannual period, of an annuity calling for the payment of $100 at the end of each of the next three semiannual periods. It would be possible, by use of Table 3, Appendix A, to find the present value of each of the $100 payments:

```
Present value of $100 due in:
    1 period is 0.94340 × $100 . . . . . . . . . . . . . . .   $ 94.34
    2 periods is 0.89000 × $100 . . . . . . . . . . . . . .     89.00
    3 periods is 0.83962 × $100 . . . . . . . . . . . . . .     83.96
            Total present value . . . . . . . . . . . . . . . . . .   $267.30
```

Such a procedure is tedious if the annuity consists of many payments. Fortunately, tables are available showing the present values of an annuity of $1 per period for varying interest rates and periods (see Table 4, Appendix A). A single figure or factor can be obtained from the table which represents the present value of an annuity of $1 per period for three (semiannual) periods at 6 percent per (semiannual) period. The figure is 2.67301. When multiplied by $100, the number of dollars in each payment, it yields the present value of the annuity as $267.30. The present value of an annuity is presented graphically in Illustration A.3.

The illustration shows that to find the present value of the three $100 cash flows, you multiply the $100 by a present value of an annuity factor, 2.67301. The 2.67301 is equal to the sum of the present value factors for $1 due in one period, $1 in two periods, and $1 in three periods. Present value factors,

Illustration A.3

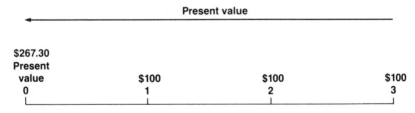

$100 × 2.67301   (2.67301* = 0.94340 + 0.89000 + 0.83962)

* Difference due to rounding.

such as the 2.67301, can be found in Table 4, Appendix A, for varying periods and interest rates.

Suppose you won a prize in a lottery that awarded you your choice of either $10,000 at the end of each of the next five years or $35,000 cash immediately. You believe you can earn interest on invested cash at 15 percent per annum. Which option should you choose? To answer the question, you should compute the present value of an annuity of $10,000 per period for five years at 15 percent. The present value is $33,521.60—$10,000 × 3.35216. You should accept the immediate payment of $35,000 since it is the larger present value.

Determining the Price of a Bond

The concepts discussed above will now be employed to illustrate the computation of the price of a bond issue.

In determining the price of a bond, the life of the bond is always stated in terms of interest payment periods, and the effective rate used in seeking amounts from the interest tables is the annual effective rate divided by the number of interest periods in one year.

Assume that bonds with a face value of $100,000 and an interest rate of 10 percent (semiannual interest payments) are issued at a price which will yield the investor a return of 12 percent. The issue date is July 1, 19x1, and the maturity date is July 1, 19x4 (this unrealistically short life is used for the sake of keeping the illustration simple). The price the investor would pay is calculated as shown:

Present value of the promise to pay principal is $100,000 times the present value of $1 due in six periods at 6%, or $100,000 × 0.70496 (from Table 3, Appendix A)	$70,496.00
Present value of the promise to pay periodic interest is $5,000 times the present value of an annuity of $1 for six periods at 6%, or $5,000 × 4.91732 (from Table 4, Appendix A).	24,586.60
Total price	$95,082.60

Thus, the amount of the discount is $100,000 − $95,082.60 = $4,917.40.

The Effective Rate of Interest Method for Amortizing the Discount

The following table shows how the discount calculated would be amortized over the life of the bond. The yield rate must be known to make the calculations required under this method. Notice that the amount of the discount amortized increases each period rather than remaining constant, as it would under the straight-line method ($819.55 per six-month period under the straight-line method). This causes the periodic interest expense to increase each succeeding period. But note that the interest expense is a constant rate per period because the carrying value of the bond's face value less the unamortized bond discount increases each period. This is the basic difference that results from use of the straight-line method (a constant *amount of expense* per period) as contrasted with the effective or yield rate method (a constant *rate of expense* per period).

Discount Amortized by the Effective-Rate-of-Interest Method

Date	Cash Credit	Interest Expense Debit	Discount on Bonds Payable Credit	Value of Bonds Payable
7/1/x1.				$ 95,082.60
1/1/x2.	$ 5,000*	$ 5,704.96†	$ 704.96‡	95,787.56§
7/1/x2.	5,000	5,747.25	747.25	96,534.81
1/1/x3.	5,000	5,792.09	792.09	97,326.90
7/1/x3.	5,000	5,839.61	839.61	98,166.51
1/1/x4.	5,000	5,889.99	889.99	99,056.50
7/1/x4.	5,000	5,943.50‖	943.50	100,000.00
	$30,000	$34,917.40	$4,917.40	

* $100,000 × 10% × ½ = $5,000.
† $95,082.60 × 12% × ½ = $5,704.96.
‡ $5,704.96 − $5,000 = $704.96.
§ $95,082.60 + $704.96 = $95,787.56.
‖ Actually this came to $5,943.39, but it was increased to make the carrying value come to $100,000.

Questions

1. (*a*) What is a share of capital stock? (*b*) What are the two major classes of capital stock? (*c*) What are the common features that distinguish the two classes?
2. What are the basic rights associated with a share of common stock?
3. A corporation has outstanding 5,000 shares of 8 percent, $50 par value, cumulative preferred stock on which dividends have not been declared for the last two years. Is the corporation liable to its preferred stockholders for these dividends? How should these dividends be reported in the balance sheet, if at all?
4. (*a*) What are some of the significant similarities and differences between a 20-year bond and a share of cumulative preferred stock? (*b*) Why might an investor desire preferred stock? (*c*) Why might a corporation issue a preferred stock that is both convertible and callable?
5. (*a*) What is book value per share of common stock, and how is it computed? (*b*) Of what significance is it? (*c*) What is its relationship to market value per share?
6. (*a*) What are the two major components of stockholders' equity? (*b*) What exactly is paid-in capital in excess of par value? (*c*) What are the sources of paid-in capital?
7. (*a*) What are retained earnings? (*b*) Why might a corporation with a $4 million balance in retained earnings have to borrow money to finance a $1 million plant expansion?
8. The following dates are associated with a cash dividend of $100,000: July 15, July 31, and August 15. (*a*) Identify each of these dates. (*b*) Which is probably most significant to the investor? (*c*) What is the accounting impact of each date?

9. What is the effect of each of the following on total stockholders' equity: (a) declaration of a cash dividend, (b) payment of a cash dividend, and (c) distribution of a stock dividend?

10. (a) Distinguish between a stock dividend and a stock split. (b) Indicate the accounting for each.

11. (a) What is treasury stock? (b) How does it differ, if at all, from unissued stock? (c) Where is it reported in the financial statements? (d) If treasury stock is sold at more than its cost, what is the accounting treatment of the "gain"?

12. What types of transactions must be guarded against because they can lead to an impairment of capital? Explain.

13. (a) Why might a bond indenture limit dividends to retained earnings in excess of a stated amount? (b) How might such a limitation be reported in the financial statements?

14. (a) Why might a firm borrow money by issuing long-term notes or bonds? (b) What are some of the disadvantages of using this source of financing?

15. (a) What is a bond? (b) Why might bonds of a certain issue sell at a premium while bonds of another issue sell at a discount? (c) What is the typical accounting for premiums or discounts on bonds payable? (d) Why are they so accounted for?

16. Differentiate between a debenture and a mortgage bond.

17. What is a timing difference? Give an example.

Exercises

1. Walters Corporation received $1 million in cash by issuing its authorized 10,000 shares of stock. Show how this information is presented in the balance sheet assuming that:
   a. The stock had a par value of $50 per share.
   b. The stock had a stated value of $60 per share.
   c. The stock had no par or stated value.

2. One hundred shares of $50 par value common stock are issued to the promoters of a corporation in exchange for a tract of land to be used by the corporation as a plant site. Experienced appraisers estimated the value of the land to be $8,500. Give the T-account entries to record the issuance of the shares for the land.

3. P Corporation has 2,000 authorized, issued, and outstanding shares of 5 percent, $100 par value, cumulative preferred stock and 100,000 authorized shares of $20 par value common stock, of which 80,000 shares are outstanding (both classes were issued at par value). On January 1, 19x4, retained earnings amounted to $2,520,000 and net income for 19x4 was $18,000. P Corporation declared the annual dividend on the preferred stock and a $0.60 cash dividend on the common stock on December 27, 19x4. The dividends were paid in cash on February 1, 19x5. List all the accounts and corresponding amounts involved in recording the declaration and payment of the dividends.

4. Oliver Company has outstanding 2,000 shares of cumulative preferred stock with an annual dividend of $5 per share and 10,000 shares of common stock without par or stated value. No dividends were paid in 19x0 or 19x1. On January 1, 19x2, the Retained Earnings account had a debit balance of $6,000.

During 19x2, the company earned $92,500 and declared a $3 per share dividend on the common stock. Compute the December 31, 19x2, balance in the Retained Earnings account.

5. Haas Company's stockholders' equity consists of 25,000 authorized shares of $10 par value common stock, 10,000 of which have been issued at par value, and retained earnings of $200,000. The company now splits its stock, two for one, by issuing 10,000 additional shares of $5 par value stock and changing the par value of the outstanding shares to $5.

   a. Explain the entries to record the action.

   b. Assume instead the company declared and issued a 10 percent stock dividend. The market price of the shares is $12.50. Show the T-account entries.

6. The board of directors of the Royal Company ordered the formal recognition in the accounts of the restriction placed by a loan agreement upon $500,000 of the company's retained earnings, making them unavailable for dividends. Five years later, when the loan was repaid, the board ordered the removal of the restriction. Show the T-account entries for these actions.

7. Boone Company on December 31, 19x3, issued $100,000 principal amount of 12 percent, 10-year bonds dated December 31, 19x3. Interest is payable semiannually on June 30 and December 1. The bonds were issued for $100,000. Give the T-account entries to record the issuance of the bonds and the interest expense paid on June 30, 19x4.

8. Reeves Company issued $200,000 principal amount of 20-year, 12 percent bonds at 104 on December 31, 19x3, the date of the bonds.

   a. Was the market rate of interest for these bonds higher or lower than 12 percent?

   b. What is the amount of interest expense for 19x4, assuming straight-line amortization of the premium?

   c. If the bonds had been issued at 95, what would have been the interest expense for 19x4?

9. On July 1, 19x4, Ingle Company issued $100,000 face amount of 12 percent, 10-year bonds, interest payable semiannually on January 1 and July 1, for cash of $104,000. What would the income statement for the year ending December 31, 19x4, and the balance sheet as of December 31, 19x4, show as a result of the issuance of the bonds?

10. Artistic Company issued $100,000 face value of 10-year, 8 percent bonds calling for semiannual interest payments and received cash of $82,074.40—a price to yield 11 percent. Compute the first six months' interest expense using the effective rate method.

11. Brown Corporation reported depreciation on its tax return for 19x4 of $60,000. Depreciation on the income statement for the same year amounted to $50,000. If the income tax rate is 40 percent, compute the change in the Deferred Federal Income Taxes Payable account.

Business Decision Problem 5–1

Carson Bros., Inc., is a corporation in which all of the outstanding preferred and common stock is held by the four Carson brothers. The brothers have an agreement stating that upon the death of a brother, the remaining brothers will cause the corporation to call and retire the deceased brother's preferred stock. The surviving brothers, as individuals, will purchase his holdings of common stock from his estate at what they call "adjusted book value." The agreement stipulates that in calculating adjusted book value, the land owned by the company is to be valued at market value, the inventory is to be valued at replacement cost, and whatever other adjustments are needed to place the accounts on a sound accounting basis are to be made.

The stockholders' equity accounts of the company on June 30, 19x4, the date of James Carson's death, show:

Preferred stock—6 percent, $100 par value; $100 liquidation value; callable at $105; cumulative; 4,000 shares authorized, issued, and outstanding.	$ 400,000
Common stock—no-par value; stated value, $5; 60,000 shares authorized, issued, and outstanding.	300,000
Paid-in capital in excess of par—preferred.	20,000
Paid-in capital—stock dividends.	300,000
Retained earnings.	240,000
Total stockholders' equity.	$1,260,000

The market value of the land is $60,000 more than its recorded cost, and the current replacement cost of the inventory is $32,000 more than its recorded cost. It is also agreed by the three remaining brothers and the accountant representing Mrs. James Carson that the accounts fail to include a proper accrual of $20,000 for pensions payable to employees. No dividends have been declared on the preferred stock in the last one-half year. At the time of his death, James Carson held 2,000 shares of preferred stock and 10,000 shares of common stock.

Required:

Compute the amount that the corporation will pay for James Carson's preferred stock and the amount that the three brothers will pay for his common stock.

Business Decision Problem 5–2

Ames Company is considering ways of financing a proposed $2 million plant expansion which will also involve investing another $500,000 each in accounts receivable and inventories. This expansion would double the volume of business done and is expected to increase operating income (before interest expense and income taxes) from a current level of $800,000 to $1,320,000. Interest expense currently is $70,000. The income tax rate is 40 percent and is expected to remain at this level. Earnings per share (net income divided by the number of common shares outstanding) for the current year are $2.19 ($438,000 divided by 200,000 shares).

The company believes it can raise the necessary funds for the expansion in two alternative ways:

1. Finance entirely by issuing additional shares of common stock at $75 per share.
2. Finance two thirds of the necessary funds by issuing 20-year, 10 percent bonds, which can be issued at face value, and issue shares of common stock at $80 per share for the balance.

Required:

Present schedules comparing the earnings per share that are expected under each of the two alternatives as part of the information that should be gathered in making the decision on whether the expansion should be undertaken.

Solutions to End-of-Chapter Questions, Exercises, and Business Decision Problems

Answers to Questions

1. (*a*) A share of capital stock is a unit of ownership in a corporation. (*b*) The two major classes of capital stock are preferred stock and common stock. (*c*) These classes are distinguished by the features usually found in preferred stocks, namely, a preference over common stock as to assets in liquidation and as to dividends. Preferred stock may not have voting rights but typically has a right to dividends that accumulates through time if dividends are not declared.

2. The basic rights associated with a share of common stock are: (1) to share in profits by receiving dividends when declared; (2) to share in management by voting to elect the directors; (3) to receive corporate assets in proportion to ownership upon liquidation of the corporation; (4) to dispose of the share of stock; and (5) perhaps the preemptive right to subscribe to additional offerings of stock.

3. No, the corporation is not legally liable for these dividends. The stockholders' claim is a contingent one, which will become an actual liability of the corporation only when the board of directors declares dividends. The dividends in arrears should be disclosed in a footnote to the financial statements.

4. (*a*) Similarities: Both have a fixed rate of interest (or dividend) payable at stated intervals. Differences: (1) Interest on bonds is deductible by the corporation in computing taxable income and pretax net income. Dividends are distributions of income, not expenses. (2) The bond will eventually be redeemed, usually at a specific date. Preferred stock usually has no specific maturity date but may be subject to call. (*b*) An investor might desire a particular preferred stock because of its fixed, relatively high rate of return or, possibly, because it contains a conversion privilege that will permit the investor to participate in the future profitability of the issuing corporation. (Bonds may also contain a conversion privilege.) (*c*) A corporation might issue preferred stock simply because it is the least costly way of securing additional financing. A corporation might issue a preferred stock that is convertible to secure a much lower dividend rate on the preferred than would otherwise be obtainable. A corporation might include a call provision in such a preferred stock in order to be able to force its conversion or to retire it if at some time in the future financing is available at much more favorable terms.

5. (*a*) If there is no preferred stock outstanding, book value per share of common stock is simply the total net assets of the corporation, valued at their customary accounting bases, divided by the number of shares of common stock outstanding. (*b*) Book value is of limited significance because many assets are carried at historical costs, because alternative accounting methods may be used that yield

differing asset valuations, and because the balance sheet often fails to show valuable intangible assets. (c) There is little, if any, direct relationship between book value and market value per share because they are based on different factors. Stocks often sell at prices greatly in excess of book value, less frequently at prices that are fractions of book value.

6. (a) The two major components of stockholders' equity are paid-in (or contributed) capital and retained earnings. (b) Paid-in capital in excess of par value usually consists of capital actually contributed or invested by stockholders. It is capital in excess of the par value of the shares issued, which is usually the legal or stated capital of the corporation. (c) The sources of paid-in capital include amounts contributed by stockholders, "gains" on treasury stock transactions, retained earnings capitalized by stock dividends, and donations.

7. (a) Retained Earnings is the title given to the account used to show that profits retained in the business have caused an increase in net assets (stockholders' equity). (b) A corporation might have a substantial balance in its Retained Earnings account and still have to borrow to finance a plant expansion because the existence of retained earnings indicates an increase in net assets but promises nothing about what form the assets are in. Profitable operations usually will generate cash, but the cash might have already been used to make investments in plant assets or inventories or to redeem outstanding long-term debt, among many uses.

8. (a) July 15 is the date of dividend declaration; July 31 is the date of record; and August 15 is the date of payment. (b) The date of record is probably the most significant to the investor because it is used to determine to which specific persons the dividend checks are to be mailed. (c) The liability for dividends comes into existence and is recorded on the date of declaration. The dividend is paid on the payment date.

9. (a) Cash dividend declarations reduce stockholders' equity. (b) The payment of a cash dividend reduces the dividends payable liability and has no effect on stockholders' equity. (c) Stock dividends have no effect on total stockholders' equity; they transfer an amount of retained earnings to paid-in capital accounts.

10. (a) A stock dividend is a distribution of additional shares of stock to the stockholders with no corresponding reduction in the par value per share. A stock split is designed to significantly increase the number of shares outstanding to reduce the market price per share. It does this by increasing the shares outstanding by some multiple (2 for 1, 3 for 1, etc.) and correspondingly reducing the par value per share so that total par value of the outstanding shares does not change. (b) The stock dividend is debited to Retained Earnings at fair market value and credited to the Capital Stock account for par value and to a paid-in capital account for the excess over par. No formal entry is required to record the increased number of shares outstanding following a stock split.

11. (a) Treasury stock is capital stock, either preferred or common, that has been issued and reacquired by the issuing corporation. (b) Treasury stock is stock that has been issued at least once. Unissued stock has never been issued. (c) Treasury stock is reported in the balance sheet as a deduction from total stockholders' equity. (d) "Gains" on treasury stock are recorded in a separate account entitled Paid-In Capital—Treasury Stock Transactions.

12. The payment of cash dividends and the purchase of treasury stock are two types of transactions that must be handled carefully so as not to impair legal or

stated capital. Assume a corporation has only one stockholders' equity account: common stock with a balance of $100,000 from issuing 10,000 shares of $10 par value common stock at par (no retained earnings). Typically, the $100,000 is the legal capital of the firm. In this case, the acquisition of treasury stock or the declaration and payment of a cash dividend would impair (reduce) the firm's actual capital below its legal amount. Such actions are prohibited by law in most states.

13. (a) The basic reason is to prevent the directors from "pulling the rug" from under the bondholders by declaring cash dividends that substantially reduce stockholders' equity. (b) Typically, such restrictions are disclosed via a footnote.

14. (a) A firm might engage in long-term borrowing (1) to enhance the earnings per share on the common stock through favorable leverage; (2) to tap the only capital market open to it at a reasonable cost; and (3) to avoid diluting the existing stockholders' control of the corporation by issuing more shares of stock. (b) Among the disadvantages of issuing long-term notes or bonds are: (1) fixed interest charges must be paid on the debt; (2) added claims ranking ahead of the stockholders' now exist; and (3) many restrictions upon management's right to operate the firm as it believes to be the best way may be imposed by the loan agreement or the bond indenture.

15. (a) A bond is a formal, written contract stating the legal obligations undertaken by the issuer to the bondholders in exchange for the use of the bondholders' money. (b) Bonds might sell in the market at a premium or a discount, depending upon the interest rate offered by the bonds, together with all of the other covenants in the bond indenture, relative to what is available in the market from other issuers. (c) Premiums and discounts on bonds payable are amortized to interest expense over the life of the bond issue. (d) They are accounted for in this way because they change the interest cost of borrowing from the rate offered on the face of the bonds to a rate the bondholders are willing to accept.

16. A debenture is an unsecured bond, that is, a bond supported only by the general credit of the issuer. A mortgage bond is a bond that is secured by a mortgage on specific assets, such as real estate or motor vehicles.

17. A timing difference is an item included in determining taxable income and pretax accounting income that causes these two to differ because it is recognized in different years. An example of a timing difference is the difference in depreciation when accelerated depreciation is used for tax purposes and straight-line depreciation is recorded for accounting purposes.

Solutions to Exercises

1. *a.* Capital stock—$50 par value; 10,000 shares authorized, issued,
   and outstanding . . . . $ 500,000
   Paid-in capital in excess of par value   500,000

   Total paid-in capital $1,000,000

   b. Capital stock—$60 stated value; 10,000 shares authorized, issued,
   and outstanding . . . . $ 600,000
   Paid-in capital in excess of stated value.   400,000

   Total paid-in capital $1,000,000

    c. Capital stock—no par or stated value; 10,000 shares authorized,
issued, and outstanding $1,000,000

2.

Land	Common Stock	Paid-In Capital in Excess of Par Value
Bal. xxx 8,500	Bal. xxx 5,000	Bal. xxx 3,500

3. To record the declaration of the dividend, the following accounts and amounts are involved:

Dividends Payable—Preferred..................	$10,000 (2,000 × $100 × 0.05)
Dividends Payable—Common..................	48,000 (80,000 × $.60)
Retained Earnings	58,000

The Dividends Payable accounts are credited, and the Retained Earnings Account is debited.

    To record the payment of the dividends, the Dividends Payable accounts are debited and Cash is credited:

Dividends Payable—Preferred..............	$10,000
Dividends Payable—Common	48,000
Cash	58,000

4.
Retained earnings (deficit), January 1, 19x2		$ (6,000)
Add: Net income for 19x2............................		92,500
Total.......................................		$86,500
Less: Dividends—preferred (2,000 × $5 × 3 years)	$30,000	
Dividends—common (10,000 × $3)	30,000	60,000
Retained earnings, December 31, 19x2.................		$26,500

5. *a.* No formal journal entry is needed to record the stock split; a memo entry to record the increased number of shares and the reduced par value of $5 per share is sufficient.

    b.

Retained Earnings	Common Stock	Paid-In Capital— Stock Dividends
12,500 Bal. xxx	Bal. xxx 10,000	Bal. xxx 2,500

6.

Retained Earnings	Retained Earnings Restricted by Bond Indenture
(a) 500,000 Bal. xxx (b) 500,000	(b) 500,000 (a) 500,000

Entry (*a*) creates the restriction on retained earnings. Entry (*b*) reverses entry (*a*) and eliminates the restriction.

7. The entry for issuing the bonds is:

Cash			Bonds Payable		
Bal.	xxx			Bal.	xxx
	100,000				100,000

To record payment of interest, the entry is:

Cash			Bond Interest Expense		
Bal.	xxx			6,000	
		6,000			

8. *a.* The rate was lower than 12 percent. The bonds sold at a premium.
    b. $23,600 = [($200,000 × 0.12) − ($8,000/20)].
    c. $24,500 = [($200,000 × 0.12) + ($10,000/20)].
9. Income statement shows interest expense of $5,800 [($100,000 × 0.12 × 0.5) − ($4,000/20)]. Balance sheet shows a current liability for accrued interest payable of $6,000. It also shows a long-term liability of $103,800 [$100,000 + ($4,000 − $200)] for the bonds and the unamortized premium.
10. $82,074.40 × 0.055 = $4.514.09.
11. Deferred Federal Income Taxes Payable increased $4,000 during the year: 0.4 × $10,000 of excess depreciation per tax return over income statement amount.

Solution to Business Decision Problem 5–1

Total stockholders' equity..................................		$1,260,000
Agreed-upon revisions:		
Add:		
Appreciation of land..................................	$ 60,000	
Excess of replacement cost over cost of inventory	32,000	
	$ 92,000	
Less: Unrecorded pension obligation	20,000	72,000
Revised stockholders' equity		$1,332,000
Less: Equity of preferred stockholders:		
4,000 shares at call price of $105	$420,000	
Dividends in arrears (4,000 × $3)	12,000	
Equity of preferred stockholders ($108 per share)............		432,000
Total adjusted net book value of common stock ($15.00 per share)...		$ 900,000
Amount to be paid for James Carson's preferred stock (2,000 × $108)..		$ 216,000
Amount to be paid for James Carson's common stock (10,000 × $15.00)...		150,000
Total amount to be paid for James Carson's stockholdings.....		$ 366,000

Solution to Business Decision Problem 5–2

	Alternative 1	Alternative 2
Expected operating income	$1,320,000	$1,320,000
Interest expense:		
Current	(70,000)	(70,000)
On new bonds ($2,000,000 × .10)		(200,000)
	$1,250,000	$1,050,000
Income taxes (40%)	500,000	420,000
Net income for stockholders	$ 750,000	$ 630,000
Number of shares outstanding	240,000[a]	212,500[b]
Earnings per share	$ 3.125	$ 2.96

[a] 200,000 + ($3,000,000/$75) = 240,000 shares.
[b] 200,000 + ($1,000,000/$80) = 212,500 shares.

The above estimates suggest rather strongly that the investment should be made, since either means of financing will increase earnings per share substantially. The above information also suggests that the added $3 million of capital be raised by issuing only additional shares of common stock.

6

Analysis and Interpretation of Financial Statements; the Statement of Changes in Financial Position

Chapter Goals

When you have completed Chapter 6, you should be able to:

1. Explain and illustrate how comparative financial statements may be used to analyze and appraise the financial position of a firm and the results of its operations.
2. Calculate the amount of change in financial statement items for successive periods in dollars and percentages (horizontal and trend analysis).
3. Prepare common-size financial statements (vertical analysis).
4. Perform ratio analysis using widely applied financial ratios and explain what each ratio seeks to show or measure.
5. Explain the limitations of financial analysis.
6. Prepare a statement of changes in financial position and the related statement of changes in working capital.
7. Prepare a statement of changes in financial position under the cash basis.

Previous chapters discussed accounting principles and procedures that form the basis for preparation of financial statements. This chapter presents some common methods used to analyze and interpret data in financial statements and the final major financial statement, the statement of changes in financial position.

A firm's financial statements may be analyzed by investors and creditors who must decide whether to invest in or extend credit to the firm. Analysis may also be conducted by management in seeking to evaluate, plan, and control its operations as carried out by subordinates and operating divisions. Management's analysis may lead to changes in operating policies such as credit terms, product pricing, and number of products and amounts of each maintained in inventory. But much of management's analysis relates to parts of the company rather than to the company as a whole. Further, management's analysis is more likely to involve a comparison of actual with budgeted results or position (discussed in Chapter 10). For these reasons, discussion and illustration of financial statement analysis will be in the context of outsiders relying primarily upon the company's annual report for their information about a firm.

OBJECTIVES OF FINANCIAL STATEMENT ANALYSIS

Financial statement analysis applies analytical tools and techniques to financial statements and other relevant data to obtain useful information. Financial statement analysis draws attention to significant relationships and trends. The information obtained is useful in *assessing past performance* and *current financial position* which are the results of prior decisions. But the information is most useful for *making predictions* which may have a direct effect upon decisions made by many users of financial statements.

Information needed by outside users of financial statements often relates to a firm's profitability or liquidity, or both. For example, a person considering purchase of shares of a firm's common stock may wish to predict future dividends and changes in the market price of the shares. Since both dividends and price changes are likely to be influenced by earnings, the investor may seek to predict earnings. The firm's past earnings record is the logical starting point in predicting future earnings.

On the other hand, a bank asked to extend a 90-day loan would be interested in a firm's projected short-term liquidity. Here again, the predicted ability to repay the loan is likely to be based, at least partially, upon past ability to pay off debt.

FINANCIAL STATEMENT ANALYSIS

Several types of analysis may be performed on a company's financial statements. Since comparisons or relationships enhance the utility of accounting information, these are almost always involved. For example, little useful information is conveyed by the statement that a firm's net income was $100,000 last year. Some utility is added if it is known that the prior year's net income was $25,000. And information of real value results when sales and assets employed are known for the firm under review and for its competitors. Such comparisons may be expressed as:

1. Absolute increases and decreases for an item from one period to the next.
2. Percentage increases and decreases for an item from one period to the next.
3. Trend percentages.
4. Percentages of single items to an aggregate total.
5. Ratios.

Items 1 and 2 make use of comparative financial statements. Comparative financial statements are the same firm's financial statements for two or more successive periods in side-by-side columns. Calculation of dollar or percentage changes in the statement items or totals is known as *horizontal analysis*. This type of review helps detect change in a firm's performance and highlights trends.

Trend percentages (item 3) are similar to horizontal analysis except that a base year is selected and comparisons are made to the base year. Trend percentages are useful for comparing financial statements over several years because they disclose the changes and trends occurring through time.

Information may also be gained by analyzing a financial statement of a firm for a single year. *Vertical analysis* (item 4) consists of the study of a single financial statement by expressing each item therein as a percentage of a significant total. Vertical analysis is useful in analyzing income statement data, such as the percentage of cost of goods sold to sales or the gross margin on sales. When financial statements are presented showing only percentages and no absolute amounts, they are called *common size statements*.

Ratios (item 5) are expressions of logical relationships between certain items in the financial statements. Many ratios can be computed from the same set of financial statements, with the choice of ratios prepared limited only by the requirement that the items used to construct a ratio have a logical relationship to one another.

Horizontal and Vertical Analysis: An Illustration

Illustrations 6.1 and 6.2 show comparative financial statements of the Knight Corporation for the years ended December 31, 19x4 and 19x5. These comparative statements will be analyzed to disclose certain relationships among the various items included in the balance sheet and the income statement.

Illustration 6.1
Comparative Balance Sheets

THE KNIGHT CORPORATION
Comparative Balance Sheets
December 31, 19x4 and 19x5

Exhibit A

	December 31		Increase or Decrease* 19x5 over 19x4		Percentage of Total Assets December 31	
	(1) 19x5	(2) 19x4	(3) Dollars	(4) Percent	(5) 19x5	(6) 19x4
Assets						
Current assets:						
Cash	$ 80,200	$ 55,000	$25,200	45.8	12.6	10.0
Accounts receivable, net	124,200	132,600	8,400*	6.3*	19.6	24.1
Notes receivable	55,000	50,000	5,000	10.0	8.7	9.1
Inventories	110,800	94,500	16,300	17.2	17.4	17.1
Prepaid expenses	3,600	4,700	1,100*	23.4*	0.6	0.9
Total current assets	$373,800	$336,800	$37,000	11.0	58.8ᴿ	61.1
Property, plant, and equipment:						
Land	$ 21,000	$ 21,000	$ 0	0	3.3	3.8
Building	205,000	160,000	45,000	28.1	32.3	29.0
Less: Accumulated depreciation	(27,000)	(22,400)	(4,600)	21.0	(4.3)	(4.1)
Furniture and fixtures	83,200	69,800	13,400	19.2	13.1	12.7
Less: Accumulated depreciation	(20,800)	(14,100)	(6,700)	47.5	(3.3)	(2.6)
Total property, plant, and equipment	$261,400	$214,300	$47,100	22.0	41.2ᴿ	38.9ᴿ
Total assets	$635,200	$551,100	$84,100	15.3	100.0	100.0

Liabilities and Stockholders' Equity

Current liabilities:						
Accounts payable	$ 70,300	$ 64,600	$ 5,700	8.8	11.1	11.7
Notes payable	20,000	15,100	4,900	32.5	3.1	2.7
Taxes accrued	36,800	30,200	6,600	21.9	5.8	5.5
Total current liabilities	$127,100	$109,900	$17,200	15.7	20.0	19.9
Long-term liabilities:						
Mortgage notes payable, land and building, 12%, 19x7	43,600	60,800	17,700*	28.3*	6.9	11.0
Total liabilities	$170,700	$170,700	$ 0	0.0	26.9	31.0
Stockholders' equity:						
Common stock, par value $10 per share	$240,000	$200,000	$40,000	20.0	37.8	36.3
Retained earnings	224,500	180,400	44,100	24.4	35.3	32.7
Total stockholders' equity	$464,500	$380,400	$84,100	22.1	73.1	69.0
Total liabilities and stockholders' equity	$635,200	$551,100	$84,100	15.3	100.0	100.0

R Rounding difference.
* Decrease.

Illustration 6.2
Comparative Statements of Income and Retained Earnings

THE KNIGHT CORPORATION
Comparative Statements of Income and Retained Earnings
For the Years Ended December 31, 19x4 and 19x5

Exhibit B

	Year Ended December 31		Increase or Decrease* 19x5 over 19x4		Percentage of Net Sales	
	(7) 19x5	(8) 19x4	(9) Dollar	(10) Percent	(11) 19x5	(12) 19x4
Net sales	$986,400	$765,500	$220,900	28.9	100.0	100.0
Cost of goods sold	623,200	500,900	122,300	24.4	63.2	65.4
Gross margin	$363,200	$264,600	$ 98,600	37.3	36.8	34.6
Operating expenses:						
Selling	$132,500	$ 84,900	$ 47,600	56.1	13.4	11.1
Administrative	120,300	98,600	21,700	22.0	12.2	12.9
Total operating expenses	$252,800	$183,500	$ 69,300	37.8	25.6	24.0
Net operating income	$110,400	$ 81,100	$ 29,300	36.0	11.2	10.6
Other expenses	3,000	2,800	200	7.1	0.3	0.4
Net income before federal income taxes	$107,400	$ 78,300	$ 29,100	37.2	10.9	10.2
Federal income taxes	48,300	31,700	16,600	52.4	4.9	4.1
Net income to retained earnings	$ 59,100	$ 46,600	$ 12,500	26.8	6.0	6.1R
Retained earnings, January 1	180,400	146,300	34,100	23.3		
Dividends declared	$239,500	$192,900	$ 46,600	24.2		
	15,000	12,500	2,500	20.0		
Retained earnings, December 31	$224,500	$180,400	$ 44,100	24.4		

R Rounding difference.

Analysis of balance sheet.   Columns (1), (2), and (3) in the comparative balance sheets (Illustration 6.1) show the absolute dollar amounts for each item for December 31, 19x4, and December 31, 19x5, and the change for the year. If the change between the two dates is an increase from 19x4 to 19x5, the change is shown as a positive figure. If the change is a decrease, it is indicated by an asterisk (*).

Examples of the items highlighted by the first three columns are:

a.   Current assets increased $37,000, consisting largely of a $25,200 increase in cash, while current liabilities increased only $17,200.
b.   Total assets increased $84,100, while total liabilities remained unchanged.
c.   The increase in total assets was financed by the sale of common stock, $40,000, and by the retention of earnings, $44,100.

Column (4) in Illustration 6.1 expresses the dollar change in column (3) as a percentage of column (2). Frequently, percentage increases and decreases are more informative than absolute amounts, as illustrated by the current asset and current liability changes. Although the absolute amount of current assets increased by more than twice the amount of current liabilities, the percentages reveal that current assets increased 11 percent, while current liabilities increased 15.7 percent. Thus, current liabilities are increased at a rate faster than the current assets that will be used to pay them. But, in view of the substantial amount of cash possessed, the company is not likely to fail to pay its debts as they come due. The 28.3 percent decrease in mortgage notes payable may lead the analyst to conclude that interest charges will be lower and net income higher in the coming years. The 20 percent increase in common shares outstanding may tend to reduce earnings per share.

Columns (5) and (6) express the dollar amounts of each item in columns (1) and (2) as percentages of total assets (equities). Vertical analysis of the Knight Corporation's balance sheet is used to disclose an account's relative significance to total assets, which aids in assessing the importance of changes in that account. For example, although prepaid expenses declined $1,100 in 19x5, a decrease of 23.4 percent, they represent less than 1 percent of total assets and, therefore, probably would not be investigated further. The vertical analysis also shows that long-term debt financing decreased by 4.1 percent, which is the percentage stockholder financing of the company increased.

Analysis of income statement.   The amounts in columns (7) and (8) in Illustration 6.2 are the dollar amounts for the years 19x4 and 19x5. The amounts and percentages in columns (9)–(12) are computed in the same manner as the balance sheet amounts in Illustration 6.1 except that the items in columns (11) and (12) are percentages of net sales. Examination of the comparative statements of income and retained earnings shows:

a.   Sales increased 28.9 percent in 19x5.
b.   Gross margin increased 37.3 percent in 19x5.

c. Selling expenses increased 56.1 percent in 19x5.
d. Federal income taxes rose by 52.4 percent in 19x5.
e. Net income increased 26.8 percent, while dividends increased 20.0 percent.
f. Net income per dollar of sales remained virtually constant over the two years.

Considering both horizontal and vertical analysis information, the analyst would conclude that an increase in the gross margin rate from 34.6 percent to 36.8 percent, coupled with a 28.9 percent increase in sales, resulted in a 37.3 percent increase in gross margin in 19x5. But the increase in net income was held to 26.8 percent because selling expenses increased 56.1 percent and income taxes increased 52.4 percent. Predicting net income for 19x6 would be aided if the analyst knew whether this increase in selling expenses was expected to recur. Other expenses remained basically the same, on a per-centage-of-sales basis, over the two years.

Proper analysis does not stop upon the calculation of increases and de-creases in amounts or percentages over several years. Such changes are clues that may lead to significant findings. Accurate predictions depend upon a host of factors, including economic and political conditions; management's plans regarding new products, plant expansion, and promotional outlays; and the expected activities of competitors.

Trend Percentages

Trend percentages are also referred to as index numbers. They are used for comparison of financial information over time to a base year. Trend percentages are calculated by:

1. Selecting a base year.
2. Assigning a weight of 100 percent to the amounts appearing on the base year financial statements.
3. Expressing the amounts shown on the financial statements for other years as a percentage of base year amounts. Percentages are computed by dividing nonbase amounts by base year amounts and then multiplying the result by 100.

As an example, the following information is given:

	19x4	19x5	19x6	19x7
Sales	$350,000	$367,500	$441,000	$485,000
Cost of goods sold	200,000	196,000	230,000	285,000
Gross margin	$150,000	$171,500	$211,000	$200,000
Operating expenses	145,000	169,000	200,000	192,000
Net income before taxes	$ 5,000	$ 2,500	$ 11,000	$ 8,000

Letting 19x4 be the base year, trend percentages would be calculated for each year by dividing sales by $350,000, cost of goods sold by $200,000, gross margin by $150,000, operating expenses by $145,000, and net income before income taxes by $5,000. After all divisions have been made, each result would be multiplied by 100 and the resulting trends would appear as:

	19x1	19x2	19x3	19x4
Sales....................................	100	105	126	139
Cost of goods sold	100	98	115	143
Gross margin...........................	100	114	141	133
Operating expenses	100	117	138	132
Net income before taxes.................	100	50	220	160

Trend percentages indicate the changes taking place in an organization and highlight the direction of the changes. In reviewing trend percentages, a manager or investor should pay close attention to the trends in related items, such as the cost of goods sold in relation to sales. For example, trend analysis that shows a constantly declining gross margin rate may be a signal that trouble lies ahead in diminished earnings or actual losses.

Expressing changes as percentages is usually straightforward as long as the amount in the base year is not zero or negative. A $30,000 increase in notes receivable cannot be expressed in percentages if the increase is from zero last year to $30,000 this year. Also, an increase in net income from a loss last year of $10,000 to earnings this year of $20,000 cannot be expressed in percentages.

Ratio Analysis

Logical relationships exist between certain accounts or items in a firm's financial statements. These accounts may appear on the same statement, or they may appear on two different statements. The dollar amounts of the related accounts or items are set up in fraction form and called ratios. These ratios can be broadly classified as (1) liquidity ratios, (2) equity or solvency ratios, (3) profitability tests, and (4) market tests.

Liquidity ratios. Liquidity ratios are used to indicate a firm's debt-paying ability, especially its short-term debt-paying ability. The liquidity ratios discussed are the current ratio, acid-test ratio, accounts receivable turnover, number of days' sales in accounts receivable, inventory turnover, and total assets turnover.

Current or working capital ratio. *Working capital* is the excess of current assets over current liabilities. The ratio which relates these two categories is known as the current or working capital ratio. This ratio indicates the ability of a company to pay its current liabilities from current assets and, in this way, shows the strength of the company's working capital position.

The current ratio is computed by dividing total current assets by total current liabilities:

$$\text{Current ratio} = \frac{\text{Current assets}}{\text{Current liabilities}}$$

The ratio usually is stated in terms of the number of dollars of current assets to $1 of current liabilities (although the dollar signs are omitted). Thus, if current assets total $75,000 and current liabilities total $50,000, the ratio is expressed as 1.5 : 1 or simply 1.5.

The current ratio provides a better index of a firm's ability to pay current debts than does the absolute amount of working capital. To illustrate, assume that Company A and Company B have the following current assets and current liabilities on December 31, 19x4:

	Company A	Company B
Current assets	$11,000,000	$200,000
Current liabilities	10,000,000	100,000
Working capital	$ 1,000,000	$100,000
Current ratio.................	1.1 : 1	2 : 1

Company A has 10 times as much working capital as Company B. But Company B has a superior debt-paying ability since it has $2 of current assets for each $1 of current liabilities. Company A has only $1.10 of current assets for each $1 of current liabilities.

Short-term creditors are interested in the current ratio. They expect to receive payment from conversion of inventories and accounts receivable into cash. Long-term creditors are also interested in the current ratio because a firm that is unable to pay short-term debts may be forced into bankruptcy. For this reason, many bond indentures contain a provision requiring the borrower to maintain a minimum current ratio. A firm can increase its current ratio by issuing long-term debt or capital stock or by selling noncurrent assets.

A firm must also guard against a current ratio that is too high, especially if caused by idle cash, slow-paying customers, and slow-moving inventory. Decreased net income and rates of return on assets and stockholders' equity follow when too much capital that could be used profitably elsewhere is tied up in current assets.

Referring to the Knight Corporation data in Illustration 6.2, the current ratios for the two years are:

	December 31		Amount of Increase
	19x5	19x4	
Current assets (a).......	$373,800	$336,800	$37,000
Current liabilities (b)	127,100	109,900	17,200
Working capital (a − b)..	$246,700	$226,900	$19,800
Current ratio (a ÷ b)	2.94 : 1	3.06 : 1	

Thus, although Knight's working capital increased by $19,800, or 8.7 percent, its current ratio fell from 3.06 to 2.94 because its current liabilities increased faster than its current assets.

Acid-test or quick ratio.   The current ratio is not the only measure of a firm's short-term debt-paying ability. Another measure is the *acid-test* or *quick ratio,* which is the ratio of the firm's "quick assets" (cash, marketable securities, and net receivables) to its current liabilities.

$$\text{Acid-test ratio} = \frac{\text{Quick assets}}{\text{Current liabilities}}$$

Inventories and prepaid expenses are excluded from this computation because they might not be readily convertible into cash. Short-term creditors are interested particularly in this ratio since it relates the "pool" of cash and immediate cash inflows to immediate cash outflows.

The acid-test ratios for 19x4 and 19x5 for the Knight Corporation are:

	December 31		Amount of Increase
	19x5	19x4	
Quick assets (a)...................	$259,400	$237,600	$21,800
Current liabilities (b)	127,100	109,900	17,200
Net quick assets (a − b)...........	$132,300	$127,700	$ 4,600
Acid-test ratio (a ÷ b).............	2.04 : 1	2.16 : 1	

While the absolute value of the acid-test ratio is important, so too is the quality of the marketable securities and receivables. An accumulation of poor quality temporary investments or receivables, or both, could cause an acid-test ratio to appear deceptively favorable. Poor quality marketable securities means securities likely to generate losses on disposition; poor quality receivables are those which may be uncollectible or not collectible until long past due. The quality of receivables depends primarily upon their age, which can be assessed by preparation of an aging schedule or by calculating the accounts receivable turnover.

Accounts receivable turnover.   Turnover is the relationship between the amount of an asset and some measure of its use. *Accounts receivable turnover* is the number of times per year that the average amount of receivables is collected. The ratio is calculated by dividing net credit sales by average net accounts receivable, that is, accounts receivable after deducting the allowance for doubtful accounts.

$$\text{Accounts receivable turnover} = \frac{\text{Net credit sales}}{\text{Average net accounts receivable}}$$

When a ratio compares an income statement item with a balance sheet item, the balance sheet item usually is an average. Ideally, the denominator in the accounts receivable turnover should be computed by averaging the end-of-month balances or end-of-week balances of net accounts receivable outstanding during the period. The greater the number of observations used, the more accurate is the resulting average. Often, though, only the beginning-of-the-year and end-of-the-year balances are averaged because this information is easily obtainable from comparative financial statements. Sometimes a formula calls for the use of an average balance, but only the year-end amount is available. Then the analyst must use the year-end amount.[1]

The numerator should contain only sales on account because those are the only sales which appear in accounts receivable. But if cash sales are relatively small, or if their proportion to total sales remains fairly constant, reliable results can be obtained by using total net sales. In most cases, the analyst may have no choice in the matter because the amounts of cash and credit sales are not reported.

Accounts receivable turnover for the Knight Corporation is shown below assuming net accounts receivable on January 1, 19x4, were $121,200.

	19x5	19x4	Amount of Increase or Decrease*
Net sales (a)............................	$986,400	$765,500	$220,900
Accounts receivable:			
January 1	132,600	121,200	11,400
December 31	124,200	132,600	8,400*
Total...........................	$256,800	$253,800	3,000
Average accounts receivable (b)..........	$128,400	$126,900	
Turnover of accounts receivable (a ÷ b)............................	7.68	6.03	

The accounts receivable turnover ratio provides an indication of how quickly the receivables are being collected and is valuable for comparison

---

[1] These general comments about the balance sheet item in a ratio apply to the other ratios involving balance sheet items discussed in this chapter.

purposes. For the Knight Corporation in 19x5, the turnover ratio indicates that accounts receivable are collected or "turned over" slightly more than seven times per year. This ratio may be better understood and more easily compared with a firm's credit terms if it is converted into the average number of days it takes to collect accounts receivable.

Number of days' sales in accounts receivable. This ratio, which is also called the *average collection period,* is calculated as:

$$\text{Number of days' sales in accounts receivable (average collection period)} = \frac{\text{Number of days in year (365)}}{\text{Accounts receivable turnover}}$$

For the Knight Corporation, the number of days' sales in accounts receivable decreased from about 60 days (365/6.03) in 19x4 to 48 days (365/7.68) in 19x5 (the average collection period of the corporation's accounts receivable decreased from 60 days to 48 days). This ratio measures the average liquidity of accounts receivable and thus gives an indication of their quality. Quality is defined as the probability of collection in full. The quality of an account receivable decreases with age. A comparison of the average collection period with the credit terms extended customers by the firm will provide further insight into the quality of the accounts receivable. For example, receivables arising under terms 2/10, n/30 which have an average collection period of 75 days need to be investigated further.

Inventory turnover.   A firm's inventory turnover ratio shows the number of times its average inventory is sold during a period. *Inventory turnover* is calculated as:

$$\text{Inventory turnover} = \frac{\text{Cost of goods sold}}{\text{Average inventory}}$$

Inventory turnover relates a measure of sales volume to the average amount of goods on hand to produce this sales volume.

As shown by the following schedule, inventory turnover for the Knight Corporation increased slightly, to 6.07 times per year in 19x5 from 5.57 times per year in 19x4. These turnover ratios also mean that the company sold its average inventory in about 60 days (365/6.07) in 19x5 as contrasted to about 66 days (365/57) in 19x4.

	19x5	19x4	Amount of Increase
Cost of goods sold (a)	$623,200	$500,900	$122,300
Inventories:			
January 1	$ 94,500	$ 85,100	$ 9,400
December 31	110,800	94,500	16,300
Total	$205,300	$179,600	$ 25,700
Average inventory (b)	$102,650	$ 89,850	
Turnover of inventory (a ÷ b)	6.07	5.58	

In attempting to secure satisfactory earnings, the costs of storage, obsolescence, and implicit interest incurred in owning inventory must be balanced against the possible loss of sales from not having enough inventory to sell. Other things equal, the management that is able to maintain the higher inventory turnover ratio is considered more efficient. Yet other things are not always equal. For example, a firm that achieves a high inventory turnover ratio by keeping extremely small inventories may incur larger ordering costs, lose quantity discounts, and lose sales due to lack of stock.

Total assets turnover. Total assets turnover relates the dollar volume of sales to the average total assets used in the business and is calculated as:

$$\text{Total assets turnover} = \frac{\text{Net sales}}{\text{Average total assets}}$$

This ratio measures the efficiency of the use of capital invested in assets, assuming a constant margin of earnings on each dollar of sales. The larger the dollar volume of sales made per dollar of invested capital, the larger will be the earnings on each dollar invested in the assets of the business. For the Knight Corporation, the total assets turnover ratios for 19x5 and 19x4 are shown below. (Assume total assets as of January 1, 19x4, were $510,200.)

	19x5	19x4	Amount of Increase
Net sales (a)........................	$ 986,400	$ 765,500	$220,900
Total assets:			
January 1	$ 551,100	$ 510,200	$ 40,300
December 31	635,200	551,100	84,100
Total.......................	$1,186,300	$1,061,300	$125,000
Average total assets (b)	$ 593,150	$ 530,650	
Turnover of total assets (a ÷ b)	1.66:1	1.44:1	

In 19x4, each dollar of total assets produced $1.44 of sales; and in 19x5, each dollar of total assets produced $1.66 of sales, or an increase of $0.22 of sales per dollar of investment in the assets.

Equity or solvency ratios. Equity or solvency ratios indicate the financial structure of the firm. Equity ratios show the relationship of debt and equity financing or how highly leveraged a firm is. Leverage in this case refers to the proportion of debt used in financing the business. The equity or solvency ratios presented include the equity ratio and the owners' equity to debt ratio.

Equity (or owners' equity) ratio. The two basic sources of assets are owners (stockholders) and creditors, and the sum of the interests of both groups is referred to as total equities. But in ratio analysis, the term *equity* generally refers only to owners' equity. Thus, the *equity ratio* indicates the proportion of total assets provided by owners (stockholders) on any given date.

$$\text{Equity ratio} = \frac{\text{Owners' equity}}{\text{Total assets}}$$

The Knight Corporation's liabilities and stockholders' equity, taken from Illustration 6.1, are shown below. The schedule shows that the company's stockholders increased their proportionate equity in the firm's assets by additional investment in the company's common stock and by retention of income earned during the year.

	December 31, 19x5		December 31, 19x4	
	Amount	Percent	Amount	Percent
Current liabilities................	$127,100	20.0	$109,900	20.0
Long-term liabilities.............	43,600	6.9	60,800	11.0
Total liabilities............	$170,700	26.9	$170,700	31.0
Common stock.................	$240,000	37.8	$200,000	36.3
Retained earnings..............	224,500	35.3	180,400	32.7
Total stockholders' equity	$464,500	73.1	$380,400	69.0
Total equity (equal to total assets).................	$635,200	100.0	$551,100	100.0

The Knight Corporation's equity ratio increased from 69.0 percent in 19x4 to 73.1 percent in 19x5.[2] The equity ratio must be interpreted carefully. From a creditor's point of view, a high proportion of owners' equity is desirable. A high percentage indicates the existence of a large protective buffer of owners' investment for creditors in the event the company suffers a loss. But from an owner's point of view, a high proportion of owners' equity may or may not be desirable. If borrowed funds can be used by the business to generate earnings in excess of the net aftertax cost of the interest on such borrowed funds, a lower percentage of owners' equity may be desirable.

Following is a brief illustration of the effect on the Knight Corporation if it were more highly leveraged (i.e., had a larger proportion of debt). Assume that the Knight Corporation could have financed its present operations with $40,000 of 12 percent bonds instead of 4,000 shares of common stock. The

---

[2] Ratios are sometimes left in decimal form; in other situations, they are converted into percentages (which involves multiplying the decimal ratio by 100). As a rough general guide, ratios of less than one are often converted to their percentage equivalent, while ratios greater than one are usually left in decimal form (such as a current ratio of 2.73).

effect on earnings for 19x5 would be as follows, assuming a marginal federal income tax rate of 50 percent:

Net income as presently stated (Illustration 6.2)	$59,100
Additional interest on debt (0.12 × $40,000)	4,800
	$54,300
Reduced tax due to interest deduction (0.5 × $4,800)	2,400
Adjusted net income	$56,700

As shown, net income would be less. But there would be 4,000 fewer shares outstanding. As a result, earnings per share would increase to $2.84 ($56,700/20,000) from $2.46 ($59,100/24,000). Since investors place heavy emphasis upon earnings per share, many companies in recent years have introduced larger portions of debt into their capital structures to increase earnings per share. This practice is not without its dangers since financial leverage magnifies losses as well as earnings per share because there are fewer shares of stock over which to spread the losses.

Too low an equity ratio (too much debt) may be hazardous from the owners' standpoint. A business recession may result in operating losses and shrinkages in the values of assets (such as receivables and inventories), leading to an inability to meet fixed payments for interest and principal on debt. This in turn may cause stockholders to lose control of the company. The company may be forced into liquidation.

Owners' equity/debt ratio. The relative financial interests of owners and creditors may be expressed in several ways. To say creditors hold a 26.9 percent interest in the assets of the Knight Corporation on December 31, 19x5, is equivalent to saying stockholders hold a 73.1 percent interest. In many cases, the relationship is expressed as a ratio: owners' equity/debt. Such a ratio for the Knight Corporation would be 2.23 : 1 ($380,400/$170,700) on December 31, 19x4, and 2.72 : 1 ($464,500/$170,700) on December 31, 19x5. This ratio is sometimes inverted and called the debt/equity ratio. Some analysts use only long-term debt rather than total debt in calculating these ratios.

Profitability tests. Profitability is an important indicator of a firm's operating success. Generally, there are two areas of concern when judging profitability: (1) relationships on the income statement which indicate a company's ability to recover costs and expenses and (2) relationships of income to some balance sheet measure which indicates the relative ability to earn income on assets employed. There are six profitability tests presented here: earning power, net income to net sales, net income to average stockholders' equity, earnings per share, times interest earned ratio, and times preferred dividends earned ratio.

Earning power ratio or percentage (return on operating assets). The best measure of earnings performance without regard to sources of assets is the relationship of net operating income to operating assets, which is known as the *earning power ratio* or *percentage*. There are two elements in the determination of this ratio: operating margin and turnover of operating assets.

Operating margin.   Operating margin reflects the percentage of each dollar of net sales which becomes net operating income. Net operating income excludes nonoperating revenues (such as extraordinary items) and nonoperating expenses, such as interest and income taxes. The formula for operating margin is:

$$\text{Operating margin} = \frac{\text{Net operating income}}{\text{Net sales}}$$

Turnover of operating assets.   Turnover of operating assets shows the dollars of sales for each dollar invested in operating assets. Year-end operating assets typically are used, even though an average is better. Operating assets are all assets actively used in producing operating revenues. Examples of nonoperating assets are land held for future use, a factory building rented to another company, and long-term investments. Total assets should not be used in evaluating earnings performance due to the inclusion of nonoperating assets which do not contribute to the generation of sales. The formula for the turnover of operating assets is:

$$\text{Turnover of operating assets} = \frac{\text{Net sales}}{\text{Operating assets}}$$

The earning power ratio of a firm is equal to operating margin multiplied by turnover of operating assets. The more a company earns per dollar of sales and the more sales it makes per dollar invested in operating assets, the higher will be the return per dollar invested. Earning power may be expressed by the following formulas:

$$\text{Earning power} = \text{Operating margin} \times \text{Turnover of operating assets,}$$

$$\text{Earning power} = \frac{\text{Net operating income}}{\text{Net sales}} \times \frac{\text{Net sales}}{\text{Operating assets}}$$

Since net sales appears as both a numerator and a denominator, it is canceled and the formula for the earning power ratio becomes:

$$\text{Earning power ratio} = \frac{\text{Net operating income}}{\text{Operating assets}}$$

It is more useful for analytical purposes to leave the formula in the form which shows margin and turnover separately.

Securing desired earning power.   Companies that are to survive in the economy must attain some minimum level of earning power. But this minimum can be obtained in many different ways. To illustrate, consider a grocery store and a jewelry store, each with an earning power of 8 percent on operating assets. The grocery store normally would have a low margin and a high turnover, while the jewelry store would have a higher margin and a lower turnover:

	Margin × Turnover =	Earning Power Percentage
Grocery store............	1% × 8.0 times	8%
Jewelry store...........	20% × 0.4 times	8%

The earning power ratios for the Knight Corporation for 19x5 and 19x4 are calculated below.

	19x5	19x4	Amount of Increase
Net operating income (a)...............	$110,400	$ 81,100	$ 29,300
Net sales (b)	$986,400	$765,500	$220,900
Operating margin [(a ÷ b) × 100 = c]......	11.19%	10.59%	
Net sales (d)	$986,400	$765,500	$220,900
Total assets (all operating assets) (e).......	$635,200	$551,100	$ 84,100
Turnover of operating assets (d ÷ e = f).........................	1.55:1	1.39:1	
Earning power percentage (c × f).........	17.34%	14.72%	

Earning power ratio or rate of return on operating assets is designed to show the earning power of the company as a bundle of assets, not to determine which sources of assets are favored in the generation of income. By disregarding both nonoperating assets and nonoperating income, earning power percentage measures the profitability of the firm in carrying out its primary business functions.

Net income to net sales. Net income as a percentage of net sales is obtained by dividing net income for the period by net sales for the period:

$$\text{Net income to net sales} = \frac{\text{Net income}}{\text{Net sales}}$$

This ratio measures the proportion of the sales dollar which remains after deduction of all expenses. The computations for the Knight Company are:

	19x5	19x4	Amount of Increase
Net income (a)....................	$ 59,100	$ 46,600	$ 12,500
Net sales (b × 100)	$986,400	$765,500	$220,000
Ratio of net to net sales (a ÷ b)	5.99%	6.09%	

Although the ratio of net income to net sales indicates the net amount of profit on each sales dollar, a great deal of care must be exercised in the use and interpretation of this ratio. Net income includes nonoperating items such as extraordinary items and interest charges. Thus, a period which contains an extraordinary item will not be comparable to a period which does not. Also, since interest expense is deductible in the determination of income, while dividends are not, net income is affected by the methods used to finance the firm's assets.

Net income to average stockholders' equity. From the stockholders' point of view, an important measure of the income-producing ability of a company is the relationship of *net income to average stockholders' equity* or the *rate of return on average stockholders' equity*. The ratio also is often referred to simply as ROE—*return on equity*. Stockholders are interested in the ratio of operating income to operating assets as a measure of the efficient use of assets by management. But stockholders are even more interested in knowing what return was earned by the company on each dollar of owners' equity invested.

$$\text{Net income to average stockholders' equity} = \frac{\text{Net income}}{\text{Average stockholders' equity}}$$

The ratios for the Knight Company are shown below. Assume that total stockholders' equity on January 1, 19x4, was $321,500.

	19x5	19x4	Amount of Increase
Net income (a)	$ 59,100	$ 46,600	$ 12,500
Total stockholders' equity:			
January 1	$380,400	$321,500	$ 8,900
December 31	464,500	380,400	84,100
Total	$844,900	$701,900	$143,000
Average total stockholders' equity (b)	$422,450	$350,950	
Ratio of net income to stockholders' equity [(a ÷ b) × 100]	13.99%	13.28%	

The increase in the ratio from 13.28 percent to 13.99 percent would be regarded favorably by stockholders. This ratio indicates that for each average dollar of capital invested by a stockholder, the company earned 14 cents in 19x5.

Earnings per share. The measure used most widely to appraise a firm's operating ability is earnings per share of common stock (hereafter simply EPS). *EPS* is usually computed only for common stock and is equal to earnings available to common stockholders divided by weighted average number of shares of common stock outstanding. The financial press regularly publishes actual and forecast EPS amounts for many corporations, together with period-to-period comparisons. *Accounting Principles Board Opinion No. 15* requires that earnings per share be reported on the face of the income statement.

Calculation of EPS may be a simple or complex problem, depending upon the corporation's capital structure. A firm has a simple capital structure if it has no outstanding securities that can be exchanged for common stock such as convertible bonds, convertible preferred stocks, warrants, or options. If a firm has such securities outstanding, it has a complex capital structure. A firm with a simple capital structure reports a single EPS amount calculated as:

$$\text{Earnings per share of common stock} = \frac{\text{Earnings available to common stockholders}}{\text{Weighted average number of common shares outstanding}}$$

The numerator in the EPS fraction is equal to net income less preferred dividends, whether declared or not.

Weighted average number of shares. The denominator in the EPS fraction is the weighted average number of common shares outstanding for the period. If the number of shares outstanding changed during the period, the change in shares must be weighted for the fractional period. For example, assume that 20,000 shares were outstanding at the beginning of the year and that 4,000 shares were issued on June 30. The 4,000 shares are weighted by ½ for the half year they were outstanding. The weighted average number of shares outstanding for the year is 22,000 : 20,000 shares outstanding all year, plus 4,000 shares outstanding for a half year (which is the equivalent of 2,000 shares outstanding all year). If the company had purchased 400 shares of treasury stock on September 30, the calculation would read:

20,000 shares × ½ year (January–June)	10,000
24,000 shares × ¼ year (July–September)	6,000
23,600 shares × ¼ year (October–December).	5,900
Weighted average number of common shares outstanding.	21,900

A weighted average for the common shares outstanding is computed whenever shares are issued or acquired during a period. Such changes increase or decrease the capital invested in the company, which should affect earnings available to stockholders. Shares should be considered outstanding only during those periods that the related capital investment was available to help produce income.

EPS for the Knight Corporation, which has a simple capital structure, is shown below. The weighted average number of shares for 19x5 is computed under the assumption that 4,000 shares were issued on June 30.

	19x5	19x4	Amount of Increase
Net income (a)..........................	$59,100	$46,600	$12,500
Average number of shares of common stock outstanding (b)	22,000	20,000	2,000
Earnings per share of common stock (a ÷ b)..	$ 2.69	$ 2.33	

The better than 15 percent increase in EPS from $2.33 to $2.69 would probably be viewed quite favorably by the Knight Corporation's stockholders.

EPS and stock dividends or splits.   Increases in shares outstanding as a result of a stock dividend or split do not require weighting for fractional periods. Such shares do not increase capital invested in the business and therefore do not affect earnings. All that is required is to restate all prior calculations of EPS using the increased number of shares. For example, a firm reported EPS for 19x4 of $1 ($100,000/100,000 shares) and earned $150,000 in 19x5. The only change in common stock over the two years was a two-for-one stock split on December 1, 19x5, which doubled the shares outstanding to 200,000. EPS would be restated at $0.50 ($100,000/200,000 shares) for 19x4 and would be $0.75 ($150,000/200,000 shares) for 19x5.

Times interest earned ratio.   Creditors, especially long-term creditors, want to know whether a borrower can meet its required interest payments when they become due. A ratio that provides some indication of this ability is the *times interest earned ratio* (or *interest coverage ratio*). It is computed as:

$$\text{Times interest earned} = \frac{\text{Income before interest and taxes}}{\text{Interest expense}}$$

Analysts disagree on whether the denominator should be interest on long-term debt or all interest expense. Since failure to make any required interest payment is a serious matter, the calculations here will use all interest expense. Assume that a company has income before interest expense and income taxes of $100,000, and interest expense for the period of $10,000. The times interest earned ratio is 10; the company earned its interest expense 10 times during the period. Income before interest and income taxes is used in the ratio since there would be no income taxes if interest expense is equal to or greater than income before interest and taxes. The ratio is a rough measure of cash flow from operations and cash flow out as interest on debt. Very low or negative interest coverage ratios suggest that the borrower is in danger of defaulting on interest payments. A firm is not likely to be able to continue interest payments over many periods if it fails to earn enough income to cover them. On the other hand, interest coverage of 10 to 20 times suggests that the company is not likely to default on interest payments.

Times preferred dividends earned ratio. Preferred stockholders, like bondholders, must usually be satisfied with a fixed dollar return on their investments. They are interested in the company's ability to make preferred dividend payments each year. This can be measured by computing the number of times preferred dividends are earned:

$$\text{Times preferred dividends earned ratio} = \frac{\text{Net income}}{\text{Preferred dividends}}$$

Suppose a company has net income of $48,000 and has $100,000 (par value) of 8 percent preferred stock outstanding. The number of times the preferred dividends are earned would be:

$$\frac{\$48,000}{\$8,000} = 6 \text{ times}$$

The higher the rate, the higher is the probability that the preferred stockholders will receive their dividends each year.

Market tests. Certain ratios are computed using information from the financial statements and market prices for the company's stock. These tests help investors and potential investors assess the relative merits of the various stocks in the marketplace. The market tests included here are: yield on common stock, price-earnings ratio, dividend yield, dividend payout ratio, and yield on preferred stock.

Yield on common stock and price-earnings ratio. The *yield* on a stock investment is the annual earnings or dividends per share as a percentage of the current market price per share. Thus, a firm's earnings yield per share of common stock is calculated:

$$\text{Earnings yield on common stock} = \frac{\text{Earnings per share}}{\text{Current market price per share}}$$

Suppose, for example, that a company had earnings per share of common stock of $2 and that the market price of the stock was $30. The *earnings yield* on common stock would be:

$$\frac{\$2}{\$30} = 0.0667 \text{ or } 6\frac{2}{3} \text{ percent}$$

The ratio of market price to EPS is called the *price-earnings* (or PE) *ratio.* In the case just cited, the price-earnings ratio is:

$$\text{Price-earnings ratio} = \frac{\text{Current market price per share}}{\text{Earnings per share}} = \frac{\$30}{\$2} = 15:1$$

Investors would say that this stock is selling at 15 times earnings or at a multiple of 15. They might have a multiple in mind as being the proper one that should be used to judge whether the stock was underpriced or overpriced. Different investors will have different estimates of the proper price-earnings ratio for a given stock and also different estimates of the future earnings prospects of the firm. These are two of the factors which cause one investor to sell stock at a particular price and another investor to buy at that price.

Dividend yield and dividend payout ratios.   The dividend paid per share of common stock is of interest to common stockholders. When the dividend is divided by the current market price per share, the result is called the *dividend yield*.

If the company referred to immediately above paid a $1.50 per share dividend, the dividend yield would be:

$$\text{Dividend yield on common stock} = \frac{\text{Dividend per share}}{\text{Current market price per share}}$$

$$= \frac{\$1.50}{\$30.00} = 0.05 \text{ or 5 percent}$$

One additional step is to divide the dividend per share by the earnings available per share to determine the *payout ratio on common stock* as:

$$\text{Payout ratio} = \frac{\text{Dividend per share}}{\text{Earnings per share}} = \frac{\$1.50}{\$2.00} = 0.75 \text{ or 75 percent}$$

A payout ratio of 75 percent means that the company paid out 75 percent of the earnings per share in the form of dividends. Some investors are attracted by the stock of companies that pay out a large percentage of their earnings. Other investors are attracted by the stock of companies that retain and reinvest a large percentage of their earnings. The tax status of the investor has a great deal to do with this. Investors in very high tax brackets often prefer to have the company reinvest the earnings, with the expectation that this will result in share price appreciation which would be taxed at capital gains rates when the shares are sold. Dividends are taxed at ordinary income rates, which are much higher than capital gains rates.

Yield on preferred stock.   Preferred stockholders compute dividend yield in a manner similar to the computation of dividend yield for common stockholders. Suppose a company has 2,000 shares of $100 par value, 8 percent preferred stock outstanding which has a current market price of $110 per share. The dividend yield would be computed as:

$$\text{Dividend yield on preferred stock} = \frac{\text{Dividend per share}}{\text{Current market price per share}}$$

$$= \frac{\$8}{\$110} = 0.0727 \text{ or 7.27 percent}$$

Through the use of dividend yield rates, different preferred stocks having different annual dividends and different market prices can be compared.

Final Considerations in Financial Statement Analysis

Standing alone, a single financial ratio may not be very informative. Greater insight can be obtained by computing and analyzing several related ratios for a company. The ratios presented in this chapter are summarized in Illustration 6.3.

Illustration 6.3
Summary of Ratios

Ratio	Formula	Significance
Liquidity ratios:		
Current ratio	Current assets ÷ Current liabilities	Test of debt-paying ability
Acid-test (quick) ratio	(Cash + Net receivables + Marketable securities) ÷ Current liabilities	Test of immediate debt-paying ability
Accounts receivable turnover	Net sales ÷ Average net accounts receivable	Test of quality of accounts receivable
Number of days' sales in accounts receivable (average collection period)	Number of days in year ÷ Accounts receivable turnover ratio	Test of quality of accounts receivable
Inventory turnover	Cost of goods sold ÷ Average inventory	Test of whether or not a sufficient volume of business is being generated relative to inventory
Total assets turnover	Net sales ÷ Average total assets	Test of whether or not volume of business generated is adequate relative to amount of capital invested in business
Tests of equity position and solvency:		
Equity ratio	Owners' (stockholders') equity ÷ Total equities	Index of long-run solvency and safety
Owners' equity to debt	Owners' (stockholders') equity ÷ Debt	Index of long-run solvency and safety
Profitability tests:		
Earning power	Net operating income ÷ Operating assets	Measure of managerial effectiveness
Net income as a percentage of sales	Net income ÷ net sales	Measure of net income as a percentage of sales
Net income to stockholders' equity	Net income ÷ Average stockholders' equity	Measure of what a given company earned for its stockholders from all sources as a percentage of the stockholders' investment

Illustration 6.3 (*concluded*)

Ratio	Formula	Significance
Earnings per share (of common stock)	Net income available to common stockholders ÷ Average number of shares of common stock outstanding	Tends to have an effect on the market price per share
Times interest earned	Net income before interest and taxes ÷ Interest expense	Indicates likelihood that bondholders will continue to receive their interest payments
Times preferred dividends earned	Net income ÷ Preferred dividends	Indicates the probability that preferred stockholders will receive their dividend each year
Market tests:		
Earnings yield on common stock	Earnings per share ÷ Current market price per share	Useful for comparison with other stocks
Price-earnings ratio	Current market price per share ÷ Earnings per share	Index of whether a stock is relatively cheap or expensive
Dividend yield	Dividend per share ÷ Current market price per share	Useful for comparison with other stocks
Payout ratio on common stock	Dividend per share ÷ Earnings per share	Index of whether company pays out large percentage of earnings as dividends or reinvests most of its earnings

By comparing one company's financial data and ratios over time, an indication can be gained as to changes and trends of that company. But to evaluate these trends, standards for comparison are needed.

Sources of comparative standards.   The possible sources of comparative standards include:

1. Records of past performance and position of the company as gained from comparative financial statements of the past three to five years. Such records are often used by an investor contemplating purchase of common stock. For a current stockholder, the most common comparisons are likely to be EPS for the most recent quarter and year to date as compared with the same data for last year.
2. Trade associations, governmental agencies such as the Federal Trade Commission, and financial reporting services such as Dun & Bradstreet and Robert Morris Associates.
3. Ratios and financial data of a firm's major competitors.
4. The analyst's personal experience and observation.

5. Traditional rules of thumb, which must be applied with caution because the firm may be unique. An example is the ageless rule that a firm's current ratio should be at least 2:1.

Financial statement analysis must be carried out with knowledge of industry characteristics. Acceptable current ratios, gross margin rates, debt-to-equity ratios, and so on, vary widely depending on environmental conditions within an industry. Even within an industry, legitimate variations may exist.

Need for comparable data.   Analysts must be sure that their comparisons are valid—whether the comparisons are of items for different periods or for different companies. Consistent accounting practices must be followed if valid interperiod comparisons are to be made. Comparable interfirm comparisons are more difficult to secure. Accountants cannot do much more than disclose the fact that one firm is using FIFO and another is using LIFO. Such a disclosure alerts analysts that interfirm comparisons of, for example, inventory turnover ratios may not be strictly comparable.

Also, when comparing a firm's ratios to industry averages provided by an external source such as Dun & Bradstreet, the analyst must calculate the firm's ratio in the same manner as the reporting service. Thus, if Dun & Bradstreet uses sales (rather than cost of goods sold) to compute inventory turnover, so should the analyst. Net sales is used because cost of goods sold amounts are not computed and reported in the same manner by all companies.

Influence of external factors.   Financial analysis relies heavily upon informed judgment. Percentages and ratios are guides to aid comparison and are useful in uncovering potential strengths and weaknesses. But the financial analyst should seek the basic causes behind changes and established trends. Quite often, facts and conditions not disclosed by the financial statements may affect their interpretation. A single important event may have been largely responsible for a given relationship. For example, a new product may have been unexpectedly put on the market by competitors, making it necessary for the company under study to sacrifice its inventory of a product suddenly rendered obsolete. Such an event would affect the gross margin rate. Yet there may be little or no chance that such an event would happen again.

General business conditions within the business or industry of the company under study must be considered. A downward trend in earnings, for example, is less alarming if the industry trend or the general economic trend is also downward rather than limited to a single corporation.

Consideration should be given to the possible seasonal nature of the businesses under study. If the balance sheet date represents the seasonal peak in the volume of business, for example, the ratio of current assets to current liabilities may acceptably be much lower than if the balance sheet date is one in a season of low activity.

The potential investor should realize that acquiring the ability to make informed judgments is a long process and does not occur overnight. Using ratios and percentages mechanically is a sure road to wrong conclusions.

THE STATEMENT OF CHANGES IN FINANCIAL POSITION

The income statement, statement of retained earnings, and balance sheet often do not provide ready answers to such questions as: How much cash was generated by operations? Why is such a profitable firm only able to pay such meager dividends? How much money was spent on plant and equipment, and where did it come from? The statement of changes in financial position—the fourth major financial statement—provides answers to such questions. This statement is required whenever an income statement and balance sheet are presented. The statement reports the flow of funds into and out of a business and is often called a *funds statement*.

The Concept of Funds

Funds can mean cash or working capital. If funds are defined as cash, every transaction that increases or decreases cash will be included in the statement of changes in financial position. If funds are defined as working capital, every transaction that increases or decreases working capital will be included in the funds statement. Under the working capital definition of funds, the issuance of stocks or bonds for cash would be included; the payment of an account payable or collection of a receivable would not. With either definition, the funds statement would report transactions that did not actually involve cash or working capital. For example, an exchange of stock for land would be treated as if the stock were issued for cash which was then spent for land. Thus, no matter how funds are defined, the objectives of the funds statement are: (1) to summarize the significant financing and investing activities of the firm, including disclosure of funds from operations; and (2) to explain and disclose the change in financial position that occurred during the period.

The fund flows are reported in a statement of changes in financial position that has two sections. One section may be headed "Financial resources (or cash or working capital) provided"; the other may be headed "Financial resources (or cash or working capital) applied." For an example, see Illustration 6.6.

Major Sources and Uses of Funds

When funds are defined as working capital, the major sources of funds are: (1) operations, (2) issuance of stock, (3) borrowing, and (4) sales of noncurrent assets. The major uses of funds include: (1) investment in plant, equipment, and other noncurrent assets; (2) redemption of debt or acquisition of treasury stock; (3) dividends; and (4) operations, under certain conditions, as discussed below.

Funds from Operations

The major source of funds in a firm usually is operations. Revenues (sales) increase working capital (by increasing cash or accounts receivable), while expenses decrease working capital (by decreasing cash or increasing a current liability). The reporting of net income for a period generally means the firm had a positive flow of funds from operations.

But funds provided by operations differ from net income because certain items are included in net income that do not affect funds (working capital). The most common example is depreciation expense. The entry to record depreciation debits an expense account and credits an accumulated depreciation account. Neither account is a working capital account, which means the transaction has no effect on working capital. But depreciation was deducted in arriving at net income. As a result, net income understates funds from operations. And, in the almost universal practice of using net income as the starting point in measuring funds from operations, depreciation expense must be added back to net income.

Consider the following example. Company A reported net income for the year of $20,000, while Company B reported a net loss of $4,000. Both companies deducted $10,000 of depreciation in calculating net income. Although A earned net income, while B suffered a loss, both companies have a positive flow of working capital from operations:

	Company A	Company B
Net income (loss)	$20,000	($ 4,000)
Add depreciation expense (which did not require use of funds)	10,000	10,000
Positive funds flow from operations	$30,000	$ 6,000

Only if B's loss had exceeded $10,000 would B have applied funds to operations rather than generating funds from operations. Other expenses and losses that are added back to net income for the same reason as depreciation in determining funds from operations include depletion expense, amortization of intangible assets and of discount on bonds payable, and losses from disposals of noncurrent assets. These addbacks are often called *nonworking capital (nonfund) charges or expenses*.

Statement of Changes in Financial Position—Working Capital Basis

The financial statements and additional data for the Welby Company, Illustration 6.4, are used to prepare the company's statement of changes in

Illustration 6.4
Financial Statements and Other Data

WELBY COMPANY
Balance Sheets

	December 31	
Assets	19x4	19x3
Cash......................................	$ 21,000	$ 10,000
Accounts receivable..............................	30,000	20,000
Inventory.......................................	26,000	30,000
Plant assets....................................	70,000	50,000
Accumulated depreciation.........................	(10,000)	(5,000)
Total assets.....................................	$137,000	$105,000
Liabilities and Stockholders' Equity		
Accounts payable................................	$ 10,000	$ 15,000
Accrued liabilities................................	2,000	–0–
Common stock ($10 par value).....................	90,000	60,000
Retained earnings	35,000	30,000
Total liabilities and stockholders' equity..............	$137,000	$105,000

WELBY COMPANY
Income Statement
For the Year Ended December 31, 19x4

Sales		$140,000
Cost of goods sold..............................		100,000
Gross margin		$ 40,000
Operating expenses and taxes	$ 25,000	
Depreciation	5,000	30,000
Net income		$ 10,000

Additional data:

1. Plant assets purchased for cash during 19x4, $20,000.
2. Common stock with a par value of $30,000 was issued at par for cash.
3. Cash dividends declared in 19x4, $5,000.

financial position on a working capital basis. Two steps are involved in preparing the statement: (1) determine the change in working capital; and (2) analyze all noncurrent accounts for changes that affect working capital, including in the statement of changes those that do.

Determining the change in working capital. A statement of changes in working capital, as in Illustration 6.5, should accompany the statement of changes in financial position. Or a schedule of changes in working capital components may be presented under the statement of changes in financial position, as in Illustration 6.6.

Illustration 6.5
Statement of Changes in Working Capital

				WELBY COMPANY		

WELBY COMPANY
Statement of Changes in Working Capital
For the Year Ended December 31, 19x4

	December 31		Working Capital	
	19x4	19x5	Increase	Decrease
Current assets:				
Cash	$21,000	$10,000	$11,000	
Accounts receivable	30,000	20,000	10,000	
Inventory	26,000	30,000		$ 4,000
Total current assets.........	$77,000	$60,000		
Current liabilities:				
Accounts payable	$10,000	$15,000	5,000	
Accrued liabilities..............	2,000	–0–		2,000
Total current liabilities	$12,000	$15,000		
Working capital..................	$65,000	$45,000		
Increase in working capital........				20,000
			$26,000	$26,000

Illustration 6.6
Statement of Changes in Financial Position—Working Capital Basis

WELBY COMPANY
Statement of Changes in Financial Position—Working Capital Basis
For the Year Ended December 31, 19x4

Financial resources provided:		
Working capital from operations:		
Net income		$10,000
Add nonworking capital expenses:		
Depreciation......................................		5,000
Total working capital from operations		$15,000
Issuance of common stock.........................		30,000
Total financial resources provided		$45,000
Financial resources applied:		
Purchase plant assets	$20,000	
Dividends...	5,000	25,000
Increase in working capital..........................		$20,000
Schedule of changes in working capital components:		
Increase (decrease) in current assets:		
Cash...		$11,000
Accounts receivable		10,000
Inventory		(4,000)
		$17,000
Increase (decrease) in current liabilities:		
Accounts payable	$ (5,000)	
Accrued liabilities...............................	2,000	(3,000)
Increase in working capital..........................		$20,000

Illustrations 6.5 and 6.6 show that changes in current assets cause working capital to change in the same direction, while changes in current liabilities cause working capital to change in the opposite direction. Thus, the $10,000 increase in accounts receivable and the $5,000 decrease in accounts payable both increased working capital. The $4,000 decrease in inventory and the $2,000 increase in accrued liabilities both decreased working capital. Both illustrations show that Welby's working capital increased by $20,000. The causes of this change will be reported in the company's statement of changes in financial position (see Illustration 6.6).

Analyzing the noncurrent accounts.   At first, it may seem quite unusual to seek causes of changes in working capital in the noncurrent (nonworking capital) accounts. But a transaction recorded solely in two working capital accounts can never increase or decrease working capital. Collections of accounts receivable, payment of accounts payable, and purchases of merchandise *change the composition but not the amount* of working capital. And there are many such transactions. As a result, it is easier to find transactions that changed the amount of working capital by analyzing the noncurrent accounts. In the Welby case, there are four noncurrent accounts to analyze: Plant Assets, Accumulated Depreciation, Common Stock, and Retained Earnings.

1.   Because of the importance of working capital provided by operations, the preparation of the statement of changes usually begins with net income. The amount of net income can be found in the Retained Earnings account. This account increased $5,000 ($10,000 net income, less $5,000 dividends). Both are entered in the funds statement in Illustration 6.6. The $5,000 of dividends reduced working capital when they were declared and credited to Dividends Payable, a current liability account. The declaration of dividends is a use of working capital, or more broadly, a financial resource applied. The $10,000 net income is used as the starting figure in determining working capital from operations and is entered on the statement in the "Financial resources provided" section under "Working capital from operations."

2.   Plant assets increased as a result of a $20,000 purchase. Such a purchase is a use of funds and is entered under "Financial resources applied."

3.   The $5,000 increase in accumulated depreciation resulted from the recording of an equal amount of depreciation expense. Because depreciation does not affect or use up working capital, it must be added back to net income to convert net income to working capital from operations.

4.   The $30,000 increase in common stock resulted from the issuance of stock at par value. The $30,000 is entered as a source of working capital under "Financial resources provided."

Every noncurrent account has now been analyzed, and changes in such accounts that affected working capital or net income as a measure of working capital from operations have been included in the statement of changes in financial position. The current accounts were not analyzed individually.

Only the change in working capital is reported as the final item in the statement.

The completed statement of changes in financial position in Illustration 6.6 shows that $15,000 of working capital was provided by operations and $30,000 was provided by issuance of stock. Of the $45,000 provided, $20,000 was used to acquire plant assets, $5,000 was used for dividends, and the remaining $20,000 increased working capital.

Statement of Changes in Financial Position—Cash Basis

A cash basis statement of changes in financial position differs from one focusing on working capital primarily in the "Funds from operations" section. A cash basis statement usually reports both cash and working capital from operations. Cash from operations is the net amount of cash received or spent on items which normally appear in the income statement. It is obtained by converting accrual basis net income to a cash basis amount.

Cash provided by operations. Two steps are involved in converting net income to cash basis income. First, convert net income to working capital from operations by adding back to net income those items deducted that did not use up working capital. Second, convert working capital from operations to cash from operations by including the changes that occurred in current accounts other than cash. Applying these two steps to the Welby Company information in Illustration 6.4 yields:

Net income...		$10,000
Add expenses not reducing working capital—depreciation		5,000
Working capital from operations..........................		$15,000
Effects of changes in components of working capital on cash:		
Increase in accounts receivable.........................	$(10,000)	
Decrease in inventory	4,000	
Decrease in accounts payable	(5,000)	
Increase in accrued liabilities...........................	2,000	(9,000)
Cash provided by operations.............................		$6,000

Cash basis conversion summary. These conversion procedures can be summarized as:

	Make these Adjustments to Convert Accrual Basis Net Income to Cash Basis Net Income	
For items classified as:	Add	Deduct
Current assets...............	Decrease	Increase
Current liabilities	Increase	Decrease

Notice in the summary that, in converting from accrual to cash basis, all changes in current assets are handled in a similar manner. All changes in current liabilities are handled in the opposite manner.

The completed cash basis statement of changes in financial position is presented in Illustration 6.7. It shows $6,000 of cash provided by operations

Illustration 6.7
Statement of Changes in Financial Position—Cash Basis

WELBY COMPANY
Statement of Changes in Financial Position—Cash Basis
For the Year Ended December 31, 19x4

Financial resources provided:
Cash from operations:		
Net income....................................		$10,000
Add nonworking capital expenses:		
Depreciation..............................		5,000
Working capital from operations.............		$15,000
Effects of changes in components of working capital on cash:		
Increase in accounts receivable.................	$(10,000)	
Decrease in inventory.........................	4,000	
Decrease in accounts payable..................	(5,000)	
Increase in accrued liabilities...................	2,000	(9,000)
Cash from operations...........................		$ 6,000
Issuance of common stock......................		30,000
Total financial resources provided............		$36,000
Financial resources applied:		
Purchase plant assets...........................	$ 20,000	
Dividends......................................	5,000	25,000
Increase in cash...............................		$11,000
Cash, December 31, 19x3........................		10,000
Cash, December 31, 19x4........................		$21,000

and $30,000 provided by issuance of common stock. Of the $36,000 provided, $20,000 was spent for plant assets and $5,000 for dividends, leaving an $11,000 increase in cash. Note the similarity of the statements in Illustrations 6.6 and 6.7—they differ only in the "Funds from operations" section. The main reason for this similarity is that most sources and uses of funds involve cash receipts and disbursements and would be reported in the same way whether cash or working capital was the focus of attention.

Questions

1. Distinguish between horizontal and vertical analysis of financial statements.
2. What are common-size financial statements? What is the major purpose served by such statements?
3. What were the changes, absolute and percentage, if net income in 19x5 was $40,000 after a loss of $10,000 in 19x4? What were the changes if the loss was sustained in 19x5 after income was earned in 19x4?
4. Of what significance is the equity ratio? What are the alternative ways of conveying the same information?
5. The higher the accounts receivable turnover rate, the better off is the company. Do you agree? Why?
6. Illustrate a situation where the current ratio is misleading as an indicator of short-term debt-paying ability. Does the quick ratio offer a remedy to the situation you have described? Describe a situation where the quick ratio will not suffice either.
7. Before the John Company issued $10,000 of long-term notes (due more than a year from the date of issue) in exchange for a like amount of accounts payable, its acid-test ratio was 2:1. Will this transaction increase, decrease, or have no effect on (1) the current ratio and (2) the equity ratio?
8. Through the use of turnover ratios, explain why a firm might seek to increase the volume of its sales even though such an increase can be secured only at reduced prices.
9. Indicate which of the relationships illustrated in Chapter 6 would be best to judge:
    a. The short-term debt-paying ability of the firm.
    b. The overall efficiency of the firm without regard to the sources of assets.
    c. The return to owners of a corporation.
    d. The safety of bondholders' interest.
    e. The safety of preferred stockholders' dividends.
10. Indicate how each of the following ratios or measures is calculated:
    a. Payout ratio.
    b. Earnings per share of common stock.
    c. Price-earnings ratio.
    d. Yield on common stock.
    e. Yield on preferred stock.
    f. Times interest earned.
    g. Times preferred dividends earned.
    h. Return on stockholders' equity.
11. How is earning power on operating assets determined? Is it possible for two companies with "operating margins" of 5 percent and 1 percent, respectively, to both have an earning power of 20 percent on operating assets? How?
12. What are the major sources of funds in a business? What are the major uses of funds?
13. Why might a company have a positive inflow of cash (or working capital) from operations even though operating at a net loss?
14. Depreciation is often referred to as a source of funds. Is it a source of funds? Explain.

Exercises

1. Income statement data for White Company for 19x4 and 19x5 are:

	19x5	19x4
Net sales	$725,000	$538,000
Cost of goods sold	508,000	349,000
Selling expenses	110,000	97,000
Administrative expenses............	65,000	55,000
Income taxes	16,000	15,000

   Prepare a horizontal and vertical analysis of the above income data in a form similar to that in Illustration 6.2. Comment on the results of this analysis.

2. Under each of the three conditions listed below, compute the current ratio after each of the transactions described. (Consider each transaction independently of the others.) Current assets are now $100,000. Current ratio before the transaction is:
   a. 1:1.
   b. 2:1.
   c. 1:2.

   Transactions:
   1. $100,000 of merchandise purchased on account.
   2. Purchased $50,000 of machinery for cash.
   3. Issued stock for $50,000 cash.

3. A company has sales of $912,500 per year. Its average accounts receivable balance is $182,500. What is the average number of days an account receivable is outstanding?

4. From the following partial income statement, calculate the inventory turnover for the period.

Net sales		$521,450
Cost of goods sold:		
Beginning inventory	$ 50,000	
Purchases	370,000	
Goods available for sale................	$420,000	
Less: Ending inventory................	58,000	
Cost of goods sold................		362,000
Gross margin..........................		$159,450
Operating expenses		75,000
Net operating income....................		$ 84,450

5. The Korner Company had 40,000 shares of common stock outstanding on January 1, 19x1. On April 1, 19x1, it issued 10,000 additional shares for cash. The earnings available for common stockholders for 19x1 were $200,000. What amount of earnings per share of common stock should the company report?

6. A company paid interest of $4,000, incurred federal income taxes of $11,000, and had net income (after taxes) of $21,000. How many times was the interest earned?

7. The Field Company had 4,000 shares of $100 par value, 5 percent, preferred stock outstanding. Net income after taxes was $120,000. The market price per share was $80.
   a. How many times were the preferred dividends earned?
   b. What was the yield on the preferred stock, assuming the regular preferred dividends were declared and paid?
8. Indicate how the following data should be reported in a working capital basis statement of changes in financial position. A company purchased land valued at $20,000 and a building valued at $40,000 by paying $10,000 by check; signing a $15,000, six-month, interest-bearing note for $15,000; and assuming a mortgage on the property of $35,000.
9. Given that net income for 19x4 is $20,000, patent amortization expense is $500, loss on sale of patents is $1,000, depreciation is $2,000, and the Accumulated Depreciation on Equipment account shows a year-end balance of $10,000. Compute working capital from operations.
10. A company's financial statements for a given year show sales of $500,000, net income of $50,000, and accounts receivable on 1/1 of $44,000 and on 12/31 of $47,000. Compute the effect of the above information on net income as a measure of cash from operations.
11. The income statement of a company shows net income of $50,000 and cost of goods sold of $350,000. Inventory was $51,000 on 1/1 and $63,000 on 12/31; accounts payable for merchandise purchases were $38,000 on 1/1 and $42,000 on 12/31. Compute the effects of the above information on net income as a measure of cash from operations.
12. The operating expenses and taxes (including depreciation of $10,000) of a company for a given year were $100,000. Net income was $50,000. Prepaid insurance decreased from $3,000 to $2,000 and accrued wages payable increased from $4,000 to $6,000 during the year. Compute the effects of the above information on net income as a measure of cash from operations.
13. Assume that the data in Exercises 10, 11, and 12 are for the same company. Prepare the section of the statement of changes in financial position showing conversion of net income to cash from operations. Show both working capital and cash from operations.

Business Decision Problem 6–1

Shown below are the comparative balance sheets of the Bradley Corporation for December 31, 19x2 and 19x1:

BRADLEY CORPORATION
Comparative Balance Sheets
December 31, 19x2 and 19x1

	December 31, 19x2	December 31, 19x1
Assets		
Cash	$ 50,000	$10,000
Accounts receivable	9,000	12,000
Inventory	40,000	42,000
Plant and equipment	28,000	30,000
Total assets	$127,000	$94,000

	December 31, 19x2	December 31, 19x1
Liabilities and Stockholders' Equity		
Accounts payable	$ 10,000	$10,000
Common stock	70,000	70,000
Retained earnings.................................	47,000	14,000
Total liabilities and stockholders' equity.........	$127,000	$94,000

Required:

a. What was the net income for 19x2, assuming no dividend payments?
b. What was the primary source of the large increase in the cash balance from 19x1 to 19x2?
c. What were the two main sources of assets for the Bradley Corporation?
d. What other comparisons and procedures would you use to complete the analysis of the balance sheet begun above?

Business Decision Problem 6–2

The information below was obtained from the annual reports of the Morley Manufacturing Company:

	19x0	19x1	19x2	19x3
Net accounts receivable..............	$ 45,000	$ 90,000	$120,000	$165,000
Net sales	400,000	550,000	625,000	800,000

Required:

a. Assume a 360-day year. If cash sales account for 30 percent of all sales and credit terms are always 1/10, n/60, determine all turnover ratios possible and the number of days' sales in accounts receivable at all possible dates. (The number of days' sales in accounts receivable should be based on year-end accounts receivable and net credit sales.)
b. How effective is the company's credit policy?

Business Decision Problem 6–3

Barbra Hansen is interested in investing in one of three companies (A, B, or C) by buying its common stock. The companies' shares are selling at about the same price. The long-term capital structures of the companies are as follows:

	Company A	Company B	Company C
Bonds with a 10% interest rate.....................			$ 500,000
Preferred stock with an 8% dividend rate		$ 500,000	
Common stock, $10 par.............................	$1,000,000	500,000	500,000
Retained earnings.................................	80,000	80,000	80,000
Total long-term equity.....................	$1,080,000	$1,080,000	$1,080,000
Number of common shares outstanding	100,000	50,000	50,000

Ms. Hansen has consulted two investment advisers. One adviser believes that each of the companies will earn $80,000 per year before interest and taxes. The other adviser believes that each company will earn about $250,000 per year before interest and taxes.

Required:

a. Compute each of the following, assuming first that the estimate made by the first adviser is used and then that the estimate made by the second adviser is used:

   1. Earnings available for common stockholders, assuming a 40 percent corporate tax rate.
   2. Earnings per share of common stock.
   3. Rate of return on total stockholders' equity.

b. Which stock should Ms. Hansen select if she believes the first adviser?
c. Are the stockholders as a group (common and preferred) better off with or without the use of long-term debt in the above companies?

Business Decision Problem 6–4

Following are comparative ledger balances for the Clayton Company:

	December 31	
	19x4	19x3
Debit Balances		
Cash.	$ 35,000	$ 25,000
Accounts receivable.	40,000	30,000
Inventory	60,000	35,000
Land.	50,000	40,000
Building.	60,000	60,000
Equipment.	190,000	150,000
Goodwill	80,000	100,000
Total	$515,000	$440,000
Credit Balances		
Accumulated depreciation—building	$ 20,000	$ 18,000
Accumulated depreciation—equipment	35,000	32,000
Accounts payable.	50,000	30,000
Accrued liabilities.	20,000	15,000
Capital stock.	210,000	200,000
Paid-in capital—stock dividends	50,000	45,000
Paid-in capital—land donation.	10,000	–0–
Retained earnings	120,000	100,000
Total	$515,000	$440,000

An analysis of the Retained Earnings account for the year reveals the following:

Balance, December 31, 19x3...................		$100,000
Add: Net income for the year		65,000
		$165,000
Less:		
Cash dividends	$30,000	
Stock dividends.........................	15,000	
		45,000
Balance, December 31, 19x4.................		$120,000

Additional data:

Depreciation on building was $2,000 for the year, while depreciation on equipment was $21,000. Equipment with a cost of $20,000 on which $18,000 of depreciation had been accumulated was sold during the year at a loss of $1,000.

The President of Clayton Company has set two goals for 19x5: (1) increase working capital by $40,000; and (2) increase cash dividends to $60,000. The company's activities in 19x5 are expected to be quite similar to those of 19x4.

Required:

Prepare a schedule showing working capital and cash provided by operations in 19x4. Does it appear that the company can meet its president's goals for 19x5? Explain.

Solutions to End-of-Chapter Questions, Exercises, and Business Decision Problems

Answers to Questions

1. Horizontal analysis consists of determining the period-to-period changes in financial statement items in both absolute and percentage terms. Vertical analysis involves showing the items on the financial statement for a single period as an amount and as a percentage of a significant total.
2. Common-size financial statements are financial statements expressed solely in percentages; no absolute amounts are reported. The major purpose of such statements is to aid in comparing financial statements, especially when the dollar amounts differ sharply from period to period or between firms.
3. If net income rose to $40,000 in 19x5 after a loss of $10,000 in 19x4, the absolute change was a $50,000 increase; a percentage change cannot be calculated. The absolute change in net income was a decrease of $50,000 and the percentage change was a decrease of 125 percent when net income fell from $40,000 in 19x4 to a $10,000 net loss in 19x5.
4. The equity ratio shows what proportion of a firm's total assets is provided by stockholders (owners). It also describes the firm's capital structure and shows the extent of leveraging. The same information can be obtained from the debt-to-equity and the equity-to-debt ratios.
5. The company is not necessarily better off. It depends on what is done to make the turnover rate higher. The turnover rate is computed by dividing average net accounts receivable into net credit sales. Through the use of very stringent screening policies or collection policies, or both, the average balances of net

accounts receivable may have been reduced. It is likely that net sales would have been reduced also. If net sales were reduced less than proportionally to the decrease in net accounts receivable, the turnover ratio would increase, but the effect on earnings *could* be negative.

6. The current ratio is misleading as an indicator of debt-paying ability when:
   a. A large proportion of the current assets is composed of slow-moving inventory and of prepaid expenses.
   b. The current liabilities are due immediately and the noncash current assets are slow in being converted into cash.
   c. Some of the current assets are carried at amounts greater than their net realizable values.

   The quick ratio is similarly misleading when:
   a. Accounts receivable are slow-moving and current liabilities are due almost immediately.
   b. Accounts receivable and marketable securities are carried at amounts greater than their net realizable values.

7. Since current liabilities are decreased, both the current ratio and the acid-test ratio will increase. The equity ratio will remain unchanged since both stockholders' equity and the total of liabilities and stockholders' equity remain unchanged.

8. In general, the objective sought is to increase the absolute amount of net income by securing increased volume even if this means lowering prices. Then, if investment can be held constant, all rates of return on investment (assets or stockholders' equity) will increase. Thus, a firm might have a rate of return on assets of 8 percent consisting of a 2 percent rate of net income to sales and a total assets turnover of 4. If, by reducing prices, the rate of net income to sales is cut to 1.8 percent but the turnover is increased to 5, the rate of return on assets is increased to 9 percent.

9. a. Acid-test ratio (or possibly the current ratio):

$$\frac{\text{Quick assets}}{\text{Current liabilities}}$$

   b. The earning power computation:

$$\text{Earning power} = \frac{\text{Net operating earnings}}{\text{Operating assets}}$$

   c. The return on total stockholders' equity:

$$\frac{\text{Net income}}{\text{Average stockholders' equity}}$$

   If there were no preferred stockholders, the only "owners" would be the common stockholders. In that case, one might prefer earnings per share or earnings rate on market price:

$$\text{Earnings per share} = \frac{\text{Net income of common stockholders}}{\text{Number of shares of common stock outstanding}}$$

$$\text{Earnings rate on market price} = \frac{\text{Earnings per share of common stock}}{\text{Current market price per share}}$$

    d. Number of times bond interest is earned:

$$\frac{\text{Net income before interest and taxes}}{\text{Interest expense}}$$

    e. Number of times preferred dividends earned:

$$\frac{\text{Net income}}{\text{Preferred dividends}}$$

10. The ratios are calculated as follows:
    a. Dividends per share ÷ Earnings per share.
    b. Earnings of common stockholders ÷ Average number of common shares outstanding.
    c. Current market price of common stock ÷ Earnings per share of common stock.
    d. Earnings per share of common stock ÷ Current market price per share of common stock.
    e. Annual preferred dividend ÷ Current market price per share of preferred stock.
    f. (Pretax net income + interest) ÷ Interest expense.
    g. Net income after taxes ÷ Preferred dividends.
    h. Net income ÷ Average stockholders' equity.

11.   Earning power = Net operating margin × Turnover of operating assets

$$\text{Earning power} = \frac{\text{Net operating}}{\text{Net sales}} \times \frac{\text{Net sales}}{\text{Operating assets}}$$

$$\text{Earning power} = \frac{\text{Net operating income}}{\text{Operating assets}}$$

The companies with operating margins of 5 percent and 1 percent, respectively, could each have a 20 percent earning power rate as follows:

	Operating Margin	×	Turnover of Operating Assets	=	Earning Power
Company 1..............	5%	×	4 times	=	20%
Company 2..............	1%	×	20 times	=	20%

The one with the higher operating margin would have a lower turnover of operating assets, and vice versa.

12. The major sources of funds in a business are operations, stock issuances, borrowing, and disposals of noncurrent assets. The major uses of funds are the redemption of debt and the acquisition of treasury stock, investment in noncurrent assets, dividends, and operations. The last use is necessary if the addback of nonfund items is not large enough to yield inflow of funds from operations.

13. The addback of nonfund items may convert a net loss to a positive amount, thus showing that there was an excess of funds from revenues over funds used for expenses.

14. Depreciation is not a source of funds. It just seems to be from the way the accountant adds depreciation to net income to determine funds from operations. This is a shortcut that could easily be replaced by a method that deducts only fund-consuming expenses from fund-producing revenues to get funds from operations. In this way, sales, not depreciation, would be clearly shown as the source of funds. Under this approach, depreciation would never appear on the funds statement.

Solutions to Exercises

1.

WHITE COMPANY
Comparative Income Statements
For the Years Ended December 31, 19x4 and 19x5

	Year Ended December 31		Increase or Decrease* 19x5 over 19x4		Percentage of Net Sales	
	19x5	19x4	Dollar	Percent	19x5	19x4
Net sales	$725,000	$538,000	$187,000	34.8	100.0	100.0
Cost of goods sold..........	508,000	349,000	159,000	45.6	70.1	64.9
Gross margin.	$217,000	$189,000	$ 28,000	12.9	29.9	35.1
Expenses:						
Selling	$110,000	$ 97,000	$ 13,000	13.4	15.2	18.0
Administrative	65,000	55,000	10,000	18.2	9.0	10.2
Total expenses........	$175,000	$152,000	$ 23,000	15.1	24.2	28.2
Net operating income........	$ 42,000	$ 37,000	$ 5,000	13.5	5.7	6.9
Income taxes..............	16,000	15,000	1,000	6.7	2.2	2.8
Net income	$ 26,000	$ 22,000	$ 4,000	18.2	3.6^D	4.1

^{D} = Rounding difference.

The benefits of a strong surge in sales in 19x5 over 19x4 were substantially offset by a sharp increase in the cost of goods sold—a sharp decrease in the gross margin rate, from 35.1 percent to 29.9 percent—which suggests that the increase in sales may have resulted from cuts in selling prices. Holding selling and administrative expenses to increases well below the increase in sales raised a 12.9 percent increase in gross margin to an 18.2 percent increase in net income.

2.

Current ratio before transaction (current assets = $100,000) ...	(a) 1:1	(b) 2:1	(c) 1:2
After transaction 1	$1:1\left(\dfrac{\$200,000}{\$200,000}\right)$	$4:3\left(\dfrac{\$200,000}{\$150,000}\right)$	$2:3\left(\dfrac{\$200,000}{\$300,000}\right)$
2	$1:2\left(\dfrac{\$50,000}{\$100,000}\right)$	$1:1\left(\dfrac{\$50,000}{\$50,000}\right)$	$1:4\left(\dfrac{\$50,000}{\$200,000}\right)$
3	$3:2\left(\dfrac{\$150,000}{\$100,000}\right)$	$3:1\left(\dfrac{\$150,000}{\$50,000}\right)$	$3:4\left(\dfrac{\$150,000}{\$200,000}\right)$

3. $182,500/$912,500 = 20\%; 20\%$ of $365 = 73$ days.
4. Average inventory $= \$50,000 + \$58,000/2 = \$54,000$.
   Inventory turnover $= \$362,000/\$54,000 = 6.7$ times.
5. Earnings per share of common stock:

$$\frac{\$200,000}{0.25(40,000) + 0.75(50,000)} = \frac{\$200,000}{47,500} = \$4.21 \text{ per share}$$

6. $\dfrac{(\$21,000 + \$11,000 + \$4,000)}{\$4,000} = \dfrac{\$36,000}{\$4,000} = 9$ times.

7. *a.* $\$120,000/\$20,000 = 6$ times.
   b. $\$5/\$80 = 0.0625$ or 6.25%.

8. Under "Financial resources provided":

Liability for mortgage on land and building	$35,000

   Under "Financial resources applied":

Land and building acquired	$60,000

9.
Net income		$20,000
Add: Nonfund expenses not using funds:		
Depreciation	$2,000	
Loss on sale of patent	1,000	
Patent amortization	500	3,500
Working capital from operations.		$23,500

10.
Net income	$50,000
Less: Increase in accounts receivable.	3,000
Cash from operations	$47,000

11.
Net income	$50,000
Less: Increase in inventory	(12,000)
Add: Increase in accounts payable	4,000
Cash from operations	$42,000

12.
Net income	$50,000
Add: Nonfund item—depreciation	10,000
Working capital from operations.	$60,000
Add: Increase in accrued wages payable	2,000
Decrease in prepaid insurance	1,000
Cash from operations	$63,000

13.
Financial resources provided:.	
Cash from operations:	
Net income.	$50,000
Add: Depreciation	10,000
Working capital from operations	$60,000
Increase in accounts receivable	(3,000)
Increase in inventory	(12,000)
Increase in accounts payable	4,000
Decrease in prepaid insurance	1,000
Increase in accrued wages	2,000
Cash from operations	$52,000

Solution to Business Decision Problem 6-1

a.
Retained earnings, December 31, 19x2	. . . .	$47,000
Retained earnings, December 31, 19x1	. . . .	14,000
Net income for 19x2	. . . .	$33,000

b. The primary source of the large ($40,000) increase in the cash balance from 19x1 to 19x2 was the retention of $33,000 of net income. Other sources were the $3,000 reduction in accounts receivable, the $2,000 reduction in inventory, and the $2,000 reduction in plant and equipment.

c. The two main sources of assets for the Bradley Corporation in both 19x1 and 19x2 were the common stockholders' original investment and the retention of earnings in the business.

d. To complete the analysis of the balance sheets begun above, a thorough ratio analysis should be prepared for each year so that relative as well as absolute changes may be observed. Furthermore, both the absolute change analysis begun above and the suggested ratio analysis should include the information contained in the earnings statement for each year. Finally, the ratio analysis, and possibly the absolute change analysis, should include comparisons with other firms in the same industry, comparisons with industry-wide statistics, and consideration of general economic conditions.

Solution to Business Decision Problem 6-2

a. Accounts receivable turnover = Net credit sales ÷ Average net accounts receivable.

19x0: Since average net accounts receivable cannot be determined from the data, neither can the accounts receivable turnover. An estimate would be $280,000 ÷ $45,000 = 6.22.

19x1: $385,000 ÷ [($45,000 + $90,000) ÷ 2] = 5.70

19x2: $437,500 ÷ [($90,000 + $120,000) ÷ 2] = 4.17

19x3: $560,000 ÷ [($120,000 + $165,000) ÷ 2] = 3.93

Number of days' sales in accounts receivable = (Net accounts receivable ÷ Net credit sales) × 360.

19x0: ($45,000 ÷ $280,000) × 360 = 57.86.

19x1: ($90,000 ÷ $385,000) × 360 = 84.16.

19x2: ($120,000 ÷ $437,500) × 360 = 98.74.

19x3: ($165,000 ÷ $560,000) × 360 = 106.07.

b. The credit policy has apparently lost its effectiveness. The net accounts receivable are increasing at a faster rate than the net credit sales. This could indicate that the discount is not large enough to cause buyers to take advantage of it. The company is not even enforcing the upper limit of the credit policy (60 days).

Solution to Business Decision Problem 6-3

		Co. A	Co. B	Co. C
a.	1.			

Using first adviser's estimate:

	Co. A	Co. B	Co. C
Income before interest and taxes	$ 80,000	$ 80,000	$ 80,000
Less: Interest (10% of $500,000)			50,000
	$ 80,000	$ 80,000	$ 30,000
Less: Taxes (40%)	32,000	32,000	12,000
Net income after taxes	$ 48,000	$ 48,000	$ 18,000
Less: Preferred dividends.		40,000	
Earnings available for common stockholders	$ 48,000	$ 8,000	$ 18,000

Using second adviser's estimate:

	Co. A	Co. B	Co. C
Income before interest and taxes	$ 250,000	$ 250,000	$250,000
Less: Interest (10% of $500,000)			50,000
	$ 250,000	$ 250,000	$200,000
Less: Taxes (40%)	100,000	100,000	80,000
Net income after taxes	$ 150,000	$ 150,000	$120,000
Less: Preferred dividends.		40,000	
Earnings available for common stockholders	$ 150,000	$ 110,000	$120,000

2. *Using first adviser's estimate:*

	Co. A	Co. B	Co. C
Earnings available to common stockholders.	$ 48,000	$ 8,000	$ 18,000
Number of shares of common stock outstanding. . .	100,000	50,000	50,000
Earnings per share	$ 0.48	$ 0.16	$ 0.36

Using second adviser's estimate:

	Co. A	Co. B	Co. C
Earnings available for common stockholders	$ 150,000	$ 110,000	$120,000
Number of shares of common stock outstanding. . .	100,000	50,000	50,000
Earnings per share	$ 1.50	$ 2.20	$ 2.40

3. *Using first adviser's estimate:*

	Co. A	Co. B	Co. C
Net income after taxes	$ 48,000	$ 48,000	$ 18,000
Total stockholders' equity.	$1,080,000	$1,080,000	$580,000
Rate of return on total stockholders' equity	4.44%	4.44%	3.10%

Using second adviser's estimate:

	Co. A	Co. B	Co. C
Net income after taxes	$ 150,000	$ 150,000	$120,000
Total stockholders' equity.	$1,080,000	$1,080,000	$580,000
Rate of return on total stockholders' equity	13.89%	13.89%	20.69%

b. If Ms. Hansen believes the first adviser, she probably should not buy stock in any of the companies. If things become only a little worse for Company B, there will be no earnings available to common stockholders. If she is determined to buy stock in one, Company A would be preferable because of the higher earnings per share.

Incidentally (although the question does not require this information), if Ms. Hansen believes the second adviser, she probably should select Company C's stock because of the higher earnings per share. But there are other considerations. The equity-to-debt ratio is only slightly greater than 1 : 1 (assuming that short-term debt is negligible). There is greater risk involved as a result. Preferred dividends can usually be delayed or avoided completely, while interest on bonds must be paid each year (or the creditors may take over the assets).

c. The computation in part a3 above merely indicates whether stockholders (common and preferred) are better off with or without long-term debt. The results indicate that the answer depends on the level of income before interest and taxes.

Solution to Business Decision Problem 6-4

CLAYTON COMPANY
Schedule of Working Capital and Cash Provided by Operations
For the Year Ended December 31, 19x4

Working capital from operations:
Net income	$ 65,000
Add nonworking capital charges:	
Depreciation of building	2,000
Depreciation of equipment	21,000
Loss on sale of equipment	1,000
Amortization of goodwill	20,000
Working capital provided by operations	109,000
Effects of changes in working capital on cash:	
Increase in accounts receivable.	(10,000)
Increase in inventories	(25,000)
Increase in accounts payable.	20,000
Increase in accrued liabilities.	5,000
Cash provided by operations	$ 99,000

The president's goals appear to be attainable, provided there is no intention of spending the $60,000 again on equipment in 19x5. Working capital increased $109,000 in 19x4, which is greater than the $40,000 increase in working capital and the $60,000 increased dividends sought. The goal of being able to pay $60,000 in cash dividends also appears feasible since the cash flow from operations is $99,000. This is only $1,000 less than the increase in working capital plus cash dividends planned. But since the entire $40,000 increase in working capital need not be in cash form, we need only be concerned with whether sufficient cash is generated by operations to cover the cash dividends. Such is the case here.

7

Income Measurement in Manufacturing Companies

Chapter Goals

When you have completed Chapter 7, you should be able to:

1. Explain the three broad classifications of costs incurred by a manufacturing firm.
2. Illustrate and contrast the three basic elements of manufacturing cost incurred to produce a product.
3. Discuss the general pattern of the flow of costs through the accounting system of a manufacturing firm.
4. Explain the financial reporting of costs incurred by a manufacturing firm and prepare the statement of cost of goods manufactured and sold.
5. Explain how and why financial reporting is heavily dependent upon the distinction drawn between product costs and period costs.
6. Explain the concept of a predetermined overhead rate and show how such a rate is used to apply overhead to production.
7. Explain how and why the use of an overhead rate leads to underapplied or overapplied overhead and illustrate the accounting treatments of such overhead.
8. Explain the way overhead rates are influenced by the level of capacity used in setting the rate and the consequence of varying overhead rates.
9. Contrast the two major types of cost systems used by manufacturing companies and illustrate the kinds of operations in which each is likely to be used.

All firms—merchandising, service, or manufacturing—incur three types of expenses:

Cost of goods sold.
Selling or marketing.
Administrative.

How accountants accumulate and present these expenses was treated earlier and will be mentioned only briefly for manufacturing firms. But the determination of cost of goods sold (and therefore inventory values) is significantly different for manufacturing firms than for other firms. Further, job performance of managers in manufacturing firms is frequently evaluated on the basis of their ability to control the costs of manufacturing. Therefore, the nature of cost accumulation for manufacturing is important not only for accurate financial statement purposes but also for understanding how and why cost of manufacturing affects the evaluation of a manager. This chapter and the next are focused on the costs of manufacturing products.

COST CLASSIFICATIONS IN MANUFACTURING FIRMS

The objective of a manufacturer is to use resources to produce a product that can be sold at a profit. To achieve this objective, raw materials are converted into finished products delivered to customers. For example, a furniture manufacturer converts lumber, cloth, foam rubber, and other raw materials into chairs, tables, sofas, and so on.

One objective in measuring the costs of a manufacturer is to provide information on the cost per unit of goods manufactured so that the cost of goods sold used in income determination and the cost of inventories for reporting on financial position can be ascertained. Costs also are measured for other purposes, such as product pricing, planning, and performance evaluation.

Costs are called by many (and sometimes conflicting) names. The types of cost discussed in this section are:

Product costs.
Selling and administrative costs (period costs).
Variable and fixed costs.

Manufacturing Costs

Cost is a money measurement of the resources used or the sacrifice made for a stated purpose. The product cost concept will be discussed further, but it is important to recognize the significance of product cost now. Classifying a cost as a product cost means it will be treated as an expense when the product is *sold,* not when the cost is incurred. Thus, the purchase of direct materials is an acquisition of an asset often called raw material inventory;

the use of the direct materials creates another asset often called finished goods inventory; the direct materials used are recognized as an expense when the finished product is sold.

The total cost of manufacturing a product includes the costs of (1) materials used (called direct materials), (2) labor directly related to converting or processing (called direct labor), and (3) costs that do not directly go into conversion or processing (called manufacturing overhead). These three elements of total cost are referred to as *product cost, manufacturing cost,* or *factory cost.*

Direct materials.   *The basic materials that are included in the finished product, which are clearly traceable to the product, and whose manufacture caused their usage are called direct materials.* Thus, iron ore is a direct material to a steel company, while steel is a direct material to the auto manufacturer. But some minor direct materials are often not accounted for as direct materials. For example, glue and thread used in manufacturing furniture may not be accounted for as direct materials, although they could be, simply because it is not economically practical to trace these items to the finished product. They would be described as *supplies* or *indirect materials* and accounted for as manufacturing overhead.

Direct materials costs include the cost of the actual quantity of materials used, priced at net invoice price, plus delivery costs. Some firms also include storage and handling costs. The method of costing inventories, such as FIFO, LIFO, and average cost, discussed in Chapter 3, also affects the measurement of direct materials costs.

Direct labor.   *The services of employees who actually work on the materials to turn them into finished products are called direct labor.* The direct labor costs of a product include those labor costs that are clearly traceable to or readily identifiable with the product or are caused by its manufacture. Evidence that a labor cost is directly related to a product can be established by showing that the amount of labor cost incurred varies with the number of units produced. Thus, the services of the machinist, the assembler, the cutter, and the painter are classified as direct labor. But some labor services may not be accounted for as direct labor, even though they vary directly with the number of units produced. These services are broadly described as *indirect labor* and are accounted for as manufacturing overhead. Materials handling costs may be an example.

Direct labor cost is usually measured by multiplying the number of hours of direct labor services received by the hourly wage rate. The actual cost of direct labor is considerably higher because of other costs such as employer's payroll taxes, pension costs, paid vacations, paid sick leaves, and other "fringe benefits." These may amount to as much as 25 to 50 percent of the hourly wage paid. Although sometimes accounted for as part of direct labor cost, these are commonly included in manufacturing overhead.

Manufacturing overhead. There are many alternative names for this cost category, including factory indirect costs, factory burden, and manufacturing expense. However named, *the category includes all costs incurred in making a product, except those costs accounted for as direct materials and direct labor costs.* These manufacturing overhead costs are manufacturing costs that must be incurred but cannot be traced directly to the units produced, and may include certain direct materials and direct labor costs because it is not economically practical to trace them to the units produced.

Some of the more common types of manufacturing overhead costs incurred include indirect materials, indirect labor, repairs and maintenance, depreciation of factory buildings and machinery, pensions, payroll taxes and other fringe benefits, utilities, insurance and taxes on factory property, and overtime wage premiums paid to direct laborers. Indirect labor includes the salaries and wages earned by factory employees who do not work directly on the products produced but serve indirectly in their manufacture. This includes the services of timekeepers, inspectors, janitors, engineers, supervisors, materials handlers, and toolroom personnel. Overtime wage premiums are usually included in manufacturing overhead rather than being included as direct labor cost traced directly to the products worked on. The reason is that the need to work overtime can usually be traced to all production, not the manufacture of a given product that, by chance, happened to be the one worked on during the overtime period.

Other manufacturing cost terminology. The sum of the direct materials costs and direct labor costs incurred to manufacture a product is the *prime cost.* The sum of the direct labor costs and the manufacturing overhead costs related to a product is the *conversion cost.* As stated, the sum of the three elements of cost (direct materials, direct labor, and manufacturing overhead) is called *product cost, manufacturing cost,* or *factory cost.* The costs incurred to manufacture the product are "attached" to units of the product and determine the amount at which each unit of completed goods is carried in inventory until sold. The total of these costs assigned to units of product determine the amount used to measure the expense, cost of goods sold, when the products are actually sold. These cost relationships are shown in Illustration 7.1.

Selling and Administrative Costs

Selling and administrative costs differ from manufacturing costs. Selling and administrative costs are incurred in the general administration of the organization and in *disposing* of the product, not in producing it.

Selling (marketing) costs. *Selling or marketing costs* generally are classified as order-getting and order-filling costs. *Order-getting costs* are costs incurred in seeking orders for products or services. They include the cost of

Illustration 7.1
Cost Relationships

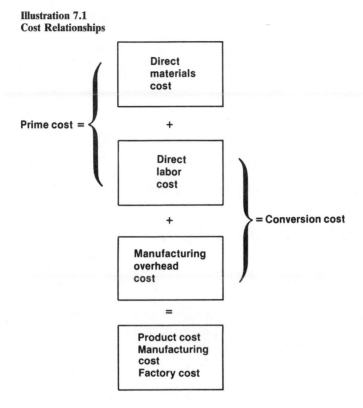

advertising, market research, selection and training of personnel, and maintaining sales offices, as well as the cost of sales salaries and commissions. *Order-filling costs* are the costs incurred after completion of a product until it is delivered to a customer and the resulting account receivable collected. They include the costs of warehousing, delivering, installing, and servicing the product as well as the costs of billing the customer, processing payments received, and bad debts.

Administrative (general) costs. All costs not classified as manufacturing or selling costs are classified as *administrative or general costs*. This category includes the costs of the top administrative functions plus those of various staff departments—accounting, finance, personnel, legal, and so on. Also included are executives' salaries and executive office expenses, donations, litigation costs, and research and development costs. How these costs are classified will differ among firms.

A cost classified as a selling and administrative cost is often called a *period cost,* as contrasted to a product cost. This means that selling and administrative costs are recorded in the period incurred and not attached to products or carried in inventory accounts. A sales manager's salary, for example, will be recorded as an expense in the period incurred. And this will hold even though the sales manager may be working on projects that will benefit future periods. The salary will be treated as a period cost and charged immediately to expense (because the amount that would otherwise be carried forward is not material in amount or is difficult to measure, or both).

Variable and Fixed Costs

Another of the most useful ways to classify costs is by their behavior—that is, according to how they change as activity (output) changes. A cost may increase or decrease in total amount as activity increases or decreases (variable), or it may remain constant (fixed) despite changes in the level of activity.

Variable costs. *Variable costs are costs that vary in total amount directly with changes in the level of activity or output.* For example, every electric washing machine produced has an electric motor. If the motors cost $5 each, then the motor cost of one machine is $5, of two machines $10, of 100 machines $500, and so on. If the plan is to produce 10,000 washing machines, then the planned cost of the motors is $50,000. Similarly, the labor cost to install the motors is a variable cost. In merchandising firms, examples of variable costs are cost of goods sold and sales commissions. Both will vary with the dollar volume of sales.

Fixed costs. *Fixed costs are costs that remain constant in total amount over wide variations in the level of activity.* For example, the annual license for an automobile may cost $50 whether the auto is driven 1,000 or 100,000 miles during the year. The same may hold for the premium on an insurance policy on the auto. Property taxes, depreciation, rent, executives' salaries, and advertising are further examples of fixed costs. Fixed costs are called time-related costs to distinguish them from volume-related costs.

Fixed costs present a special type of problem in determining the unit cost of producing a certain product. Since the total cost is fixed, cost *per unit* may vary widely if output varies. If the site on which a factory building is located is rented at an annual rent of $100,000, then the rental cost per ton of output is $1 if 100,000 tons are produced, $0.50 if 200,000 tons are produced, and only $0.10 if 1 million tons are produced. Thus, unit cost decreases with increases in output and increases with decreases in output.

THE GENERAL COST ACCUMULATION MODEL

In manufacturing companies, a primary cost objective is to measure the cost per unit to manufacture a product. Unit product costs are measured under the principle that such costs consist of (1) direct materials and direct labor plus (2) a fair share of the other factory indirect costs incurred. This cost information is needed for financial reporting and pricing and is required for income tax purposes. The accountant in a manufacturing firm will use a certain system to accumulate costs. The system is called a "cost accumulation model." The model is based on the physical flow of goods and their costs.

Product and Cost Flows

The accounting systems of manufacturing firms tend to have a similar general framework because the products manufactured flow through each firm in a similar order. Raw or direct materials are acquired; direct labor services and other factory services are used to process the materials into completed products ready for sale. The accounting records are set up in such a way as to show a flow of costs through the records that matches the physical flow of product through the firm. These relationships are shown in Illustration 7.2.

Illustration 7.2
Product and Cost Flows

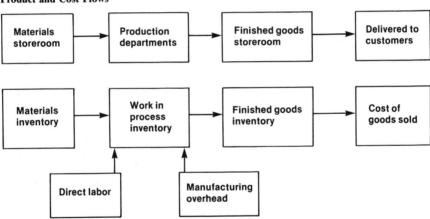

Physically, the products move from the raw materials warehouse to the production department. During production, they are partially completed manufactured products and are called *work in process*. Eventually they become completed manufactured products and are called *finished goods*. They are then moved to the finished goods warehouse and then delivered to customers. The accounting records show the flow of costs from the Materials Inventory into Work in Process Inventory where the costs of direct labor and other factory services are added. When the products are completed, their costs are moved to the Finished Goods Inventory account, and upon the sale of the products, the costs are transferred to the Cost of Goods Sold account.

Because a manufacturer has products in various stages of completion, the accounts and financial statements of the manufacturer typically will show three types of inventories: Materials, Work in Process, and Finished Goods. At any given time, the amount or balance in each of these accounts will depend upon many factors, including the availability of materials and the level of customer demand.

Accounting for Cost and Revenue Flows

Knowledge of the general flow of costs and revenues through a manufacturing firm is of value in understanding a cost system. For this reason, an example using dollar amounts is presented below and summarized graphically in Illustration 7.3. The lines running between accounts show the transfer or flow of costs from one account to the next.

To begin the illustration, it is assumed that the inventories of the Brice Company as of July 1, 19x3, were:

Materials inventory	$10,000
Work in process inventory	20,000
Finished goods inventory	40,000

The company's activities for July are summarized below, together with further explanation.

The flow of direct materials costs. During July, $40,000 of materials were purchased on account and $30,000 of materials were issued to production from the storeroom. The entries required (numbered to key to the entries in the T-accounts in Illustration 7.3) are (1) and (2):

Materials Inventory				Work in Process Inventory		
Beginning balance	10,000	(2) Used	30,000	Beginning balance	20,000	
(1) Purchased	40,000			(2) Materials	30,000	

	Accounts Payable	
	Bal.	xxx
	(1)	40,000

(Note: In order to focus attention upon cost and revenue flows, the credit to Accounts Payable is not included in Illustration 7.3.)

The flow of labor costs. Two groups of employees are likely to be involved in the accounting for labor costs. One group is concerned with *payroll accounting*—that is, determining the total wages earned, the various deductions, and the net pay of each employee. The second group engages in *labor cost accounting*—that is, determining which accounts are to be charged with what amount of labor costs. Under such a procedure, an account common to both groups is needed to tie together the separate accounting activities. In Illustration 7.3, this account is called Payroll Summary. It is a temporarily established clearing account. It is debited when payrolls are prepared by the payroll department and credited when labor costs are distributed by the factory accounting department. Normally, the Payroll Summary account will have a zero balance at the end of any accounting period. During the period, it will have a balance only because of the time lag between preparation and distribution of the payroll.

The factory payrolls for July amounted to $75,000—$60,000 of direct labor and $15,000 indirect. Payroll withholdings amounted to $3,500 of social security taxes, $8,000 of federal income taxes, and $500 of union dues. The entries required (keyed [3] and [4] in Illustration 7.3) are:

Payroll Summary				Work in Process Inventory	
(3) Incurred	75,000	(4) Distributed	75,000	Beginning balance	20,000
				(2) Materials	30,000
				(4) Direct labor	60,000

Manufacturing Overhead	
(4) Indirect labor	15,000

The accrued payroll will be paid in cash to the employees, while the amounts withheld will be paid on their behalf to the federal government and the union at a later date (entries showing such payments are omitted here as not being relevant to this discussion, as are various credits in entry 3, which records the various liabilities incurred upon receipt of factory employee services). Entry 4 adds to Work in Process Inventory the cost of the labor traceable to the products being manufactured and transfers those labor costs not traceable to products to Manufacturing Overhead.

The flow of overhead costs. The indirect costs of operating the factory during the period included repairs of $1,000, property taxes of $1,500, equipment rent of $2,500, payroll taxes of $3,500, utilities of $4,000, insurance of $2,000, and factory building depreciation of $5,500. Entry 5 shows the recording of these costs:

Manufacturing Overhead	
(4) Indirect labor	15,000
(5) Other costs	20,000

Entries would also be made in supporting accounts or records maintained for each type of manufacturing overhead cost incurred. The credits assumed

Illustration 7.3
Cost and Revenue Flowchart

Materials Inventory

Beginning balance	10,000	(2)	Used*	30,000
(1) Purchased	40,000			

Payroll Summary

(3) Incurred	75,000	(4)	Distributed	75,000

Manufacturing Overhead

(4) Indirect labor	15,000	(6)	Applied	35,000
(5) Other costs	20,000			

Selling Expenses

(10) Incurred	23,000	(16)	Closed	23,000

Administrative Expenses

(11) Incurred	19,000	(16)	Closed	19,000

Interest Expense

(12) Incurred	3,000	(16)	Closed	3,000

Federal Income Taxes

(13) Incurred	15,000	(16)	Closed	15,000

* If any of the material had been indirect materials, that portion would have been transferred to manufacturing overhead.

Work in Process Inventory

Beginning balance	20,000	(7)	Completed	110,000
(2)	Materials	30,000			
(4)	Direct labor	60,000			
(6)	Overhead	35,000			

Finished Goods Inventory

Beginning balance	40,000	(8)	Sold	125,000
(7)	Completed	110,000			

Cost of Goods Sold

(8)	Sold	125,000	(15)	Closed	125,000

Sales

(14)	Closed	200,000	(9)	Sold	200,000

Income Summary

(15)		125,000	(14)	200,000
(16)		60,000		

to accompany the $20,000 debit to manufacturing overhead are omitted from Illustration 7.3 as not being relevant to the showing of cost flows.

The manufacturing overhead costs are as much a part of the cost of the period's production as are the costs of direct materials and direct labor. These costs are added to the costs already in the Work in Process Inventory account, and illustrated in entry 6:

Manufacturing Overhead

(4) Indirect labor	15,000	(6) Applied	35,000
(5) Other costs	20,000		

Work in Process Inventory

Beginning balance	20,000	
(2) Materials	30,000	
(4) Direct labor	60,000	
(6) Overhead	35,000	

The assignment of overhead to work in process is a problem that is dealt with later. For purposes of Illustration 7.3, it is assumed that the overhead incurred during a period is to be assigned to the production of the period.

The flow of finished goods. As shown in Illustration 7.3, for product costing purposes, Work in Process Inventory is charged with the materials, labor, and overhead costs of producing goods. When the goods are completed and transferred out of production, an entry is made to transfer their cost from Work in Process Inventory to Finished Goods Inventory. Assuming that goods costing $110,000 were completed and transferred, the entry needed is (7):

Work in Process Inventory

Beginning balance	20,000	(7) Completed	110,000
(2) Materials	30,000		
(4) Direct labor	60,000		
(6) Overhead	35,000		

Finished Goods Inventory

Beginning balance	40,000	
(7) Completed	110,000	

Now assume that goods costing $125,000 were sold on account for $200,000. Entries are now required to record the sale of the goods and to record the transfer out of the Finished Goods Inventory account of the cost of the goods sold. The required entries are 8 and 9:

Finished Goods Inventory

Beginning balance	40,000	(8) Sold	125,000
(7) Completed	110,000		

Cost of Goods Sold

(8) Sold	125,000

Sales

(9) Sold	200,000

Once again, since concern is only with costs and revenues, the debit to Accounts Receivable in entry 9 is omitted from Illustration 7.3.

To complete the explanation of the entries in the accounts in Illustration 7.3, assume that selling expenses of $23,000, administrative expenses of $19,000, interest expense of $3,000, and federal income taxes of $15,000 were incurred in July. The required entries are 10, 11, 12, and 13:

Selling Expenses

(10) Incurred	23,000

Administrative Expenses

(11) Incurred	19,000

Interest Expense

(12) Incurred	3,000

Federal Income Taxes

(13) Incurred	15,000

Subsidiary records or accounts would be kept for the various types of selling and administrative expenses incurred but, for brevity, are omitted here. The credits in entries 10 and 11 would be to accounts such as Cash, Accounts Payable, Salaries Payable, and Accumulated Depreciation. They are omitted from Illustration 7.3, as are the credits in entries 12 and 13, to keep attention directed toward costs, expenses, and revenues.

Although the accounts are usually formally closed only at the end of the accounting year, entry 14 records the closing of the Sales revenue account for the month of July as an illustration of the annual entry, and entries 15 and 16 are required to close the expense accounts:

Selling Expenses				Cost of Goods Sold			
(10) Incurred	23,000	(16) Closed	23,000	(8) Sold	125,000	(15) Closed	125,000

Administrative Expenses				Sales			
(11) Incurred	19,000	(16) Closed	19,000	(14) Closed	200,000	(9) Sold	200,000

Interest Expense				Income Summary			
(12) Incurred	3,000	(16) Closed	3,000	(15) (16)	125,000 60,000	(14)	200,000

Federal Income Taxes			
(13) Incurred	15,000	(16) Closed	15,000

The closing process would, of course, be completed by debiting the Income Summary account and crediting the Retained Earnings account for $15,000. Here again, this entry is omitted for brevity.

As a technical matter, the accounting for the costs of manufacturing operations ends with entry 7. The other entries are included to provide a complete set of illustrative entries for a manufacturing company.

FINANCIAL REPORTING BY MANUFACTURING COMPANIES

Typically, it is difficult to determine from a statement of retained earnings and a statement of changes in financial position whether the issuing company was a merchandiser or a manufacturer. But it is easy to make the determination from a balance sheet or an income statement.

The Balance Sheet

The balance sheet (or the accompanying notes) will typically disclose separately the manufacturer's inventories of materials, work in process, and finished goods as well as factory supplies. By way of contrast, a merchandiser will report a single merchandise inventory amount and, perhaps in prepaid expenses, the cost of supplies on hand. The manufacturer's statement may also show, as intangible assets, patents and trademarks relating to the products manufactured and sold. And it may contain greater detail in the "Property, plant, and equipment" section because of the ownership of assets used in manufacturing.

The Income Statement

A manufacturer's income statement is more complex than a merchandiser's. The manufacturer incurs many more additional costs in producing goods than a merchandiser does in buying them ready for sale. Because of this greater detail, a question arises as to how detailed an income statement should be. To a large extent, the answer depends on for whom the statement is prepared.

If the income statement is to be published in an annual report, it is usually condensed, differing little from a merchandiser's income statement. Such a statement is shown in Illustration 7.4, which reports on the Brice Company

Illustration 7.4
Income Statement of a Manufacturer

BRICE COMPANY		
Income Statement		
For the Month Ended July 31, 19x3		
Sales...		$200,000
Cost of goods sold	$125,000	
Selling expenses......................	23,000	
Administrative expenses................	19,000	
Interest expense	3,000	
Federal income taxes	15,000	185,000
Net income..........................		$ 15,000

activities which were summarized in Illustration 7.3. Although it is common practice to include comparative data (the income statement for July 19x2) when financial statements are released to the public, such data are omitted here.

The same type of income statement could be used in reporting to top management and to the board of directors. When so used, it is likely to be in comparative form, containing data for the same period last year, and to contain budgeted data. It is also likely to be supported by a statement of cost of goods manufactured and sold and with the schedules showing the details of the selling and administrative expenses, complete with comparative and budgeted data.

The Statement of Cost of Goods Manufactured and Sold

Illustration 7.5 contains the statement of cost of goods manufactured and sold for the Brice Company for the month of July 19x3. It shows the costs incurred during the month for materials, labor, and overhead and describes this total as *"Cost to manufacture."* By adding to this amount the July 1 inventory and subtracting the July 31 inventory of work in process, the *"Cost of goods manufactured"* (completed) during the period is shown. When the July 1 finished goods inventory is added to this amount, the *"Cost of goods available for sale"* is obtained. This amount less the July 31 fin-

Illustration 7.5
Statement of Cost of Goods Manufactured and Sold

BRICE COMPANY
Statement of Cost of Goods Manufactured and Sold
For the Month Ended July 31, 19x3

Direct materials		$ 30,000
Direct labor		60,000
Manufacturing overhead:		
Indirect labor	$15,000	
Building depreciation	5,500	
Utilities	4,000	
Payroll taxes	3,500	
Equipment rent	2,500	
Insurance	2,000	
Property taxes	1,500	
Repairs	1,000	35,000
Cost to manufacture		$125,000
Work in process, July 1, 19x3		20,000
		$145,000
Work in process, July 31, 19x3		35,000
Cost of goods manufactured		$110,000
Finished goods, July 1, 19x3		40,000
Cost of goods available for sale		$150,000
Finished goods, July 31, 19x3		25,000
Cost of goods sold		$125,000

ished goods inventory yields the *"Cost of goods sold."* At this stage, note the following similarity:

Merchandiser: Beginning merchandise inventory + Purchases − Ending merchandise inventory = Cost of goods sold.

Manufacturer: Beginning finished goods inventory + Cost of goods manufactured − Ending finished goods inventory = Cost of goods sold.

Careful attention should be paid to the terminology used in the statement of cost of goods manufactured and sold. Note the similarity between "Cost to manufacture" and "Cost of goods manufactured." *"Cost to manufacture"* consists of the costs of all the resources put into production in the period. *"Cost of goods manufactured"* consists of the cost of the goods completed and includes "Cost to manufacture" and the change in the work in process inventory from the beginning to the end of the period.

A Graphic Summary

The discussion of a manufacturer's activities that lead to the recognition of net income is summarized in Illustration 7.6. Several implications of the accounting for such activities are worth stressing again.

Illustration 7.6
A Manufacturing Company's Total Operations

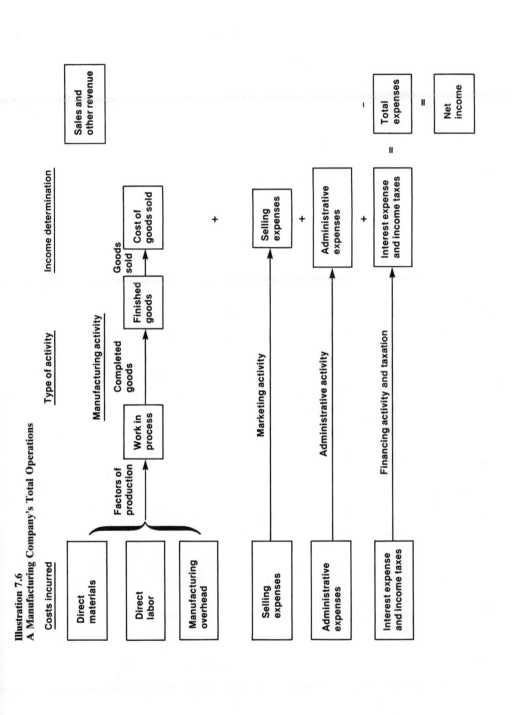

First, the accounting for the costs of manufacturing operations is an integral part of the overall accounting system of the manufacturer. No separate system is used to accumulate manufacturing cost information.

Second, as Illustration 7.6 shows, manufacturing costs are considered product costs, are attached to the products manufactured, and are run through work in process and finished goods inventories. They are recognized as expenses when the products to which they attach are sold. Selling and administrative costs are treated as period costs and expensed in the period in which they are incurred.

MANUFACTURING OVERHEAD RATES

To focus on the general pattern of cost flows shown in Illustration 7.3, certain problems in accounting for manufacturing overhead were not discussed. These problems arise primarily because the costs of a wide variety of factory services having no common physical basis of measurement must be allocated to many different products. By their nature and for practical reasons, such costs are not traceable to or identifiable with any given unit of product.

Before attention is directed to these problems, the terms *cost center, production center,* and *service center* must be introduced and defined. A *cost center* is an accounting unit of activity for accumulating costs spent for a common objective. For example, the costs incurred in the assembly department of a furniture manufacturer resulted from the assembly of furniture and can, therefore, be allocated to the products assembled. A cost center in which work is performed on units of product is called a *production center.* A *service center* is a cost center in which work indirectly related to the goods produced is performed. A toolroom, maintenance department, power plant, and even the company cafeteria are examples of service centers.

Predetermined Overhead Rates

Most medium and large manufacturing firms plan and, as a part of their planning, use budgets as goals or guides for managers. In those firms, overhead costs may be predetermined or estimated at the beginning of a period and included in a budget rather than calculated at the end of a period, as was assumed in the previous discussion. In the following discussion, predetermined or budgeted *overhead rates* are examined.

A *predetermined* overhead rate is used to allocate only overhead to production and is set at the beginning of the year. The reasons for this common practice include:

1. Overhead costs are seldom incurred uniformly throughout the year as, for example, heating costs will be large in winter. No useful purpose is served in allocating less cost to a unit produced in the summer than to one produced in the winter.

2. The volume of goods produced may vary from month to month, with accompanying sharp fluctuations in average unit cost if some overhead costs are fixed.
3. Unit costs of production are known sooner. Using a predetermined rate, overhead costs can be assigned to production when direct materials and direct labor costs are assigned. Without a predetermined rate, unit costs would not be known until the end of the month or even much later if bills for overhead costs are late.
4. Some overhead costs may be better viewed as losses due to inefficiencies rather than costs properly assigned to units of product.

How predetermined overhead rates are computed. The mechanics of computing predetermined overhead rates are the same as those used for actual rates except for the use of budgeted rather than actual levels of costs and levels of activity. Budgeted overhead costs are estimated and charged to various cost centers. Budgeted service center costs are then reassigned to production centers. Budgeted production center costs are then divided by the estimated activity to compute the predetermined rates. These budget estimates will normally be available as part of the company's budgeting process.

As an example, if the expected level of activity is 60,000 direct labor-hours and budgeted overhead is $570,000, the predetermined overhead rate is:

$$\text{Predetermined overhead rate} = \frac{\text{Total estimated overhead}}{\text{Total expected direct labor-hours}}$$

$$= \frac{\$570,000}{60,000 \text{ hours}} = \$9.50 \text{ per direct labor-hour}$$

Sometimes direct labor costs or machine-hours are used as the activity base in the determination.

Underapplied or overapplied overhead. When overhead is applied to production using predetermined rates, the manufacturing overhead account is credited with *estimated* amounts applied to work in process inventory because the rate is based on estimates when it is established. Under these circumstances, it is highly unlikely that the actual costs debited to the account will exactly equal the overhead credited to the account. A *debit balance* will remain if actual overhead exceeds applied overhead and overhead will be *underapplied* or *underabsorbed*. A *credit balance* will remain if applied overhead exceeds actual overhead, and overhead will be *overapplied* or *overabsorbed*.

Referring to Illustration 7.3, if overhead is allocated to production using a predetermined rate of 50 percent of direct labor cost, entry 6, given earlier, would be:

Work in Process Inventory		Manufacturing Overhead	
Bal. xxx			30,000
30,000			

Since $35,000 of actual overhead costs were charged to Manufacturing Overhead, the account would have a $5,000 debit balance representing underapplied overhead for the period.

Reasons for underapplied or overapplied overhead. Underapplied or overapplied overhead may result from unexpected events such as price changes, a severe winter, or excessive repairs. Or it may result from the inefficient use of overhead items. But underapplied overhead is more likely to be caused by incurring costs at a higher level than that set in the typical "tight" budget. On the other hand, overapplied overhead is likely to result from operations at a higher actual level than that used in setting the overhead rate and from the existence of fixed overhead costs.

Disposition of underapplied or overapplied overhead. Any under- or overapplied overhead balance may be carried forward in interim balance sheets if the probability exists that it will be reduced or offset by future operations. At year-end, any remaining balance could be allocated to Work in Process Inventory, Finished Goods Inventory, and Cost of Goods Sold by recomputing the cost of production for the year, using actual overhead rates.

As an alternative, charging underapplied overhead off as a period loss is possible if it results from idle capacity or from unusual circumstances. But, as a practical matter, underapplied or overapplied overhead is frequently transferred to Cost of Goods Sold by accountants. Little distortion of net income or of assets results from this treatment if the amount transferred is small or if most of the goods produced during the year were sold.

COST ACCUMULATION SYSTEMS

This chapter has dealt with (1) manufacturing costs and their general flow pattern, (2) the application of overhead to production, and (3) the reporting of operations of a manufacturing company. Little attention was paid to the procedures and accounting records used by accountants in accumulating costs or to the determination of unit costs for units of product. How these costs are determined depends upon the type of cost system employed.

Attention now is directed to the two major types of cost accumulation systems—the *job order cost* system and the *process cost* system. In each system, the goal is to determine the unit costs of the products manufactured. Unit costs are needed not only to determine the cost of the goods sold and the cost of the ending inventories of work in process and finished goods but also to determine payments to be received under contracts based on "full" cost and to set selling prices.

Job Order Cost Systems

When a *job order cost system* (job costing) is used, costs are accumulated by individual jobs or batches of output. A job may consist of 1,000 chairs, 10 sofas, 5 miles of highway, a single machine, a dam, or a building. A job cost system is generally used when the products being manufactured can be separately identified or when goods are produced to meet a customer's particular needs, such as constructing a house. Job costing is also used in other types of construction, motion pictures, and job printing.

Under job order costing, an up-to-date record of the costs incurred on a job is kept on a job order cost sheet in order to provide management with cost data on a timely basis (see Illustration 7.7). For example, a manager

Illustration 7.7
Job Order Cost Sheet

Job Order Sheet (Product DG)   Job No. 106

Date	Direct Materials	Direct Labor	Manufacturing Overhead
July 1 During July	$4,200 3,000 ——— $7,200	$ 5,000 5,000 ——— $10,000	$4,000 4,000 ——— $8,000
	Job completed (4,000 units of Product DG @ $6.30). Total cost, $25,200.		

may want to know the cost of producing 100 units of product "DG" when the units are completed. The manager can also receive reports as often as desired, even daily, on such matters as materials used, labor costs incurred, goods completed, total and detailed production costs, and whether production costs are in line with expectations.

The job order cost sheet is the key document or record in the job order cost system. It serves as a backup source (subsidiary record) for the Work in Process account and is used to accumulate all of the costs incurred in the manufacture of a job. After the job is complete, the job order sheet is transferred to the completed job file with its information on units and unit costs recorded in subsidiary finished goods records.

The general flow of costs through the accounting system of a firm using a job order cost system is shown in Illustration 7.8. This illustration is similar to Illustration 7.3, which showed how the *dollars* of cost flow through a job order system.

Illustration 7.8
Job Order System Cost Flows

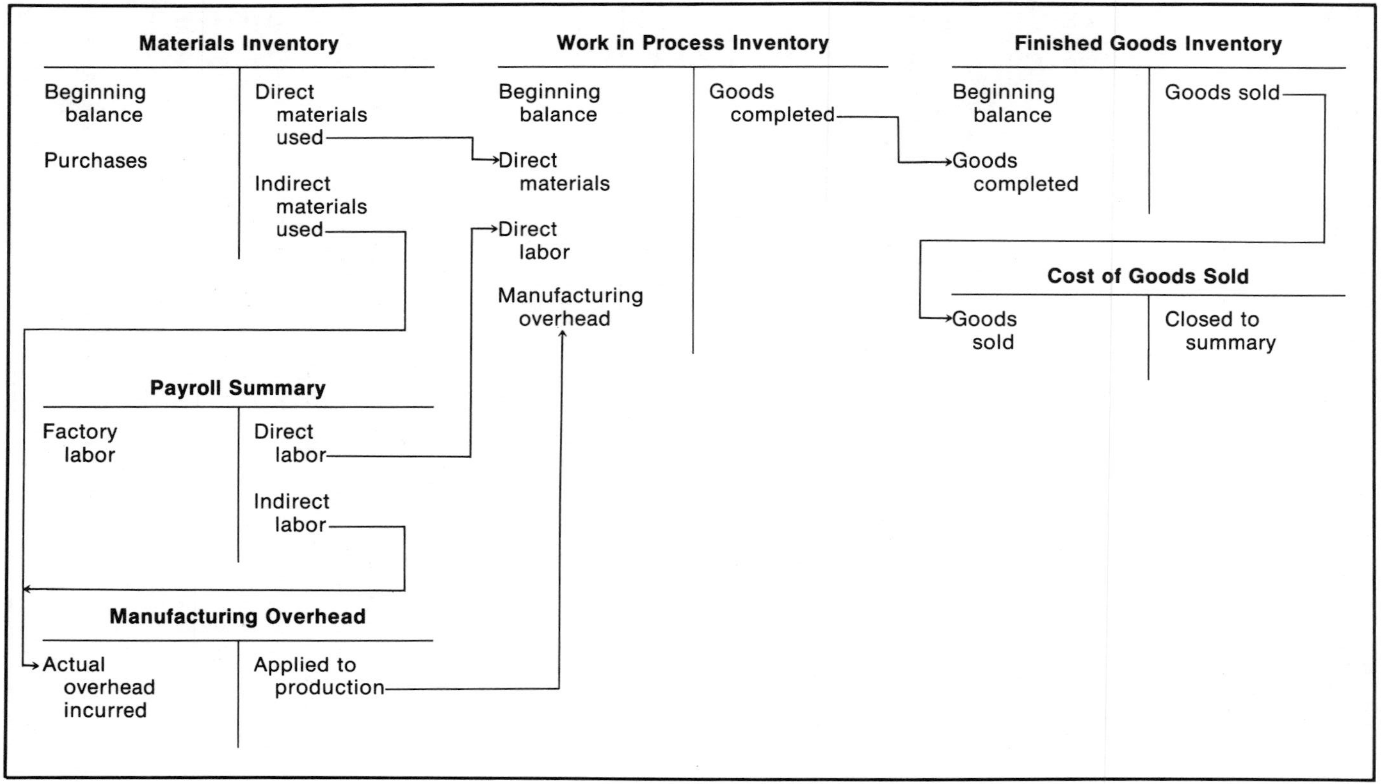

Process Cost Systems

Many business firms manufacture huge quantities of a single product or similar products (paint, paper, chemicals, gasoline, rubber, and plastics) continually over long periods of time. There is no separate job or specific batch of units. Since there is no job, job costs cannot be accumulated. Rather, costs must be accumulated for each process which a product undergoes on its way to completion. This calls for another type of cost system, one that yields unit costs by *processes* or by departments for *stated periods of time* rather than by jobs without regard to time periods. Here the processes or departments serve as cost centers for which costs are accumulated for the entire period (month, quarter, or year). These costs are divided by the number of equivalent whole units (tons, pounds, gallons, or feet) produced to get a broad, average unit cost. Such a system is known as a *process cost system* (*process costing*).

Basic system design.   Process cost systems have the same general design as that shown in Illustration 7.8. Costs of the factors of production are first recorded in separate accounts for materials inventory, labor, and overhead. These costs are then transferred to work in process inventory. A process cost system usually has more than one work in process inventory account. Such an account is kept for each processing center in order to determine the unit cost of each process. All products manufactured may be subjected to the same processing in a specified *sequential* order, as depicted in Illustration 7.9. The products are started in Department A, processed, transferred to Department B, processed further, and then transferred to finished goods inventory.

Cost of production report.   A cost of production report is prepared for each processing center at the end of each period (usually one month). It shows how many units have been charged to a department and whether these units have been completed and transferred out or remain in ending work in process inventory. Similarly, it shows the costs charged to a department (either currently or brought forward from previous periods). The report may also contain computations of equivalent whole units, the costs of units transferred, and the cost of the ending work in process inventory. An example of a cost of production report is shown in Illustration 7.10. All amounts are assumed.

Equivalent units.   Essentially, the concept of *equivalent units* shown in Illustration 7.10 involves expressing a given number of partially completed units as a smaller number of fully completed units. For example, if 1,000 units are brought to a 50 percent state of completion, they are the equivalent of 500 units that are 100 percent complete. The assumption is that the same amount of costs must be incurred to bring 1,000 units to a 50 percent level of completion as would be required to complete 500 units.

Illustration 7.9
Cost Flows in a Process Cost System

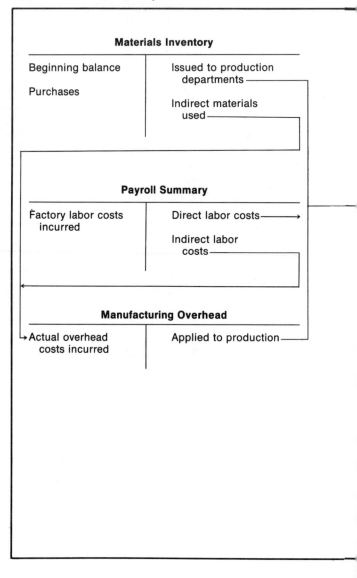

In Illustration 7.10, the equivalent units for materials and conversion (labor and overhead) may vary. The 24,000 units in the ending work in process inventory are 100 percent complete as to materials and 60 percent complete as to conversion. Thus, the equivalent whole units in the May 31 inventory are 24,000 units for materials and 14,400 (24,000 × 0.6) for conversion. Under the average cost method, the total equivalent units for materials and for conversion consist of the units completed and transferred plus the

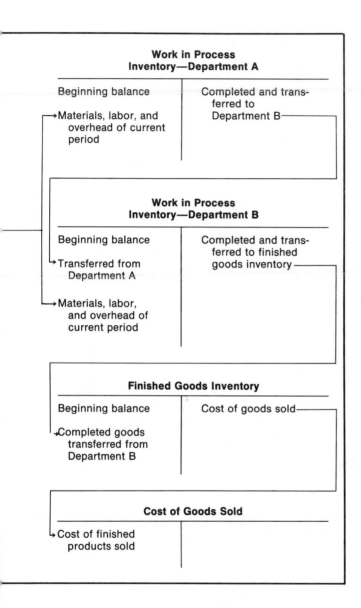

**Work in Process
Inventory—Department A**

Beginning balance	Completed and trans- ferred to Department B
Materials, labor, and overhead of current period	

**Work in Process
Inventory—Department B**

Beginning balance	Completed and trans- ferred to finished goods inventory
Transferred from Department A	
Materials, labor, and overhead of current period	

Finished Goods Inventory

Beginning balance	Cost of goods sold
Completed goods transferred from Department B	

Cost of Goods Sold

Cost of finished products sold	

equivalent whole units in ending work in process inventory for that compo-
nent. The equivalent whole units are then divided into costs to be accounted
for in arriving at unit costs for the month. These unit costs are used to
determine the cost of units in the ending inventory and the cost of units
transferred out. For instance, in Illustration 7.10, the cost of units transferred out is 106,000 units × $7.80 = $826,800. The cost of the ending
inventory is:

	Equivalent Units	Unit Cost	
Transferred in...............	24,000	$6.00	$144,000
Materials..................	24,000	0.60	14,400
Conversion	14,400	1.20	17,280
Total cost.............			$175,680

Illustration 7.10
Cost of Production Report

AFA, INC.
Finishing Department
Cost of Production Report
For the Month Ended May 31

		Equivalent Units		
	Actual Units	Transferred In	Materials	Conversion
Units:				
Units in May 1 inventory	30,000			
Units transferred in	100,000			
Units to be accounted for.......	130,000			
Units completed and transferred...............	106,000	106,000	106,000	106,000
Units in May 31 inventory*....	24,000	24,000	24,000	14,400
Units accounted for....	130,000	130,000	130,000	120,400

* Inventory is complete as to materials, 60 percent complete as to conversion.

	Transferred-In Costs	Cost of Materials Used in Conversion	Conversion Costs	Total Cost
Costs:				
Costs to be accounted for:				
Costs in May 1 inventory ...	$180,000	$ 25,000	$ 35,000	$ 240,000
Costs transferred in	600,000			600,000
Costs added in department		53,000	109,480	162,480
Costs to be accounted for.......	$780,000	$ 78,000	$144,480	$1,002,480
Equivalent units (as above)...	130,000	130,000	120,400	
Unit costs	$6.00	$0.60	$1.20	$7.80
Costs accounted for:				
Costs in May 31 inventory ..	$144,000	$ 14,400	$ 17,280	$ 175,680
Costs transferred out	636,000	63,600	127,200	826,800
Costs accounted for ...	$780,000	$ 78,000	$144,480	$1,002,480

The transferred-in units shown in Illustration 7.10 represent the units transferred into the Finishing Department from some other department which worked on the units previously. The transferred-in costs are the costs which were incurred in that other department and are now passed on to the Finishing Department as a cost of the units to be included in total cost of the units.

Questions

1. Identify the three broad classifications of costs incurred by manufacturing firms. Indicate why it is important that these costs be correctly classified.
2. Identify the three elements of cost incurred in manufacturing a product, and indicate the distinguishing characteristics of each.
3. Why might a firm claim that the total cost of employing a person is $10.30 per hour even though the employee's wage rate is $6.50 per hour? How should this difference be classified, and why?
4. In general, what is the relationship between cost flows in the accounts and the flow of physical products through a factory?
5. What is meant by the term *product cost*? State the general principle under which product costs are accumulated.
6. What is the general content of a statement of cost of goods manufactured and sold? What is its relationship to the income statement?
7. What is the typical accounting for the overtime wage premium paid a direct laborer? Why? Under what circumstances might an alternative accounting be considered preferable?
8. Why are certain costs referred to as period costs? What are the major types of period costs incurred by a manufacturer?
9. What deficiencies do you see in an accounting system that assigns the actual overhead incurred in a month to the production of that month?
10. Why would the manufacturing overhead rate be determined prior to the year in which it is used?
11. What is a manufacturing overhead rate? Why is the application of overhead to production through the use of such a rate almost a necessity?
12. What is the reason, other than errors in estimating costs, for overapplied overhead?
13. When overhead is applied to production via a predetermined overhead rate, is it correct to speak of the per unit product costs computed as actual costs?
14. Indicate the possible dispositions of a balance in the Manufacturing Overhead account and the reasoning or circumstances in which each would seem preferable.
15. What is the basic purpose of any costing system?
16. In what respects does a process cost system differ from a job order cost system? What factors should be taken into consideration in determining which type of system should be employed?
17. What is a job order sheet? Explain how it is used.
18. What is the basic information reported in a cost of production report?

Exercises

1. During a given week, $60,000 of direct materials and $5,000 of indirect materials were issued by the storeroom to the production department. Give the required T-account entries.

2. As prepared by the payroll department, the week's factory labor payroll amounted to $116,000. Analysis of the payroll shows that it consists of $98,000 of direct labor and the following wages and salaries: inspectors, $3,800; supervisors, $2,200; electricians, $3,200; timekeepers, $2,400; janitors, $3,600; warehousemen, $2,800; and the Payroll Summary account has the $116,000 as a debit balance. Give the T-account entries to distribute the labor costs and their distribution to the proper accounts.

3. Given below are some costs incurred by an automobile manufacturer. Classify these costs as direct materials, direct labor, manufacturing overhead, selling, or administrative.

   a. Salary of the cost accountant.
   b. Cost of automobile radios installed in autos.
   c. Cost of stationery used in president's office.
   d. Supplies used in cost accountant's office.
   e. Wages of a factory inspector.
   f. Payroll taxes on assembly-line worker's wages.
   g. Repair parts used to repair factory machine.
   h. Cost of labor services to install radios in autos.
   i. Depreciation on automobiles driven by company's top executives.
   j. Cost of magazines purchased for the engineering department.

4. Review the list of costs in Exercise 3, and indicate which of the listed costs is likely to vary directly with the number of autos produced.

5. The following data pertain to the Z Company for the year ended June 30, 19x2:

Direct materials used	$200,000
Direct labor	400,000
Work in process, 7/1/x1	40,000
Work in process, 6/30/x2	60,000
Finished goods, 7/1/x1	100,000
Finished goods, 6/30/x2	140,000
Manufacturing overhead	600,000

   Compute the cost of goods manufactured and sold.

6. Joe Smith was paid for 48 hours of work as a carpenter for Home Constructors, Inc., for last week. His total wages amounted to $312—40 hours at $6 per hour plus 8 hours of Saturday work at $9 per hour (time and a half). He worked 32 hours of regular time on House 124 and 8 hours of regular time and 7 hours of overtime on House 125. He was idle one hour on Saturday waiting for materials to be delivered. Saturday work is common in the construction industry during good weather.

   How much of the wages paid Joe Smith should be considered a cost of House 124? Of House 125? As manufacturing overhead? Explain.

7. Ace Company sells 25-inch television sets which it assembles from purchased parts. In 19x1, it purchased 10,000 picture tubes at $30 each. Of these 10,000 tubes, 25 were used by Ace in testing their product life (an indirect factory cost), 5 were used to replace burned-out tubes in display models, and 9,000

were issued to production. Of the 9,000 placed in production, 7,000 were in units completed, of which 6,000 were sold.

As of December 31, 19x1, how much of the $300,000 cost of purchased picture tubes would appear in each of the following accounts?
  a. Materials Inventory.
  b. Work in Process Inventory.
  c. Finished Goods Inventory.
  d. Manufacturing Overhead.
  e. Selling Expense.
  f. Cost of Goods Sold.

8. Z company estimated its overhead for 19x1 at $400,000 ($100,000 fixed and $300,000 variable) based on a normal activity of 200,000 direct labor-hours. At the end of 19x1, manufacturing overhead was overapplied by $3,000, while actual direct labor-hours amounted to 202,000. Analyze the $3,000 as to the reasons for its existence.

9. Assume that at the end of 19x1, in Exercise 8, the costs of the 202,000 actual direct labor-hours were lodged in the following accounts: Work in Process, 20,200 hours; Finished Goods, 50,500 hours; and Cost of Goods Sold, 131,300. Allocate the overhead balances to these accounts.

10. For each of the following cases (a through e), fill in the missing data as indicated by the blank spaces. Assume that overhead rates are based on estimated fixed overhead for long-run normal production.

Case	Overhead Rate	Estimated Overhead	Estimated Production (in Units)	Actual Production (in Units)	Overhead Applied
a.	$5	$ _____	25,000	_____	$130,000
b.	___	90,000	_____	27,000	81,000
c.	___	210,000	30,000	31,000	_____
d.	6	_____	40,000	35,000	_____
e.	8	160,000	_____	_____	144,000

11. Job No. 210 has, at the end of the second week in February, an accumulated total cost of $4,200. In the third week, $1,000 of direct materials were used on the job, together with $10 of indirect materials; 200 hours of direct labor were charged to the job at $5 per hour; and manufacturing overhead was applied on the basis of $2.50 per direct labor-hour for fixed overhead and $2 per hour for variable overhead. Job No. 210 was the only job completed in the third week. Compute the cost of Job No. 210.

12. In Department A, materials are added uniformly throughout processing. The ending inventory was considered 50 percent complete as to materials and conversion. There were 3,000 units in the ending inventory, and 16,000 units were completed and transferred. If average unit costs are to be computed, what is the equivalent production for the period?

13. In Exercise 12, the total costs charged to the department amounted to $70,000, including the cost of the beginning inventory, what is the cost of units completed and transferred?

Business Decision Problem 7–1

A number of costs that would affect business decisions in the factory operations of different companies are listed below. These costs may be fixed or variable with respect to some measure of volume or output and may be classified as direct materials (DM), direct labor (DL), or manufacturing overhead (MO).

1. Glue used to attach labels to bottles containing a patented medicine.
2. Compressed air used in operating machines turning out products.
3. Insurance on factory building and equipment.
4. A production department supervisor's salary.
5. Rent on factory machinery.
6. Iron ore and coke in a steel mill.
7. Oil, gasoline, and grease for forklifts.
8. Services of painters in building construction.
9. Cutting oils used in machining operations.
10. Cost of food in a factory employees' cafeteria.
11. Payroll taxes and fringe benefits related to direct labor.
12. The plant electricians' salaries.
13. Sand in a glass manufacturer.
14. Copy editor's salary in a book publisher.

Required:

a. List the numbers 1 through 14 down the left side of a sheet of paper. After each number, write the letters V (for variable) or F (for fixed) and DM (for direct materials), DL (for direct labor), or MO (for manufacturing overhead) to show how you would classify the similarly numbered cost item given above for your firm.
b. With which of your own answers given for part *a* could you take issue? Discuss.

Business Decision Problem 7–2

Partial income statements for the Detroit division of Clair Company for 19x1 and 19x2 have shown identical results, as follows:

Sales (5,000 units @ $80)		$400,000
Cost of goods sold:		
Variable costs (at $20 per unit)	$100,000	
Fixed costs	240,000	340,000
Gross margin		$ 60,000

Other expenses of the division have amounted to slightly more than $60,000 so that the division has contributed small losses to overall corporate earnings.

A new manager, June O'Donnell, has been placed in charge of the division. She believed it would be possible to reduce the division's inventory from its current level of 2,000 units (at $68 each) to 1,000 units because of some changes made in production processing. Therefore, she ordered the production of 4,000 units in 19x3. Sales volume, selling prices, and fixed overhead are expected to remain unchanged, but variable costs are expected to run $19 per unit because of the changes made. The company sets overhead rates based on expected activity for the coming year, and uses the FIFO inventory method.

Required:

a. Assuming expectations for 19x3 are realized exactly, prepare a partial income statement for the year.

b. Explain why the actions taken by Ms. O'Donnell did (or did not) lead to increased income for the division.

Solutions to End-of-Chapter Questions, Exercises, and Business Decision Problems

Answers to Questions

1. A manufacturing firm's costs may be broadly classified as (1) manufacturing or production, (2) selling or marketing, and (3) administrative or general. In general, costs should be correctly classified according to cost objectives, or the wrong decisions may be made. More specifically, selling and administrative costs should not be misclassified as manufacturing costs since the latter are inventoried, while the former are expensed as incurred. Assets and net income may be misstated as a result.

2. Manufacturing, factory, or product cost consists of the cost of direct materials, direct labor, and manufacturing overhead. Direct materials are the ingredients physically incorporated into the product and traceable to the product. Direct labor consists of the services of employees actually working on the product and traceable to or identifiable with the product. Manufacturing overhead includes all other services, supplies, and materials incurred to produce a product.

3. Many costs other than the wages paid are incurred in employing a person. These include: payroll taxes, pensions, medical and life insurance plan premiums, and vacation pay. These costs generally should be classified as manufacturing overhead, especially those that are incurred on only the first few thousands of dollars of wages earned within a year, such as unemployment insurance. If these costs are traced directly to production, a different labor cost rate would be used for products manufactured early in the year compared with those manufactured later in the year, after the cutoff level is reached.

4. The flow of costs through the accounts such as Work in Process Inventory, Finished Goods Inventory, and Cost of Goods Sold parallels the flow of physical products through the production department to the finished goods warehouse and on to delivery to customers.

5. Product cost consists of those costs incurred to create or manufacture the finished product, as distinguished from costs incurred to sell the product or to administer the activities of a firm. The general product costing principle states that the cost of manufacturing a product consists of the direct materials costs and direct labor costs, plus a fair share of the indirect costs incurred to produce it.

6. The statement of cost of goods manufactured and sold shows the costs of direct materials used, direct labor, and manufacturing overhead, together with beginning and ending work in process inventories to yield cost of goods manufac-

tured. This figure together with the change in finished goods inventory yields cost of goods sold. The statement is a supporting schedule to the income statement, giving the details of the cost of goods sold item.

7. The overtime wage premium paid a direct laborer is accounted for as part of manufacturing overhead. This is done to avoid penalizing the products that *by chance* happened to be produced in the overtime period with a cost that should be borne by all of the units produced. But overtime premiums paid on rush orders for customers could be charged to those orders, especially if the customer were willing to pay for them.

8. Certain costs are referred to as period costs because their relationship to the products manufactured is quite remote and difficult to trace and measure. For this reason, such costs are matched against revenue on a time basis rather than a product basis. All of a manufacturer's selling and administrative costs are generally accounted for as period costs. Interest expense and federal income taxes are also period costs.

9. The basic deficiencies of assigning the actual overhead incurred in a month to that month's production are: (1) per unit costs may fluctuate sharply because of seasonal patterns in production volume or in overhead cost incurrence; and (2) product cost information (available under actual costs only after the end of the month) may be too late to be of maximum utility. Also, the procedure outlined applies to product costs that may be better viewed as losses from inefficiencies or idle capacity.

10. When an overhead rate is predetermined, product costs are available when production is completed. This makes it less likely that monthly per unit costs will be computed. Such costs are subject to wide variation, as noted in the answer to Question 9.

11. An overhead rate is a means of applying indirect factory costs to the units of product manufactured. Such a rate must be used (either actual or predetermined) because there are few situations where the units produced are homogeneous enough to permit applying overhead to products by dividing total overhead for a period by units produced. Thus, some indirect method must be used—an overhead rate.

12. Overapplied overhead usually results from charging too much fixed costs because the production level was higher than the level used in setting overhead rates.

13. Probably the best that can be said is that the per unit product costs computed are approximations of the actual costs. The per unit costs obtained are actual costs only in the sense that they are averages for a year (or longer). Such costs may exclude some minor costs represented by underapplied overhead and may include what some accountants would consider idle capacity losses. Whether they are actual costs may be questioned also by noting the difficulty in determining the periodic amount of some overhead costs, such as depreciation.

14. Underapplied overhead, if due to inefficiencies or idle capacity, is best viewed as a period loss and charged off immediately. It can be carried forward if future operations are expected to absorb any overhead balance, either under- or overapplied. If underapplied overhead results from sources beyond the control of the firm, such as price changes, it should be allocated to the production of the period as a valid cost of such production. The practical treatment of charging such underapplied overhead, then, is theoretically proper only if it results from

noncontrollable additions to cost, if it is not due to idle capacity, and if all of the units produced during the year were sold.

15. The basic purpose of any costing system is to accumulate costs incurred in order to compute per unit costs of manufactured products. This information is needed for financial reporting and income taxation, and it may be useful for other purposes, such as pricing and determining reimbursement under contracts.

16. A process cost system accumulates unit product costs for each of the various processes a product undergoes on its way to completion in a given time period. In a job order system, costs are accumulated by jobs or by batches of product rather than by processes. A process cost system would accumulate costs to determine the cost of assembling all of the washing machines produced in a given period of time, for example. On the other hand, the job order system would be concerned with the total cost and the unit cost of all the washing machines produced as a given lot or batch, without specific regard to the cost of the assembly operation.

   The volume of production and the homogeneity of product are the two main criteria to be taken into consideration in determining whether to employ a process cost system or a job order cost system. The process cost system is especially suitable for accumulating costs when a standard product is mass-produced. Manufacturing cigarettes is an excellent example.

17. The job order sheet is the key document or record in the job order cost system. It serves as a subsidiary record to the Work in Process account and is used to accumulate all of the costs, direct and indirect, incurred in the manufacture of a job. After the job is completed, the job order sheet is transferred to the completed job file, with its information on units and unit costs recorded in subsidiary finished goods records.

18. A cost of production report shows the total units charged to a department and how these units were accounted for. Similarly, it shows the costs charged to a department (either currently or brought forward from previous periods) and how these costs were accounted for. The report may also contain as supplementary information computations of equivalent units, the cost of units transferred, and the cost of the ending inventory.

Solutions to Exercises

1.

Work in Process Inventory		Manufacturing Overhead		Materials Inventory	
Bal. xxxx		5,000		Bal. xxxx	
60,000					65,000

2.

Work in Process Inventory		Manufacturing Overhead		Payroll Summary	
Bal. xxxx				Bal. 116,000	
98,000		18,000			116,000

3. Direct materials: *b*.
   Direct labor: *h*.
   Manufacturing overhead: *a, d, e, f, g,* and *j*.
   Selling: None.
   Administrative: *c* and *i*.
4. The variable costs probably include only *b* and *h*, and *f* up to a certain point.

5.

Direct materials used	$ 200,000
Direct labor	400,000
Manufacturing overhead	600,000
Cost to manufacture	$1,200,000
Work in process, 7/1/x1	40,000
	$1,240,000
Work in process, 6/30/x2	60,000
Cost of goods manufactured	$1,180,000
Finished goods, 7/1/x1	100,000
Goods available for sale	$1,280,000
Finished goods, 6/30/x2	140,000
Cost of goods sold	$1,140,000

6.

Labor cost charged to House 124: 32 × $6		$192
Labor cost charged to House 125: 15 × $6		90
Labor cost charged to manufacturing overhead:		
Overtime premium: 8 × $3	$24	
Idle time: 1 × $6	6	30
Total wages earned		$312

The overtime premium and the idle-time pay are both treated as manufacturing overhead so as not to burden specific projects with costs that were not caused directly by the projects.

7. The following accounts should contain the following amounts of the $300,000:

Materials inventory, 970 × $30	$ 29,100
Work in process inventory, 2,000 × $30	60,000
Finished goods inventory, 1,000 × $30	30,000
Manufacturing overhead, 25 × $30	750
Selling expense, 5 × $30	150
Cost of goods sold, 6,000 × $30	180,000
Total cost of tubes purchased	$300,000

8. Assuming fixed costs were incurred at their budgeted level, the $3,000 of overabsorbed overhead appears to be due to:

Overabsorbed fixed overhead (2,000 hours @ $0.50)	$1,000
Excess of variable overhead applied over actual variable overhead	2,000
Total overabsorbed overhead	$3,000

9.

Cost of goods sold (131,300/202,000)	$1,950
Work in process (20,000/202,000)	300
Finished goods (50,500/202,000)	750
	$3,000

10. The missing data for each case are:
    a. $125,000; 26,000.
    b. $3; 30,000.
    c. $7; $217,000.
    d. $240,000; $210,000.
    e. 20,000; 18,000.

11.

Accumulated total cost at beginning of third week............		$4,200
Costs added to complete:		
Direct materials	$1,000	
Direct labor (200 hours @ $5)	1,000	
Variable overhead (200 hours @ $2)	400	
Fixed overhead (200 hours @ $2.50)....................	500	2,900
Total cost of completed job........................		$7,100

12. For computation of average unit costs, equivalent production is 17,500 [16,000 + (0.5 × 3,000)].

13. 16,000 × ($70,000/17,500) = 16,000 × $4 = $64,000 cost of units transferred.

Solution to Business Decision Problem 7–1

a.

1.	V	MO.	8.	V	DL.
2.	V	MO.	9.	V	MO.
3.	F	MO.	10.	V	MO.
4.	F	MO.	11.	V	MO.
5.	F	MO.	12.	F	MO.
6.	V	DM.	13.	V	DM.
7.	V	MO.	14.	F	MO.

b. This problem is certain to evoke considerable discussion and probably some disagreement with the above classification. Certain costs, such as 1, 2, and 9, are direct materials costs that are accounted for frequently as manufacturing overhead. Other costs, such as 7 and 11, may be partially variable or at least not directly variable with number of hours of operation and with direct labor cost, respectively.

Solution to Business Decision Problem 7–2

a.

CLAIR COMPANY
Detroit Division
Partial Income Statement
For Year Ended December 31, 19x3

Sales (5,000 at $80).............................		$400,000
Cost of goods sold:		
2,000 at $68 (beginning inventory)..............	$136,000	
3,000 at $79*...............................	237,000	373,000
Gross margin.................................		$ 27,000

* Per unit production costs for 19x1 are:		
Variable costs—4,000 × $19......................	$ 76,000	
Fixed costs	240,000	
Total ($79 each for 4,000 units)................	$316,000	

b. The new manager's action did not lead to increased income because per unit production costs increased from $68 to $79. This was caused by an increase of $12 per unit [($240,000/4,000) − ($240,000/5,000)] in the amount of fixed overhead allocated to each unit produced, which was offset by the $1 per unit decrease in variable costs per unit, leaving a net increase of $11. Since 3,000 of the higher-cost units were sold, $33,000 of additional costs were included in cost of goods sold. This $33,000 reduced the gross margin of $60,000 to $27,000.

   Note: The problem automatically leads to another question: How might the accounting for the above have been changed in order to avoid showing such a negative result from what is apparently such a desirable action? A partial answer is: By the use of a normalized overhead rate (a rate utilizing an average of the level of activity that is expected to prevail over a longer period of time such as three to five years). But this is not a complete answer. With normalized rates, the question remains of what to do with the underabsorbed overhead for the year. If production and sales are stabilized at 5,000 units per year, it will never be absorbed. This may lead to a special write-off later.

PART THREE

Planning and Performance Analysis

8

Control through Standard Costs

Chapter Goals

When you have completed Chapter 8, you should be able to:

1. Explain (*a*) what standard costs are, (*b*) how standard costs are set, and (*c*) the advantages of using standard costs in a cost system.
2. Compute six variances from standard for materials, labor, and overhead.
3. Explain reasons for the existence of variances and how the principle of management by exception is applied through the use of standard costs.
4. Illustrate theoretical and practical ways of disposing of variances from standard after they have attracted management attention that may have resulted in corrective action.

STANDARD COSTS

Some managers have *standard costs* for the entire cost of products to be manufactured over upcoming accounting periods. The cost systems discussed thus far are called actual cost systems and gather and allocate historical cost data. Some believe these historical data provide neither adequate information about how efficiently operations were conducted nor a good measure of a manager's performance. Therefore, standard costs are used so that actual costs may be compared with them. Standard costs can be used in both job order cost systems and process cost systems. This introductory section discusses the nature and advantages of using standard costs.

Nature of Standard Costs

A *standard cost* is a carefully predetermined measure of what a cost *should be* under stated conditions. It is more a goal than a mere estimate of what a cost will be. If a standard is properly set, achieving the standard represents a reasonable level of performance.

Standards may be set in many ways, but to be of any value they must be more than mere estimates derived from extending historical trends into the future. Usually, engineering and time and motion studies are undertaken to determine the material, labor, and services required to produce a unit of product. Knowledge of the actual working conditions in a plant is required. Also, general economic conditions must be studied because they will affect the costs of the materials and services that must be purchased.

The goal is to set a standard cost for each unit of product to be manufactured by determining the "proper" or standard costs of the direct materials, direct labor, and factory overhead needed to produce it. The standard direct materials cost is made up of a standard number of units of each material required multiplied by a standard price for each. Similarly, the standard direct labor cost consists of the standard number of hours of direct labor needed multiplied by the standard labor or wage rate. The standard overhead cost of a unit is usually based upon a predetermined rate which is computed from standard (budgeted) overhead costs and standard production, although it may be expressed as a rate per unit of some measure of activity such as direct labor-hours. In both a standard cost system and an actual cost system, overhead is assigned to production through use of a predetermined rate. The two systems differ in that an actual cost system collects actual costs for materials and labor, while a standard cost system gathers standard costs and transfers these costs through the system into finished goods.

Advantages of Using Standard Costs

A number of benefits result from the use of a standard cost system, including: (1) cost control, (2) provision of information useful in managerial planning and decision making, (3) more reasonable inventory measurements, (4) cost savings in record keeping, and (5) possibly some reductions in the costs incurred.

Cost control is secured largely by setting standards for each type of cost incurred—materials, labor, and overhead. Accountants record the amounts by which actual costs differ from standard in *variance* accounts. These variances provide a starting point in judging the effectiveness of managers in controlling the costs they incur and for which they may be held responsible. For such purposes, for example, it is far more useful to know that actual direct materials costs of $52,015 in a certain center exceeded standard by $6,015 than merely to know that actual materials costs amounted to $52,015. Thus, a standard cost system highlights *exceptions,* that is, instances where things are not going as planned. Further investigation will show whether an exception is caused by factors under management's control or not. For example, the exception (the variance) may be caused by inefficient use of materials, or it may be the result of inflation. In either case, the standard cost system has served as an early warning system by highlighting a potential problem for management. On the other hand, little attention is usually paid to actual costs when such costs differ only slightly from standard.

If management develops appropriate standards and succeeds in controlling costs, future actual costs should be fairly close to standard. When this is true, standard costs can be used in preparing budgets and in estimating costs for bidding on jobs.

In a standard cost system, all units of a given product are carried in inventory at the same unit cost. It seems logical that physically identical units should have the same cost. Cost savings in record keeping may result through use of printed forms containing standard quantities and standard costs. But under an actual cost system, unit costs for batches of identical products may differ because more labor and overhead were assigned to one batch simply because a machine was out of adjustment when the batch was produced. Under a standard cost system, such costs would not be included in inventory. Rather, they would be charged to variance accounts, discussed below.

The use of standard costs as a managerial efficiency tool may cause employees to become cost-conscious and to seek improved methods of completing their tasks. This, hopefully, will result in cost savings.

COMPUTING VARIANCES

A variance exists when actual costs differ from standard costs. A variance is *favorable* when actual costs are less than standard costs, and *unfavorable* when actual costs exceed standard. It does not follow automatically that these terms should be equated with good and bad, as will be explained. Such an appraisal should be made only after the causes of the variance are known.

Variances cannot serve as essential elements in cost control until they have been isolated. Therefore, attention is directed first to the computation of the dollar amount of a variance. The discussion and illustrations that follow are based upon the activities of the Gamma Company which manufactures and sells a single product with the following standard costs:

Materials—5 sheets @ $6	$30
Direct labor—2 hours @ $10.	20
Manufacturing overhead—2 direct labor-hours @ $5	10
Total standard cost per unit	$60

Additional data regarding the productive activities of the company is presented as needed. The six cost variances examined are:

Material price and usage.

Labor rate and efficiency.

Overhead volume and budget.

Materials Variances

The standard materials cost of any product is simply the standard *quantity* of materials that should be used multiplied by the *price* that should be paid for those materials. Actual costs may differ from standard costs for materials because of the *quantity* of materials used or the *price* paid for the materials. This suggests the need to isolate two variances for materials—*price* and *usage*. But there are other reasons for isolating these two variances. First, different individuals may be responsible for each—a purchasing agent for the price variance and a production manager for the usage variance. Second, the materials may not be purchased and used in the same period. For good cost control, the variance associated with the purchase should be isolated in the period of purchase and the variance associated with usage should be isolated in the period of use. As a general rule, the sooner a variance can be isolated, the greater is its value in cost control. And, finally, it is unlikely that a single materials variance—the difference between the standard cost and the actual cost of the materials used—would be of any real value to management, because the variance may arise from either price or usage.

Materials price variance. The standard price for material meeting certain engineering specifications is usually set by the purchasing and accounting departments. Consideration should be given to such factors as market conditions, vendors' quoted prices, and the optimum size of a purchase order. Purchasing materials at a price other than standard gives rise to a *materials price variance*. The materials price variance (MPV) is the difference between actual price (AP) and standard price (SP) multiplied by the actual quantity (AQ) of materials purchased. In equation form, the materials price variance is:

$$MPV = (AP - SP) \times AQ$$

To illustrate, assume that the Gamma Company was able, because of the entry into the market of a new foreign supplier, to purchase 60,000 sheets of material at a price of $5.90 each, for a total cost of $354,000. Since the standard price is $6 per sheet, the materials price variance, using the formula, is:

$$
\begin{aligned}
\text{MPV} &= (\text{AP} - \text{SP}) \times \text{AQ} \\
&= (\$5.90 - \$6.00) \times 60,000 \\
&= -\$0.10 \times 60,000 \\
&= -\$6,000
\end{aligned}
$$

The materials price variance of $6,000 is considered favorable since the materials were acquired for a price less than standard. If the actual price had exceeded the standard price, the variance would be considered unfavorable because more costs were incurred than were allowed by the standard. The accountant's entry to record the purchase of the materials is:

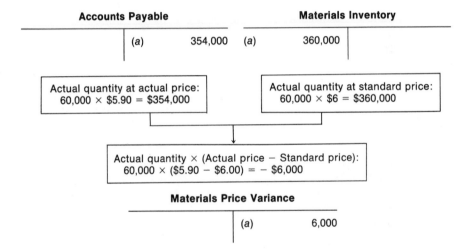

The Accounts Payable account shows the actual debt owed to suppliers; the Materials Inventory account shows the *standard price* of the actual quantity of materials purchased; and the Materials Price Variance account shows the difference between actual price and standard price multiplied by the actual quantity purchased.

Materials usage variance.   Since the standard quantity of materials to be used in making a product is largely a matter of physical aspects or product specifications, that quantity is usually set by the engineering department. But if the quality of materials used varies with price, the accounting and purchasing departments may take part in special studies to find the "right" quality.

The *materials usage variance* shows whether the amount of materials used was more or less than the standard amount. It shows only differences from standard caused by the quantity of materials used; it does not include price variances. The materials usage variance (MUV) is equal to actual quantity used (AQ) minus standard quantity prescribed (SQ) multiplied by standard price (SP):

$$MUV = (AQ - SQ) \times SP$$

To illustrate, assume that the Gamma Company used 55,500 sheets of materials to produce 11,000 units of a product for which the standard quantity is 55,000 sheets (5 × 11,000). Since the standard price of the material is $6 per sheet, the materials usage variance of $3,000 would be computed as:

$$
\begin{aligned}
MUV &= (AQ - SQ) \times SP \\
&= (55,500 - 55,000) \times \$6 \\
&= 500 \times \$6 \\
&= \$3,000
\end{aligned}
$$

The variance is unfavorable because more materials than the standard were used to complete the job. If the standard quantity had exceeded the quantity actually used, the materials usage variance would have been favorable. The entry used by the accountant to record the use of materials is:

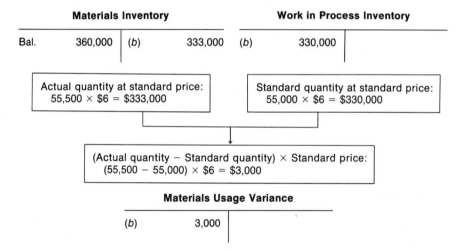

The Materials Usage Variance account shows the standard cost of the excess materials used. The Work in Process Inventory account contains standard quantities and standard prices.

The equations for both of the materials variances were expressed so that positive amounts were unfavorable variances and negative amounts were favorable variances. But greater understanding is achieved if a variance is determined to be favorable or unfavorable by reason or logic. If more materials than standard had been used, or if a price greater than standard had been paid, the variance is unfavorable. If the reverse had been true, the variance would have been favorable.

Labor Variances

The standard labor cost of any product is equal to the standard quantity of labor time prescribed multiplied by the wage rate that should be paid for this time. The actual labor cost may differ from the standard labor cost because of the *quantity* of labor used or the *wages* paid for labor, or both. Both of the labor variances relate to the same accounting period because labor services cannot be purchased in one period, stored, and then used in the next period.

Labor rate variance.   The *labor rate variance* shows how much the actual labor cost of a product differed from its standard cost because actual pay rates differed from standard rates. In this respect, it is similar to the materials price variance. Typically, actual wage rates are set in bargaining between a firm and the employees' union.

The labor rate variance (LRV) is computed by multiplying the difference between the actual rate (AR) paid and the standard rate (SR) by the actual hours (AH) of labor services received:

$$LRV = (AR - SR) \times AH$$

To continue the Gamma Company example, assume that the direct labor payroll of the company consisted of 22,200 hours and a total cost of $233,100 (an average actual hourly rate of $10.50). With a standard labor rate of $10 per hour, the labor rate variance is:

$$
\begin{aligned}
LRV &= (AR - SR) \times AH \\
&= (\$10.50 - \$10.00) \times 22{,}200 \\
&= \$0.50 \times 22{,}200 \\
&= \$11{,}100
\end{aligned}
$$

The variance is positive and unfavorable since the actual rate paid exceeded the standard rate allowed. If the reverse had been true, the variance would have been favorable. How an accountant would record the variance will be shown after the labor efficiency variance has been illustrated and discussed.

Labor efficiency variance.   The *labor efficiency (or time) variance* is, in effect, a quantity variance. It shows whether the actual labor time required to complete a period's output or a given job was more or less than the standard amount allowed. The standard amount of labor time needed to complete a product is usually set by the firm's engineering department. It may be based on time and motion studies, and it may be the subject of bargaining with the employees' union.

The labor efficiency variance (LEV) is computed by multiplying the difference between the actual hours (AH) required and the standard hours (SH) prescribed by the standard rate (SR) per hour, or:

$$LEV = (AH - SH) \times SR$$

To illustrate, assume that the 22,200 hours of labor time received from its employees by the Gamma Company resulted in production with a standard labor time of 22,000 hours. Since the standard labor rate is $10 per hour, the labor time variance is $2,000 (unfavorable), computed as:

$$
\begin{aligned}
LEV &= (AH - SH) \times SR \\
&= (22,200 - 22,000) \times \$10 \\
&= 200 \times \$10 \\
&= \$2,000
\end{aligned}
$$

The variance is unfavorable because more hours than standard were required to complete the period's production. If the reverse had been true, the variance would have been favorable.

A graphic illustration may aid in understanding the relationship between standard and actual labor cost and the computation of the labor variances. Illustration 8.1 (deliberately not drawn to scale) is based upon the following data relating to the Gamma Company:

Standard labor time per unit..	2 hours
Equivalent units produced in period	11,000 units
Standard labor rate per direct labor-hour........................	$10
Total direct labor wages paid (at average rate of $10.50 per hour)....	$233,100
Actual direct labor-hours received..............................	22,200 hours

The standard labor time for the period's output was 22,000 hours (11,000 units at 2 hours per unit). The standard labor cost of the output was $220,000

Illustration 8.1
Computation of the Labor Variances

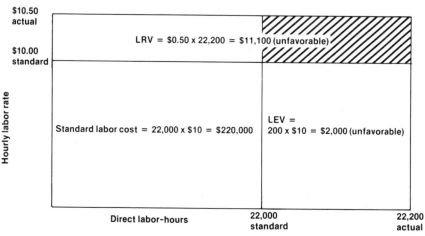

(22,000 hours at $10 per hour, the standard labor rate). The labor efficiency variance is the standard cost of the extra hours of labor required [(22,200 − 22,000) × $10], or $2,000. The actual labor rate is $10.50 per hour. The labor rate variance, then, is the 50 cents per hour ($10.50 − $10.00) of above-standard wages paid multiplied by the standard hours allowed (22,000), and, by common practice, the above-standard wages paid per hour on the extra hours required (200) represented by the shaded area in the upper right-hand corner of the rectangle. The variation from standard shown by this shaded area is actually caused by both extra hours and above-standard wages per hour. But, as shown, it is included in the labor rate variance, since this variance is based on actual hours worked.

The entry used by accountants to charge the Work in Process Inventory account with direct labor cost and to set up the two labor variances for the Gamma Company would be:

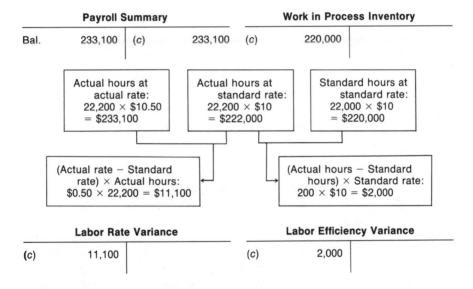

With the above entry, the gross wages earned by direct production employees ($233,100) are distributed as follows: $220,000 (the standard labor cost of the production) to the Work in Process Inventory account and the balance to the two labor variance accounts. The labor rate variance is not necessarily caused by paying employees more wages than they are entitled to receive. The more likely reason is that employees with different pay rates can complete the same task and that too much of the higher hourly rated employee time was used on a given job. Also, if some overtime premium pay is expected in setting standards, then variation from expected amounts can cause a labor rate variance. But, typically, the hours of labor employed are more likely to be under the control of management, and for this reason the labor efficiency variance is watched more closely.

Summary of labor variances. The accuracy of the computation of the two labor variances can be checked readily by comparing their sum with the difference between actual and standard labor cost for a period. In the Gamma Company illustration, this difference was:

Actual labor cost incurred	$233,100
Standard labor cost allowed..........................	220,000
Total labor variance (unfavorable)	$ 13,100

This $13,100 is made up to two labor variances, both unfavorable:

Labor efficiency variance (200 × $10)...................	$ 2,000
Labor rate variance (22,200 × $0.50)...................	11,100
Total labor variance (unfavorable)	$13,100

Overhead Variances

In a standard cost system, overhead is applied to the goods produced by means of a standard overhead rate. This rate is set prior to the start of the period through use of a flexible overhead budget. This budget is called a flexible (or variable) budget because it shows the budgeted amount of overhead for various levels of output or volume. Total budgeted overhead will vary as output varies because some overhead costs are variable. But the fixed nature of some overhead costs means that total overhead will not vary in direct proportion with output.

The flexible budget for the Gamma Company for the period is shown in Illustration 8.2. It shows the overhead costs expected to be incurred at three levels of activity: 90 percent, 100 percent, and 110 percent of capacity. For product costing purposes, one level of activity is chosen and a rate set based on that level. The level chosen is called the standard volume of output. This standard volume of output may be expressed in terms of percent of capacity, units of output, and/or direct labor-hours. In the Gamma Company example, it is assumed to be at 100 percent of capacity, at which level 10,000 units are expected to be produced and 20,000 direct labor-hours of services are expected to be used. The standard overhead rate, then, is $5 per direct labor-hour (and consists of $2 per hour of variable overhead and $3 per hour of fixed overhead). Standard overhead rates per direct labor-hour at 100 percent of capacity are:

Variable ($40,000 ÷ 20,000 hours)	$2
Fixed ($60,000 ÷ 20,000 hours)	3
Total standard manufacturing overhead rate per hour..............	$5

To continue the illustration, assume that the Gamma Company incurred $108,000 of actual manufacturing overhead costs in the period in which 11,000 units of product were produced and for which the standard labor allowed is 22,000 hours. These actual costs would be debited to Manufactur-

Illustration 8.2
Flexible Overhead Budget

GAMMA COMPANY
Flexible Manufacturing Overhead Budget

	90%	100%	110%
Percent of capacity	90%	100%	110%
Direct labor-hours	18,000	20,000	22,000
Units of output.....................	9,000	10,000	11,000
Variable overhead:			
Indirect materials	$ 7,200	$ 8,000	$ 8,800
Power...........................	9,000	10,000	11,000
Royalties	1,800	2,000	2,200
Other	18,000	20,000	22,000
Total variable overhead	$36,000	$ 40,000	$ 44,000
Fixed overhead:			
Insurance........................	$ 4,000	$ 4,000	$ 4,000
Property taxes.....................	6,000	6,000	6,000
Depreciation	20,000	20,000	20,000
Other	30,000	30,000	30,000
Total fixed overhead.............	$60,000	$ 60,000	$ 60,000
Total manufacturing overhead..........	$96,000	$100,000	$104,000

ing Overhead and credited to a variety of accounts such as Accounts Payable, Accumulated Depreciation, Unexpired Insurance, and Accrued Property Taxes Payable. The entry to record the application of $110,000 of overhead to production (22,000 hours @ $5 per hour) would be:

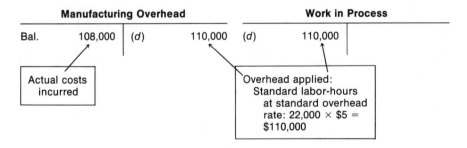

The $2,000 credit balance in the Manufacturing Overhead account shows that manufacturing overhead has been overapplied to production. This balance is also called the *net overhead variance*. It can be divided into a number of variances, two of which are illustrated: the overhead volume variance and the overhead budget variance.

The overhead volume variance. The *overhead volume variance* (OVV) results from a combination of two factors: (1) the existence of fixed overhead costs and (2) operation at a level of activity different from that used in setting the standard overhead rate. It shows whether plant assets were used more or less than expected. It is computed as the difference between (*a*) the budgeted overhead (BO) for the standard direct labor allowed for the actual volume achieved and (*b*) the applied overhead (App. O). Hence:

Overhead volume variance = Budgeted overhead − Applied overhead
$$OVV = BO - App. O$$

In the Gamma Company illustration, the 11,000 units produced in the period have a standard labor allowance of 22,000 hours. The flexible budget in Illustration 8.2 shows that the budgeted overhead for 22,000 direct labor-hours is $104,000. The applied overhead is 22,000 hours at $5 per hour, or $110,000. The overhead volume variance is:

$$
\begin{aligned}
OVV &= BO - App. O \\
&= \$104,000 - \$110,000 \\
&= -\$6,000
\end{aligned}
$$

This variance is considered favorable because applied fixed overhead absorbed in the period's output exceeded the budgeted fixed overhead for the period. That the variance is favorable can also be seen from the fact that the period's output (11,000 units) exceeded the standard volume (10,000) that was used in setting the standard overhead rate.

The overhead budget variance. The *overhead budget variance* (also called the spending or controllable variance) shows in one amount how efficiently operations were conducted in the sense of the prices paid for and the amounts of the overhead services used. It shows for overhead a variance that is similar to a combined price and usage variance for materials or labor. The overhead budget variance (OBV) is equal to the difference between total actual overhead costs (Act. O) and total budgeted overhead costs (BO) for the *actual* output attained. Since the total actual overhead was $108,000 and the total budgeted overhead was $104,000 (from Illustration 8.2) for 11,000 units (22,000 standard direct labor-hours), the overhead budget variance is computed as:

$$
\begin{aligned}
OBV &= Act. O - BO \\
&= \$108,000 - \$104,000 \\
&= \$4,000
\end{aligned}
$$

The variance is unfavorable because the actual overhead costs were $108,000, while, according to the flexible budget, they should have amounted to only $104,000.

If desired, a formal entry can be made in the accounts showing the two parts of the net overhead variance ($4,000 from OBV and −$6,000 from OVV). The overhead budget variance is recorded as a debit in an account of that title because the $4,000 variance is unfavorable. And the $6,000 favorable overhead volume variance is recorded as a credit in an account of that title. The accounts then contain an analysis of the net overhead variance.

Investigating Variances from Standard

Once variances have been isolated, management must decide which ones should be investigated. Since so many variances occur, they cannot all be investigated. Management selects some guidelines to examine variances. Possible guidelines include: (1) the absolute size of the variance; (2) the size of the variance relative to the cost incurred; and (3) the type of cost incurred, that is, whether it is considered controllable or noncontrollable. The opinions of knowledgeable operating personnel are usually sought in setting guidelines.

Statistical analysis may also be used in deciding which variances to investigate. For instance, the mean (average) value of actual costs would be determined for a period of time and only future variances which deviate from the mean by more than a certain amount or percentage would be investigated.

Any analysis of variances is likely to disclose some variances that are controllable within the company and others that are not. Prices paid for materials purchased may be largely beyond the control of the buyer. But amounts used may be controllable internally. Also, although separate variances are isolated, they are not always as independent as they may appear. An unfavorable labor rate variance may result from using higher-paid employees in a certain task; but this may result in a favorable labor efficiency variance from greater productivity and possibly a favorable materials usage variance because the more skilled employees caused less spoilage. Variances should be investigated carefully before being used to appraise the performance of a given individual or department.

Disposing of Variances from Standard

At the end of the year, variances from standard may be (1) viewed as losses due to inefficiency and closed to the Income Summary account; (2) allocated as adjustments of the recorded cost of work in process inventory, finished goods inventory, and cost of goods sold; or (3) closed to the Cost of Goods Sold account. As a practical matter, and especially if they are small, the variances are usually closed to the Cost of Goods Sold account rather than allocated. They typically are unfavorable (due to the common practice of setting "tight" standards). This tends to reduce reported net income for the period below the amounts that would otherwise be reported if the variances were treated as cost elements and allocated to the inventory accounts and Cost of Goods Sold.

Variances are not reported separately in statements released to the public. They are simply included in the reported amount for cost of goods sold.

In statements prepared for internal use, the variances may be listed separately after the amount for cost of goods sold at standard cost.

Questions

1. Is a standard cost an estimated cost? What is the primary advantage of employing standard costs in a cost system? What are some other advantages of using standard costs?
2. How does the use of standard costs permit the application of the principle of management by exception?
3. What are some of the problems surrounding the interpretation of variances in a standard cost system?
4. Describe how to compute the materials price and usage variances from the following data:

   Standard—1,000 units at $20 per unit.
   Purchased—1,200 units at $20.25; used—995 units.

5. What might be a plausible explanation for a given company having a substantial favorable materials price variance and a substantial unfavorable materials usage variance?
6. What is the usual cause of a favorable or unfavorable labor-rate variance? What other labor variance is isolated in a standard cost system? Of the two variances, which is more likely to be under the control of management? Explain.
7. Identify the type of variance indicated by each situation below and whether it is a favorable or unfavorable variance.
   a. The cutting department of a company during the week ending July 15 cut 12 size S cogged wheels out of three sheets of 12-inch high-tempered steel. Usually, three wheels of such size are cut out of each sheet.
   b. A company purchased and installed a new expensive cutting machine to handle expanding orders. This purchase and the related depreciation had not been anticipated when the overhead rate was set.
   c. Edwards, the band saw operator, was on vacation last week. Lands took his place for the normal 40-hour week. Edwards' wage rate is $5.40 per hour, while Lands's is $5.20 per hour. Production was at capacity last week and the week before.
8. Is the overhead budget variance essentially a "price" or a "usage" variance? Explain.
9. Theoretically, how should variances from standard be disposed of? What is their usual practical disposition?
10. Would you expect the overhead volume variance normally to be favorable or unfavorable? Explain.
11. How do standard costs aid in control?

Exercises

1. During the month of May, a department completed 2,000 units of a product which had a standard material cost of 4,000 square feet at $0.40 per square foot. The actual material used consisted of 4,050 square feet at a cost of $1,660.50.

Compute the materials usage and materials price variances, and indicate clearly whether each is favorable or unfavorable.

2. Compute the labor variances in the following circumstances:

Actual direct labor payroll (19,800 hours)	$81,180
Standard labor allowed per unit, 4 hours at $4.............	16
Equivalent production for the month (in units).............	5,000

3. During March, 100 units of a given product were produced. These units have a standard labor cost of one hour in Process A at $4 per hour and of two hours in Process B at $3.50 per hour. Assume that Couch worked 95 hours on Process A during the month for which he earned $418 and that Willard worked 205 hours on Process B for which he earned $697. Compute the labor cost variances for each process.

4. The following relate to the manufacturing activities of the Winter Company for the month of May 19x1:

Standard activity (units)	50,000
Actual production (units)	40,000
Budgeted fixed overhead	$30,000
Variable overhead rate (per unit)..............	2
Actual fixed overhead	30,400
Actual variable overhead.....................	78,300

Compute the overhead budget variance and the overhead volume variance.

5. In Exercise 4, if the actual production had been 65,000 units, what would the overhead volume variance have been?

Business Decision Problem 8–1

The standard cost variance accounts of the Martin Company at the end of its fiscal year had the following balances:

Materials usage variance (unfavorable).................	$ 4,000
Materials price variance (unfavorable)	5,000
Labor rate variance (favorable).......................	3,000
Labor efficiency variance (unfavorable)	11,000
Overhead volume variance (unfavorable)	6,000
Overhead budget variance (favorable).................	1,000

Give a possible reason for the existence of each of the variances listed.

Business Decision Problem 8–2

Dave Walker, the president of the Korner Company, has a problem. It does not involve substantial dollar amounts, but it does involve the important question of responsibility for variances from standard costs. He has just received the following report:

Total materials costs for the month of May (6,900 pounds @ $2.40 per pound)	$16,560
Unfavorable materials price variance ($2.40 − $2.00) × 6,900 pounds	(2,760)
Unfavorable materials usage variance (6,900 pounds − 6,000 pounds) × $2...	(1,800)
Standard materials at standard price for the actual production in May	$12,000

Dave has discussed the unfavorable price variance with Betty Branch, the purchasing officer. She agrees that under the circumstances she should be held responsible for most of the materials price variance. But she objects to the inclusion of $360 (900 pounds of excess materials used @ $0.40 per pound). This, she argues, is the responsibility of the production department. If it had not been so inefficient in the use of materials, she would not have had to purchase the extra 900 pounds. On the other hand, Mike Volan, the production manager, agrees that he is basically responsible for the excess quantity of materials used. But he does not agree that the above materials usage variance should be revised to include the $360 of unfavorable price variance on the excess materials used. "That's Betty's responsibility," he says.

Dave now turns to you for help. Specifically, he wants you to tell him:

a. Who is responsible for the $360 in dispute?
b. If responsibility cannot be clearly assigned, in which price variance should the accounting department include the variance? Why?
c. Are there likely to be other circumstances where materials variances cannot be considered the responsibility of the person who is most likely to be considered responsible for them? Explain.

Solutions to End-of-Chapter Questions, Exercises, and Business Decision Problems

Answers to Questions

1. A standard cost is not an estimate in the sense of being an estimate of what a cost *will be*. Rather, it is a projection or model of what a cost *should be*. Thus, a much higher degree of sophistication in approach is implied in establishing the standard than would normally be employed in making an estimate.

   The primary advantage of using standard costs is to give management criteria against which to compare the actual costs incurred either as production takes place or shortly thereafter. With variances isolated and subject to further investigation that may lead to corrective action, costs are kept under control.

   Other advantages of using standard costs include some clerical cost savings; provision of information that may be useful in managerial planning, especially as it relates to incremental analysis and budgeting; and, perhaps, some overall reduction in total costs through greater awareness of costs on the part of employees.

2. Through the system of isolating variances from standard in separate accounts, management attention is directed toward the exception rather than the routine in the production process; and it is the exception rather than the routine that may require further management action.

3. The first problem is simply that of deciding which variances are to be investigated, since there are so many that management cannot deal with all of them individually. A second problem is that the cause of a variance may lie far afield from the department or center in which it is brought to light; for example, the purchase of inferior material may cause a favorable price variance on materials but may also cause an unfavorable labor time variance because the inferior material is hard to process.

4. The materials price variance is an unfavorable $300 (1,200 × $0.25). The materials usage variance is a favorable $100 (5 × $20).

5. The company may have purchased inferior materials at a substantial reduction from the standard price. But when the materials were placed in production, substantial quantities may have been discarded in attempting to secure the necessary amount having the desired quality. Thus, an unfavorable usage variance emerges.

6. The rates paid to an employee are usually determined well in advance of the time he or she actually works. Thus, a labor rate variance will usually result from temporarily assigning an employee with an hourly rate different from standard to a given task.

   A labor efficiency variance is also isolated that emerges when the standard labor cost of the production for a period or on a given job is more or less than the standard amount allowed.

   The labor efficiency variance is more likely to be under management control, since pay rates are often set in collective bargaining. Actual production could be influenced by such things as working conditions, employee attitude and morale, production scheduling, quality of materials used, and similar factors under management control.

7. (a) Favorable materials usage variance; (b) unfavorable overhead budget variance; (c) favorable labor rate variance.

8. Actually the overhead budget variance is both a "price" and a "usage" variance combined into one variance. It shows the difference between actual variable overhead and budgeted variable overhead for the actual production of the period, and this difference could arise from both "price" and "usage" factors. Similarly, it includes the "price" variance on the fixed overhead.

9. Theoretically, each variance should be analyzed and the reason for its existence determined. Then, if it can be determined, for example, that the variance was completely beyond management control, such as a materials price variance might be, the variance should be allocated to the production of the period. If, on the other hand, the variance emerges because of mistakes and inefficiencies in using materials or in scheduling production, the variance should be treated as a loss due to inefficiency and charged to the Income Summary account. Because it is often difficult to draw this distinction, the practical approach of charging variances to the period emerges.

10. There is a probability of both favorable and unfavorable variances if expected activity is used, but the probabilities seem to favor unfavorable variances since expectations may be set a little high to motivate employees.

11. A standard cost system highlights exceptions, instances where things are not going as planned. The identification of variances serves as an early warning system for management. It points out potential problem areas for closer analysis. In this way, it assists management in controlling operations.

Solutions to Exercises

1. Materials price variance:
   4,050 × $0.01 ($1,660.50 ÷ 4,050 = $0.41; $0.41 − $0.40 = $0.01) . . . $40.50 U*
   Materials usage variance:
   (4,050 − 4,000) × $0.40 . . . .   20.00 U

   Total variance . . . . $60.50 U

   * U denotes unfavorable variance.

2. Labor rate variance:
    19,800 × $0.10 ($81,180 ÷ 19,800 = $4.10; $4.10 − $4.00 = $0.10) .. $1,980 U
    Labor usage variance:
    (19,800 − 20,000) × $4.00 .... 800 F*
       Total variance ($81,180 − $80,000) .... $1,180 U

3. Process A (Total variance is $418 − $400 = $18 unfavorable):
    Labor efficiency variance: 5 hours @ $4 .... $20.00 F
    Labor rate variance: ($4.40 − $4.00) × 95 hours .... 38.00 U
       Total variance .... $18.00 U

   Process B (Total variance is $700 − $697 = $3 favorable):
    Labor efficiency variance: 5 hours @ $3.50 .... $17.50 U
    Labor rate variance: ($3.50 − $3.40) × 205 hours .... 20.50 F
       Total variance .... $ 3.00 F

4. Overhead budget variance:
    Actual fixed overhead .... $ 30,400
    Actual variable overhead   78,300
       Actual overhead $108,700
    Budgeted fixed overhead $30,000
    Budgeted variable overhead (40,000 × $2) 80,000   110,000
       Overhead budget variance (favorable) ....   −$ 1,300

    Overhead volume variance:
    Budgeted overhead $110,000
    Applied overhead (40,000 × $2.60)   104,000
       Overhead volume variance (unfavorable) .... $ 6,000

5. Budgeted overhead $160,000
   Applied overhead (65,000 × $2.60)   169,000
       Overhead volume variance (favorable) ....   −$ 9,000

   * F denotes favorable variance.

Solution to Business Decision Problem 8–1

Variance	Possible Reasons
Unfavorable materials usage variance	Employees used wasteful work habits in performing the work.
Unfavorable materials price variance	The purchasing agent did not investigate the best sources for acquiring the materials.
Favorable labor rate variance	The work was performed by less skilled, lower-paid workers than were envisioned when the standard rate was set.
Unfavorable labor efficiency variance	Less skilled workers performed the work.
Unfavorable overhead volume variance	A strike was called, causing actual production to be less than the level planned when the standard overhead rate was set.
Favorable overhead budget variance	Employees turned off lights when these were not needed, and the thermostat was turned down from 72° to 68°.

There are other plausible explanations for variances which might be mentioned.

Solution to Business Decision Problem 8–2

a. Both the purchasing officer and the production manager are responsible for the $360 cost of excess materials used since it was caused by paying too much per pound and by using too many pounds.

b. This variance is generally attached to the materials price variance. The materials price variance is calculated when the materials are purchased. By assigning any difference in cost (from standard cost) to the materials price variance, the accountant is able to carry the standard cost of the materials in the Materials Inventory account. The materials usage variance is not calculated until the materials are placed in production. If the combination price-quality variance of $360 were to be charged to the materials usage variance, the accountant would have to record more than the actual quantity times the standard price in the Materials Inventory account when the materials are purchased. Under a standard cost system, the inventory accounts generally are maintained at standard cost.

c. Yes. Such a situation exists where the purchasing agent buys inferior materials and the workers use more than the standard quantity as a result.

9

Responsibility Accounting and Segmental Analysis

Chapter Goals

When you have completed Chapter 9, you should be able to:

1. Explain the nature and purposes of a responsibility accounting system.

2. Differentiate among expense centers, earnings centers, and investment centers and explain the conditions under which each is used as a responsibility center.

3. Illustrate concepts which are used in segmental analysis, such as direct cost, indirect cost, net income of a segment, and contribution to indirect expenses.

4. Illustrate how responsibility reports are prepared for different levels of management and how these reports relate to each other, and explain how responsibility reports motivate individuals and facilitate control over operating results.

5. Explain the arbitrary nature of allocations of indirect fixed expenses.

6. Calculate return on investment (ROI) and explain the various meanings of *earnings* and *investment* and when each set of definitions should be used.

7. Explain how the concepts of margin and turnover are used in ROI calculations.

8. Illustrate how to calculate residual income (RI) and how residual income is used to prevent suboptimization.

9. Explain how transfer prices are established for segmental reporting purposes.

RESPONSIBILITY ACCOUNTING

Introduction

Supervisors, managers, and executives are often judged on their total job performance rather than just on their ability to control certain costs (such as overhead or standard costs). To meet the need for a broader benchmark for job performance, responsibility accounting systems have been developed. Responsibility accounting will be described first in this chapter, and then segmental analysis, the method of analysis used to develop responsibility accounting system reports, will be explained.

A *responsibility accounting* system seeks to provide information to evaluate each manager on the revenue or expense items over which that manager has primary *control* (the authority to influence). The fundamental principle of responsibility accounting is that *each accounting report contains only (or at least clearly segregates) those items which are controllable by the responsible manager.*

The business entity must be well organized so that responsibility is assignable to individual managers. Clear lines of authority and responsibility must exist throughout the organization—as shown in Illustration 9.1. If clear

Illustration 9.1
Illustration of a Corporate Functional Organization Chart Including Four Levels of Management

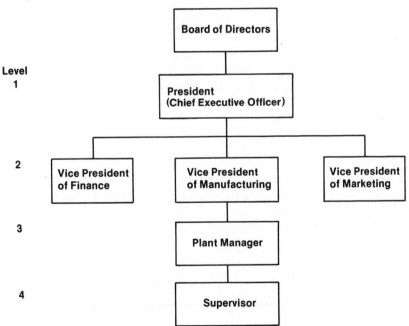

areas of authority cannot be determined, it is doubtful that responsibility accounting will be worthwhile or helpful.

Lines of authority should follow a specified path. For example, a plant supervisor may report to a plant manager, who reports to a vice president of manufacturing, who is responsible to the president (or chief executive officer—CEO). The CEO is ultimately responsible to the stockholders or their elected representatives, the board of directors. In a sense, the CEO is responsible for all revenue and expense items of the firm since at the CEO level all items are considered to be controllable. But the CEO will usually delegate authority to various managers since the CEO cannot keep fully apprised of the day-to-day operating details of each segment of the firm.

Reference here is made to levels of management. The CEO is usually considered the first-level manager. All the managers who report directly to the CEO are second-level managers. On the organization chart in Illustration 9.1, the individuals within a given level are on a horizontal line across the chart, but all managers within a certain level do not necessarily have equal authority and responsibility. The relative authority of certain types of managers will vary from firm to firm.

While the CEO may delegate much decision-making power, there are some revenue and expense items that may be exclusively under the CEO's control. For example, the CEO may be the only one who can approve large capital (plant and equipment) expenditures. In this case, depreciation, property taxes, and other related expenses should not be designated as the plant manager's responsibility since these costs are not primarily under the plant manager's control. The controllability of revenues and/or expenses criterion is crucial to the content of the reports for each manager. For example, at the supervisor level, perhaps only direct materials and direct labor are controllable items for measuring performance. But at the plant manager level, many other costs, not controllable at a lower level, are controllable and are therefore included in the responsibility accounting report and the performance evaluation of the plant manager.

The Concept of Control

A manager must be able to exercise primary control over an item before being held responsible for it. Unfortunately, controllability is rarely absolute. Frequently, some factors which change the amount of a budgeted item are beyond the control of a manager. For example, the imposition of a 10 percent excise tax by a governmental authority may decrease the sales of certain items in a particular segment. Even though the manager is given authority to control the sales revenue, external factors beyond the manager's control have altered the results, in this case. Internal factors may also be present. For example, raw material usage may be excessive because, in an effort to save money, the purchasing department bought low-quality materials. Most revenue or expense items have some elements of noncontrollability in them.

The theoretical requirement that a manager have absolute control over items for which that manager is held responsible is often compromised. The manager is usually responsible for items where *relative* control is present. *Relative control means that the manager has the predominant control over most of the factors which influence a given budget item.* The use of relative control may lead to some motivational problems, since managers are evaluated on results that may not reflect their efforts. Nevertheless, most plans recognize control on a relative basis in order to develop and use responsibility accounting.

Responsibility Reports

Responsibility accounting leads to reports on how managers are doing in the financial aspects of their job performance. These reports are typically referred to as *responsibility reports.* Any manager being judged by these reports must understand how reports issued for each level of management relate to each other, how noncontrollable items are handled in the reports, and the need for timeliness and simplicity in reporting.

How responsibility reports relate to each other.   A unique feature of a responsibility accounting system is the amount of detail in the various reports issued to the different levels of management. For example, a performance report to a particular supervisor would include the dollar amounts, actual and budgeted, of all the revenue and expense items under that supervisor's control. Thus, it may show the *controllable earnings of a segment.* But the report issued to the plant manager would show only the totals from all the supervisors' reports and any additional items subject to the plant manager's control, such as the plant administrative expense. The report to the vice president of manufacturing would contain only the totals of all the plants. Because a responsibility accounting system selectively condenses data, the report to the CEO shows only the summary totals of the reports from the subordinate levels (see Illustration 4.4). This lack of detail, which seems a hindrance to performance analysis, actually results in the practice of "management by exception." Since modern business enterprises are complex, it is necessary to filter and condense accounting data so that they may be analyzed quickly. Most executives do not have the time to study detailed accounting reports searching for problem areas. Reporting only summary totals highlights those areas that need attention so that the executive can make efficient use of available time.

The reports issued under the responsibility accounting system are interrelated since the totals from one level are carried forward in the report to the next higher management level. The reports submitted to the CEO include all revenue and expense items (in summary form) since the CEO is responsible for controlling the profitability of the entire firm.

The condensation which occurs at successively higher levels of management is justified on the basis that the appropriate subordinate manager will take the necessary corrective action. Hence, performance details need not be reported except to the particular manager. The manager should be able to describe to the immediate supervisor the action taken to correct an undesirable situation. For example, if direct labor cost has been excessively high in a particular department, the supervisor should seek to correct the cause of this variance. The plant manager, upon noticing the unfavorable total budget variance of the department, will investigate. The supervisor should be able to respond that appropriate corrective action was taken. Hence, it is not necessary to report to the vice president of manufacturing that a particular department within the plant is not operating satisfactorily, since the plant manager has already attended to the matter. If the plant as a whole under a plant manager has been performing poorly, then the summary totals which have been reported to the vice president of manufacturing will disclose this situation and an investigation of the plant manager's problems might be indicated.

Noncontrollable items.   There are two basic ways in which noncontrollable revenue or expense items at the manager's level are handled. First, these items may be omitted entirely from the reports and included only at the management level at which they become controllable. As a result, each report contains only those items which are controllable at that level. But some believe there is appeal in including all revenue and expense items which can be traced directly or allocated indirectly to a particular manager. This second method represents a full-costing approach. When full-costing reports are used, care must be taken to be sure that controllable items are separated from noncontrollable items.

Timeliness of reports.   For responsibility accounting reports to be of maximum benefit, they should be prepared as soon as possible after the end of the performance measurement period. Timely reports allow prompt corrective action to be taken. Reports that are delayed lose their effectiveness as control devices. For example, a report on the previous month's operations received at the end of the current month is virtually useless for taking corrective action. Reports should be issued promptly and regularly. Regular reports are desirable since such reports enable trends to be spotted. Thus, the appropriate management action can be initiated before major problems occur. Regularity is also an important means of getting managers to rely on the reports and become familiar with their contents.

Simplicity of reports.   The reports should be relatively simple and should avoid confusing terminology. Particularly at lower levels of management, aggregate dollar amounts may not be sufficient. Results should also be expressed in physical units when appropriate. It is desirable for a report to contain both budgeted and actual amounts. Often a year-to-date analysis is included in addition to material on the current period so that the manager can see performance to date. The use of variances is helpful in analyzing managerial performance and applying the management by exception principle. By carefully analyzing budget variances, the significant deviations from the budgeted plan are highlighted. Variance analysis allows management to spot problem areas quickly.

An illustration.   The following illustration is designed to show how responsibility accounting reports in an organization are interrelated.

Assume an organization with four management levels—the president, (CEO), vice president (manufacturing), plant manager, and supervisor (see Illustration 9.2). The fourth level is considered to be the supervisor, and so on, up to the first level, the president (as shown in Illustration 9.3).

The reports shown in Illustration 9.4 contain only the controllable expenses at each level. Only the totals from the supervisor's responsibility report are included in the plant manager's report. In turn, only the totals on

Illustration 9.2
Organization Chart

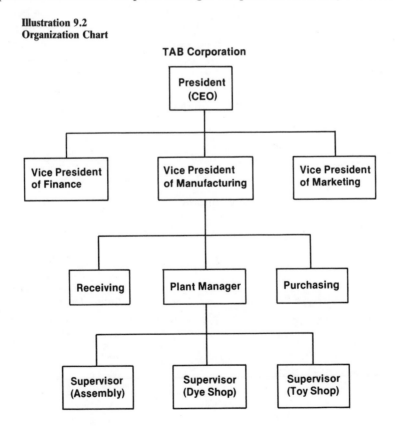

Illustration 9.3
Responsibility Reports

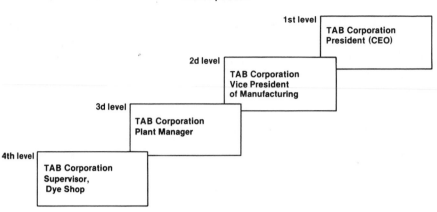

TAB Corporation

the plant manager's report are included in the report for the vice president, and so on. Detailed data from lower-level reports are summarized and carried onto the report for the next higher level. Also, new controllable costs are introduced into the reports for levels 3, 2, and 1 which were not included in the level 1 report. For instance, the president's office expense (included as the first item on the president's report) and the vice presidents' salaries were not reported at levels 1, 2, or 3 because these costs were not controllable at a lower level.

The reports also show variation from the budgeted amounts for the month and for the year to date.

Illustration 9.4
Responsibility Reports for TAB Corporation

TAB CORPORATION

Fourth level:
Supervisor, Dye Shop

Controllable Expenses	Amount		Over or (under) Budget	
	This Month	Year to Date	This Month	Year to Date
Repairs and maintenance...................	$200	$1,000	$ 10	$ 40
Supplies................................	180	850	80	95
Tools..................................	100	300	(10)	81
Overtime...............................	200	450	80	14
Total (include in report for next higher level)	$680	$2,600	$160	$230

Illustration 9.4 (*concluded*)

TAB CORPORATION

Third level:
  Plant manager

Controllable Expenses	Amount		Over or (under) Budget	
	This Month	Year to Date	This Month	Year to Date
Plant manager's office expense	$ 800	$ 9,100	$ (50)	$(100)
Dye shop costs	680	2,600	160	230←
Toy shop costs	1,000	5,000	80	130
Assembly	400	1,300	60	240
Salaries of supervisors..............	5,000	25,000	0	0
Total (include in report for next higher level)	$7,880	$43,000	$250	$ 500 ⌐

TAB CORPORATION

Second level:
  Vice president of manufacturing

Controllable Expenses	Amount		Over or (under) Budget	
	This Month	Year to Date	This Month	Year to Date
Vice president's office expense.........	$ 2,840	$ 9,500	$ (50)	$(800)
Plant departmental costs..............	7,880	43,000	250	500 ←
Purchasing.........................	380	2,500	100	200
Receiving..........................	700	3,000	300	900
Salaries of plant manager and heads of purchasing and receiving	7,000	35,000	0	0
Total (include in report for next higher level)	$18,800	$93,000	$600	$ 800⌐

TAB CORPORATION

First level:
  President

Controllable Expenses	Amount		Over or (under) Budget	
	This Month	Year to Date	This Month	Year to Date
President's office expense.............	$ 1,000	$ 5,000	$ 100	$ 200
Vice president, manufacturing	18,800	93,000	600	800←
Vice president, sales.................	8,700	19,000	400	800
Vice president, finance...............	4,000	15,000	800	900
Vice presidents' salaries..............	9,000	45,000	0	0
Total.......................	$41,500	$177,000	$1,900	$2,700

On the basis of the reports (Illustration 9.4), it is probable that the supervisor would take immediate action to determine why supplies and overtime were significantly over the budget this month. The plant manager might ask the supervisor what the problems were and whether they are now under control. The vice president might ask the same question of the plant manager (and of the head of receiving). And the president might ask each of the vice presidents why the budget was exceeded this month.

Responsibility Centers

Various references have been made to the *segments* of a business enterprise. Examples of segments are divisions, departments, product lines, and service centers. The organization of appropriate business segments is crucial to successful responsibility accounting. The segments of a business enterprise must be defined according to function or product line. For example, companies have traditionally been organized along functional lines. The segments or departments performed a specified function (e.g., marketing, finance, purchasing, production, shipping). Recently, large firms have tended to organize segments according to product line (e.g., the electrical products division, the shoe department, the food division). These segments are to a degree autonomous, self-contained units, each with the various functional units contained within itself. The responsibility accounting system should be structured to gather information for each segment. There are three possible types of *responsibility center* for evaluating business segments:

1. The expense (or cost) center.
2. The earnings (or profit) center.
3. The investment center.

The characteristics of a specific segment will limit the selection of an appropriate reporting basis.

Expense or cost centers. The distinguishing feature of expense (or service) centers is that they produce no direct revenue from the sale of goods or services. Examples of expense centers are the maintenance department, the computer section, the accounting department, or intermediate production facilities which produce parts for assembly into a finished product. *Managers of expense centers are held responsible only for specified expense items.*

The appropriate goal of an expense center is not necessarily the short-run minimization of expense for any given level of output, but rather the long-run minimization of expense. The time period examined must also be specified. For example, a production supervisor could eliminate maintenance costs during a short period of time. This would cause total short-term costs to be lower, but long-run costs might be higher due to more frequent machine breakdowns.

Earnings centers. Because many managers are motivated with rewards based on earnings, segmental earnings are often calculated when a responsibility center has control over both revenues *and* expenses. Accordingly, in an increasing number of firms, the segments are organized as *earnings centers*. Since segmental earnings are usually defined as segmental revenue minus related expenses, the manager must be able to *control* both of these categories. That is, the manager must have the authority to attempt to control selling price, sales volume, and all of the reported expense items. The manager's authority over all of these measured items is essential to proper performance evaluation. If the earnings center approach is chosen, a problem may arise with those centers which earn no revenues.

Transfer prices. When a division or segment, such as a maintenance department, does not sell its output to outside parties, it is necessary to establish a *transfer price* which must be "paid" by the other division so that the producing division can have a measured "revenue." This enables the producing unit to become an earnings center rather than an expense center.

In effect, the transfer price is recorded as revenue of one segment and a cost or expense of the other segment. No cash changes hands, and the accounting entry on the corporate books is an internal adjustment. For example, a segment that manufactures a specialized part used in the assembly of a finished product may have no outside market for that part. A transfer price such as $20 per unit must be charged to the assembly segment in order to measure segmental revenue for the segment manufacturing the part. It is essential that the segmental manager have some degree of control over the transfer price. If the manager does not have any control over the transfer price and output volume, the use of a profit measure may be undesirable for motivational purposes. Ideally, a transfer price would represent the cost of the part or service if it were purchased from an outside party. But this market "price" often is not available and sometimes is determined on some cost basis such as standard full cost or standard variable cost. These costs may or may not have a predetermined profit margin added to compute the transfer price. In still other cases, transfer prices are negotiated between the two segments.

Investment centers. Closely related to the earnings center concept is the concept of an investment center. An *investment center* is a segment which is evaluated on the basis of the rate of return that it can earn on a specified investment base. Rate of return is computed by dividing segmental earnings by the appropriate investment base. For example, a segment that earns $100,000 on an investment base of $1 million is said to have a rate of return on investment of 10 percent. There is a question as to the appropriate investment base that should be used in calculating return on investment.

The logic for using investment centers as bases for performance evaluation is that segments with larger amounts of resources should produce more earnings than segments with smaller amounts of resources. By calculating rates of return for performance evaluation, the relative effectiveness of a segment is measured. Thus, the segment with the highest percentage return is presumably the most effective in utilizing its resources. When the absolute amount of earnings is used to measure performance, larger segments will have a distinct advantage over smaller segments.

Normally, the assets available to the division make up the base. But there are differences of opinion as to whether depreciable assets should be shown at cost less accumulated depreciation, at cost, or at current replacement cost. Use of these bases will be discussed later in the chapter.

After the appropriate investment base is selected and valued to the satisfaction of the manager, problems can remain since most segment managers have limited control over certain items. For instance, capital expenditure decisions often are made by the top-level management of the company. Another problem area may exist if the firm has a centralized credit and collection segment. The manager may have little control over the amount of accounts receivable shown as segment assets. It is usually argued that all segments are treated the same and that the inclusion of noncontrollable items in the investment base is therefore appropriate. But it is important that the segment managers agree to this proposition in order to avoid adverse reactions.

With the fundamentals of responsibility accounting described, the investment center concept will be examined.

SEGMENTAL ANALYSIS

The more decentralized the decision making in an organization, the more applicable is the investment center concept to the segments of the company. The more centralized the decision making, the more likely is one to find responsibility centers established as expense centers. *Decentralization* refers to the extent to which management decision making is delegated to lower echelons of the organization. In other words, the extent of decentralization refers to the degree of control which segmental managers have over the revenues, expenses, and assets of their segments. When a segment manager has control over all three of these, the investment center concept can be used.

Typical investment centers are large, autonomous segments of very large companies. These segments are often separated from one another by location, types of products, functions, and/or necessary management skills. But the investment center concept can be applied wherever the manager has control over revenues, expenses, and assets—even in relatively small companies, divisions, or departments.

Four advantages of decentralization of decision making and use of investment centers are:

1. Increased control over their segment gives managers experiences which train them for high-level positions in the company. The added responsibility and authority also represent "job enlargement" and often result in increased job satisfaction and motivation.
2. Top management can be more removed from day-to-day decision making at the lower echelons of the company and can manage by the exception principle. By removing top management from everyday problem solving, that group can better concentrate on long-range planning and on control of the most significant problem areas.
3. Decisions can be made at the point where problems arise. Members of top management often find it difficult to make appropriate decisions when they are not intimately involved with the problem they are trying to solve.
4. Since decentralization enables the investment center concept to be applied, performance evaluation criteria such as return on investment and residual earnings can be used. These concepts are explained later in the chapter.

Concepts Used in Segmental Analysis

The concepts of variable cost, fixed cost, direct cost, indirect cost, net income of a segment, and contribution to indirect expenses need to be understood before the investment center analysis can begin. Variable cost and fixed cost were discussed in Chapter 7.

Direct cost and indirect cost.   Costs may be either directly or indirectly related to a particular segment, product, process, or other category which management designates as an accounting cost accumulation unit (called a *costing unit* here). In other words, a cost is not "direct" or "indirect" in and of itself. It is only "direct" or "indirect" in relation to a given costing unit.

A cost is a *direct cost* (*expense*) of a costing unit if it is traceable to that costing unit. It is an *indirect cost* (*expense*) to a costing unit if it is not traceable to that costing unit but has been allocated to it. A particular cost may be direct to one costing unit and indirect to another costing unit. For instance, the salary of the manager of a segment of a company may be a direct cost of that segment but an indirect cost of one of the products manufactured by that segment.

Since a direct cost is traceable to a costing unit, it is likely that the cost will be eliminated if the costing unit is eliminated. For instance, if the plastics segment of a business is eliminated, it is likely that the salary of the manager of that segment will be eliminated. It is possible to find a direct cost which would not be eliminated if the costing unit were eliminated, but this is the exception rather than the rule.

An indirect cost is not traceable to a costing unit. Therefore, it only becomes an expense of the costing unit through allocation. An example is where depreciation expense on the company headquarters building is allocated as an expense to each of the segments of the company. If a particular segment is eliminated, it is not likely that the expense will disappear; it will be allocated to the remaining segments. Again, it may be possible in a given situation to identify an indirect cost which would be eliminated if the costing unit were eliminated, but this would be an exception to the general rule.

Since direct costs of a unit are clearly identified with that unit, there is a *tendency* for these items also to be controllable by the manager of the unit. And since indirect costs become costs of a unit only through allocation, there is a *tendency* for these items to be noncontrollable by the manager of the unit. They are controllable at some higher level, as is true for all costs. But care must be taken not to equate direct and controllable costs. A cost such as the salary of the supervisor of a unit may be direct to that unit and noncontrollable by that supervisor. But many costs are direct to a given unit and controllable by the manager of that unit.

Net income of a segment. To measure the contribution which a segment makes to overall company earnings, the income statement shown in Illustration 9.5 may be used.

Illustration 9.5
Segmental Net Income

	Segment		
	A	B	Total
Sales....................................	$1,000,000	$700,000	$1,700,000
Less: Variable expenses (all direct expenses)....	500,000	410,000	910,000
Contribution margin...........................	$ 500,000	$290,000	$ 790,000
Less: Direct fixed expenses..................	120,000	170,000	290,000
Contribution to indirect expenses..............	$ 380,000	$120,000	$ 500,000
Less: Indirect fixed expenses.................	90,000	160,000	250,000
Net income.......................................	$ 290,000	$ (40,000)	$ 250,000

Contribution margin. The *contribution margin* is equal to sales less variable expenses. The same concept can be expressed on a per unit basis, and is used that way in Chapter 11. In Illustration 9.5, all variable expenses are direct expenses. Some fixed expenses are direct, while others are indirect.

An alternative format which could be used in reporting for a segment is one which shows gross margin, as would be done in an income statement, but does not show the contribution margin:

Sales	$XX
Less: Cost of goods sold.	XX
Gross margin	$XX
Less: Other direct expenses	XX
Total*.	$XX
Less: Indirect fixed expenses	XX
Net income	$XX

*This total may be labeled "contribution to indirect expenses" only if there are no indirect fixed manufacturing costs included in cost of goods sold.

This format includes a portion of the fixed direct manufacturing expenses in cost of goods sold. Since some fixed costs are being deducted from sales immediately, the contribution margin figure cannot be shown. Also, some variable costs (selling and administrative) move down with the other direct expenses.

To illustrate, assume that detailed data for Segment A of Illustration 9.5 are as shown in the center column in Illustration 9.6. These data can be grouped to show a *contribution margin format* (shown on the left-hand side of Illustration 9.6) or a *gross margin format* (shown on the right-hand side). Indirect fixed expenses could be deducted using either format to arrive at net income.

In determining the contribution which a segment makes to company income, it is tempting to use net income of the segment since this figure is used in evaluating the performance of an entire company. But there is a problem with using this means of evaluation for segments within a company. Certain indirect fixed expenses are allocated to the segment, and the bases of allocation are often arbitrary.

Arbitrary allocations of indirect fixed expenses. Indirect fixed expenses, such as depreciation on the home office administrative building or on the computer facility maintained at the home office, can only be allocated to segments on some arbitrary basis. An attempt is often made to allocate these expenses on the basis of benefit received, but this is not always possible. For instance, how does one determine the benefit a given segment received because the company made a charitable contribution to a worthy cause? Yet costs such as these must be allocated to the segments on some basis if a net income approach is used.

For certain indirect expenses, the allocation can be made on the basis of benefit received. For instance, if Segment A of Illustration 9.5 utilized 4,000 hours of the total of 10,000 hours of computer time, it could be charged with 40 percent of the total cost of the computer facility since this is proportional to the benefit received. (Where the benefit received is very clear-cut, it could be argued that the expense should be treated as a direct expense.)

For certain other expenses, the allocation may be made on the basis of responsibility for incurrence. For instance, assume that Segment A contracts with a magazine to run an advertisement which will benefit it and

Illustration 9.6
Alternative Formats for Arriving at Contribution to Indirect Expenses

Contribution Margin Format

Sales....................		$1,000,000
Less: Variable expenses.........	500,000	
Contribution margin.............		$ 500,000
Less: Direct fixed expenses.....		120,000
Contribution to indirect expenses..............		$ 380,000

Given:

Sales....................		$1,000,000
Variable manufacturing expenses...........		450,000
Fixed direct manufacturing expenses...........		20,000
Variable selling and administrative expenses...........		50,000
Fixed direct selling and administrative expenses...........		100,000

Gross Margin Format

Sales....................		$1,000,000
Less: Cost of goods sold............		470,000
Gross margin..............		$ 530,000
Less: Other direct expenses..........		150,000
Contribution to indirect expenses*...		$ 380,000

* In situations where indirect fixed manufacturing costs are included in cost of goods sold, this title should not be used. Instead, the title "Total" is used.

various other segments of the company. Often, the entire cost of the advertisement will be allocated to Segment A since it had the responsibility for incurring that portion of the total advertising expense.

When neither "benefit" nor "responsibility" can be used to allocate indirect fixed expenses, some other basis which seems reasonable in the circumstances must be found. Often, such expenses are allocated on the basis of net sales for lack of a better basis for allocation. For instance, if Segment A's net sales are 60 percent of total company sales, then 60 percent of a certain indirect expense would be allocated to Segment A.

Due to the arbitrary nature of allocations of indirect fixed expenses, many companies do not allocate these expenses to their segments. Instead, they calculate the contribution to indirect fixed expenses and use this figure to determine the earnings contribution of each segment.

Contribution to indirect expenses.   The net income figure for a segment does not show the amount by which company earnings would decrease if the segment were discontinued.

If management relied on the net income figure for a segment to judge its contribution to earnings, it might conclude that Segment B in Illustration 9.5 should be eliminated. But what would have been the effect on earnings if Segment B had been eliminated? This action would have had the following effect:

Reduction in revenues		$700,000
Reduction in expenses:		
Variable expenses	$410,000	
Direct fixed expenses	170,000	580,000
Reduction in earnings of the company		$120,000

The reduction in earnings of $120,000 which would have resulted from eliminating Segment B is also shown by Segment B's contribution to indirect expenses in Illustration 9.5.

The *contribution to indirect expenses* is a useful figure for determining whether or not a segment should be retained. For this reason and because the allocations of indirect fixed expenses usually are arbitrary, many companies use an income statement (for internal use) which uses the format shown in Illustration 9.7.

The contribution margin format was used, but the gross margin format could have been used. No attempt is made to allocate indirect fixed expenses to the segments. This format focuses attention on the amount of dollars which a segment contributes toward covering indirect expenses. If all indirect expenses are covered, there is net income for the period.

Investment Centers Using Segmental Analysis

Consideration of the investment base transforms the performance criteria into an investment center analysis. For a responsibility center to be treated

Illustration 9.7
Segmental Contribution to Indirect Expenses

	Segment		
	A	B	Total
Sales	$1,000,000	$700,000	$1,700,000
Less: Variable expenses	500,000	410,000	910,000
Contribution margin	$ 500,000	$290,000	$ 790,000
Less: Direct fixed expenses	120,000	170,000	290,000
Contribution to indirect expenses	$ 380,000	$120,000	$ 500,000
Less: Indirect fixed expenses			250,000
Net income			$ 250,000

as an investment center, the manager of that center has to have control over revenues, expenses, and assets (investment). Two performance criteria frequently used include the concept of investment base in the analysis: ROI (return on investment) and RI (residual income).

Return on investment (ROI). A segment that has a large amount of assets should earn more (in an absolute sense) than a segment that has a small amount of assets. Return on investment gives consideration to this by calculating the return (earnings) as a percentage of the assets employed (investment):

$$\text{ROI} = \frac{\text{Earnings}}{\text{Investment}}$$

To illustrate, assume the facts shown in Illustration 9.8 for a company with three segments.

Using ROI as a criterion for evaluating the segments, Segment 3 is per-

Illustration 9.8
Computation of Return on Investment

	Segment			
	(1)	(2)	(3)	Total
a. Earnings.	$ 100,000	$ 250,000	$ 500,000	$ 850,000
b. Investment.	1,000,000	1,250,000	2,000,000	4,250,000
Return on investment (a ÷ b)	10%	20%	25%	20%

forming the best (25 percent), Segment 2 is next (20 percent), and Segment 1 is performing the worst (10 percent).

Definitions of earnings and investment. Although ROI appears to be simple and straightforward, there are several difficulties involved with its use. These difficulties center on what is considered to be "earnings" and what is considered to be "investment." Illustration 9.9 shows the possible

Illustration 9.9
Possible Definitions of "Earnings" and "Investment"

Possible Definitions of "earnings"	Possible Definitions of "investment"	When to Use the Definitions
1. Net income of the segment*	Total assets† directly or indirectly related to the segment (including those related to indirect fixed expenses allocated to the segment)	Not recommended for segmental evaluation, but to evaluate the earning power of an entire company
2. Contribution to indirect expenses	Assets directly used by and identified with the segment	To evaluate the *rate* of earnings contribution of a segment
3. "Controllable" earnings—this would start with contribution to indirect expenses and would eliminate any of the revenues and direct expenses which were not under the "control" of the segment manager. (An example of an item to exclude would be the segment manager's own salary.)	Assets under the "control" of the segment manager	To evaluate the earnings *performance* of the *manager* of the segment

* Often, *net operating* income is used. This is defined as earnings before interest and taxes (EBIT).
† *Operating assets* are often used in the calculation. Assets not used in normal operations, such as land held for future use, are excluded.

combinations of definitions of these terms which may be used and the situations in which they are appropriate.

The first set of definitions could conceivably be used for segmental evaluation, but are not recommended. The indirect fixed expenses which are allocated to a segment prevent its use for evaluating the earnings contribution of the segment. The presence of expenses which are not under the control of the manager prevent its use for evaluating the performance of the manager. Only if an evaluation of the earning power of an entire company is being made should this set of definitions be used. Even then, it may be preferable to use an ROI calculation which measures earning power without regard to the sources of assets. This can be done by dividing *net operating income* by *operating assets,* as was shown in Chapter 6. For definitions of these terms see the bottom of Illustration 9.9.

The second set of definitions is useful in evaluating the *rate* of earnings contribution of a segment. Indirect fixed expenses allocated to the segment are eliminated from the computation, and assets not directly used by the segment are eliminated from the investment base. This set of definitions is not useful in evaluating the performance of the *manager* because items not under the control of the manager are included.

The third set of definitions is useful in evaluating the earnings performance of the manager of a segment because all items not under the control of the manager are eliminated (a fundamental principle of responsibility accounting is to evaluate responsibility center managers only on items under their control).

Valuation base. Another problem with the denominator of ROI is with the *valuation base* to use for plant assets. Some possibilities include original cost less accumulated depreciation, original cost, and current replacement cost.

Original cost less accumulated depreciation (book value) is probably the most widely used valuation base. *Original cost* is the price paid to acquire an asset. One advantage of this method is that the amount can readily be determined. Several disadvantages exist. The first is that many different methods of depreciation exist (straight line, sum-of-the-years' digits, double-declining balance, and so on). This leads to different income amounts and different asset amounts for two segments which would otherwise be identical. Thus, meaningful interfirm and intrafirm comparisons with other segments are hampered. Also, with this method, the older the plant assets, the higher the ROI tends to be because the book value of the plant assets decreases as accumulated depreciation increases and earnings remain about the same or increase as a result of inflation. Also, when a segment with old plant assets is compared to a segment with new plant assets, the former will have a further advantage in that the original cost of the assets was lower.

The use of *original cost* eliminates the problem of decreasing book values resulting from the growth in accumulated depreciation. But it does not solve the price-level problem. The ROI may still increase over time because earnings tend to increase due to inflation. Also, the income on old assets needs to be much less than on new assets to achieve the same *rate* of return.

When *current replacement cost* is used, the problem of differing depreciation methods and the price-level problem disappear. Current replacement cost is the cost of replacing the present assets with similar assets which are in the same condition as those now in use. The one disadvantage is that current replacement costs are often difficult to determine.

Expanded form of ROI computation. It is useful at times to break the ROI formula into two parts:

$$\text{ROI} = \frac{\text{Earnings}}{\text{Sales}} \times \frac{\text{Sales}}{\text{Investment}}$$

The first term, Earnings/Sales, is called *margin*. It is the percentage relationship of earnings to sales. This percentage also shows the number of cents of earnings that attach to each dollar of sales.

The second term, Sales/Investment, is called *turnover*. It is the number of times by which sales per year exceeds the investment in assets.

Breaking the ROI formula into these two components is useful in determining a strategy for increasing the margin or the turnover or the net effect of the two in a particular case. For instance, assume that the manager of a segment is faced with the following return on investment for the past year.

$$\text{ROI} = \text{Margin} \times \text{Turnover}$$

$$= \frac{\text{Earnings}}{\text{Sales}} \times \frac{\text{Sales}}{\text{Investment}}$$

$$= \frac{\$100,000}{\$2,000,000} \times \frac{\$2,000,000}{\$1,000,000}$$

$$= 5 \text{ percent} \times 2 \text{ times}$$

$$= 10 \text{ percent}$$

The manager desires to increase ROI for the coming year. Three illustrated strategies, independent of each other, are:

1. Concentrate on increasing the margin while holding turnover constant. Pursuing this strategy would involve leaving selling prices as they are and making every effort to increase efficiency so as to reduce expenses. Possibly expenses could be reduced by $40,000 without affecting sales and investment. If so, the new ROI would be:

$$\text{ROI} = \frac{\text{Earnings}}{\text{Sales}} \times \frac{\text{Sales}}{\text{Investment}}$$

$$= \frac{\$140,000}{\$2,000,000} \times \frac{\$2,000,000}{\$1,000,000}$$

$$= 7 \text{ percent} \times 2 \text{ times}$$

$$= 14 \text{ percent}$$

2. Concentrate on increasing the turnover by reducing the investment in assets while holding income and sales constant. Possibly working capital could be reduced or some land could be sold, reducing investment in assets by $200,000 without affecting sales and earnings. If so, the new ROI would be:

$$\text{ROI} = \frac{\text{Earnings}}{\text{Sales}} \times \frac{\text{Sales}}{\text{Investment}}$$

$$= \frac{\$100,000}{\$2,000,000} \times \frac{\$2,000,000}{\$800,000}$$

$$= 5 \text{ percent} \times 2.5 \text{ times}$$

$$= 12\frac{1}{2} \text{ percent}$$

3. Possibly actions could be taken which affect both margin and turnover. An advertising campaign would probably increase sales and earnings. (Getting rid of nonproductive depreciable assets would decrease investment while increasing earnings.) Assume that an advertising campaign increased sales by $500,000 and earnings by $50,000. ROI would then be:

$$\text{ROI} = \frac{\text{Earnings}}{\text{Sales}} \times \frac{\text{Sales}}{\text{Investment}}$$
$$= \frac{\$150,000}{\$2,500,000} \times \frac{\$2,500,000}{\$1,000,000}$$
$$= 6 \text{ percent} \times 2.5 \text{ times}$$
$$= 15 \text{ percent}$$

In the third example, both margin and turnover were increased as a result of the advertising campaign. But sometimes an increase in one is accompanied by a decrease in the other. For instance, assume that the advertising campaign increased sales by $500,000 but only increased earnings by $12,500. The resulting ROI would be:

$$\text{ROI} = \frac{\text{Earnings}}{\text{Sales}} \times \frac{\text{Sales}}{\text{Investment}}$$
$$= \frac{\$112,500}{\$2,500,000} \times \frac{\$2,500,000}{\$1,000,000}$$
$$= 4.5 \text{ percent} \times 2.5 \text{ times}$$
$$= 11.25 \text{ percent}$$

In this illustration, the margin decreased from 5 percent to 4.5 percent, but turnover increased from 2 times to 2.5 times. The net result was an increase in ROI from 10 percent to 11.25 percent.

Residual income. The use of return on investment (ROI) can result in what is called *suboptimization*. This term is defined as the situation where segment managers take an action which is in their own (their segment's) interest but not in the best interests of the company as a whole.

To illustrate, assume that the manager of Segment 3 in Illustration 9.8 has an opportunity to take on a project involving an investment of $100,000 which will return 22 percent (or $22,000). Since the segment is already realizing a return on investment of 25 percent, the manager may decide to reject the project. But the overall company rate of return of 20 percent would be increased by accepting the project.

To prevent suboptimization, the *residual income* concept is sometimes applied. *Residual income* is defined as the amount of earnings of a segment in excess of the desired minimum rate of return. This desired minimum rate is always equal to or greater than the cost of capital (the cost of raising capital). In formula form, residual income is:

Residual income = Earnings − (Investment × Desired minimum ROI)

When evaluating the earnings contribution of a segment, "earnings" would be "contribution to indirect expenses" and "investment" would be "assets directly used by and identified with the segment." When evaluating the earnings performance of a segment manager, "earnings" would be "controllable earnings" and "investment" would be "assets under the control of the segment manager." The residual income concept is generally not used for evaluating an entire company, since the problem of suboptimization does not exist (by definition).

Using the data from Illustration 9.8, residual income would be found as shown in Illustration 9.10 (assuming a desired minimum ROI of 10 percent).

Illustration 9.10
Computation of Residual Income

	Segment			
	(1)	(2)	(3)	Total*
a. Earnings	$ 100,000	$ 250,000	$ 500,000	$ 850,000
b. Investment	1,000,000	1,250,000	2,000,000	4,250,000
c. Desired minimum ROI— b × 10%	100,000	125,000	200,000	425,000
d. Residual income (a − c)	0	125,000	300,000	425,000

* Depending on the set of definitions used for *earnings* and *investment*, the total column may include amounts which do not equal the total when adding across. This is because some expenses will not be allocated and some assets will not be assigned to the segments if definition sets 2 or 3 in illustration 9.9 are used.

If the manager of Segment 3 were to accept the proposal mentioned above (a 22 percent return on an investment of $100,000), the last two columns of Illustration 9.10 would be changed to:

	Segment 3	Total
a. Earnings	$ 522,000	$ 872,000
b. Investment	2,100,000	4,350,000
c. Desired minimum ROI—b × 10%	210,000	435,000
d. Residual (a − c)	312,000	437,000

This example shows that the use of the residual income concept will prevent suboptimization in situations like this. The segment rated as the best is the one with the greatest amount of residual income rather than the one with the highest ROI rate. Segment managers will take those actions which will increase their residual income.

In evaluating the performance of a segment manager, comparisons should be made not only with the current budget and with other segments within the company but also with past performance in that manager's segment and with similar segments in other companies. Consideration must be given to general economic conditions, market conditions for the product being produced, and so on. A superior manager in Company A may be earning a return of 12 percent, which is above the return of similar segments in other companies but below the return of other segments in Company A. The other segments in Company A may be more profitable because of market conditions and the nature of the products rather than the performance of the segment manager. Careful judgment must be used when evaluating the performance of the manager of a responsibility center.

Questions

1. What is the fundamental principle of responsibility accounting?
2. Name three possible reporting bases for evaluating business segments.
3. What is the logic of using investment centers as a basis for performance evaluation?
4. How soon after the end of the performance measurement period should accounting reports be prepared? Explain.
5. Compare and contrast an expense center and an investment center.
6. Which categories of items must a segment manager have control over for the investment center concept to be applicable?
7. What connection is there between the extent of decentralization and the investment center concept?
8. Differentiate between a direct cost and an indirect cost of a segment. What happens to each category if the segment to which it is related is eliminated?
9. Is it possible for a cost to be "direct" to one costing unit and "indirect" to another costing unit? Explain.
10. Indicate how each of the following is calculated for a segment:
    a. Gross margin.
    b. Contribution margin.
    c. Contribution to indirect expenses (under the two different formats).
    d. Net income.
11. Describe some of the methods by which indirect expenses are usually allocated to a segment.
12. Give the general formula for return on investment (ROI). How is this split into two components?
13. Give the three sets of definitions for *earnings* and *investment* which may be used in ROI calculations and when each set is applicable.
14. Give the various valuation bases that could be used for plant assets in investment center calculations. Discuss some of the advantages and disadvantages of these methods.

15. In what way is the use of the residual income (RI) concept superior to the use of return on investment (ROI)?
16. How is residual income determined?
17. If the residual income for Segment Manager X is $50,000 while the residual income for Segment Manager Y are $100,000, does this necessarily mean that X is a better manager than Y?
18. What purpose is served by setting transfer prices?

Exercises

1. Describe a segment of a business enterprise that is best treated as an expense center. List four indirect expenses that may be allocated to such an expense center.
2. Barrow Company manufactures refrigerators. Below are listed several costs that occur. Indicate whether or not the shop supervisor can control each of the listed items.
   a. Depreciation.
   b. Repairs.
   c. Small tools.
   d. Supplies.
   e. Bond interest.
3. List five important factors that should be considered in designing reports for a responsibility accounting system.
4. Given the following data, prepare a schedule which shows contribution margin, contribution to indirect costs, and net income of the segment:

Direct fixed expenses	$ 60,000
Indirect fixed expenses.	50,000
Sales	500,000
Variable expenses	340,000

What would be the effect on company earnings if the segment were eliminated?
5. Three segments (1, 2, and 3) of the Wilkes Company have net sales of $600,000, $400,000, and $200,000, respectively. A decision is made to allocate the pool of $60,000 of administrative overhead expenses of the home office to the segments based on net sales.
   a. How much should be allocated to each of the segments?
   b. If Segment 3 were eliminated, how much would be allocated to 1 and 2?
6. Two segments (balls and bats) showed the following data for the most recent year:

	Balls	Bats
Contribution to indirect expenses	$ 100,000	$ 288,000
Assets directly used by and identified with the segment	500,000	1,200,000
Sales	2,000,000	3,600,000

   a. Calculate return on investment (ROI) for each segment in the most direct manner.
   b. Calculate return on investment (ROI) utilizing the margin and turnover components.

7. Determine the effect of each of the following on the margin, turnover, and ROI of the balls segment in Exercise 6. Consider each change independently of the others.

   a. Direct variable expenses were reduced by $10,000, and indirect expenses were reduced by $15,000. Sales and assets were unaffected.

   b. Assets used by the segment were reduced by $100,000, while earnings and sales were unaffected.

   c. An advertising campaign increased sales by $200,000 and earnings by $32,000. Assets directly used by the segment remained unaffected.

8. The Bowman Company has three segments: Stars, Stripes, and Dots. Data concerning "earnings" and "investment" are as follows:

	Stars	Stripes	Dots
Contribution to indirect expenses	$ 20,000	$ 45,000	$ 70,000
Assets directly used by and identified with the segment	100,000	300,000	800,000

Assuming that the minimum desired return on investment is 10 percent, calculate the residual earnings of each of the segments. Do the results indicate that any of the segments should be eliminated?

9. Assume that for the Stars segment in Exercise 8, $5,000 of the direct expenses and $20,000 of the segmental assets are not under the control of the segment manager. Top management wishes to evaluate the segment manager's earnings performance. Calculate the manager's return on investment and residual income. (Because certain expenses and assets are not controllable by the segment manager, the minimum desired ROI is 15 percent.)

Business Decision Problem 9-1

Respond to each of the following situations.

a. The Poindexter Company manufactures swimsuits. The company's business is seasonal, so that between August and December 10 skilled manufacturing employees are usually "laid off." In order to improve morale, the financial vice president suggests that these 10 employees not be laid off in the future. Instead, it is suggested that they work in general labor from August to December but still be paid their manufacturing wages of $6 per hour. General labor personnel earn $3 per hour. What are the implications of this plan for the assignment of costs to the various segments of the business?

b. The Inman Company builds new homes. Wheeler is in charge of the construction department. Among other things, Wheeler hires and supervises the carpenters and other workers who build the homes. The Inman Company does not do its own foundation work. The construction of the foundation is done by subcontractors hired by Ruez of the procurement department.

   The Inman Company was about to start the development of a 500-home community. Ruez hired the Peak Company to build the foundations on the homes. On the day construction was to begin, the Peak Company went out of business. Consequently, construction was delayed six weeks while Ruez hired a new subcontractor. Which department should be charged with the cost of the delay in construction? Why?

c. Howard Johnson is supervisor of Department 6 of the Fustino Company. The annual budget for the department is:

	Annual Budget for Department 6
Small tools.............................	$ 9,000
Setup	10,000
Direct labor	11,000
Direct materials........................	20,000
Supplies...............................	5,000
Supervision	30,000
Property taxes.........................	5,000
Property insurance	1,000
Depreciation, machinery.................	2,000
Depreciation, building	2,000
Total...........................	$95,000

Identify the budget items that are controllable by Johnson. Johnson's salary of $20,000 is included in supervision. The remaining $10,000 in supervision is the salary of the assistant supervisor, who is directly responsible to Johnson.

Solutions to End-of-Chapter Questions, Exercises, and Business Decision Problems

Answers to Questions

1. The fundamental principle of responsibility accounting is to evaluate each manager only on those items over which the manager has control.
2. Three possible reporting bases for evaluating business segments are:
    a. The expense center.
    b. The earnings or profit center.
    c. The investment center.
3. The logic for using investment centers as a basis for performance evaluation is that segments with large amounts of resources should produce more earnings than segments with smaller amounts of resources. By calculating rates of return for performance evaluation, the relative efficiency of a division is measured.
4. Accounting reports should be prepared as soon after the end of the performance measurement period as possible. Timely reports allow corrective action to be taken quickly.
5. In an expense center, only expense items are measured. In an investment center, the manager is responsible for earnings and the use of assets.
6. The segment manager must have control over revenues, expenses, and assets. If control exists only for expenses, then the expense center concept is applicable. If there is control of only revenues and expenses, then the earnings center concept could be used.
7. The more decentralization of decision making, the more likely is a segment manager to have control over revenues, expenses, and assets. Thus, the investment center concept can be applied.

8. A direct cost of a segment is traceable to that segment. An indirect cost is *not* traceable to that segment, but, instead, becomes a cost of the segment through allocation. Direct costs usually disappear when a segment is eliminated, while indirect costs usually do not. In a given situation, there could be an exception to this general rule.

9. Yes, it is possible for a given cost (the segment manager's salary) to be direct to one costing unit (the segment) and indirect to another costing unit (a product manufactured in the segment). Costs are only "direct" or "indirect" in relation to a costing unit.

10.   *a.*   Sales − Cost of goods sold = Gross margin
     b.   Sales − Variable expenses = Contribution margin
     c.   Gross margin − Other direct expenses = Contribution to indirect expenses or contribution margin
                                      − Direct fixed expenses
                                    = Contribution to indirect expenses
     d.   Contribution to indirect expenses − Indirect fixed expenses = Net income

11. The allocations may be made on the basis of "benefit," "responsibility," or some other basis (such as net sales) which seems reasonable in the circumstances. The use of "benefit" is preferable. In fact, if benefit can be shown with considerable accuracy, an argument could be made for treating the expense as a direct expense. Where benefit cannot be used, responsibility for incurring the expense is recommended. If neither benefit nor responsibility can be used, then some other basis must be used.

12. The general formula is:

$$\text{ROI} = \frac{\text{Earnings}}{\text{Investment}}$$

The formula split into two components is:

$$\text{ROI} = \text{Margin} \times \text{Turnover}$$
$$= \frac{\text{Earnings}}{\text{Sales}} \times \frac{\text{Sales}}{\text{Investment}}$$

13. To evaluate the earning power of an entire company, the formula is:

$$\text{ROI} = \frac{\text{Net income}}{\text{Total assets}}$$

or

$$\text{ROI} = \frac{\text{Net operating income}}{\text{Operating assets}}$$

To evaluate the rate of earnings contribution of a segment, the formula is:

$$\text{ROI} = \frac{\text{Contribution to indirect expenses}}{\text{Assets directly used by and identified with the segment}}$$

To evaluate the earnings performance of a segment manager, the formula is:

$$\text{ROI} = \frac{\text{Controllable earnings}}{\text{Assets under the control of the segment manager}}$$

14. The various valuation bases that could be used for plant assets in investment center calculations are:
    a. Original cost less accumulated depreciation is probably the most widely used base in spite of its several disadvantages. One problem is that various depreciation methods may be used, yielding different results for different segments. Also, the investment base gets smaller and smaller each year because the increasing accumulated depreciation causes book value to decline. Another problem is that inflation may cause the earnings numerator to increase while the investment denominator declines. This can cause ROI to increase even faster over time without any real change in performance. An advantage is the easy access to this amount since it is already contained in the accounting records.
    b. Use of original cost (without deducting accumulated depreciation) gets rid of the problems of varying depreciation methods and a shrinking book value. The problem caused by inflation mentioned above still remains. Another advantage of this method is the easy access to the data since they are already contained in the accounting records.
    c. Current replacement cost is an alternative which gets rid of all the problems associated with the first two methods. It is the cost of replacing the present assets with similar ones in the same condition as those now in use. The one disadvantage is that reliable data may be difficult to obtain.
15. The use of the residual income concept avoids the problem of suboptimization. For instance, assume Segment A has an ROI of 30 percent. It has an opportunity to go ahead with a project which will earn 20 percent. The minimum desired return on projects is 15 percent. If ROI is used as a basis for evaluating the earnings performance of segments, the project will probably be rejected, since ROI of Segment A would decline. But if the residual income concept is used, Segment A will accept the project because doing so would enable it to increase its residual income.
16. Residual income is determined:

Residual income = Earnings − (Investment × Desired minimum ROI)

17. No. A manager's performance must be evaluated in its context. Maybe the earnings opportunities for Y were much greater than those for X (new product in great demand, no competition, etc.). Each manager's performance should be compared with budgeted amounts and with past performance as well as with that of managers of similar segments in other companies.
18. When segments within a company supply their output of goods or services to other segments within that company, no revenues are created. Therefore, artificial revenues must be created by setting a "price" at which the goods or services will be transferred. The setting of a transfer price allows the investment center concept (or the earnings center concept) to be used in these situations.

Solutions to Exercises

1. Service centers are best treated as expense centers. Accounting or EDP departments are examples of such service centers. Examples of indirect expenses include maintenance, property taxes, depreciation, and corporate administration expense.

2. *a.* Noncontrollable.
   b. Controllable.
   c. Controllable.
   d. Controllable.
   e. Noncontrollable.
3. *a.* The reports should be articulated so that totals from one level are carried forward in the report to the next higher management level.
   b. Reports should be timely. They should be prepared as soon after the end of the performance measurement period as possible.
   c. Reports should be relatively simple.
   d. Confusing accounting terminology should be avoided.
   e. Results should be expressed in physical units when appropriate.
   f. It is desirable to report the budget standard as well as actual results.

4.

Sales....................................	$500,000
Less: Variable expenses....................	340,000
Contribution margin..........................	$160,000
Less: Direct fixed expenses..................	60,000
Contribution to indirect expenses...............	$100,000
Less: Indirect fixed expenses.................	50,000
Net income..................................	$ 50,000

The effect on earnings if the segment were eliminated would be a reduction of $100,000, assuming that direct expenses would be eliminated and indirect expenses would not.

5. *a.*

Segment	Net Sales	Portion of Total	Allocation of Administrative Overhead
1...................	$ 600,000	½	$30,000(½ × $60,000)
2...................	400,000	⅓	20,000(⅓ × $60,000)
3...................	200,000	⅙	10,000(⅙ × $60,000)
	$1,200,000		$60,000

   b.

Segment	Net Sales	Portion of Total	Allocation of Administrative Overhead
1...................	$ 600,000	⅗	$36,000(⅗ × $60,000)
2...................	400,000	⅖	24,000(⅖ × $60,000)
	$1,000,000		$60,000

6. *a.*

	Balls	Bats
$\text{ROI} = \dfrac{\text{Earnings}}{\text{Investment}}$	$\dfrac{\$100,000}{\$500,000} = 20\%$	$\dfrac{\$288,000}{\$1,200,000} = 24\%$

   b. ROI = Margin × Turnover

$$= \frac{\text{Earnings}}{\text{Sales}} \times \frac{\text{Sales}}{\text{Investment}}$$

Balls		Bats	
$\dfrac{\$100,000}{\$2,000,000}$ ×	$\dfrac{\$2,000,000}{\$500,000}$	$\dfrac{\$288,000}{\$3,600,000}$ ×	$\dfrac{\$3,600,000}{\$1,200,000}$
5%	× 4 times = 20%	8%	× 3 times = 24%

7. $$\text{ROI} = \text{Margin} \times \text{Turnover}$$
$$= \frac{\text{Earnings}}{\text{Sales}} \times \frac{\text{Sales}}{\text{Investment}}$$

   a. $$\text{ROI} = \frac{\$110,000^*}{\$2,000,000} \times \frac{\$2,000,000}{\$500,000}$$
   $$= \quad 5.5\% \quad \times \quad 4 \text{ times} = 22\%$$

   b. $$\text{ROI} = \frac{\$100,000}{\$2,000,000} \times \frac{\$2,000,000}{\$400,000}$$
   $$= \quad 5\% \quad \times \quad 5 \text{ times} = 25\%$$

   c. $$\text{ROI} = \frac{\$132,000}{\$2,200,000} \times \frac{\$2,200,000}{\$500,000}$$
   $$= \quad 6\% \quad \times \quad 4.4 \text{ times} = 26.4\%$$

   * The reduction in indirect expenses would not affect contribution to indirect expenses.

8.

		Stars	Stripes	Dots	Total
a.	"Earnings"	$ 20,000	$ 45,000	$ 70,000	$ 135,000
b.	"Investment"	100,000	300,000	800,000	1,200,000
c.	Desired minimum ROI—b × 10%	10,000	30,000	80,000	120,000
d.	Residual income (a − c)	10,000	15,000	−10,000	15,000

The residual income concept does not give useful information in determining whether a segment should be eliminated. If the Dots segment were eliminated, company earnings would decline by $70,000 (the amount of its contribution to indirect expenses). However, the Dots segment is making less than the desired minimum rate of return ($70,000 ÷ $800,000 = 8.75%). It should attempt to find a strategy which will increase its rate of return. Efforts to increase margin or turnover, or both, might be considered.

9. $$\text{ROI} = \frac{\text{Controllable income}}{\substack{\text{Assets under the control} \\ \text{of the segment manager}}}$$
$$= \frac{\$25,000}{\$80,000} = 31.25\%$$

$$\substack{\text{Residual} \\ \text{earnings}} = \substack{\text{Controllable} \\ \text{income}} - \left(\substack{\text{Assets under} \\ \text{segment manager's} \\ \text{control}} \times \substack{\text{Desired} \\ \text{minimum} \\ \text{ROI}} \right)$$
$$= \quad \$25,000 \quad - \quad (\$80,000 \quad \times \quad 15\%)$$
$$= \quad \$25,000 \quad - \quad \$12,000 = \$13,000$$

Business Decision Problem 9–1

   a.   General labor should be charged the regular $3 per hour rate. The remaining $3 should be charged somewhere else, possibly to the executive who decided not to temporarily lay off the workers.

b. The cost of the delay should be charged to Ruez. Wheeler should not be charged with the delay over which he has no control. Had Ruez originally hired another subcontractor, the delay might not have occurred.

c. Items controllable by Johnson:

Small tools.	$ 9,000
Setup	10,000
Direct labor	11,000
Direct materials.	20,000
Supplies.	5,000
Supervision	10,000
Total.	$65,000

10

Budgeting

Chapter Goals

When you have completed Chapter 10, you should be able to:

1. Explain the concept of the budget as a tool for planning, control, and evaluation.
2. Describe the characteristics of the various types of budgets and the uses for each type.
3. Illustrate the principles of budgeting and the procedures of budget preparation.
4. Explain the limitations of budgeting, especially as a substitute for effective management.

THE BUDGET—FOR PLANNING AND CONTROL

Time and money are scarce resources, and effective use of both requires planning. But planning alone is insufficient. Control must also be exercised to determine whether the plan is feasible, and to see that it is carried out. A budget is a tool used to plan and control the use of scarce resources.

There are various types of budgets. *Responsibility budgets,* covered in the preceding chapter, are designed to judge the performance of an individual manager. *Capital budgets,* covered in Chapter 12, are prepared to evaluate particular long-term projects such as the addition of equipment or the relocation of a plant. Another type of budget, the *master budget,* is the topic of this chapter. The master budget is made up of two parts, the *operating budget* and the *financial budget.* The operating budget is a projected income statement. The financial budget is a projected balance sheet. Before the master budget is discussed, some considerations involved with budgeting in general are presented.

Purposes of Budgets

In business, a *budget* is simply a *plan* showing (1) how management intends to acquire and use resources and (2) how it intends to *control* the acquisition and use of resources over the planning period. The budget often is referred to as a formal quantitative expression of management plans. Yet it is much more than that. It forces all levels of management to think ahead, anticipate results, and take action to remedy possible poor results.

Budgets, such as the responsibility budget, are also used to *motivate* individuals to achieve stated goals and to *appraise the performance* of individuals. For instance, the standard variable cost of producing a given part in a given cost center is a budget figure against which actual performance can be compared in order to evaluate the performance of that cost center.

Many other benefits result from the preparation and use of budgets. The activities of the business are better *coordinated*; individual members of management *become aware of the problems of other members* of management; employees may become *cost-conscious* and seek to *conserve* resources; the organization plan of the enterprise may be *reviewed* more often and changed where needed; and a breadth of *vision,* which might not otherwise be developed, is fostered. Another important benefit is that a properly prepared budget will allow management to manage by the exception principle by devoting attention to areas where activities are deviating from their planned levels.

Considerations in Preparing Budget

Uncertainty about the future is a poor excuse for not budgeting; in fact, the less stable the conditions, the more necessary and desirable budgeting is.

Stable operating conditions permit greater reliance upon past experience as a basis for budgeting. But budgets are based on more than past results. Plans must also be considered.

A budget plan should explicitly spell out management's assumptions relating to such things as (1) the state of the economy over the planning period; (2) plans for adding, deleting, or changing product lines; (3) the nature of the industry's competition; and (4) the effect of existing or possible government regulations. If the nature of the assumptions should change during the budget period, an analysis of the effects should be made and reflected in the evaluation of the company's performance.

In the preparation of a budget, accounting data play an important part. The details of the budget must be in agreement with the company's accounts. The accounts, in turn, must be designed to facilitate the preparation of the budget and the usual financial statements as well as the numerous reports—cost and financial—that are prepared quarterly, monthly, weekly, or even daily to help exercise operational control.

During the budget period, repeated comparisons of accounting data and budgeted projections should be made and the differences investigated. But budgeting is not a substitute for management, and a budget is not self-operating. Instead, the budget is designed as an important tool for managerial planning and control.

Budget periods vary in length, but they usually coincide with the accounting period. Normally, the budget period is broken into months or quarters, and the greater the uncertainty faced, the more likely it is that shorter budget periods will be used.

General Principles of Budgeting

Budgeting involves the coordination of financial and nonfinancial planning to satisfy the goals and objectives of the organization. Although there is no foolproof way to prepare an effective budget, the following are accepted practices:

Top-management support.   All levels of management must be aware of the importance of the budget to the firm. Plans must be stated explicitly, and overemphasis on pure mechanics avoided. Overall broad objectives of the corporation must be decided and communicated through the organization.

Participation in goal setting.   It is generally accepted that an employee is more likely to strive to achieve organization goals if the employee participates in the goal setting.

Responsibility accounting.   People should know their own performance goals. Only those costs over which an individual has predominant control should be used in the evaluation of that individual's performance.

Communication of results.   People should be informed of their own progress in a timely and meaningful manner. Effective communication implies (1) timeliness, (2) reasonable accuracy, and (3) understandability. Results should be communicated in such a manner that adjustments can be made, if needed.

Flexibility. As basic assumptions underlying the preparation of the budget are altered during operations over the planning period, the budget should be restated so that the efficiency of the actual level of operations can be analyzed.

Behavioral Implications

Too often, the term *budget* has negative connotations to personnel who feel *subjected to* a budget. Too often, a budget is imposed by management without consideration of the opinions and feelings of the personnel affected. Such imposed budgets may bring both overt and subtle resistance to the budget. There may be a number of reasons why such resistance is encountered. These reasons might include a lack of understanding about the program, concern about status, expectation of increased pressure, a feeling that the method of performance evaluation is unfair, a feeling that the goals are unrealistic and unattainable, lack of confidence in the manner in which accounting figures are generated, and a preference for more informal communication and evaluation. Often, these fears are completely unfounded, but the important thing is that the employees may not believe they are and that because of their beliefs it is difficult to accomplish the objectives of budgeting. The problems encountered by such *imposed* budgets have led to greater use of *participatory budgeting.*[1]

Budget participation includes the active involvement of all levels of management in the setting of operating goals for the forthcoming period. Managers are much more likely to understand, accept, and pursue those goals which they were actively involved in formulating.

Managers should prepare budgets, and accountants should be the *compilers* or coordinators of budgets. Accountants should be on hand during the preparation process to present and explain significant financial data and their relationships. They should identify the relevant cost data that will enable management's objectives to be quantified into dollar terms. Accountants have the responsibility for meaningful budget reports. Everyone must have confidence in the accounting system, and accountants should strive to make the accounting system responsive to managerial needs.

THE MASTER BUDGET

The remainder of this chapter will concentrate on the master budget. The main emphasis will be on one part of the master budget, the operating

---

[1] Studies have shown that budget participation is not effective in some types of organizations. The effectiveness of participation as a tool will vary according to leadership style, organization structure, and organization size. Thus, participation is not a panacea for all the problems of budget preparation. Rather, it should be considered as a possible means of achieving better results in most organizations in which the philosophy of participation fits in with the actual managerial philosophy of the organization.

budget, because of that budget's importance in the financial planning and control of the business entity. Illustration 10.1 presents in simplified information flow form the major elements in the preparation of the master budget. Some of the more important aspects are:

1. The flow (in preparation) proceeds from the top of the chart to the bottom, with each lower level derived in part as a function of the previous level.
2. The end result is the preparation of the projected income statement and balance sheet. The elements making up these statements are contained in the previously prepared budgets.
3. The budgeting process starts with management's plans and objectives for the planning period. These plans result in various policy decisions concerning selling price, distribution network, advertising expenditures, and environmental influences from which the sales forecast (by product or product line) for the period is made.
4. Conversion from units to selling price forms the sales budget in dollars.
5. Projected cost of goods sold is based upon expected volume and inventory policy. Detailed budgets are made for each of the major types of manufacturing expenses both on a cost center (responsibility) basis and in the aggregate. Volume and inventory policy influence the preparation of the purchasing budget.
6. The projected balance sheet is derived from the operating budget, but it is also influenced by policy decisions pertaining to dividends, inventory, and credit, along with capital expenditures and financing plans.

This chapter will not cover all the areas of budgeting in detail, as whole books are devoted to the subject. The presentation that follows provides an overview of a budgeting procedure that has been used successfully by many business enterprises. As the presentation proceeds, it may be useful to refer to Illustration 10.1 and examine it in more detail, since it sets a frame of reference for the discussion.

Since the projected balance sheet in the master budget depends upon many items in the projected income statement, the starting place in the preparation of a master budget is the projected income statement. The projected income statement in budgetary terminology is often called the *operating budget,* while the projected balance sheet is called the *financial budget.* A number of supporting budgets are usually prepared.

Deriving the Operating Budget

The operating budget is derived from the sales budget and the production and selling, administrative, and other expense budgets.

The sales budget.   Because of the sales budget's primary importance, careful study and analysis must precede its preparation. The expected general level of economic activity in the budget period must be taken into

Illustration 10.1
A Flowchart of the Financial Planning Process (an Overview)

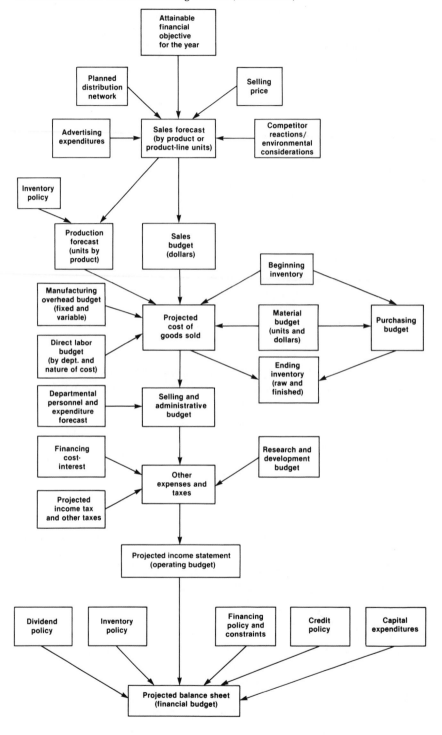

consideration. The prospects of the industry of which the company is a member must be considered. These prospects may be influenced in varying degrees by population growth, per capita income, new construction, population migration, and so forth. The relative position of the company in the industry must be considered and reviewed in the light of any expected or actively sought changes.

Allowance must be made for the strength of competitors and for varying conditions which affect different products or different territories. Allowance must also be made for any changes in the expected level of promotional expenditures. Quotas may be developed for salespersons as a result of sales analyses according to territories, customers, products, and so on. The sales budget is usually the responsibility of the sales manager. Based on expected selling prices, the sales budget may be prepared in units and later converted to dollars. Or a goal in dollars may be set first. Then estimates of selling prices and units of sales are made and a reasonable combination decided, based on management's goal regarding profit maximization, market penetration, or some other objective. In any event, the sales budget should eventually be stated in units to serve as a frame of reference for preparing the rest of the budget.

The production budget.   The production budget is affected by the sales budget and the company's inventory policy. It is first developed in terms of units. Unit costs can seldom be developed until production volume is known. The principal objective of the production budget is to achieve agreement in terms of time and quantity between the production of goods and their sale. Careful scheduling must be undertaken to maintain certain minimum quantities of inventory on hand while excessive accumulation is avoided. Also, the cost of carrying inventory on hand must be compared with the higher unit costs frequently encountered in producing relatively small batches of a product.

The production budget is often subdivided into budgets for materials, labor, and overhead. Usually, materials and labor will vary directly with production within a given *relevant range* of production. Overhead costs may not vary directly with production, but may be constant in total across the relevant range of production.

Selling, administration, and other expense budgets (schedules).   Departmental personnel and expenditure forecasts are used to budget the amounts of selling and administration expenses. Other expenses, such as interest expense, income tax expense, and research and development expenses, are also estimated.

Deriving the Financial Budget

The preparation of a projected balance sheet would ordinarily involve an analysis of each account appearing in that statement. The beginning balance would be taken from the balance sheet at the start of the budget period. The effect of any planned activities upon each account would then be taken into consideration. Many of the accounts will be affected by items appearing in the operating budget and by either cash inflows or outflows.

These cash inflows and outflows are usually shown in a cash budget. The complexities encountered in preparing the financial budget often will require the preparation of worksheets. These analyses include such things as planned accounts receivable collections and balances, planned material purchases, planned inventories, changes in all accounts affected by operating costs, and the amount of federal income taxes payable. Dividend policy, financing policy and constraints, credit policy, and any planned capital expenditures also affect amounts shown in the financial budget.

The preparation of a master budget for the Keller Company will now be illustrated.

The Master Budget Illustrated

Preparing the operating budget in units for the Keller Company. The operating budget may be first developed in terms of units rather than dollars. Since revenues and the bulk of the costs to be incurred will vary with volume, forecasts of revenues and costs can be derived more easily after quantities have been established. After performing the analysis for sales budgets, assume that sales for the year are forecast at 100,000 units. Quarterly sales are expected to be 20,000, 35,000, 20,000, and 25,000 units. In line with company policy of stabilizing production, the 100,000 units will be produced uniformly throughout the year at the rate of 25,000 units per quarter. A simplifying assumption made at this time is to assume an ending finished goods inventory but no beginning or ending work in process inventories. A more realistic assumption would be that work in process inventories remain stable throughout the year.

From the above data, a schedule of budgeted sales and production in terms of units is prepared (Illustration 10.2). Note the fluctuation in the ending inventory which must be accepted if sales vary and the management policy of stable production is to be implemented. Thus, the finished goods inventory serves the function of absorbing the difference between production and sales. In this case, a management decision has been made that it is less costly to deal with fluctuating inventories than with fluctuating production.

Preparing the operating budget in dollars. The operating budget is converted from units into dollars. A forecast of expected selling prices is made. In addition, an analysis of costs must be made along the lines previously outlined. The forecast selling prices and costs are shown in Illustration 10.3. The costs are classified as either variable or fixed and are budgeted accordingly. From Chapter 9, variable costs are those which vary in total directly

Illustration 10.2
Planned Sales and Production in Units

KELLER COMPANY
Planned Sales and Production

	Quarter Ending	
	March 31, 19x2	June 30, 19x2
	(in Units of Product)	
Sales forecast...............................	20,000	35,000
Production planned..........................	25,000	25,000
Increase (decrease) in finished goods inventory ...	5,000	(10,000)
Planned beginning finished goods inventory......	10,000*	15,000
Planned ending finished goods inventory.........	15,000	5,000

* Actual on January 1.

Illustration 10.3
Budget Estimate of Selling Price and Costs

KELLER COMPANY
Budget Estimates of Selling Price and Costs
For the Quarters Ending March 31 and June 30, 19x2

Forecast selling price............................	$	20
Manufacturing costs:		
Variable (per unit manufactured):		
Raw material		2
Direct labor		6
Overhead		1
Fixed overhead (total each quarter)..............		75,000
Selling and administrative expenses:		
Variable (per unit sold)........................		2
Fixed (total each quarter)		100,000

with production or sales and fixed costs are unaffected by the relative level of production or sales. Therefore, variable costs are budgeted as a constant dollar amount *per unit,* while fixed costs are budgeted only in total. Individual responsibility budgets could be prepared for each of the identifiable units of the entity and accumulated to form the overall budget. This is true for each budget area to be discussed in the remainder of the chapter.

A schedule showing the development of the forecast cost of goods manufactured and sold is prepared (Illustration 10.4).

Separate schedules are prepared for all of the selling and administrative expenses and their totals entered for each of the first two quarters, as shown in Illustration 10.5.

Illustration 10.4
Planned Cost of Goods Manufactured and Sold

KELLER COMPANY
Planned Cost of Goods Manufactured and Sold

	Quarter Ending	
	March 31, 19x2	June 30, 19x2
Beginning finished goods inventory	$130,000*	$180,000
Cost of goods manufactured:		
Raw materials (25,000 × $2)	$ 50,000	$ 50,000
Direct labor (25,000 × $6)	150,000	150,000
Variable overhead (25,000 × $1).............	25,000	25,000
Fixed overhead (per illustration 10.3).........	75,000	75,000
Cost of goods manufactured (25,000 units at $12)	$300,000	$300,000
Goods available for sale	$430,000	$480,000
Ending finished goods inventory:		
(15,000 at $12)†..........................	180,000	
(5,000 at $12)............................		60,000
Cost of goods sold.........................	$250,000	$420,000

* Actual on January 1.
† First-in, first-out procedure assumed.

Illustration 10.5
Projected Income Statements

KELLER COMPANY
Projected Income Statements
For Quarters Ending March 31 and June 30, 19x2

	Quarter Ending	
	March 31, 19x2	June 30, 19x2
Forecast sales (20,000 and 35,000 at $20) (per Illustration 10.3).....................	$400,000	$700,000
Cost of goods sold (per Illustration 10.4)........	250,000	420,000
Gross margin...............................	$150,000	$280,000
Selling and administrative expenses:		
Variable (20,000 and 35,000 at $2) (per Illustration 10.3).....................	$ 40,000	$ 70,000
Fixed (per Illustration 10.3)	100,000	100,000
Total expenses	$140,000	$170,000
Net income before income taxes	$ 10,000	$110,000
Estimated federal income taxes (assumed to be 50%).....................	5,000	55,000
Net income	$ 5,000	$ 55,000

All of the items appearing in the operating budget (Illustration 10.5) except the income tax accrual have been explained. Income taxes are budgeted in this case at an assumed level of 50 percent of net before taxes.

Illustration 10.5 shows the resulting operating budgets. If the operating budgets do not reveal the desired net income, new plans will have to be formulated and new budgets developed. But the purpose of preparing such a plan is to gain some knowledge of what the outcome of a period's activities will be prior to their actual occurrence.

The flexible operating budget. One of the basic principles of budgeting is to adjust the budget for changes in assumptions or changes in the level of operations. To cope with such changes, a technique known as flexible budgeting has been developed. Preparation of a flexible operating budget will include detailed estimates of expenses at various levels of output. For example, a flexible budget of manufacturing overhead costs at varying levels of output could be as in Illustration 10.6.

Illustration 10.6
Flexible Budget

Element of Overhead	Volume (Percent of Capacity)			
	70%	80%	90%	100%
Supplies	$ 4,200	$ 4,800	$ 5,400	$ 6,000
Power	11,500	13,000	14,500	16,000
Insurance	4,500	4,500	5,000	5,000
Maintenance.	12,000	13,000	14,000	14,800
Depreciation.	20,000	20,000	20,000	20,000
Supervision	28,000	28,000	28,000	28,000
	$80,200	$83,300	$86,900	$89,800

In Illustration 10.6, supplies are considered a strictly variable cost, although there are probably few costs that vary in an exact linear relationship with output. Power is considered here as a semivariable cost (it varies but not directly with volume), as it is assumed that beyond a minimum level it varies directly with output. Depreciation and supervision are fixed costs, while insurance and maintenance are semivariable costs. When a flexible budget is prepared, the amount of costs considered to be the budgeted amount in appraising performance is read from the flexible budget for the actual level of output experienced.

Budget variances. A *budget variance* is defined as the difference between an actual cost experienced at a certain level of operations and the budgeted amount for that same level of operations. Budget variances may thus be viewed as indicators or indices of efficiency since they emerge from a comparison of "what was" with "what should have been." To compute a budget variance, a flexible operating budget must be used. As an illustration of a way in which a flexible operating budget may be used, assume that the departmental budget in Illustration 10.6 is prepared based on the expectation of producing 100,000 units of product—the 100 percent of capacity level. Under such expectations, the budgeted amount for supplies would be $6,000, or $0.06 per unit. If at the end of the period, the actual amount of supplies consumed was $5,600, the first impression would be that of a favorable variance of $400. But if the production for the period was only 90,000 units, there was actually an unfavorable variance of $200. The flexible operating budget shows that at 90 percent of capacity, the supplies that should have been consumed amount to only $5,400. Consequently, there appears to have been some inefficiency in the use of supplies, and an unfavorable budget variance of $200 ($5,600 − $5,400) exists.

In another situation, maintenance may have been budgeted at $13,000 for a given period in the expectation that 80,000 units of product would be produced. This is at the 80 percent of operating capacity level. If actual maintenance costs total $13,900 for the period, this does not mean that an unfavorable variance of $900 has been incurred. Production volume must be known; assume it to be 90,000 units. At this level, maintenance costs are budgeted at $14,000; therefore, a favorable variance of $100 was experienced.

The main advantage of flexible operating budgets is to allow for appraisal of performance on two levels. First, the deviation from expected output can be analyzed. Then, given the actual level of operations, actual costs can be compared with expected costs for that level of output. The use of flexible or formula operating budgets makes it unnecessary to revise budget estimates when production volume differs from the volume expected. A formula budget is a projection stated in a mathematical formula instead of a formal document. In the case of variable costs, the expected cost at any level can be computed easily. In the case of certain semivariable costs, the budget amount for any level of operations other than those presented can be computed from the following formula:

Budget amount = Fixed costs + (Variable costs per unit × Units of output)

More complicated formulas are needed if the relationship between costs and volume above a minimum level of costs is not linear, that is, if the costs do not vary proportionately with production.

Other semivariable costs may change only when a sufficiently large increase in production occurs as, for example, when one additional inspector must be added for each 20 percent of capacity utilized. Such semivariable costs usually can be read directly from the flexible budget.

The preparation of budgets for selling expenses and for general administrative expenses is similar to the preparation of the manufacturing overhead budget. Several supporting budgets may be involved, such as budgets for advertising, office expenses, and payroll department expenses. In each case, the supporting budget may show the fixed expenses and the variable expenses at various levels of sales volume.

The flexible operating budget and budget variances illustrated. The Keller Company has prepared a detailed flexible operating budget for the quarter ending March 31, 19x2. The budget is based on the data in Illustration 10.3. The budget based on expected sales of 20,000 units and expected production of 25,000 units and actual results for the quarter ending March 31, 19x2, are shown in Illustration 10.7.

Illustration 10.7
Comparison of Expected Budget and Actual Results

KELLER COMPANY
Comparison of Expected Budget and Actual Results
Quarter Ending March 31, 19x2

	Budget	Actual
Sales	$400,000	$380,000
Cost of goods sold:		
Beginning finished goods inventory	$130,000	$130,000
Cost of goods manufactured:		
Raw materials	$ 50,000	$ 62,500
Direct labor	150,000	143,750
Variable overhead.............................	25,000	31,250
Fixed overhead	75,000	75,000
Cost of goods manufactured	$300,000	$312,500
Goods available for sale	$430,000	$442,500
Ending finished goods inventory	180,000	200,000
Cost of goods sold	$250,000	$242,500
Gross margin	$150,000	$137,500
Selling and administrative expenses:		
Variable	$ 40,000	$ 28,500
Fixed	100,000	95,000
Total expenses	$140,000	$123,500
Net income before income taxes	$ 10,000	$ 14,000
Estimated federal income taxes (50%).............	5,000	7,000
Net income	$ 5,000	$ 7,000

Assume that (1) the actual selling price of all units was $20 per unit, (2) actual production was 25,000 units, and (3) actual sales were 19,000 units.

The comparison of the original budget with actual results yields some useful information where actual performance deviated from planned performance. Sales were 1,000 units lower than expected; gross margin was $12,500 less than expected; and net income was $2,000 more than expected.

But the comparison does not show the expected expenditures for the actual level of output attained, a comparison useful for expense control.

Since the company expected to sell 20,000 units but only sold 19,000, a better analysis for expense control purposes can be made by using a flexible operating budget for 19,000 units (see Illustration 10.8). In such analyses,

Illustration 10.8
Comparison of Flexible Operating Budget and Actual Results

KELLER COMPANY
Comparison of Flexible Operating Budget and Actual Results
For Quarter Ending March 31, 19x2

	Budget	Actual	Budget Variance (Unfavorable)
Sales..........................	$380,000	$380,000	0
Cost of goods sold:			
Beginning finished goods inventory...	$130,000	$130,000	0
Cost of goods manufactured:			
Raw materials...................	$ 50,000	$ 62,500	$(12,500)
Direct labor....................	150,000	143,750	6,250
Variable overhead	25,000	31,250	(6,250)
Fixed overhead.................	75,000	75,000	0
Cost of goods manufactured....	$300,000	$312,500	$(12,500)
Goods available for sale............	$430,000	$442,500	$(12,500)
Ending finished goods inventory......	192,000	200,000	8,000
Cost of goods sold.............	$238,000	$242,500	$ (4,500)
Gross margin......................	$142,000	$137,500	$ (4,500)
Selling and administrative expenses:			
Variable.........................	$ 38,000	$ 28,500	$ 9,500
Fixed...........................	100,000	95,000	5,000
Total expenses	$138,000	$123,500	$ 14,500
Net income before income taxes......	$ 4,000	$ 14,000	$ 10,000
Estimated federal income taxes (50%)	2,000	7,000	(5,000)
Net income......................	$ 2,000	$ 7,000	$ 5,000

beginning and ending inventories often are not shown. Instead, the number of units *sold* times the unit cost of materials, labor, and overhead are shown.

A number of items become apparent when a comparison is made between actual expenses incurred and expected expenses for the actual level of output. The flexible operating budget (Illustration 10.8) reveals some inefficiencies. For instance, raw materials cost $2.50 ($62,500/25,000) instead of the $2 expected. Direct labor cost was only $5.75 ($143,750/25,000) per unit instead of the $6 expected. Variable overhead was $1.25 ($31,250/25,000) per unit instead of the $1 expected.

Net income was $5,000 more than expected at a sales level of 19,000 units. The main reason for the increase in net income was the lower-than-expected amounts of selling and administrative expenses. Variable selling and administrative expenses were only $1.50 ($28,500/19,000) per unit instead of the $2 expected; fixed selling and administrative expenses were only $95,000 instead of the $100,000 expected.

Preparing the financial budget for the Keller Company. The starting point in preparing the financial budget is to examine the balance sheet which existed at the beginning of the budget period. The balance sheet as of December 31, 19x1, is shown in Illustration 10.9.

The operating budget, shown in Illustration 10.5, as well as the other previous illustrations are helpful in preparing the financial budget.

Illustration 10.9
Balance Sheet at Beginning of Period

KELLER COMPANY
Balance Sheet
December 31, 19x1

Assets

Current assets:

Cash		$ 130,000
Accounts receivable		200,000
Inventories:		
Raw materials	$ 40,000	
Finished goods	130,000	170,000
Prepaid expenses		20,000
Total current assets		$ 520,000
Plant and equipment:		
Land		$ 60,000
Buildings	$1,000,000	
Less accumulated depreciation	400,000	600,000
Equipment	$ 600,000	
Less accumulated depreciation	180,000	420,000
Total plant and equipment		$1,080,000
Total assets		$1,600,000

Liabilities and Stockholders' Equity

Current liabilities:

Accounts payable		$ 80,000
Accrued liabilities		160,000
Federal income taxes payable		100,000
Total current liabilities		$ 340,000
Stockholders' equity:		
Capital stock (100,000 shares of $10 par value)		$1,000,000
Retained earnings		260,000
Total stockholders' equity		$1,260,000
Total liabilities and stockholders' equity		$1,600,000

Accounts receivable. To prepare a financial budget, schedules other than the ones already prepared in connection with the operating budget are usually prepared. The first of these is shown in Illustration 10.10. This schedule is prepared under the assumption that 60 percent of the current quarter's

Illustration 10.10
Planned Accounts Receivable Collections and Balances

KELLER COMPANY		
Planned Accounts Receivable Collections and Balances		
	Quarter Ending	
	March 31, 19x2	June 30, 19x2
Planned balance at beginning of quarter...............	$200,000*	$160,000
Planned sales for period (per Illustration 10.5)	400,000	700,000
Total......................................	$600,000	$860,000
Projected collections during quarter (per discussion in text)	440,000	580,000
Planned balance at end of quarter	$160,000	$280,000

* Actual on January 1.

sales are collected in that quarter plus all of the uncollected sales of the prior quarter. Thus, collections for the first quarter are estimated as 0.6($400,000) + $200,000 = $440,000. For the second quarter, they are estimated as 0.6($700,000) + $160,000 = $580,000. Several other simplifying assumptions are made, such as all sales are on credit and there are no sales returns or allowances, or discounts, or uncollectible accounts. Obviously, in an actual planning situation, allowance may have to be made for these items.

Inventories. A schedule of inventories should be prepared, starting with the planned purchases and inventory of raw materials. The planned usage and cost per unit are calculated from the production schedules. Assuming no work in process, the ending inventories will consist of raw materials and finished goods.

Illustration 10.11 shows the planned purchases and inventories of raw materials. The raw materials inventory had been built up above the normal level of one half of next quarter's planned usage because of a strike threat in the supplier company. This threat has now passed, and the inventory will be reduced in the first quarter to the normal planned level.

The calculation of planned ending finished goods inventories is included in Illustration 10.4.

Accounts affected by operating costs. Although individual schedules could be prepared for each of the accounts affected by operating costs, for illustrative purposes a schedule combining the analyses of all the accounts

Illustration 10.11
Planned Materials Purchases and Inventories

KELLER COMPANY
Planned Materials Purchases and Inventories

	Quarter Ending	
	March 31, 19x2	June 30, 19x2
Planned usage (25,000 × $2) (per Illustration 10.4)........	$50,000	$50,000
Planned ending inventory (½ × 25,000 × $2) (per discussion in text)	25,000	25,000
Planned raw materials available for use	$75,000	$75,000
Inventory at beginning of quarter	40,000*	25,000
Planned purchases for the quarter	$35,000	$50,000

* Actual on January 1.

affected by material purchases or operating costs is presented in Illustration 10.12.

The following assumptions were made:

1. All purchases of raw materials will be made on account.
2. Direct labor incurred will be credited to accrued liabilities.
3. Manufacturing overhead incurred will be credited to the following accounts:

	Quarter Ending	
	March 31	June 30
Accounts Payable.............................	$ 16,000	$ 13,000
Accrued Liabilities	60,000	64,000
Prepaid Expenses.............................	6,000	5,000
Accumulated Depreciation—Building	5,000	5,000
Accumulated Depreciation—Equipment	13,000	13,000
Total..................................	$100,000	$100,000

4. Selling and administrative expenses incurred will be credited to the following accounts:

	Quarter Ending	
	March 31	June 30
Accounts Payable.............................	$ 5,000	$ 10,000
Accrued Liabilities	130,000	154,000
Prepaid Expenses.............................	2,000	3,000
Accumulated Depreciation—Building	1,000	1,000
Accumulated Depreciation—Equipment	2,000	2,000
Total..................................	$140,000	$170,000

Illustration 10.12
Analyses of Accounts Credited for Materials Purchases and Operating Costs

KELLER COMPANY
Analyses of Accounts Credited for Materials Purchases and Operating Costs

	Total	Accounts Payable (Cr.)	Accrued Liabilities (Cr.)	Prepaid Expenses (Dr.)	Accumulated Depreciation Building (Cr.)	Accumulated Depreciation Equipment (Cr.)
Purchases or operating costs quarter ending March 31:						
Raw materials (per Illustration 10.11)	$ 35,000	$ 35,000				
Direct labor (per Illustration 10.4)	150,000		$150,000			
Overhead (per Illustration 10.4)	100,000	16,000	60,000	$ 6,000	$ 5,000	$ 13,000
Selling and administrative expense (per Illustration 10.5)	140,000	5,000	130,000	2,000	1,000	2,000
Total	$425,000	$ 56,000	$340,000	$ 8,000	$ 6,000	$ 15,000
Beginning balances (per Illustration 10.9)		$ 80,000	$160,000	$20,000	$400,000	$180,000
		$136,000	$500,000	$12,000	$406,000	$195,000
Planned cash payments		80,000	330,000			
Planned balances, March 31		$ 56,000	$170,000	$12,000	$406,000	$195,000
Purchases or operating costs quarter ending June 30:						
Raw materials (per Illustration 10.11)	$ 50,000	$ 50,000				
Direct labor (per Illustration 10.4)	150,000		$150,000			
Overhead (per Illustration 10.4)	100,000	13,000	64,000	$ 5,000	$ 5,000	$ 13,000
Selling and administrative expense (per Illustration 10.5)	170,000	10,000	154,000	3,000	1,000	2,000
Total	$470,000	$ 73,000	$368,000	$ 8,000	$ 6,000	$ 15,000
Total including March 31 balances		$129,000	$538,000	$ 4,000	$412,000	$210,000
Planned cash payments		56,000	354,000	10,000		
Planned balances, June 30		$ 73,000	$184,000	$14,000	$412,000	$210,000

5. Planned cash payments will be:

	Quarter Ending	
	March 31	June 30
Accounts Payable	$ 80,000	$ 56,000
Accrued Liabilities.............................	330,000	354,000
Prepaid Expenses	0	10,000
	$410,000	$420,000

Illustration 10.12 shows the analysis of accounts credited as a result of the above data. It provides a considerable amount of information needed in constructing financial budgets for the quarters ended March 31, 19x2, and June 30, 19x2. The balances for both dates for Accounts Payable, Accrued Liabilities, Prepaid Expenses, Accumulated Depreciation—Building, and Accumulated Depreciation—Equipment are computed in the schedule.

Federal income taxes payable.   A separate schedule could be prepared showing the changes in the Federal Income Taxes Payable account (it will be omitted here). The balances reported in the financial budgets are derived under the assumption that one half of the $100,000 liability shown in the December 31, 19x1, balance sheet is paid in each of the first two quarters of 19x2 (see Illustration 10.12). The accrual for the current quarter is added

Illustration 10.13
Planned Cash Flows and Cash Balances

KELLER COMPANY Planned Cash Flows and Cash Balances		
	Quarter Ending	
	March 31, 19x2	June 30, 19x2
Planned balance at beginning of quarter	$130,000*	$ 90,000
Planned cash receipts:		
Collections of accounts receivable (per Illustration 10.10)	440,000	580,000
	$570,000	$670,000
Planned cash disbursements:		
Payment of accounts payable (per Illustration 10.12)...	$ 80,000	$ 56,000
Payment of accrued liabilities (per Illustration 10.12) ..	330,000	354,000
Payment of federal income tax liability	50,000	50,000
Payment of dividends.............................	20,000	40,000
Expenses prepaid (per Illustration 10.12).............	0	10,000
Total disbursements	$480,000	$510,000
Planned balance at end of quarter....................	$ 90,000	$160,000

  * Actual on January 1.

Illustration 10.14
Projected Balance Sheet

KELLER COMPANY
Projected Balance Sheet

	March 31, 19x2	June 30, 19x2
Assets		
Current assets:		
Cash (per Illustration 10.13).....................	$ 90,000	$ 160,000
Accounts receivable (per Illustration 10.10).......	160,000	280,000
Inventories:		
Raw materials (per Illustration 10.11)	25,000	25,000
Finished goods (per Illustration 10.4)	180,000	60,000
Prepaid expenses (per Illustration 10.12).........	12,000	14,000
Total current assets	$ 467,000	$ 539,000
Plant and equipment:		
Land (per Illustration 10.9).....................	$ 60,000	$ 60,000
Buildings ($1,000,000 less accumulated depreciation of $406,000 and $412,000) (per Illustrations 10.9 and 10.12)	594,000	588,000
Equipment ($600,000 less accumulated depreciation of $195,000 and $210,000) (per Illustrations 10.9 and 10.12)	405,000	390,000
Total plant and equipment	$1,059,000	$1,038,000
Total assets	$1,526,000	$1,577,000
Liabilities and Stockholders' Equity		
Current liabilities:		
Accounts payable (per Illustration 10.12).........	$ 56,000	$ 73,000
Accrued liabilities (per Illustration 10.12)........	170,000	184,000
Federal income taxes payable (per discussion in text).......................................	55,000	60,000
Total current liabilities...................	$ 281,000	$ 317,000
Stockholders' equity:		
Capital stock (100,000 shares of $10 par value) (per Illustration 10.9)........................	$1,000,000	$1,000,000
Retained earnings (see below)	245,000*	260,000†
Total stockholders' equity...............	$1,245,000	$1,260,000
Total liabilities and stockholders' equity	$1,526,000	$1,577,000

* $260,000 (per Illustration 10.9) + earnings of $5,000 less dividends of $20,000.
† $245,000 + earnings of $55,000 less dividends of $40,000.

(see Illustration 10.5). Thus, the balance at March 31, 19x2, is $100,000 − $50,000 + $5,000 = $55,000. The balance at June 30, 19x2, is $55,000 − $50,000 + $55,000 = $60,000. At June 30, the balance is equal to the accrual for the current year of $5,000 for the first quarter and $55,000 for the second quarter.

Cash budget. After the analyses have been prepared, there should be enough information to prepare the cash budget to determine the balance of the Cash account at both dates. Illustration 10.14 refers to where the information came from with the exception of payment of federal income tax liability and payment of dividends.

It was assumed that the company would pay one half of the $100,000 income tax liability shown in the December 31, 19x1, balance sheet in each of the first two quarters ($50,000 in each quarter). It was also assumed that $20,000 of dividends would be paid in the first quarter and $40,000 in the second quarter. For the Keller Company, the cash budget would be as in Illustration 10.13.

The financial budgets illustrated.   The financial budgets for the quarters ended March 31, 19x2, and June 30, 19x2, are now prepared and are shown in Illustration 10.14.

The completion of the financial budgets for the two quarters completes the preparation of the master budget. Management now has on hand information which will assist it in appraising the results of the policies it instituted. If the results of these policies, as shown by the master budget, are unsatisfactory, the policies can be changed before serious difficulty is encountered. For example, the Keller Company management decided to stabilize production. The master budget shows that production can be stabilized even though sales fluctuate widely. The planned ending inventory at June 30 may be considered somewhat low in view of the fluctuations in sales, but management does have advance information of this fact.

Questions

1. What are the three main objectives of budgeting?
2. What is meant by the term *management by exception?* How does management by exception relate to budgeting?
3. What are five basic principles which, if followed, should improve the possibilities of preparing a meaningful budget? Why is each important?
4. What is the difference between an "imposed" budget and a "participatory" budget?
5. Define and explain a budget variance. Budget variances imply the use of what kind of budget?
6. What are the two major budgets in the master budget? Which should be prepared first? Why?

7. Distinguish between master and responsibility budgeting.
8. What is a flexible budget?
9. The budget established at the beginning of a given period carried an item for supplies in the amount of $40,000. At the end of the period, the supplies used amounted to $44,000. Can it be concluded from these data that either there was inefficient use of supplies or care was not exercised in purchasing the supplies?
10. Management must make certain assumptions about the business environment when preparing a budget. What areas should be considered?
11. Why is budgeted performance better than past performance as a basis for judging actual results?

Exercises

1. The Barry Slacks Company has decided to produce 60,000 pairs of slacks at a uniform rate throughout 19x2. The sales department of Barry Slacks Company has estimated sales for 19x2 according to the following schedule:

	Sales in Units
First quarter	16,000
Second quarter	13,000
Third quarter	15,000
Fourth quarter	21,000
Total for 19x2	65,000

If the December 31, 19x1, inventory is estimated to be 8,000 pairs of slacks, prepare a schedule of planned sales and production (in units) for the first two quarters of 19x2.

2. Labor and materials of Slocum Company are considered to be variable costs. Expected production for the year is 100,000 units. At that level of production, labor cost is budgeted at $375,000 and materials cost is expected to be $165,000. Prepare a flexible budget for labor and materials for possible production levels of 70,000, 80,000, and 90,000 units of production.

3. Assume that in Exercise 2, actual production was 80,000 units and material cost was $135,000 while labor cost was $297,000. What is the budget variance?

4. The following data apply to the collection of accounts receivable for the Lunatti Company.

Current balance—February 28—$100,000 (of which $60,000 relates to February sales).
Planned sales for March—$500,000.

Assumptions: 70 percent of sales are collected in the month of sale, 20 percent in the following month, and the remaining 10 percent in the second month after the sale. Prepare a schedule of planned collections and ending balance for accounts receivable as of March 31, 19x2.

5. The Welsh Company expects to sell 30,000 units of gadgets during the next quarter at a price of $10 per unit. Production costs (all variable) are $3.50 per unit. Selling and administrative expenses are: variable, $2.50 per unit; and fixed, $80,000 in total. What is the budgeted net income? (Do not consider taxes.)

6. Fixed production costs for the Roiz Company are budgeted at $80,000 assuming 40,000 units of production. Actual sales for the period were 35,000 units, while actual production was 40,000 units. Actual fixed costs used in computing cost of goods sold were $70,000. What is the budget variance?

Business Decision Problem 10–1

The Mackle Company has applied at a local bank for a short-term loan of $25,000 starting on October 1. The loan will be repaid with interest at 10 percent on December 31. The bank's loan officer has requested a cash budget from the company for the quarter ending December 31. The following budget information is needed to prepare the cash budget for the quarter ending December 31:

Sales	$108,000
Purchases	60,000
Salaries and wages to be paid	21,000
Rent payments	1,200
Supplies (payments for)	800
Insurance payments	300
Other cash payments	3,700

A cash balance of $4,000 is planned for October 1. Accounts receivable are expected to be $8,000 on October 1. All of these accounts will be collected in the quarter ending December 31. Sales are collected 90 percent in the quarter of sale and 10 percent in the quarter after sale. Accounts payable will be $80,000 on October 1 and will be paid during the quarter ending December 31. All purchases are paid for in the quarter after purchase.

Required:

a. Prepare a cash budget for the quarter ending December 31. Assume that the $25,000 loan will be made on October 1 and will be repaid with interest at 10 percent on December 31.
b. Will the company be able to repay the loan on December 31? If the company desires a minimum cash balance of $3,000, will the company be able to repay the loan as planned?

Solutions to End-of-Chapter Questions, Exercises, and Business Decision Problems

Answers to Questions

1. Many objectives may be sought through budgeting. The three main objectives are:
   a. Planning for future.
   b. Controlling earnings through timely variance analysis and responsibility accounting.
   c. Motivating employees.
2. Management by exception is a method that devotes attention to items which do not turn out as expected, that is, deviations from the normal. To make the method operational, a careful analysis of expected results must be made before-

hand. The master budget is a quantification of expected results for the forthcoming period.

3. The principles and their importance are:

   a. Top-management support—the budget must be viewed as worthwhile.

   b. Participation—gives employees a voice in setting standards; develops a greater awareness of firm goals.

   c. Responsibility accounting—individuals are held accountable for costs, revenues, and assets over which they have control.

   d. Timeliness—results must be communicated on a basis that permits corrective action to be taken.

   e. Flexibility—as basic assumptions underlying the preparation of the budget are altered during the year, the budget should be able to reflect those changes.

4. Imposed budgets and participatory budgets are not necessarily different. The terms refer to the process of preparing a budget. An imposed budget is prepared at the top and handed down to the employees, who are expected to perform within the budget. A participatory budget implies that all levels which have control or responsibility for given performance levels are involved in the budgetary process, including the formulation of reasonable goals for the forthcoming period.

5. A budget variance is the difference between actual expenses at a given level of operation and the expected expenses for that level of operation. Budget variances imply the use of flexible budgets and are considered indices of efficiency.

6. The two budgets included in the master budget are the operating budget and the financial budget. The operating budget should be prepared first, since many of the elements in it will affect the financial budget.

7. Master budgeting is the preparation of the projected financial statements, that is, the expression of the company's objectives in terms of a projected income statement and balance sheet. Responsibility budgeting can be practiced within the confines of master budgeting, but its essential feature is that budgets are established for individuals or cost centers that contain only those costs within the control of the individual or the supervisor of the cost center. Under responsibility budgeting, all costs are deemed to be the responsibility of someone.

8. A flexible budget is one in which the various costs are budgeted for a number of different levels of output rather than for a single level.

9. The data given are not sufficient to allow this conclusion. Actual production may have exceeded planned production by more than 10 percent. In such an instance, there would be a favorable variance relative to the use of supplies.

10. Assumptions should be explicitly spelled out. Areas which have particular relevance are:

    a. The expected state of the economy.

    b. Plans for adding, deleting, or changing product lines.

    c. The nature of competition.

    d. The effect of government regulations.

11. Budgeted performance is, in part, based upon past performance. However, it is much more than that. It spells out what the expected results are from this year's managerial, production, and sales activities. Budget performance is better than past performance as a basis for judging actual results because it relates to the current year's expected activities under the current year's conditions.

Solutions to Exercises

1.

BARRY SLACKS COMPANY
Planned Sales and Production
(in Pairs of Slacks)

	Quarter Ending	
	March 31, 19x2	June 30, 19x2
Production planned..................................	15,000	15,000
Estimated sales	16,000	13,000
Increase (decrease) in finished goods inventory............	(1,000)	2,000
Planned beginning finished goods inventory...............	8,000	7,000
Planned ending finished goods inventory	7,000	9,000

2. As variable expenses, labor and material cost should vary directly with production.

Labor cost per unit = $375,000 ÷ 100,000 units = $3.75/unit
Material cost per unit = $165,000 ÷ 100,000 units = $1.65/unit

SLOCUM COMPANY
Flexible Budget

Production Volume	Labor	Materials
100,000 units................	$375,000	$165,000
90,000 units................	337,500	148,500
80,000 units................	300,000	132,000
70,000 units................	262,500	115,500

3.

SLOCUM COMPANY

	Actual Cost	Budgeted Cost	Budget Variance (Unfavorable)
Labor....................	$297,000	$300,000	$3,000
Materials	135,000	132,000	(3,000)
Total	$432,000	$432,000	$ 0

4.

LUNATTI COMPANY
Planned Accounts Receivable Collection and Balance
Month Ending March 31, 19x2

Balance at beginning of month	$100,000	
Sales during month..................................	500,000	$600,000
Less collections for the month:		
Collections relating to current balance:		
Remainder of January sales......................	$ 40,000	
February sales (⅔ of $60,000)....................	40,000	$ 80,000
Collections relating to March sales ($500,000 × 0.7)....		350,000
Total collections		$430,000
Balance—March 31, 19x2.............................		$170,000
Composition of ending balance:		
From February sales	$ 20,000	
From March sales.................................	150,000	
	$170,000	

5.

WALSH COMPANY
Planned Sales and Net Income

Sales—30,000 × $10		$300,000
Cost of goods sold—30,000 × $3.50		105,000
Gross margin		$195,000
Selling and administrative expenses:		
Variable—30,000 × $2.50	$75,000	
Fixed	80,000	155,000
Budgeted net income		$ 40,000

6. There is no budget variance. Fixed cost per unit of production is $2. Actual production equaled expected production. Since production was greater than sales, $10,000 of the fixed cost (5,000 units × $2) goes into the cost of inventory.

Solution to Business Decision Problem 10–1

a.

MACKLE COMPANY
Cash Budget
For the Quarter Ending December 31, 19x2

Planned balance at beginning of quarter		$ 4,000
Planned cash receipts:		
Short-term note		25,000
Collection of accounts receivable $8,000 + 0.9($108,000)		105,200
		$134,200
Planned cash disbursements:		
Payment of accounts payable	$80,000	
Salaries and wages	21,000	
Rent	1,200	
Supplies	800	
Insurance	300	
Other	3,700	
Repayment of loan	25,000	
Payment of interest on loan	625	132,625
Planned balance at end of quarter		$ 1,575

b. The company will be able to repay the loan on December 31. If the company desires a minimum cash balance of $3,000, it will not be able to repay all of the loan and interest because the resulting cash balance will be only $1,575.

11

Cost-Volume-Profit Analysis for Short-Term Decision Making

Chapter Goals

When you have completed Chapter 11, you should be able to:

1. Explain how costs are separated into fixed and variable categories.
2. Identify the behavior of costs in relation to changes in level of activity.
3. Compute the break-even point in terms of sales dollars, units, and percentage of capacity.
4. Describe and use the techniques in cost-volume-profit analysis (including the contribution margin and break-even charts) and explain the circumstances in which they may be applied.
5. Explain the practical aspects of cost-volume-profit analysis, including the multiproduct situation and the types of fixed costs (committed and discretionary).
6. List the assumptions made in cost-volume-profit analysis.

Although cost-volume profit analysis alone is insufficient to support managerial decision making, basic cost-volume-profit relationships should be understood by management. Knowledge of cost-volume-profit relationships can be used to determine the effect on income of any change in fixed costs, variable costs, or sales price. Such knowledge, for instance, may help management to determine (1) whether to increase sales promotion costs in an effort to increase sales volume, (2) whether an order at a lower-than-usual price should be accepted, and (3) whether plant facilities should be expanded. Planning, in general, is facilitated by careful study of break-even charts. Indeed, it has been said that, to be successful, management must become "break-even minded."

Cost-volume profit analysis is a means of predicting what effect changes in costs and volume will have on a company's net income in the *short run*. In the short run, plant capacity and certain costs are assumed to be fixed, although all costs are subject to variation in the long run.

Cost-volume-profit analysis can be used to answer such questions as: At what level of sales will a company break even (i.e., have neither net income nor a net loss)? What volume of sales is required to generate a certain level of net income? What effect will a change in selling prices, sales volume, or costs have on net income?

The relevant income statement format for cost-volume-profit analysis is:

Revenues...........................	$xx
Less: Variable costs	xx
Contribution margin.................	$xx
Less: Fixed costs...................	xx
Net income.........................	$xx

Variable costs, fixed costs, and contribution margin all have been discussed.

THE BEHAVIOR OF COSTS

Knowledge of the behavior and nature of costs is crucial to management for decision making. Two basic categories of costs are generally used—variable and fixed.

Fixed and Variable Costs

Variable costs (Illustration 11.1, part *a*) are those which vary directly with changes in volume. For example, if volume increases 10 percent, variable costs increase 10 percent. Certain production costs, such as raw materials and the labor used to convert the raw materials into finished products, vary directly with production volume, while other costs, such as sales commissions, vary directly with sales volume. *Fixed costs* (Illustration 11.1, part *b*) are those which remain constant over the entire range of output. They are often described as time-related costs. That is, they will be incurred simply

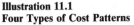

Illustration 11.1
Four Types of Cost Patterns

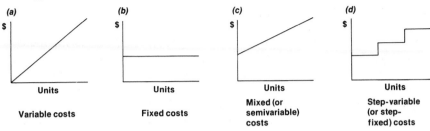

because of the passage of time if the company expects to continue to operate. Depreciation, property insurance, property taxes, and administrative salaries are examples of time-related costs and, therefore, are fixed costs. More will be said about fixed cost at the end of this chapter.

Mixed and Step-Variable Costs

Besides these two basic categories of variable and fixed costs, there are two other types of costs which are in part fixed and in part variable. These include *mixed* (or *semivariable*) costs (Illustration 11.1, part c) and *step-variable* (or *step-fixed*) costs (Illustration 11.1, part d).

Mixed costs.   An example of a *mixed cost* occurs when a given amount of maintenance cost has to be incurred while a plant is completely idle. Once production is under way, additional maintenance costs vary with production volume. These costs may be separated into their fixed and variable components as shown:

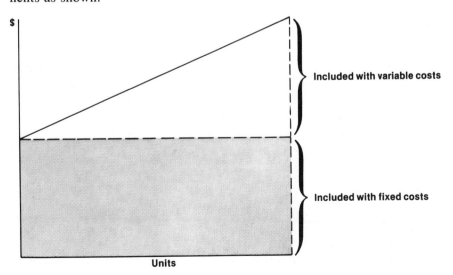

When divided in this way, the top part fits the variable cost pattern, as shown in Illustration 11.1, part *a*. The bottom part fits the fixed-cost pattern, as shown in Illustration 11.1, part *b*.

In a business situation, there may be difficulty in estimating a particular mixed cost. The fixed portion of a particular mixed cost represents the cost of having a service available for use. The variable portion is the cost associated with various levels of activity (usually defined as production or sales volume).

The scatter diagram. One method for estimating the total amount of a mixed cost at various levels of activity is to prepare a *scatter diagram* in which actual costs incurred are plotted.

Assume that Illustration 11.2 is a scatter diagram representing total maintenance costs for a firm's fleet of delivery trucks. The dots on the diagram

Illustration 11.2
Scatter Diagram

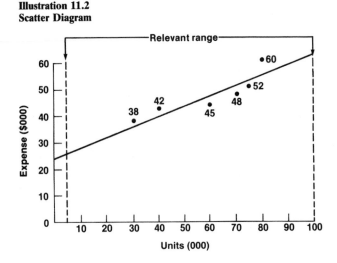

represent historical costs at various levels of activity. The line is drawn through what appears visually to be the center of the pattern of these dots. In the example, the fixed element of the mixed cost is $23,000. Since the line (called a regression line) rises from $23,000 to $63,000 over the range of 100,000 units, the slope of the variable cost portion is:

$$\frac{\$63,000 - \$23,000}{100,000 \text{ units}}$$

or $0.40 per unit. Thus, the variable portion of this cost is equal to $0.40 per unit. The data in the chart suggest that the firm's truck maintenance costs can be estimated at $23,000 plus 40 cents for every mile driven.

A more sophisticated method, called the *least squares method,* could be used to draw the regression line. This method is more precise since it involves statistical analysis, but is not presented here.

The high-low method. This is another widely used method for identifying the behavior of mixed costs. The *high-low method* involves the use of only the highest and lowest plots on a scatter diagram to determine the relationship between volume and variable cost.

Assume that in Illustration 11.2 the lowest plot is $38,000 of expense at 30,000 units of output and the highest plot is $60,000 at 80,000 units of output. The amount of variable cost per unit is found as follows:

$$\frac{\text{Change in expense}}{\text{Change in output}} = \frac{\$60,000 - \$38,000}{80,000 \text{ units} - 30,000 \text{ units}}$$

$$= \frac{\$22,000}{50,000} = \$0.44 \text{ per unit}$$

The fixed-cost portion is then found as:

Total cost at 80,000 units of output.	$60,000
Less: Variable cost at that level of output (80,000 × $0.44)	35,200
Fixed cost at all levels of output within the relevant range	$24,800

The high-low method is less precise than the scatter diagram method since it uses only two data points in the computation. Either or both points may not be representative of the data as a whole.

Step-variable costs. *Step-variable costs* can be handled in one of two ways. The first is to assume that a straight-line relationship exists, as shown below by the slanted dotted line:

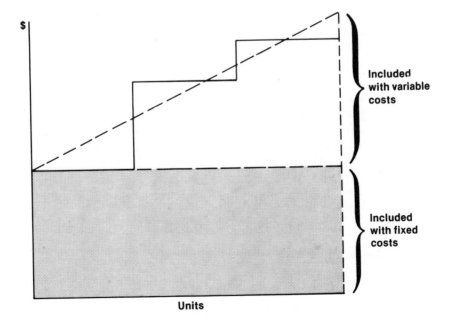

When this method is used, the costs may be separated into their fixed and variable components as for mixed costs.

When step-variable costs are present and there are very few steps (one or two usually), it is sometimes useful to treat the costs as "step-fixed." To illustrate, assume that between 0 and 40 percent of capacity a cost is $20,000 and that at over 40 percent of capacity it becomes $50,000, as shown:

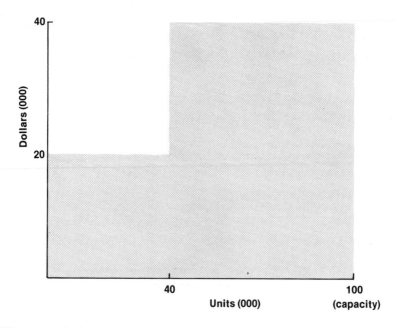

When costs behave in this step-fixed manner, the best approach to analyzing operations is to treat the fixed cost as being $20,000 for the 0 to 40 percent level of capacity and as being $50,000 for the 40 to 100 percent level of capacity.

Even though there are four different types of cost patterns, two basic categories—variable and fixed—may be used to include all of them. One other comment is in order. Some variable costs do not vary in a strictly linear relationship with volume. Rather, they vary in a curvilinear pattern— a 10 percent increase in volume may yield an 8 percent change in costs at lower output levels and an 11 percent change in costs at higher output levels. A curvilinear relationship is diagramed in Illustration 11.3 and can be handled with a mathematical formula. But, for the balance of this chapter, only linear or straight-line variable costs will be dealt with.

TOOLS FOR ANALYSIS

Of the various tools available, cost-volume-profit analysis, the break-even chart, margin of safety, and contribution margin concepts will be presented.

Illustration 11.3
Curvilinear Cost Pattern

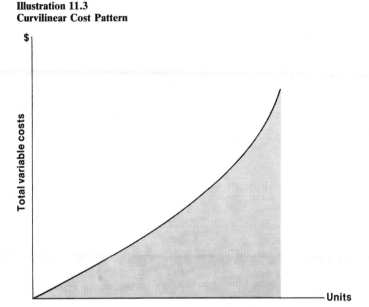

Cost-Volume-Profit Analysis

In planning future operations, a type of analysis sometimes referred to as *cost-volume-profit* (or *break-even*) *analysis* is undertaken. In such an analysis, the company's break-even point is calculated. A company is said to break even for a given period if the sales revenue and the costs charged to that period are equal. As a result, no element of income or loss remains. *The break-even point is defined as the level of operations at which revenues and costs are equal.*

To undertake a careful and accurate cost-volume-profit analysis requires knowledge of costs and their behavior as volume changes. Management must be able to distinguish among the different types of costs involved in its operations. Of course, the types and quantities of cost data accumulated will depend on the costs of obtaining the data compared to the benefits resulting from more refined information. Within this constraint, it is desirable to compute break-even points for each area of decision making within the company. Some important classifications of cost data for break-even analysis are by product, territory, salesperson, class of customer, and method of selling.

Several procedures are available for calculating a break-even point. It may be expressed (1) in dollars of sales revenue, (2) in number of units produced (sold), or (3) as a percentage of capacity.

Assume that a company manufactures a single product which it sells for $20. Fixed costs per period total $40,000, while variable costs are $12 per unit, or 60 percent of sales price. A linear relationship between variable costs and sales revenue is assumed to exist. Thus, variable costs are, within a given range of sales activity or sales volume, a constant percentage of sales. In this example, variable costs are 60 percent of sales. The sales revenue needed to break even is computed as follows:

$$\text{Sales } (S) = \text{Fixed costs } (FC) + \text{Variable costs } (VC)$$

Fixed costs are known to be \$40,000, while variable costs as a percentage of sales are equal to $0.60S$. The break-even equation becomes:

$$S = \$40,000 + 0.60S$$
$$S - 0.60S = \$40,000$$
$$0.40S = \$40,000$$
$$S = \$40,000 \div 0.40$$
$$S = \$100,000$$

Sales at the break-even point are \$100,000, and this can easily be proven. At that level, fixed costs will be \$40,000 and variable costs will be \$60,000 ($0.60 \times \$100,000$). The break-even point in units can be computed by dividing total sales revenue at the break-even point by the selling price per unit ($\$100,000 \div \$20 = 5,000$ units).

Newspaper reports often refer to the break-even point of the steel industry, or of a company in that industry, as a percentage of capacity, for example, 65 percent. If desired, the break-even point can be expressed in terms of capacity. If in the example presented above, the output capacity of the plant is 25,000 units, the break-even point in terms of plant capacity is 20 percent ($5,000 \div 25,000$).

The Break-Even Chart

The *break-even chart* in Illustration 11.4 graphically presents the break-even point for the above company. Each *break-even* chart (or analysis) is assumed valid only for a specified *relevant range* of volumes. For volumes outside these ranges, incurrence of different costs will alter the assumed relationship. For example, if only a few units were produced, the variable costs per unit would probably be quite high. Also, to produce more than 10,000 units, it may be necessary to add to plant capacity, thus incurring additional fixed costs, or to work extra shifts, thus incurring overtime charges and other inefficiencies. In either case, the cost relationships first assumed are no longer valid. Illustration 11.4 is based on data *relevant* for output from 500 to 10,000 units. Different cost and revenue patterns may exist outside these limits.

Illustration 11.4 shows that the break-even volume of sales is \$100,000 (5,000 units at \$20). At this level of sales, fixed costs and variable costs are exactly equal to sales revenue:

Revenues	$100,000
Less: Variable costs.	60,000
Contribution margin	$ 40,000
Less: Fixed costs	40,000
Net Income	$ 0

The break-even (cost-volume-profit) chart shows that a period of complete idleness would produce a loss of $40,000, the amount of fixed costs, while output of 10,000 units would produce net income of $40,000. Other points which can be read show that with sales of 7,500 units total revenue would be $150,000. At that point, total costs would amount to $130,000, generating net income of $20,000.

The break-even point can be lowered by increasing the selling price per unit, decreasing the total fixed costs, or decreasing the variable cost per unit. This can be seen by studying Illustration 11.4 and imagining that either the slope of the sales line increases (becomes steeper), or the distance between the variable costs and total costs lines diminishes, or the slope of the variable

Illustration 11.4
The Break-Even Chart

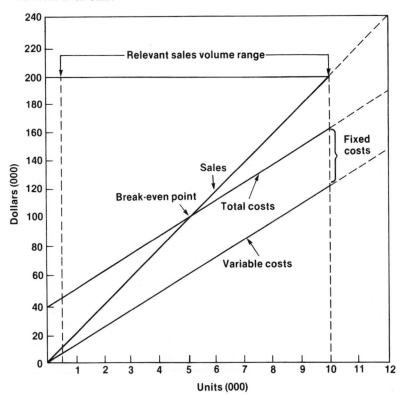

costs line decreases. The effect of each of these is to lower the break-even point. Taking opposite actions will increase the break-even point.

For example, assume that a company currently has variable costs of $15 per unit, fixed costs of $27,000, and a selling price of $60 per unit. Its break-even point is $36,000 ($27,000/0.75) or 600 ($36,000/$60) units. If the company can increase its selling price by $15 per unit while holding variable costs and fixed costs the same, the break-even point will decrease by $2,250:

$$S = FC + VC$$

$$S = \$27,000 + \frac{\$15}{\$75}\,S$$

$$S = \$27,000 + 0.2S$$

$$S - 0.2S = \$27,000$$

$$0.8S = \$27,000$$

$$S = \$27,000 \div 0.8$$

$$S = \$33,750 \text{ break-even point}$$

Original break-even point $36,000
Break-even point with $15 increase in selling prices.............. 33,750
Decrease in break-even volume of sales .... $ 2,250

Margin of Safety

If a company's current sales are above its break-even point, the company is said to have a *margin of safety* equal to the difference between current sales and sales at the break-even point. The margin of safety is the amount by which sales can decrease before a loss will be incurred. For example, assume current sales are $250,000, and sales at the break-even point are $200,000. The margin of safety is $50,000, or 20 percent of sales:

Margin of safety
(absolute) = Current sales − Break-even sales
= $250,000 − $200,000 = $50,000

or

$$\text{Margin of safety (percentage)} = \frac{\text{Current sales} - \text{Break-even sales}}{\text{Current sales}}$$

$$= \frac{\$250,000 - \$200,000}{\$250,000}$$

$$= 20 \text{ percent}$$

The Contribution Margin Concept

Contribution margin is defined as the amount by which revenue exceeds the variable costs incurred in securing that revenue. This amount often is referred to as marginal income. It may be computed for a given number of units (or dollars of sales) or per unit or dollar of sales.

Using previous data (selling price per unit of $20 and variable costs per unit of $12 with total fixed costs of $40,000), the contribution margin per unit is $8. The sale of one additional unit will add $20 to total revenues, $12 to total costs, and $8 to net income (ignoring income taxes). From this information, the break-even point in units can be computed. Each unit contributes $8 to the coverage of fixed costs, and fixed costs total $40,000. Thus, the sale of 5,000 units is necessary to cover the fixed costs:

Break-even point in units = Fixed costs ÷ Contribution margin per unit

At the break-even point, the total contribution margin will equal the total fixed costs, as shown in Illustration 11.5.

Illustration 11.5
Break-Even Chart Showing That Fixed Costs Equal Contribution Margin at Break-Even Point

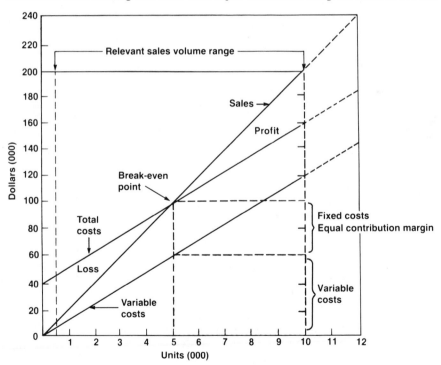

The break-even point in terms of dollars of sales can also be computed by dividing the fixed costs per period by the *contribution margin rate*. This rate is computed by dividing the contribution margin by sales price per unit. In the above data, it is 40 percent ($8 ÷ $20), and the break-even point is $100,000 of sales revenue ($40,000 ÷ 0.40).

In addition, the net income at any level of output can be computed as the contribution margin per unit multiplied by the number of units sold, less the total fixed costs. Using the above data, the net income at the 80 percent level of capacity can be determined. First, multiply 8,000 units (0.80 × 10,000) by $8, obtaining $64,000; then subtract the fixed costs of $40,000, leaving net income of $24,000. In this case, the contribution margin more than covers the total fixed costs. The remainder is net income (ignoring income taxes), as shown in Illustration 11.6.

Illustration 11.6
Break-Even Chart Showing Sales Level for Desired Net Income

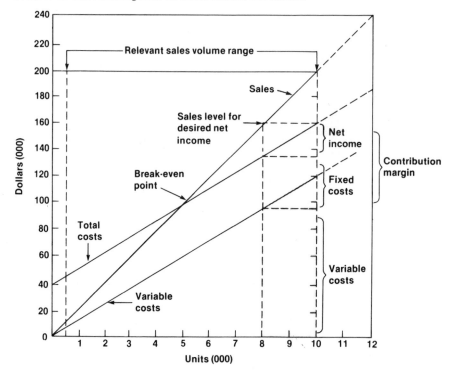

A simple example may aid in reinforcing understanding of some of these concepts. Break-even analysis can be used to analyze the cost-volume-profit relationships for a venture or project. Suppose that a major airline desires to know the number of seats that have to be sold on a certain flight to break even. To solve this problem, the costs have to be identified and separated into fixed and variable categories.

The fixed costs are those that do not vary with different levels of seats filled. These include such costs as fuel required to fly the plane with crew (no passengers) to destination; depreciation on the plane and facilities utilized on this flight; salaries of crew members, gate attendants, and maintenance and refueling personnel; and other miscellaneous fixed costs.

The variable costs include those costs that vary directly with the number of passengers. These might include such costs as extra fuel consumed per passenger, food and beverages included in the price of the ticket, baggage handling costs per passenger, and miscellaneous variable costs.

Assume that after the various costs have been analyzed and have been classified as fixed or variable, the fixed costs for a given flight are $12,000. The variable costs are $25 per passenger, and tickets are sold at $125. This yields a contribution margin per ticket of $100 ($125 − $25). Assume also that there are 300 seats on the aircraft.

The break-even point can be expressed in dollars, in number of passengers, or in percentage of capacity.

The sales revenue needed to break even is:

$$\text{Sales } (S) = \text{Fixed costs } (FC) + \text{Variable costs } (VC)$$
$$S = \$12,000 + 0.2\,S$$
$$0.8\,S = \$12,000$$
$$S = \$15,000$$

The break-even sales revenue may also be found using the contribution margin rate formula:

$$\text{BEP (dollars)} = \frac{FC}{\text{Contribution margin rate}}$$
$$= \frac{\$12,000}{80 \text{ percent}}$$
$$= \$15,000$$

The break-even point in terms of number of passengers may be found by dividing the break-even point in dollars ($15,000) by the selling price per unit ($125). Thus, $15,000/$125 = 120 passengers. It may also be found as follows:

$$\text{BEP (units)} = \frac{FC}{\text{Contribution margin}}$$
$$= \frac{\$12,000}{\$125 - \$25}$$
$$= 120 \text{ passengers}$$

The break-even point in percentage of capacity is:

$$\frac{\text{BEP (units)}}{\text{Total capacity (units)}} = \frac{120 \text{ passengers}}{300 \text{ passengers}} = 40 \text{ percent}$$

Additional Uses of Cost-Volume-Profit Analysis

Cost-volume-profit analysis may also be useful in determining the level of sales volume needed to generate some desired level of net income. To illustrate using the first set of data, if management wished to generate $24,000 of net income, Illustration 11.6 shows that sales volume must be 8,000 units, $160,000, or 80 (8,000 ÷ 10,000) percent of capacity.

Now assume that management has the opportunity to operate at 100 percent of capacity if it will increase its fixed costs by investing $10,000 in a sales promotion contract. Will it be profitable for management to make such an investment? Illustration 11.7 shows that net income would increase to

Illustration 11.7
Break-Even Chart Showing Earnings Resulting from Action Taken

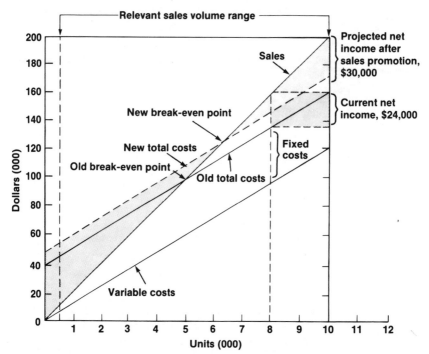

$30,000, provided the cost and revenue estimates are correct and the objective of management is to maximize net income.

Further, assume that XYZ Company's sales are currently $60,000, variable costs are $25,000, and fixed costs are $30,000. Net income is $5,000:

Net income (NI) = Sales (S) − Variable costs (VC) − Fixed costs (FC)
        = $60,000 − $25,000 − $30,000
        = $5,000

A 5 percent increase in sales price, with variable costs and fixed costs remaining the same, would have the following effect on the net income of XYZ Company:

$$NI = \$60,000(1.05) - \$25,000 - \$30,000$$
$$= \$63,000 - \$25,000 - \$30,000$$
$$= \$8,000$$

XYZ Company's net income will increase by $3,000, or 60 percent ($3,000/$5,000), if the sales price increases by 5 percent and variable and fixed costs stay the same.

Now, suppose the sales price increases by 5 percent (over $60,000) and variable costs increase by 10 percent. Net income would be $5,500:

$$NI = \$60,000(1.05) - \$25,000(1.10) - \$30,000$$
$$= \$63,000 - \$27,500 - \$30,000$$
$$= \$5,500$$

The result is a $500, or 10 percent ($500/$5,000), increase in net income.

Some of the practical aspects of cost-volume-profit analysis will be discussed in the remainder of the chapter.

SOME PRACTICAL ASPECTS OF COST-VOLUME-PROFIT ANALYSIS

The practical aspects and application of cost-volume-profit analysis to be discussed include its use for multiproduct firms, the meaning of the term *units* in the analysis, the true nature of fixed costs, and the assumptions in cost-volume-profit analysis.

Cost-Volume-Profit Analysis for the Multiproduct Firm

The previous discussion allowed calculation of the break-even point in terms of units, sales dollars, or percentage of capacity. When computing the break-even point for a multiproduct firm, only sales dollars are used. The assumption must be made that the *product mix*—that is, the number of units of each type of product sold—is known in advance.

To illustrate the situation for a multiproduct firm, assume the following historical data:

	Products							
	1		2		3		Total	
	Amt.	%	Amt.	%	Amt.	%	Amt.	%
Sales.................	$60,000	100	$30,000	100	$10,000	100	$100,000	100
Less: Variable expenses...........	40,000	67	16,000	53	4,000	40	60,000	60
Contribution margin.....	$20,000	33	$14,000	47	$ 6,000	60	$ 40,000	40

The sales mix for the products is 60 : 30 : 10, respectively, and total variable costs are 60 percent of total sales. If this sales mix can be expected to hold in the future, the break-even point for a future period can be found (assuming fixed costs are $50,000):

$$S = FC + VC$$
$$S = \$50,000 + 0.6S$$
$$0.4S = \$50,000$$
$$S = \$125,000$$

The $125,000 can be broken down into products by multiplying it by 60 percent, 30 percent, and 10 percent, respectively.

If historical patterns are not expected to hold in the future, *projected* sales and variable expenses should be used in determining the total expected percentage of variable expenses to total sales.

The Meaning of Units as a Measure of Volume

In the various cost-volume-profit charts included throughout this chapter, the horizontal axis has been labeled "units." A practical question is whether this is units of production or units sold. An implicit assumption in this type of analysis is that production is equal to sales. In other words, inventories do not vary from the beginning to the end of the period because in the long run production must equal sales. In the short run, this might not occur.

Some of the costs which a company will incur vary directly with production (e.g., supplies used in manufacturing), and some vary directly with sales (e.g., sales commissions). The nature of this problem is recognized, but it is best to assume that production is equal to sales for this type of analysis. Therefore, whether "units" is labeled units of output or units of sales is irrelevant.

The Nature of Fixed Costs

So far, fixed costs have been treated as if they were all alike. But there are two types of fixed costs which should be identified—*committed fixed costs* and *discretionary fixed costs*.

Committed fixed costs. These costs relate to the basic facilities and organization structure which a company must have to continue operations. They are not changed in the short run without seriously disrupting operations. Examples of committed fixed costs are depreciation on buildings and equipment and salaries of key executives. In the short run, costs such as these are viewed as not subject to the discretion or control of management. They result from decisions which "committed" the company for a number of years. For instance, once a company constructs a building to house production operations, it is committed to the use of the building for many years.

The depreciation on that building is not as subject to control by management as are some other types of fixed cost.

Discretionary fixed costs. In contrast to committed fixed costs, discretionary fixed costs are related to fixed-cost areas which are subject to management control from year to year. Each year, management decides how much to spend on advertising, research and development, and employee training and development programs. Since these decisions are made each year, they are said to be under the "discretion" of management. Management is not locked in or committed to a certain level of expense for more than one budget period. The next period, it may change the level of expense or eliminate it completely.

The philosophy of management can affect to some extent which fixed costs are committed and which are discretionary. For instance, during recessions some companies terminate employees in the upper levels of management, while other companies keep their "management team" intact. Thus, in some firms the salaries of top-level managers are discretionary, while in other firms they are committed.

The discussion of committed fixed costs and discretionary fixed costs is relevant to cost-volume-profit analysis. If a company's fixed costs are almost all committed fixed costs, it is going to have a more difficult time in reducing its break-even point for the next budget period than if most of its fixed costs are discretionary in nature. A company with a large proportion of discretionary fixed costs may be able to reduce fixed costs dramatically in a recessionary period. By doing this, it may be able to "run lean" and show some net income even when economic conditions are difficult. Thus, its chances of long-run survival may be enhanced.

Assumptions Made in Cost-Volume-Profit Analysis

1. Selling price and variable costs per unit remain constant throughout the relevant range. This means that more units can be sold at the same price and there is no change in technical efficiency as volume increases.
2. The number of units produced equals the number of units sold.
3. In multiproduct situations, the product mix is known in advance.
4. Costs can be accurately classified into their fixed and variable portions.

These assumptions have been described as being unrealistic in many situations. But even where there is some truth to this criticism, cost-volume-profit analysis can serve as a useful planning tool. Although it may lack precision, its use is preferable to pure intuition.

Questions

1. What format of the income statement is used in cost-volume-profit analysis?
2. Name the four types of cost patterns.

3. What is meant by the term *break-even point*? What factors must be taken into consideration in determining it?
4. What are the different ways in which the break-even point may be expressed?
5. How is relevant range related to break-even analysis?
6. Why is break-even analysis considered appropriate only for short-run decisions?
7. What is the formula for calculating the break-even point in sales revenue?
8. What formula is used to solve for the break-even point in units? How can this formula be altered to calculate the number of units which must be sold to achieve a desired level of net income?
9. Why might a business wish to lower its break-even point? How would it go about lowering the break-even point? What effect would you expect the mechanization and automation of production processes to have upon the break-even point?
10. How is the break-even point calculated for a multiproduct firm?
11. What are the various ways in which the cost line for a mixed cost can be determined? Describe each method.
12. What does the label "units" on the horizontal axis of the break-even chart mean?
13. What are committed fixed costs? Give some examples.
14. What are discretionary fixed costs? Give some examples.
15. Give an example of a fixed cost which might be considered committed for one firm and discretionary for another.
16. What assumptions are made in cost-volume-profit analysis?

Exercises

1. Compute the break-even point for a company in which fixed costs amount to $175,000 and variable costs are 65 percent of sales.
2. Martha Company is currently producing and selling 20,000 units of a given product at $10 per unit. Its average cost of production and sale is $7. It is contemplating attempting to sell 50,000 units at $8. At this level, average cost per unit will be $6.50. At which level should it seek to operate?
3. If a given company has fixed costs of $50,000 and variable costs of production of $6.75 per unit, how many units will have to be sold at a price of $9.25 each for the company to break even? How many would the company have to sell to earn $25,000? If 50,000 units represent 100 percent of capacity, what percentage of capacity does this latter level of operations represent?
4. Using the data in Exercise 3, what would be the effect on the break-even point if (consider each part separately):
    a. The price per unit were increased to $9.75?
    b. Fixed costs were lowered by $10,000?
    c. Variable costs were reduced to $6 per unit?
5. Company Q sells two products. The sales of Product 1 and Product 2 in the most recent year were $80,000 and $60,000, respectively. The variable costs of the products were $50,000 and $34,000, respectively. The company had fixed costs of $40,000. The sales mix for the next period is estimated to be the same as in the most recent year. What is the break-even point in terms of sales revenue?

6. The Mazetti Company uses the high-low method in determining the cost line for a mixed cost. Assume that the low and high plots are as follows:

Volume	Cost
4,000	$5,000
10,000	8,000

Determine the variable cost per unit and the amount of total fixed costs.

Business Decision Problem 11–1

The Dennis Company is operating at almost 100 percent of capacity. The company expects the demand for its product to increase by 25 percent next year (19x3). In order to satisfy the demand for its product, the company is considering two alternatives. The first alternative involves a capital outlay which will increase fixed costs by 15 percent but will have no effect on variable costs. The second alternative will not affect fixed costs but will cause variable costs to increase to 60 percent of the selling price of the company's product.

The Dennis Company's condensed income statement for 19x2 is shown below:

Sales		$3,000,000
Costs:		
Variable	$1,350,000	
Fixed	550,000	1,900,000
Net income before taxes		$1,100,000

Required:

a. Determine the break-even point for 19x3 under each of the alternatives.
b. Determine projected net income before taxes for 19x3 under each of the alternatives.
c. Which alternative would you recommend? Why?

Business Decision Problem 11–2

The Warm Toast Company, a leading manufacturer of toasters, incurred $210,000 of fixed costs while selling 20,000 toasters at $50 each. Variable costs amounted to $15 per toaster.

A new machine used in the production of toasters has recently become available and is more efficient than the machine currently being used. The new machine would reduce variable costs by 20 percent but would increase fixed costs by $8,000 because of additional depreciation.

Required:

a. Compute the break-even point *in units* using the old machine.
b. Compute the break-even point *in units* using the new machine.
c. Assuming total sales remain at $1 million, compute expected net income assuming the new machine is acquired.
d. Should the new machine be acquired? Why?

Business Decision Problem 11–3

The Haverty Company sells a single product at $25 per unit. The company incurs variable costs of $15 per unit and total fixed costs of $100,000 per year. The current year's sales amounted to $750,000.

The company is not satisfied with its current level of net income. In order to increase its net income, the company is considering the following alternatives:

1. Spend $30,000 per year on advertising without changing selling prices. Sales volume is expected to increase by 20 percent as a result of this action.
2. Decrease the selling price to $20 per unit. Sales volume is expected to increase by 25 percent as a result of this action.

Required:
a. Compute the company's current break-even point in units.
b. Compute the break-even point in units under each of the two alternatives.
c. Compute expected net income under each of the two alternatives. (Ignore income taxes.)
d. Which of the alternatives would you recommend? Why?

Solutions to End-of-Chapter Questions, Exercises, and Business Decision Problems

Answers to Questions

1. The format of the income statement used in cost-volume-profit analysis is:

    Revenues
       Less: Variable expenses
    Contribution margin
       Less: Fixed expenses
    Net income

2. The four types of cost patterns are variable, fixed, mixed, and step variable.
3. The break-even point is that volume of sales revenue which is just sufficient to cover all costs with no net income remaining. The two factors which must be known in order to determine it are the level of fixed costs and the percentage relationship of variable costs to sales revenue.
4. The break-even point may be expressed in dollars of sales revenue, in number of units, or as a percentage of capacity.
5. The relevant range acts as a constraint to break-even analysis in that the basic assumptions of break-even analysis are valid only within a certain production or sales volume range.
6. Fixed plant capacity is an important assumption of break-even analysis. Since fixed costs and capacity exist only in the short run, all long-term costs tend to vary with production. This situation does not lend itself to break-even analysis.
7. The formula for calculating the break-even point in sales revenue is:

$$S = FC + VC$$

8. The formula used to solve for the break-even point in units is:

$$\text{Break-even point in units} = \frac{\text{Fixed costs}}{\text{Contribution margin per unit}}$$

To solve for the number of units needed to achieve a desired level of net income, the formula is:

$$\text{Number of units} = \frac{\text{Fixed costs} + \text{Desired net income}}{\text{Contribution margin per unit}}$$

9. The lower the break-even point, the smaller is the volume of sales needed to generate net income. If all costs were variable, then a sales volume of $1 would generate some net income if variable costs were less than revenues. The break-even point can be lowered by reducing the level of fixed costs, increasing the selling price per unit, or decreasing the variable costs per unit. Generally, the mechanization and automation of production processes tend to raise the break-even point because of the increased fixed cost of depreciation.

10. The percentage relationship between total sales and total variable costs is found by assuming that a certain product mix (either historical or projected) will exist. Once that percentage relationship is found, it is used in the formula:

$$S = FC + VC$$

11. The three methods of determining the cost line for a mixed cost are the high-low method, the scatter diagram method (with visual fitting of the regression line), and the least squares method (with statistical fitting of the regression line).

    The high-low method utilizes only the highest and lowest actual costs for a mixed cost in drawing the cost line. The scatter diagram method utilizes many plots of actual costs in visually fitting the cost line to the plots. The least squares method utilizes all of the plots and employs statistical methods to obtain the best fit of the regression line to the plots.

12. The label "units" on the horizontal axis of the break-even chart means either units produced or units sold, since these are assumed to be equal.

13. Committed fixed costs are those associated with the basic facilities and organization structure which a company must have to continue operations. Examples of committed fixed costs include depreciation expense on buildings and equipment and salaries of top management.

14. Discretionary fixed costs are related to certain fixed-cost areas which are subject to management control from year to year. Examples of discretionary fixed costs are advertising expense, research and development expense, and management development expense.

15. Executive salaries might be considered committed fixed costs by one firm and discretionary fixed costs by another. Management philosophy determines the classification. In a recessionary period, some firms do not consider certain levels of their top management to be part of the basic organization structure. Some executives are laid off, and their duties are performed by the remaining officers.

16. The assumptions made in cost-volume-profit analysis are:
    a. Selling price and variable costs per unit remain constant throughout the relevant range. This means that more units can be sold at the same price and there is no change in technical efficiency as volume changes.
    b. The number of units produced equals the number of units sold.
    c. In multiproduct situations, the product mix is known in advance.
    d. Costs can be divided into their fixed and variable portions with reasonable accuracy.

Solutions to Exercises

1. $S = \$175,000 + 0.65S$; $S = \$500,000$.
2. Net income currently is $20,000 \times \$3$, or $\$60,000$. Net income at the contemplated level would be $50,000 \times \$1.50$, or $\$75,000$. Other things being equal, attempting to sell 50,000 at $8 per unit seems warranted.
3. The contribution margin per unit $= \$9.25 - \$6.75 = \$2.50$.

$$\text{BEP in units} = \frac{\text{Fixed costs}}{\text{Contribution margin per unit}}$$
$$= \frac{\$50,000}{\$2.50} = 20,000$$

Units to be sold to earn $25,000

$$= \frac{\text{Fixed costs} + \text{Desired net income}}{\text{Contribution margin per unit}}$$
$$= \frac{\$50,000 + \$25,000}{\$2.50}$$
$$= 30,000 \text{ units that must be sold to earn } \$25,000$$

This represents 60 percent of capacity (30,000 units/50,000 units).

4. The new break-even points would be as follows:

a.
$$\text{BEP in units} = \frac{\text{Fixed costs}}{\text{Contribution margin per unit}}$$
$$= \frac{\$50,000}{\$3} = 16,667 \text{ units}$$

b.
$$\text{BEP in units} = \frac{\text{Fixed costs}}{\text{Contribution margin per unit}}$$
$$= \frac{\$40,000}{\$2.50} = 16,000 \text{ units}$$

c.
$$\text{BEP in units} = \frac{\text{Fixed costs}}{\text{Contribution margin per unit}}$$
$$= \frac{\$50,000}{\$3.25} = 15,385 \text{ units}$$

5. The relationship between total sales and variable costs is found as follows:

	Products					
	1		2		Total	
	Amt.	%	Amt.	%	Amt.	%
Sales.................	$80,000	100	$60,000	100	$140,000	100
Variable expenses........	50,000	62.5	34,000	56.67	84,000	60
Contribution margin......	$30,000	37.5	$26,000	43.33	$ 56,000	40

The break-even point is as follows:

$$S = FC + VC$$
$$S = \$40,000 + 0.6S$$
$$0.4S = \$40,000$$
$$S = \$100,000$$

6.   Variable cost per unit $= \dfrac{\text{Change in costs}}{\text{Change in volume}} = \dfrac{\$3,000}{6,000 \text{ units}} = 0.50$ per unit

The fixed costs can be found as follows:

$$\text{Total cost at volume of 4,000 units} = FC + VC$$
$$\$5,000 = FC + (4,000 \times \$0.50)$$
$$\$5,000 = FC + \$2,000$$
$$\$3,000 = FC$$

Solution to Business Decision Problem 11–1

a. First alternative's break-even point:

$$S = \$632,500 + 0.45S$$
$$0.55S = \$632,500$$
$$S = \$1,150,000$$

Second alternative's break-even point:

$$S = \$550,000 + 0.6S$$
$$0.4S = \$550,000$$
$$S = \$1,375,000$$

b. First alternative:

Sales....................................		$3,750,000
Costs:		
Variable (45%)	$1,687,500	
Fixed	632,500	2,320,000
Projected net income before taxes............		$1,430,000

Second alternative:

Sales....................................		$3,750,000
Costs:		
Variable (60%)	$2,250,000	
Fixed....................................	550,000	2,800,000
Projected net income before taxes............		$ 950,000

c. The first alternative—increasing fixed costs by 15 percent—should be recommended because it has a lower break-even point and because its projected net income before taxes is $480,000 larger than the projected net income before taxes of the second alternative.

Solution to Business Decision Problem 11–2

a.
$$\text{Break-even point in units} = \frac{\text{Fixed costs}}{\text{Contribution margin}}$$
$$= \frac{\$210,000}{\$35}$$
$$= \underline{\underline{6,000}}$$

b.
$$\text{Break-even point in units} = \frac{\text{Fixed costs}}{\text{Contribution margin}}$$
$$= \frac{\$218,000}{\$50 - \$15(0.8)}$$
$$= \frac{\$218,000}{\$38}$$
$$= \underline{\underline{5,737}}$$

c.

Sales		$1,000,000
Costs:		
Variable....................................	$240,000	
Fixed	218,000	458,000
Projected net income before taxes		$ 542,000

d. The new machine should be acquired unless the company has more profitable alternatives for the funds it plans to invest in the new machine. If the new machine is acquired, the company will have a lower break-even point and higher projected net income.

Solution to Business Decision Problem 11–3

a.
$$\text{Break-even point in units} = \frac{\text{Fixed costs}}{\text{Contribution margin}}$$
$$= \frac{\$100,000}{\$10}$$
$$= \underline{\underline{10,000}}$$

b.
$$\text{Break-even point in units} = \frac{\text{Fixed costs}}{\text{Contribution margin}}$$

First alternative:

$$\text{BEP} = \frac{\$130,000}{\$10}$$
$$= \underline{\underline{13,000}}$$

Second alternative:

$$\text{BEP} = \frac{\$100,000}{\$5}$$
$$= \underline{\underline{20,000}}$$

c. *First alternative:*

Sales		$900,000
Costs:		
Variable	$540,000	
Fixed	130,000	670,000
Expected net income..............		$230,000

Second alternative:

Sales		$750,000
Costs:		
Variable	$562,500	
Fixed	100,000	662,500
Expected net income..............		$ 87,500

d. Alternative 1 should be recommended because it will increase net income by $30,000 over the current year's level, whereas alternative 2 will decrease net income by $112,500.

12

Capital Budgeting: Long-Range Planning

Chapter Goals

When you have completed Chapter 12, you should be able to:

1. Explain the nature of capital budgeting decisions.
2. Illustrate the capital budgeting decision process.
3. Explain the nature of out-of-pocket and sunk costs, net cash benefits, and the cost of capital.
4. Make capital budgeting decisions using discounting techniques.
5. Explain and calculate the various methods of project selection—payback, unadjusted rate of return, net present value, profitability index, and time-adjusted rate of return.

INTRODUCTION TO CAPITAL BUDGETING

Managers always face the problem of planning for the future. This long-range planning includes the acquisition and retirement of buildings, equipment, and other major items of property. Failure to invest enough funds in a good product can also be costly. Ford's Mustang provides an excellent example of such a situation. If Ford had known the reception the Mustang would receive at the time of the original capital budgeting decision, it would have expended more funds earlier. Some believe Ford lost or deferred additional sales because of its undercommitment of funds.

Capital budgeting is the term used to describe the planning and financing of plant assets. Capital expenditures differ from ordinary expenditures in that they—

1. Usually involve very large sums of money.
2. Do not occur as often as expenditures for items such as payroll and inventory.
3. Commit a firm to a long-term course of action.

The first two characteristics need no further explanation. But a look at the third characteristic—commitment to a long-term course of action—is necessary. Once a firm builds a plant or undertakes some other capital expenditure, it becomes less flexible. Poor capital budgeting decisions can be costly. If a poor capital budgeting decision is implemented, the firm can lose all or part of the funds originally invested. In addition, the capital budgeting decision affects other day-to-day decisions such as the decision to hire and train employees to work with new equipment. If the new equipment is not purchased, the decision to hire and train becomes irrelevant. Other efforts such as marketing and procurement are lost if the capital budgeting decision is revoked. Another price of a poor capital budgeting decision is its harmful effect on the firm's competitive position and image. Finally, the amount of funds available for investment is limited. Thus, once a capital investment decision is made, the alternatives to that investment are lost. The benefits or returns lost by rejecting the alternative investments are an opportunity cost.

PROJECT SELECTION CONCEPTS

Before examining some capital budgeting project selection techniques, some aspects common to those techniques are presented. The time value of money is reviewed, and the concepts of "net cash benefits" and "cost of capital" are introduced.

Time Value of Money

The meaning of the time value of money concept is that money received today is worth more today than is the future receipt of the same amount of money received a week, month, or year from now. This concept involves the use of compound interest, which was covered in the Appendix to Chapter 5. It is briefly reviewed here. (If you do not need this review, go directly to the section "Net cash benefits.")

Future worth (compound amount). Suppose $500 is deposited in a savings account at the beginning of a year at a rate of interest of 5 percent each year. At the end of the first year, the original deposit of $500 will have grown to $525 ($500 $\times$ 1.05). If the $525 is left in the savings account, the amount will grow to $551.25 ($525 $\times$ 1.05) by the end of the second year. Interest of $26.25 was earned in the second year, whereas interest of only $25 was earned in the first year. The reason for the increased amount of interest is that interest in the second year has been earned on the first year's interest in addition to principal. The $25 earned in the first year was left in the account and added to the original deposit. Interest for the second year was computed on the amount of $525 ($500 principal and $25 accumulated interest). Interest is said to be compounded when periodic interest is computed on principal and all accumulated interest. At simple interest, the $500 deposit would have grown to only $550 in two years. At simple interest, the interest for each year would have been $25 ($500 $\times$ 0.05).

The $551.25 amount at compound interest was calculated by multiplying $500 $\times$ 1.05 $\times$ 1.05. Since 1.05 $\times$ 1.05 is equal to $(1.05)^2$, a shortcut can be used. The *compound amount,* as it is called, at the end of two years is simply $500 $\times$ $(1.05)^2$, which equals $500 $\times$ 1.1025, or $551.25. From this, the formula for the compound amount of $1 can be derived as being $(1 + i)^n$, where i is the interest rate per period and n is the number of periods involved.

Interest tables can be used to compute the sum to which any invested amount will grow at a given rate for a stated number of periods. From Table 1, Appendix A, at the end of this book, the amount to which an investment of $1 at 6 percent for five periods will grow can be seen to be $1.33823. The amount to which an investment of $2,000 would grow would be $2,000 times 1.33823, or $2,676.46.

Present value. While future worth is the value of a current amount at some future point in time, present value is the current value of a specified amount to be received at some future date. Present value, then, is the inverse of future worth. It is found by dividing the future sum by $(1 + i)^n$. Thus, the present value of $5,000 to be received one period from now at 6 percent is equal to $5,000 $\div$ (1.06). The computation can also be expressed as $5,000 $\times$ 1/1.06, which is equal to $5,000 $\times$ 0.94340, or $4,717.00. Another way to look at the process is to note that $4,717.00 invested at 6 percent per period will grow to $5,000 in one period.

The present value of $5,000 due in two periods, then, is $5,000 $\div$ $(1.06)^2$. Here again, the computation can be expressed as $5,000 $\times$ $1/(1.06)^2$, which simplifies to $5,000 $\times$ 0.89000, or $4,450.00. Table 3, Appendix A, at the end of this book, contains the present values of $1 at different interest rates for different periods of time. The use of the table can be illustrated by determining the present value of $20,000 due in 30 periods at 12 percent. The present value of $1 due in 30 periods at 12 percent per period is $0.03338. The present value of $20,000 due in 30 periods at 12 percent per period then is $667.60 ($20,000 × 0.03338).

Present value of an annuity. An *annuity* is a series of equal payments equally spaced in time. The approach to valuing annuities can be illustrated by finding the present value, at 6 percent per period, of an annuity calling for the payment of $100 at the end of each of the next three periods. Through the use of Table 3, Appendix A, the present value of each of the $100 payments is:

```
Present value of $100 due in—
   1 period is 0.94340 × $100............................  $ 94.34
   2 periods is 0.89000 × $100 ..........................     89.00
   3 periods is 0.83962 × $100...........................     83.96
      Total present value of three $100 payments.............  $267.30
```

Such a procedure is tedious when the annuity consists of many payments. Fortunately, Table 4 in Appendix A is available showing the present values of an annuity of $1 per period for varying interest rates and periods. Thus, a single figure can be obtained from the table which represents the present value of an annuity of $1 per period for three periods at an interest rate of 6 percent per period. This figure is 2.67301. Multiplying 2.67301 by $100 (the number of dollars in each payment) yields the present value of the annuity of $267.30.

Net Cash Benefits

The *net cash benefit* (as used in capital budgeting) is the net cash inflow expected from a project in a period. It is the difference between the periodic cash inflows and the periodic cash outflows for a proposed project.

Cash inflows and outflows. Assume in Example A that a firm is considering the purchase of new equipment for $120,000. The equipment is expected to have a useful life of 15 years and no salvage value. It is expected that use of the new equipment will produce cash inflows (revenue) of $75,000 per year and cash outflows (costs) of $50,000 per year. Ignoring depreciation and taxes, the annual net cash benefit is computed as:

```
Cash inflows.......................  $75,000
Cash outflows .....................   50,000
Net cash benefit (inflow).............  $25,000
```

Depreciation and taxes.   Although depreciation does not involve a direct cash outflow, it is deductible in arriving at federal taxable income, and reduces the amount of cash outflow for income taxes. This reduction in cash outflows for income taxes is a tax savings made possible by the depreciation tax shield. A *tax shield* is the total amount of a tax-deductible item. Thus, if depreciation is $8,000, the tax shield is $8,000.

The amount of the tax savings can be found by multiplying the tax rate by the amount of the depreciation tax shield. The formula for the tax saving is:

$$\text{Tax rate} \times \text{Depreciation tax shield} = \text{Tax savings}$$

Using the data in the previous example and assuming straight-line depreciation of $8,000 per year and a 40 percent tax rate, the amount of the tax savings is $3,200 (40 percent × $8,000 depreciation tax shield). Now, considering taxes and depreciation, the annual net cash benefit (inflow) from the $120,000 of equipment is computed as:

Example A

	To Compute Net Income	To Compute Net Cash Benefit
Cash inflows..............................	$75,000	$75,000
Cash outflows.............................	50,000	50,000
Net cash benefit before taxes..................	$25,000	$25,000
Depreciation..............................	8,000	
Taxable income	$17,000	
Tax at 40%	6,800	6,800
Net income after taxes	$10,200	
Net cash benefit (after taxes)		$18,200

Considering taxes and depreciation, the net cash benefit is $18,200 instead of the $25,000 computed previously.

Asset replacement example.   Sometimes a firm has to decide whether or not to acquire new assets to replace existing assets. Such replacement decisions often occur when new and improved—faster and more efficient—machinery and equipment appear on the market.

The computation of the net cash benefits is more difficult for a replacement decision than for an addition decision. To illustrate, assume in Example B that a company operates two machines purchased four years ago at a cost of $18,000 each. The estimated useful life of each machine was expected to be 12 years (with no salvage value). Each machine will produce 30,000 units of product each year. The annual cash outflows (labor, repairs, etc.) of operating both machines total $14,000.

After the old machines have been used for four years, a new machine becomes available. The new machine can be acquired for $28,000 and has an estimated useful life of eight years (with no salvage value). It will produce 60,000 units annually with an annual cash outflow of $10,000.

There will be a $28,000 cash outflow in the first year to acquire the new machine. The additional annual cash inflow from replacement is computed as:

Example B

	To Compute Tax	To Compute Net Cash Benefit
Cash operating outflows		
Old machines............................	$14,000	
New machines	10,000	
Difference—additional taxable income	$ 4,000	$4,000
Depreciation:		
Old machines ($18,000 ÷ 12) × 2	$ 3,000	
New machine ($28,000 ÷ 8)	3,500	
Difference—additional tax deduction...........	$ (500)	
Additional taxable income	$ 4,000	
Additional tax deduction	(500)	
Net increase in taxable income................	$ 3,500	
Additional tax at 40%	$ 1,400	1,400
Additional net cash benefit....................		$2,600

The additional net cash benefit does not necessarily mean the machine should be purchased. The purchase decision is discussed later in the chapter.

This example used straight-line depreciation. If an accelerated depreciation method is used, the tax shield is larger in the earlier years of the life of the asset and smaller in the later years.

Out-of-pocket and sunk costs. There is an important distinction between out-of-pocket costs and sunk costs. An *out-of-pocket cost* is one which requires the future use of resources or a future payment. It can be avoided or changed in amount. Future labor and repair costs are examples of out-of-pocket costs.

Sunk costs are costs that have been incurred. Nothing can be done about sunk costs. They cannot be avoided or changed. The price paid for a machine the minute it is acquired represents a sunk cost (before that moment it was an out-of-pocket cost). Its amount cannot be changed regardless of whether the machine is scrapped or used. A sunk cost is a *past* cost, while an out-of-pocket cost is a *future* cost. Only the out-of-pocket costs (the future cash outlays) are relevant to capital budgeting decisions, while the sunk costs are not.

Initial cash outflows and salvage value.   Any cash outflows necessary to acquire an asset and get it ready for use are part of the *initial cash outflows* of the asset. If an investment has a salvage value, that value should be treated as a cash inflow in the year of the asset's disposal.

The cost of capital.   The cost of capital is important in project selection. Any acceptable investment proposal should offer a return that at least exceeds the cost of the funds used to finance it.

The *cost of capital,* usually expressed as a percentage rate, may be computed on an aftertax basis. It measures the cost of all sources of capital (debt and equity) employed by a firm. For convenience, most current liabilities, such as accounts payable and federal income taxes payable, are treated as being costless. Everything else on the right (equity) side of the balance sheet has a cost.

Computing the cost of capital is an inexact art, and many people offer different methods of computing it. In this text we will assume a cost of capital in each situation.

PROJECT SELECTION

The amount of capital available to an enterprise usually is limited. Given this constraint, management must select carefully among capital expenditure proposals. Techniques used to evaluate alternative proposals are: payback, unadjusted rate of return, net present value, profitability index, and time-adjusted rate of return.

Payback Period

The payback period of an outlay is often computed to help in evaluating an investment proposal. The *payback period* is that period of time during which net cash benefits from an investment must continue to recover the initial investment. In effect, it answers the question: How long will it take the new machine to pay for itself? The formula for the payback period is:

$$\text{Payback period} = \frac{\text{Initial investment}}{\text{Annual net cash benefits (or inflows)}}$$

Illustration 12.1 contains the calculation of the payback periods for Examples A and B, used earlier.

Illustration 12.1
Payback Period Calculation

	Example A	Example B
Initial investment..............	$120,000	$28,000
Annual net benefits............	18,200/year	2,600/year
Calculation:	$\dfrac{\$120,000}{\$18,200/\text{year}}$	$\dfrac{\$28,000}{\$2,600/\text{year}}$
Payback period:	6.6 years	10.8 years

Example A had an initial investment of $120,000 and an annual net cash benefit (after taxes) of $18,200 per year. Dividing the initial capital outlay, $120,000, by the annual net cash benefit of $18,200 reveals that 6.6 years would be required for the new equipment to pay for itself.

To compute the payback period for the new machine in Example B, the initial investment of $28,000 is divided by the additional annual cash benefit of $2,600. The payback is 10.8 ($28,000 ÷ $2,600) years. But the new machine will last only eight years. Since the payback period is longer than the machine's useful life, the investment will not pay for itself. Therefore, the new machine should not be purchased.

When the payback period is used to evaluate investment proposals, the decision rule may be one of the following:

1. Select the investment with the shortest payback period.
2. Select only those investments that have a payback period of less than a specified number of years.
3. Under normal circumstances, never select a payback period longer than the expected life of the project.

The payback period type of analysis has several important limitations. First, it ignores the period of time beyond the payback period. For example, consider two alternative investments, each requiring an initial outlay of $30,000. Proposal Y will return $6,000 per year for five years. Thus, it has a five-year payback period. Proposal Z will return $5,000 a year for eight years—a total return of $40,000. Thus, its payback period is six years. If the goal is to maximize net income, Proposal Y should not be accepted just because it has a shorter payback period. It will take one more year to recover the investment in Proposal Z, but the returns from Proposal Z will continue for two years after the investment has been recovered, while Proposal Y will only return its initial investment.

Second, the payback method of analysis also ignores the time value of money. For example, consider the following net cash benefits expected from two capital proposals:

	Proposal A	Proposal B
First year................	$15,000	$ 9,000
Second year.............	12,000	12,000
Third year..............	9,000	15,000
	$36,000	$36,000

If the cost of each proposal is $36,000, then each has a payback period of three years. But common sense says that the two are not equal. Money has a time value; it can be reinvested to increase net income. Since the larger amounts are received sooner under Proposal A, it is preferable to Proposal B. Despite its faults, the payback method is used extensively in capital budgeting.

When annual cash benefits are uniform, the payback period is computed by dividing the initial investment by the annual cash benefits (or savings). But, when the annual returns are uneven, a cumulative calculation must be used. For example, assume that a company is considering a proposal which requires an initial investment of $40,000 and is expected to last 10 years. The expected annual cash benefits are:

Year	Investment	Annual Net Cash Benefits	Cumulative Net Cash Benefits
0..............	$40,000	—	—
1..............	—	$8,000	$ 8,000
2..............	—	6,000	14,000
3..............	—	7,000	21,000
4..............	—	5,000	26,000
5..............	—	8,000	34,000
6..............	—	6,000	40,000
7..............	—	3,000	43,000
8..............	—	2,000	45,000
9..............	—	3,000	48,000
10..............	—	1,000	49,000

The payback period in this example is six years—the time it takes to recover the original investment.

Unadjusted Rate of Return

The *unadjusted rate of return* is computed by dividing the average future annual net income (after taxes) from the project by the average amount of the investment (original outlay ÷ 2). Notice that annual net income and not net cash benefits are used in the calculation.

To illustrate, assume that a firm is considering two proposals. The firm does not have enough funds to undertake both proposals. Both proposals have a useful life of three years.

Net Cash Benefits from Operations (before Taxes)

Proposal	Initial Cost	Year 1	Year 2	Year 3	Average Depreciation
1	$72,000	$45,000	$45,000	$45,000	$24,000
2	90,000	55,000	55,000	55,000	30,000

Assuming a 40 percent tax rate, the unadjusted rate of return is determined as:

	Proposal 1	Proposal 2
1. Average investment:		
Original outlay ÷ 2	$36,000	$45,000
Annual net cash benefit (before taxes)	$45,000	$55,000
Annual depreciation	24,000	30,000
Annual net income (before taxes)	$21,000	$25,000
Income taxes at 40%	8,400	10,000
2. Average net income	$12,600	$15,000
Rate of return (2 ÷ 1).....................................	35%	33⅓%

The unadjusted rate of return can also be computed with the following formula:

$$\text{Rate of return} = \frac{\left(\begin{array}{c}\text{Average annual} \\ \text{net cash benefit}\end{array} - \begin{array}{c}\text{Average annual} \\ \text{depreciation}\end{array}\right)(1 - \text{Tax rate})}{\text{Average investment}}$$

The unadjusted rate-of-return method does not consider the time value of money or the length of the period over which the return will be earned. In the illustration, Proposal 1 would be selected since it has the higher rate of return. The question of the timing of the cash flows is ignored. There are other variations used in the calculation of the unadjusted rate of return. For example, the rate is sometimes calculated using the gross investment (initial outlay) as the divisor.

Net Present Value Method

The *net present value* method uses the concept of the time value of money. Management requires some minimum rate of return on its investments. This required rate of return should be at least the firm's cost of capital. Since it is difficult to determine the cost of capital, management often selects a target rate of return which it believes to be at or above the cost of capital.

The required rate of return is used to discount all expected net cash benefits (after tax) from a proposed investment. The present value of the expected cash benefits is then compared with the investment amount. If the present value of the expected net cash benefits equals or exceeds the investment amount, the investment proposal is acceptable for further consideration. On the other hand, if the present value of the expected cash flows is less than the investment amount, the proposal should be rejected.

To illustrate, assume that a proposed investment will cost $25,000. It is expected that the net cash benefits (after taxes) for the next four years will be $8,000, $7,500, $8,000, and $7,500. Management requires a minimum rate of return of 14 percent. Is the project acceptable? To find out, the following analysis is needed:

	Net Cash Benefits (after Taxes)	Present Value of $1 at 14% (from Table 3, Appendix A)	Total Present Value
First year	$8,000	0.87719	$ 7,017.52
Second year.	7,500	0.76947	5,771.03
Third year.	8,000	0.67497	5,399.76
Fourth year	7,500	0.59208	4,440.60
Total.			$22,628.91

Since the present value of the net cash benefits, $22,628.91, is less than the initial outlay of $25,000, the project is not acceptable. Its net present value is equal to the present value of the benefits less the present value of its cost (the investment amount), which in this instance is −$2,371.09 ($22,628.91 − $25,000). The project is rejected because the projected net cash benefits will not generate the 14 percent (in this case) required return.

In general, a proposed investment is acceptable if it has a zero or positive net present value. For example, assume the expected benefits from the investment had been $10,000 per year for four years. Then the present value of the benefits would have been (from Table 4, Appendix A):

$$\$10,000 \times 2.91371 = \$29,137.10$$

This yields a net present value of $29,137.10 − $25,000 = $4,137.10. Since the net present value is positive, the investment proposal is acceptable. It is acceptable because the present value at 14 percent of the net cash benefits equals or exceeds the required investment. But there may be a competing project that has an even higher net present value. In general, when the net present value method is used to screen projects, those projects that have the highest net present values should be selected.

Profitability Index

The *profitability index* is the present value of the expected net cash benefits from an investment divided by the initial cash outlay:

$$PI = \frac{\text{PV of net cash benefits}}{\text{Initial cash outlay}}$$

Use of the formula allows all possible proposals to be evaluated and ranked according to their desirability. Only those proposals that have a profitability index greater than or equal to 1.00 are considered eligible for further consideration. Those with a profitability index of less than 1.00 will not yield the minimum rate of return (the present value of the expected net cash benefits of such proposals is less than their required initial cash outlay).

To illustrate, assume that a company is considering two alternative capital outlay proposals which have the following initial costs and expected net cash benefits after taxes:

	Proposal X	Proposal Y
Initial cash investment	$8,000	$9,500
Expected net cash benefits (after taxes):		
Year 1	$5,000	$9,000
Year 2	4,000	6,000
Year 3	6,000	3,000

Management's minimum desired rate of return is 20 percent. The profitability indices can be computed as (using Table 3, Appendix A):

	Present Value	
	Proposal X	Proposal Y
Year 1 (cash benefit in year 1 × 0.83333)	$ 4,166.65	$ 7,499.97
Year 2 (cash benefit in year 2 × 0.69444)	2,777.76	4,166.64
Year 3 (cash benefit in year 3 × 0.57870)	3,472.20	1,736.10
Total	$10,416.61	$13,402.71
Initial cash investment.	$ 8,000.00	$ 9,500.00

	Proposal X	Proposal Y
Profitability index:	$\frac{\$10,416.61}{\$8,000} = 1.30$	$\frac{\$13,402.71}{\$9,500} = 1.41$

Proposal Y is more desirable than Proposal X since it has a higher profitability index. But the choice of Proposal Y is not automatic. The effect of each proposal on such intangible factors as employee morale and the future flexibility of the firm should also be considered. X may be a more versatile machine than Y for use in manufacturing other products should the demand decline for the present product.

Time-Adjusted Rate of Return

The *time-adjusted rate of return* is also called the discounted rate of return or the internal rate of return. The time-adjusted rate of return is the rate of return which equates the present value of future expected net cash benefits (after tax) from an investment with the cash cost of the investment. It is the rate at which the net present value is zero. If the time-adjusted rate of return equals or exceeds the cost of capital (or target rate of return), the investment should be considered further. But if the rate of return is less than the minimum rate of return (cost of capital or target rate of return), the proposal should be rejected.

Assume that management is considering several competing proposals and that only one can be accepted. The project with the highest rate of return should be accepted, assuming the project has a rate of return above that required by management.

Present value tables can be used to approximate the time-adjusted rate of return. To illustrate, assume that a company is considering a $90,000 investment that is expected to last 25 years (with no salvage value). The investment will yield net cash benefits of $15,000 a year (after tax) for the next 25 years.

The first step in computing the rate of return involves computing the payback period. In this case, the payback period is six years ($90,000 investment ÷ $15,000 annual net cash benefit). Next, Table 4, Appendix A, is used. It gives the present value of $1 received annually for n years. Since the investment is expected to yield returns for 25 years, the 25 periods row in the table is used. In that row, the factor that is nearest to the payback period of 6 is found. It is 5.92745, and the 5.92745 present value factor involves an interest rate of 16 percent.

If the annual return of $15,000 is multiplied by the 5.92745 factor, the result is $88,911.75, which is just above the $90,000 cost of the asset. Thus, the actual rate of return is slightly less than 16.5 percent.

The example involved level net cash benefits from year to year. What happens when net cash benefits are not level? In such instances, a trial and error procedure can be used. For example, assume that a company is considering a $200,000 project that will last four years and yield the following net cash benefits (ignoring scrap value):

At the End of—	Net Cash Benefit after Taxes
Year 1	$ 20,000
Year 2	40,000
Year 3	80,000
Year 4	150,000
Total	$290,000

The average annual net cash benefit is $72,500 ($290,000 ÷ 4). Based on an average net cash benefit of $72,500, the payback period is 2.76 ($200,000 ÷ $72,500) years. Looking in the four-year row of Table 4, Appendix A, the factor 2.77048 is nearest to the payback period of 2.76. But in this case, net cash benefits are not level. The largest returns occur in the later years of the asset's life. Since the early returns have the largest present value, it is likely that the rate of return will be less than the 16.5 percent rate that corresponds to the present value factor of 2.77048. Thus, various interest rates of less than 16.5 percent are used. Several attempts may be made before the discount rate which yields the present value closest to the initial outlay of $200,000 is found. By trial and error, a rate of return slightly lower than 12.5 percent is found according to the following computation:

	Return	Present Value at 12.5%	Present Value of Net Cash Benefits
Year 1..........	$ 20,000	0.88889	$ 17,777.80
Year 2..........	40,000	0.79012	31,604.80
Year 3..........	80,000	0.70233	56,186.40
Year 4..........	150,000	0.62430	93,645.00
			$199,214.00

If the returns had been greater during the earlier years of the asset's life, the correct rate of return would have been found among rates that were higher than 16.5 percent.

The net present value method and the time-adjusted rate-of-return method theoretically are superior to the payback and unadjusted rate-of-return methods, but they are more difficult to apply. If the cost of capital could be calculated precisely, there would be no need to choose either the payback or unadjusted rate-of-return methods.

Since the cost of capital is not a precise percentage, some financial theorists argue that the time-adjusted rate-of-return method is better than the net present value method. Under the time-adjusted rate-of-return method, the cost of capital is just used as a *cutoff point* in deciding which projects are acceptable for more consideration. But, under the net present value method, the cost of capital is used in the calculation of the present value of the benefits. Thus, if the cost of capital percentage is wrong, the *ranking* of the projects will be affected. As a result, management may select projects that are really not as profitable as other projects.

Other Capital Budgeting Factors

Two more considerations must be taken into account: before a decision has been made, investments in working capital must be examined, and after the decision has been made, a postaudit should be conducted.

Investments in working capital. An investment in plant assets usually must be supported by an investment in working capital such as accounts receivable and inventory. For example, an investment in plant assets often is expected to increase sales. The increase in sales may require an increase in accounts receivable and inventory to support the higher sales level. The increases in the current assets—accounts receivable and inventory—are investments in working capital that usually are recovered in full at the end of a capital project's life. Such investments should be considered in capital budgeting decisions.

To illustrate, assume that a company is considering a capital project that will involve a $50,000 investment in machinery and a $40,000 investment in working capital. The machine, which will be used to produce a new product, has a useful life of eight years. The annual cash inflow (before taxes) is estimated at $25,000 with annual cash outflows (before taxes) of $5,000. The annual net cash benefit from the proposal is computed below (assuming straight-line depreciation and a 40 percent tax rate):

	To Compute Tax	To Compute Net Cash Benefit
Cash inflows..............................	$25,000	$25,000
Cash outflows............................	5,000	5,000
	$20,000	$20,000
Depreciation ($50,000/8)	6,250	
Taxable income	$13,750	
Tax at 40%	$ 5,500	5,500
Annual net cash benefit, years 1–8		$14,500

In addition to the $14,500 recovered each year for eight years, the $40,000 investment in working capital will be recovered in year 8.

The net present value of the proposal is computed as (assuming a 14 percent required rate of return):

Present value of net cash, years 1–8 (14,500 × 4.63886)	$67,263.47
Recovery of investment in working capital in year 8 ($40,000 × 0.35056) ..	14,022.40
Present value of net cash benefit....................................	$81,285.87
Initial cash outlay ($50,000 + $40,000)...............................	90,000.00
Net present value	$ (8,714.13)

The investment is not acceptable because it has a negative net present value. If the working capital investment had been ignored, the proposal would have had a rather large positive net present value of $17,263.47 ($67,263.47 − $50,000.00). Thus, it should be obvious that investments in working capital must be considered if correct capital budgeting decisions are to be made.

The postaudit.   The last step in the capital budgeting process is the postaudit. Ideally a disinterested party should perform this review. Management needs to know whether or not the project is living up to its expectations.

The postaudit should be performed early in the life of the project. But enough time should have passed for all of the operational "bugs" to be ironed out. Actual operating costs should be determined. Management would like to know whether estimated costs are accurate and whether all costs were considered. Also, actual net cash benefits should be compared with the estimated amounts. Any discrepancies in either costs or revenue estimates should be analyzed. This experience will help in analyzing future capital expenditure proposals.

Questions

1. How do capital expenditures differ from ordinary expenditures?
2. Why does a capital expenditure commit a firm to a long-term course of action?
3. Identify three types of capital investments.
4. What effect does depreciation have on cash flow?
5. List three types of external pressures that may affect capital budgeting decisions.
6. Give an example of an out-of-pocket cost and a sunk cost by describing a situation in which both are encountered.
7. A machine currently is being considered for purchase. The salesperson attempting to sell the machine says that it will pay for itself in five years. What is meant by this statement?
8. Discuss the limitations of the payback method.
9. What is the time-adjusted rate of return of a capital investment?
10. What role does the cost of capital play in the time-adjusted rate-of-return method and in the net present value method?
11. What is the profitability index, and of what value is it?
12. What effect would the existence of the investment credit have on the profitability index calculated for capital expenditure projects which qualify for the credit?
13. What is the purpose of a postaudit? When should a postaudit be performed?

Exercises

1. Given the following annual costs, compute the payback period for the new machine if its net cost is $80,000. (Ignore income taxes.)

	Old Machine	New Machine
Labor	$25,100	$22,000
Repairs...............	6,000	1,500
Other costs...........	4,000	1,600
	$35,100	$25,100

2. The Blanc Company is considering investing $75,000 in a new machine. The machine is expected to last five years and to have no salvage value. Yearly net cash inflows from the machine are expected to be $20,000. Calculate the unadjusted rate of return. (Ignore income taxes.)

3. Compute the profitability index for each of the following two proposals, assuming a desired minimum rate of return of 20 percent. Based upon the profitability indices, which proposal is better?

	Proposal G	Proposal H
Initial outlay..................	$16,000	$20,600
Net cash benefit (after taxes):		
First year	10,000	12,000
Second year.................	9,000	12,000
Third year..................	6,000	8,000
Fourth year.................	0	5,000

4. The Rusk Company is considering three alternative investment proposals. Using the information presented below, rank the proposals in order of desirability using (a) the payback method and (b) the unadjusted rate-of-return method. Assume the net cash benefits occur evenly throughout each year.

	J	K	L
Initial outlay....................	$ 80,000	$ 80,000	$ 80,000
Net cash benefit (after taxes):			
First year	$ 0	$ 20,000	$ 20,000
Second year...................	40,000	60,000	40,000
Third year....................	40,000	20,000	60,000
Fourth year...................	20,000	40,000	100,000
	$100,000	$140,000	$220,000

5. The Winwood Company is considering the purchase of a new machine. The machine can be bought for $45,000. It is expected to save $9,000 cash per year for 10 years. It has an estimated useful life of 10 years and an estimated salvage

value of zero. Management will not make any investment unless at least an 18 percent rate of return can be earned. (Ignore taxes.)

Using the net present value method, determine whether the proposal is acceptable.

6. Assume the same situation as described in Exercise 5. Calculate the time-adjusted rate of return.

7. Rank the following investments in the order of their desirability using (a) the payback method, (b) the net present value method, and (c) the time-adjusted rate-of-return method. Management requires a minimum rate of return of 14 percent. (Ignore taxes and depreciation.)

Investment	Initial Outlay	Expected Net Cash Benefit per Year	Expected Life of Proposal
D	$40,000	$ 6,000	8
E	50,000	8,750	20
F	80,000	16,000	10

Business Decision Problem 12–1

The Maxell Company has $500,000 which it wishes to invest in capital projects with a minimum expected rate of return of 14 percent. Five proposals are being evaluated. Acceptance of one proposal does *not* preclude acceptance of any of the other proposals. The company's criterion is to select proposals with a minimum rate of return of 14 percent.

The relevant information related to the five proposals is presented below:

Investment	Initial Outlay	Expected Net Cash per Year	Expected Life of Proposal
V	$100,000	$30,000	5 years
W	200,000	40,000	8
X	250,000	55,000	10
Y	300,000	52,000	12
Z	100,000	21,000	10

Required:

a. Compute the net present value of each of the five proposals.
b. Which projects should be undertaken? Why? In what order should they be undertaken?

Business Decision Problem 12–2

The MacIntosh Company is considering a capital project that will involve a $150,000 investment in machinery and a $30,000 investment in working capital. The machine has a useful life of 10 years and no salvage value. The annual cash inflow (before taxes) is estimated at $60,000, with annual cash outflows (before taxes) of $20,000. The company uses straight-line depreciation. The income tax rate is 40 percent.

The company's new bookkeeper computed the net present value of the project using a minimum required rate of return of 16 percent (the company's cost of capital). The bookkeeper's computations are shown below:

Cash inflow.	$ 60,000
Cash outflow	−20,000
Net cash benefit.	$ 40,000
Present value factor at 16% for 10 years	×4.83323
Present value of net cash benefits	$ 193,329
Initial outlay	150,000
Net present value.	$ 43,329

Required:

a. Are the bookkeeper's computations correct? If not, recompute the correct net present value.

b. Is this capital project acceptable to the company? Why or why not?

Business Decision Problem 12–3

The Crowell Company is trying to decide whether to purchase or lease a new factory machine. If the machine is purchased, the following costs will be incurred:

Acquisition cost	$200,000
Repairs and maintenance:	
Years 1–5.	5,000
Years 6–10.	10,000

The machine will be depreciated on a straight-line basis and will have no salvage value.

If the machine is leased, the lease payment will be $30,000 each year for 10 years. The first lease payment will be due on the day the lease contract is signed. All repairs and maintenance will be provided by the lessor.

The Crowell Company's cost of capital is 12 percent.

Required:

Do you recommend that the company lease or purchase the machine? Show computations to support your answer. (Ignore incomes taxes.)

Solutions to End-of-Chapter Questions, Exercises, and Business Decision Problems

Answers to Questions

1. In contrast to ordinary (called revenue) expenditures, capital expenditures require large sums of money, are not regularly recurring, and usually commit a firm to a long-term course of action.

2. Once an enterprise is committed to a capital project, its further flexibility is affected. It experiences a situation from which it usually cannot extricate itself without paying a price such as loss of funds invested.

3. Three types of capital investments are:
   a. Investments for replacement.
   b. Investments for cost reduction.
   c. Investments for expansion and new products.

4. Depreciation reduces the amount of cash outflow for income taxes. The reduction in income taxes is equal to the tax rate multiplied by the amount of depreciation.

5. Three types of external pressures that may affect capital budgeting decisions are the effects of competition, demand, and technology.

6. In a situation where purchase of a new machine to replace an old machine is contemplated, an out-of-pocket cost would be the direct labor costs incurred to operate both machines. The original cost of the old machine is a sunk cost which can be ignored. The cost of the new machine before it is purchased is an out-of-pocket cost.

7. To say that a machine will pay for itself in five years means that the net cash benefits (increase in sales or decrease in costs, or both) will in five years equal the net outlay for the machine.

8. The payback method does not consider the period of time beyond the payback period, nor does it consider the time value of money.

9. The time-adjusted rate of return is the rate of return that equates the present value of future expected net cash inflows (after taxes) from an investment with the cost of the investment. It is the rate at which the net present value is zero.

10. Under the time-adjusted rate-of-return method, the cost of capital is a cutoff point for deciding which projects are acceptable for more consideration. Under the net present value method, the cost of capital is the discount rate used to calculate the present value of the benefits.

11. The profitability index is the ratio of the present value of the expected net cash benefits from a project to the project's initial capital outlay. The profitability index is valuable because it makes possible a ready comparison of proposals having different patterns, amounts, and periods of time of cash flows as well as different original outlays. It expresses all proposals in a common denominator, so that they can be easily and readily compared.

12. The investment credit can be treated as a net cash inflow (benefit) in the year of acquisition or as a reduction in the initial outlay. Either way, it increases the profitability index for capital expenditure projects.

13. The purpose of a postaudit is to determine whether or not a project is living up to its expectations by comparing actual costs and benefits with estimated costs and benefits. The postaudit should be performed early in the life of a project but after the operational "bugs" have been ironed out.

Solutions to Exercises

1.

	Old Machine	New Machine
Labor..................................	$25,100	$22,000
Repairs	6,000	1,500
Other costs..........................	4,000	1,600
Annual out-of-pocket costs	$35,100	$25,100

$$\frac{\text{Cost of machine}}{\text{Annual cost savings}} = \frac{\$80,000}{\$10,000} = \text{Payback period of 8 years}$$

2.

Average annual cash inflow	$20,000
Average depreciation......................	15,000
Average annual net income.................	$ 5,000

$$\frac{\text{Average annual net income}}{\text{Average investment}} = \frac{\$5,000}{\$37,500} = 13\tfrac{1}{3}\%$$

3. The profitability indices of the two proposals are computed as follows:

	Proposal G	Proposal H
Present value of net cash benefits:		
First year (0.83333)	$ 8,333.30	$ 9,999.96
Second year (0.69444)...........	6,249.96	8,333.28
Third year (0.57870).............	3,472.20	4,629.60
Fourth year (0.48225)............	0	2,411.25
	$18,055.46	$25,374.09
Required initial outlay.............	$16,000	$20,600
Profitability index	1.13	1.23

On the basis of profitability, Proposal H is better since it will yield the higher rate of return.

4. *a.* Proposal J has a payback period of three years:

Year	Investment	Yearly Net Cash Benefit	Accumulated Net Cash Benefit
0................	$80,000	—	—
1................	—	—	—
2................	—	$ 40,000	$ 40,000
3................	—	40,000	80,000
4................	—	20,000	100,000

Proposal K has a payback period of two years:

Year	Investment	Yearly Net Cash Benefit	Accumulated Net Cash Benefit
0................	$80,000	—	—
1................	—	$ 20,000	$ 20,000
2................	—	60,000	80,000
3................	—	20,000	100,000
4................	—	40,000	140,000

Proposal L has a payback period of 2⅓ years:

Year	Investment	Yearly Net Cash Benefit	Accumulated Net Cash Benefit
0..............	$80,000	—	—
1..............	—	$ 20,000	$ 20,000
2..............	—	40,000	60,000
3..............	—	60,000	120,000
4..............	—	100,000	220,000

Using the payback method, the proposals would be ranked in order of desirability as follows:

K payback period = 2 years.
L payback period = 2⅓ years.
J payback period = 3 years.

b. Proposal J has an unadjusted rate of return of 12.5 percent:

Average annual cash benefit...............	$25,000
Average depreciation.....................	20,000
Average annual net income...............	$ 5,000

$$\frac{\text{Average annual net income}}{\text{Average investment}} = \frac{\$5,000}{\$40,000} = 12.5\%$$

Proposal K has an unadjusted rate of return of 37.5 percent:

Average annual cash benefit...............	$35,000
Average depreciation.....................	20,000
Average annual net income...............	$15,000

$$\frac{\text{Average annual net income}}{\text{Average investment}} = \frac{\$15,000}{\$40,000} = 37.5\%$$

Proposal L has an unadjusted rate of return of 87.5 percent:

Average annual cash benefit...............	$55,000
Average depreciation.....................	20,000
Average annual net income...............	$35,000

$$\frac{\text{Average annual net income}}{\text{Average investment}} = \frac{\$35,000}{\$40,000} = 87.5\%$$

Using the unadjusted rate-of-return method, the proposals would be ranked in order of desirability as follows:

L—87.5 percent.
K—37.5 percent.
J—12.5 percent.

5.

Present value of cash savings at 18%.		$40,447*
Investment		45,000
Net present value.		($4,553)

* $9,000 × 4.49409 (Table 4, Appendix A).

It appears that the investment should not be made since it has a negative net present value—that is, the cost exceeds the present value of the expected future cash benefits.

6.
$$\text{Payback} = \frac{\$45,000}{9,000} = 5$$

We noted that 5.01877 is nearest to the factor of 5 in the 10 periods row in Table 4. Also, 5.08177 × $9,000 = $45,168.93. Thus, we can say that the time-adjusted rate of return is more than 15 percent (since 5.01877 involves the 15 percent interest rate).

7. *a.* Payback period:

Proposal	Investment (a)	Net Annual Cash Benefit (b)	Payback Period (a/b)
D.	$40,000	$ 6,000	6.67 years
E.	50,000	8,750	5.71 years
F.	80,000	16,000	5.00 years

The proposals in order of rank are F, E, D.

b. Net present value:

Proposal	Net Annual Cash Benefit	Present Value Factor at 14%	Present Value of Annual Net Cash Benefit	Initial Outlay	Net Present Value
D.	$ 6,000	4.63886	$27,833	$40,000	$(12,167)
E.	8,750	6.62313	57,952	50,000	7,952
F.	16,000	5.21612	83,458	80,000	3,458

The proposals in order of rank are E, F, D. But Proposal D should be rejected since its net present value is negative.

c. Time-adjusted rate of return:

Proposal	Rate
D.	4% (slightly above)
E.	16 (slightly above)
F.	16 (slightly above)

The payback periods are used to find the approximate return for each project. For Proposal D, use the 8-year row; for E, use the 20-year row; and for F, use the 10-year row.

The proposals in order of rank are E, F, D. But Proposal D should be rejected since its time-adjusted rate of return is less than the required minimum rate of return of 14 percent.

Solution to Business Decision Problem 12–1

a.

Investment	Annual Net Cash Benefit (a)	Present Value Factor at 14% (b)	Present Value of Annual Net Cash Benefit (c)(= a × b)	Initial Outlay (d)	Net Present Value (c − d)
V............	$30,000	3.43308	$102,992	$100,000	$ 2,992
W............	40,000	4.63886	185,554	200,000	(14,446)
X............	55,000	5.21612	286,887	250,000	36,887
Y............	52,000	5.66029	294,335	300,000	(5,665)
Z............	21,000	5.21612	109,539	100,000	9,539

b. Projects V, X, and Z should be undertaken because they have positive net present values and will yield the minimum required rate of 14 percent. Only $450,000 of the $500,000 available should be expended.

Solution to Business Decision Problem 12–2

a. No, the bookkeeper's computations are not correct. The bookkeeper did not determine net cash benefit on an aftertax basis. The bookkeeper also did not consider the investment in working capital.

The correct net present value is computed below:

	To Compute Tax	To Compute Net Cash Benefit
Cash inflows	$60,000	$ 60,000
Cash outflows	20,000	20,000
	$40,000	$ 40,000
Depreciation ($150,000/10).....................	15,000	
Taxable income.............................	$25,000	
Tax at 40%.................................	$10,000	10,000
Annual net cash benefit (after taxes)		$ 30,000

Present value of annual net cash inflow ($30,000 × 4.83323).........................	$144,997
Present value of recovery of investment in working capital in year 10 ($30,000 × 0.22668).........................	6,800
Present value of net cash benefit	$151,797
Initial cash outlay ($150,000 + $30,000)...........	180,000
Net present value	$ (28,203)

b. This capital project is not acceptable to the company because it has a negative net present value and will *not* yield a minimum rate of return of 16 percent.

Solution to Business Decision Problem 12–3

Purchase:

Present value of acquisition cost	$200,000
Present value of repairs and maintenance:	
Years 1–5 ($5,000 × 3.60478	18,024
Years 6–10 [$10,000 × (5.65022 − 3.60478)]	20,454
Present value of out-of-pocket costs	$238,478

Lease:

Present value of lease payments:	
First year......................................	$ 30,000
Years 2–10 ($30,000 × 5.32825)...................	159,848
Present value of out-of-pocket costs	$189,848

The company should lease the machine because the present value of the out-of-pocket costs is less for the lease alternative than for the purchase alternative.

APPENDIX A

Compound Interest and Annuity Tables

Table 1
Future Value of $1 at Compound Interest: 0.5%–10%

$$F_{1,n} = (1 + i)^n$$

Period	.5%	1%	1.5%	2%	2.5%	3%	3.5%	4%	4.5%	5%
1	1.00500	1.01000	1.01500	1.02000	1.02500	1.03000	1.03500	1.04000	1.04500	1.05000
2	1.01003	1.02010	1.03023	1.04040	1.05063	1.06090	1.07123	1.08160	1.09203	1.10250
3	1.01508	1.03030	1.04568	1.06121	1.07689	1.09273	1.10872	1.12486	1.14117	1.15762
4	1.02015	1.04060	1.06136	1.08243	1.10381	1.12551	1.14752	1.16986	1.19252	1.21551
5	1.02525	1.05101	1.07728	1.10408	1.13141	1.15927	1.18769	1.21665	1.24618	1.27628
6	1.03038	1.06152	1.09344	1.12616	1.15969	1.19405	1.22926	1.26532	1.30226	1.34010
7	1.03553	1.07214	1.10984	1.14869	1.18869	1.22987	1.27228	1.31593	1.36086	1.40710
8	1.04071	1.08286	1.12649	1.17166	1.21840	1.26677	1.31681	1.36857	1.42210	1.47746
9	1.04591	1.09369	1.14339	1.19509	1.24886	1.30477	1.36290	1.42331	1.48610	1.55133
10	1.05114	1.10462	1.16054	1.21899	1.28008	1.34392	1.41060	1.48024	1.55297	1.62889
11	1.05640	1.11567	1.17795	1.24337	1.31209	1.38423	1.45997	1.53945	1.62285	1.71034
12	1.06168	1.12683	1.19562	1.26824	1.34489	1.42576	1.51107	1.60103	1.69588	1.79586
13	1.06699	1.13809	1.21355	1.29361	1.37851	1.46853	1.56396	1.66507	1.77220	1.88565
14	1.07232	1.14947	1.23176	1.31948	1.41297	1.51259	1.61869	1.73168	1.85194	1.97993
15	1.07768	1.16097	1.25023	1.34587	1.44830	1.55797	1.67535	1.80094	1.93528	2.07893
16	1.08307	1.17258	1.26899	1.37279	1.48451	1.60471	1.73399	1.87298	2.02237	2.18287
17	1.08849	1.18430	1.28802	1.40024	1.52162	1.65285	1.79468	1.94790	2.11338	2.29202
18	1.09393	1.19615	1.30734	1.42825	1.55966	1.70243	1.85749	2.02582	2.20848	2.40662
19	1.09940	1.20811	1.32695	1.45681	1.59865	1.75351	1.92250	2.10685	2.30786	2.52695
20	1.10490	1.22019	1.34686	1.48595	1.63862	1.80611	1.98979	2.19112	2.41171	2.65330
21	1.11042	1.23239	1.36706	1.51567	1.67958	1.86029	2.05943	2.27877	2.52024	2.78596
22	1.11597	1.24472	1.38756	1.54598	1.72157	1.91610	2.13151	2.36992	2.63365	2.92526
23	1.12155	1.25716	1.40838	1.57690	1.76461	1.97359	2.20611	2.46472	2.75217	3.07152
24	1.12716	1.26973	1.42950	1.60844	1.80873	2.03279	2.28333	2.56330	2.87601	3.22510
25	1.13280	1.28243	1.45095	1.64061	1.85394	2.09378	2.36324	2.66584	3.00543	3.38635
26	1.13846	1.29526	1.47271	1.67342	1.90029	2.15659	2.44596	2.77247	3.14068	3.55567
27	1.14415	1.30821	1.49480	1.70689	1.94780	2.22129	2.53157	2.88337	3.28201	3.73346
28	1.14987	1.32129	1.51722	1.74102	1.99650	2.28793	2.62017	2.99870	3.42970	3.92013
29	1.15562	1.33450	1.53998	1.77584	2.04641	2.35657	2.71188	3.11865	3.58404	4.11614
30	1.16140	1.34785	1.56308	1.81136	2.09757	2.42726	2.80679	3.24340	3.74532	4.32194

5.5%	6%	6.5%	7%	7.5%	8%	8.5%	9%	9.5%	10%
1.05500	1.06000	1.06500	1.07000	1.07500	1.08000	1.08500	1.09000	1.09500	1.10000
1.11303	1.12360	1.13423	1.14490	1.15563	1.16640	1.17723	1.18810	1.19903	1.21000
1.17424	1.19102	1.20795	1.22504	1.24230	1.25971	1.27729	1.29503	1.31293	1.33100
1.23882	1.26248	1.28647	1.31080	1.33547	1.36049	1.38586	1.41158	1.43766	1.46410
1.30696	1.33823	1.37009	1.40255	1.43563	1.46933	1.50366	1.53862	1.57424	1.61051
1.37884	1.41852	1.45914	1.50073	1.54330	1.58687	1.63147	1.67710	1.72379	1.77156
1.45468	1.50363	1.55399	1.60578	1.65905	1.71382	1.77014	1.82804	1.88755	1.94872
1.53469	1.59385	1.65500	1.71819	1.78348	1.85093	1.92060	1.99256	2.06687	2.14359
1.61909	1.68948	1.76257	1.83846	1.91724	1.99900	2.08386	2.17189	2.26322	2.35795
1.70814	1.79085	1.87714	1.96715	2.06103	2.15892	2.26098	2.36736	2.47823	2.59374
1.80209	1.89830	1.99915	2.10485	2.21561	2.33164	2.45317	2.58043	2.71366	2.85312
1.90121	2.01220	2.12910	2.25219	2.38178	2.51817	2.66169	2.81266	2.97146	3.13843
2.00577	2.13293	2.26749	2.40985	2.56041	2.71962	2.88793	3.06580	3.25375	3.45227
2.11609	2.26090	2.41487	2.57853	2.75244	2.93719	3.13340	3.34173	3.56285	3.79750
2.23248	2.39656	2.57184	2.75903	2.95888	3.17217	3.39974	3.64248	3.90132	4.17725
2.35526	2.54035	2.73901	2.95216	3.18079	3.42594	3.68872	3.97031	4.27195	4.59497
2.48480	2.69277	2.91705	3.15882	3.41935	3.70002	4.00226	4.32763	4.67778	5.05447
2.62147	2.85434	3.10665	3.37993	3.67580	3.99602	4.34245	4.71712	5.12217	5.55992
2.76565	3.02560	3.30859	3.61653	3.95149	4.31570	4.71156	5.14166	5.60878	6.11591
2.91776	3.20714	3.52365	3.86968	4.24785	4.66096	5.11205	5.60441	6.14161	6.72750
3.07823	3.39956	3.75268	4.14056	4.56644	5.03383	5.54657	6.10881	6.72507	7.40025
3.24754	3.60354	3.99661	4.43040	4.90892	5.43654	6.01803	6.65860	7.36395	8.14027
3.42615	3.81975	4.25639	4.74053	5.27709	5.87146	6.52956	7.25787	8.06352	8.95430
3.61459	4.04893	4.53305	5.07237	5.67287	6.34118	7.08457	7.91108	8.82956	9.84973
3.81339	4.29187	4.82770	5.42743	6.09834	6.84848	7.68676	8.62308	9.66836	10.83471
4.02313	4.54938	5.14150	5.80735	6.55572	7.39635	8.34014	9.39916	10.58686	11.91818
4.24440	4.82235	5.47570	6.21387	7.04739	7.98806	9.04905	10.24508	11.59261	13.10999
4.47784	5.11169	5.83162	6.64884	7.57595	8.62711	9.81822	11.16714	12.69391	14.42099
4.72412	5.41839	6.21067	7.11426	8.14414	9.31727	10.65277	12.17218	13.89983	15.86309
4.98395	5.74349	6.61437	7.61226	8.75496	10.06266	11.55825	13.26768	15.22031	17.44940

350

Table 1 (*concluded*)
Future Value of $1 at Compound Interest: 10.5%–20%

Period	10.5%	11%	11.5%	12%	12.5%	13%	13.5%	14%	14.5%	15%
1	1.10500	1.11000	1.11500	1.12000	1.12500	1.13000	1.13500	1.14000	1.14500	1.15000
2	1.22103	1.23210	1.24323	1.25440	1.26563	1.27690	1.28822	1.29960	1.31102	1.32250
3	1.34923	1.36763	1.38620	1.40493	1.42383	1.44290	1.46214	1.48154	1.50112	1.52088
4	1.49090	1.51807	1.54561	1.57352	1.60181	1.63047	1.65952	1.68896	1.71879	1.74901
5	1.64745	1.68506	1.72335	1.76234	1.80203	1.84244	1.88356	1.92541	1.96801	2.01136
6	1.82043	1.87041	1.92154	1.97382	2.02729	2.08195	2.13784	2.19497	2.25337	2.31306
7	2.01157	2.07616	2.14252	2.21068	2.28070	2.35261	2.42645	2.50227	2.58011	2.66002
8	2.22279	2.30454	2.38891	2.47596	2.56578	2.65844	2.75402	2.85259	2.95423	3.05902
9	2.45618	2.55804	2.66363	2.77308	2.88651	3.00404	3.12581	3.25195	3.38259	3.51788
10	2.71408	2.83942	2.96995	3.10585	3.24732	3.39457	3.54780	3.70722	3.87307	4.04556
11	2.99906	3.15176	3.31149	3.47855	3.65324	3.83586	4.02675	4.22623	4.43466	4.65239
12	3.31396	3.49845	3.69231	3.89598	4.10989	4.33452	4.57036	4.81790	5.07769	5.35025
13	3.66193	3.88328	4.11693	4.36349	4.62363	4.89801	5.18736	5.49241	5.81395	6.15279
14	4.04643	4.31044	4.59037	4.88711	5.20158	5.53475	5.88765	6.26135	6.65697	7.07571
15	4.47130	4.78459	5.11827	5.47357	5.85178	6.25427	6.68248	7.13794	7.62223	8.13706
16	4.94079	5.31089	5.70687	6.13039	6.58325	7.06733	7.58462	8.13725	8.72746	9.35762
17	5.45957	5.89509	6.36316	6.86604	7.40616	7.98608	8.60854	9.27646	9.99294	10.76126
18	6.03283	6.54355	7.09492	7.68997	8.33193	9.02427	9.77070	10.57517	11.44192	12.37545
19	6.66628	7.26334	7.91084	8.61276	9.37342	10.19742	11.08974	12.05569	13.10039	14.23177
20	7.36623	8.06231	8.82058	9.64629	10.54509	11.52309	12.58686	13.74349	15.00064	16.36654
21	8.13969	8.94917	9.83495	10.80385	11.86323	13.02109	14.28608	15.66758	17.17573	18.82152
22	8.99436	9.93357	10.96597	12.10031	13.34613	14.71383	16.21470	17.86104	19.66621	21.64475
23	9.93876	11.02627	12.22706	13.55235	15.01440	16.62663	18.40369	20.36158	22.51781	24.89146
24	10.98233	12.23916	13.63317	15.17863	16.89120	18.78809	20.88818	23.21221	25.78290	28.62518
25	12.13548	13.58546	15.20098	17.00006	19.00260	21.23054	23.70809	26.46192	29.52141	32.91895
26	13.40971	15.07986	16.94910	19.04007	21.37793	23.99051	26.90868	30.16658	33.80202	37.85680
27	14.81772	16.73865	18.89824	21.32488	24.05017	27.10928	30.54135	34.38991	38.70331	43.53531
28	16.37359	18.57990	21.07154	23.88387	27.05644	30.63349	34.66443	39.20449	44.31529	50.06561
29	18.09281	20.62369	23.49477	26.74993	30.43849	34.61584	39.34413	44.69312	50.74101	57.57545
30	19.99256	22.89230	26.19667	29.95992	34.24330	39.11590	44.65559	50.95016	58.09846	66.21177

15.5%	16%	16.5%	17%	17.5%	18%	18.5%	19%	19.5%	20%
1.15500	1.16000	1.16500	1.17000	1.17500	1.18000	1.18500	1.19000	1.19500	1.20000
1.33402	1.34560	1.35722	1.36890	1.38063	1.39240	1.40422	1.41610	1.42802	1.44000
1.54080	1.56090	1.58117	1.60161	1.62223	1.64303	1.66401	1.68516	1.70649	1.72800
1.77962	1.81064	1.84206	1.87389	1.90613	1.93878	1.97185	2.00534	2.03926	2.07360
2.05546	2.10034	2.14600	2.19245	2.23970	2.28776	2.33664	2.38635	2.43691	2.48832
2.37406	2.43640	2.50009	2.56516	2.63164	2.69955	2.76892	2.83976	2.91211	2.98598
2.74204	2.82622	2.91260	3.00124	3.09218	3.18547	3.28117	3.37932	3.47997	3.58318
3.16706	3.27841	3.39318	3.51145	3.63331	3.75886	3.88818	4.02139	4.15856	4.29982
3.65795	3.80296	3.95306	4.10840	4.26914	4.43545	4.60750	4.78545	4.96948	5.15978
4.22493	4.41144	4.60531	4.80683	5.01624	5.23384	5.45989	5.69468	5.93853	6.19174
4.87980	5.11726	5.36519	5.62399	5.89409	6.17593	6.46996	6.77667	7.09654	7.43008
5.63617	5.93603	6.25045	6.58007	6.92555	7.28759	7.66691	8.06424	8.48037	8.91610
6.50977	6.88579	7.28177	7.69868	8.13752	8.59936	9.08528	9.59645	10.13404	10.69932
7.51879	7.98752	8.48326	9.00745	9.56159	10.14724	10.76606	11.41977	12.11018	12.83918
8.68420	9.26552	9.88300	10.53872	11.23487	11.97375	12.75778	13.58953	14.47167	15.40702
10.03025	10.74800	11.51370	12.33030	13.20097	14.12902	15.11797	16.17154	17.29364	18.48843
11.58494	12.46768	13.41346	14.42646	15.51114	16.67225	17.91480	19.24413	20.66590	22.18611
13.38060	14.46251	15.62668	16.87895	18.22559	19.67325	21.22904	22.90052	24.69575	26.62333
15.45460	16.77652	18.20508	19.74838	21.41507	23.21444	25.15641	27.25162	29.51143	31.94800
17.85006	19.46076	21.20892	23.10560	25.16271	27.39303	29.81035	32.42942	35.26615	38.33760
20.61682	22.57448	24.70839	27.03355	29.56618	32.32378	35.32526	38.59101	42.14305	46.00512
23.81243	26.18640	28.78527	31.62925	34.74026	38.14206	41.86043	45.92331	50.36095	55.20614
27.50335	30.37622	33.53484	37.00623	40.81981	45.00763	49.60461	54.64873	60.18134	66.24737
31.76637	35.23642	39.06809	43.29729	47.96327	53.10901	58.78147	65.03199	71.91670	79.49685
36.69016	40.87424	45.51433	50.65783	56.35684	62.66863	69.65604	77.38807	85.94045	95.39622
42.37713	47.41412	53.02419	59.26966	66.21929	73.94898	82.54240	92.09181	102.69884	114.47546
48.94559	55.00038	61.77318	69.34550	77.80767	87.25980	97.81275	109.58925	122.72511	137.37055
56.53216	63.80044	71.96576	81.13423	91.42401	102.96656	115.90811	130.41121	146.65651	164.84466
65.29464	74.00851	83.84011	94.92705	107.42321	121.50054	137.35111	155.18934	175.25453	197.81359
75.41531	85.84988	97.67373	111.06465	126.22227	143.37064	162.76106	184.67531	209.42916	237.37631

Table 2
Future Value of an Ordinary Annuity of $1 per Period: 0.5%–10%

$$F_{A_{i,n}} = \frac{(1+i)^n - 1}{i}$$

Period	.5%	1%	1.5%	2%	2.5%	3%	3.5%	4%	4.5%	5%
1	1.00000	1.00000	1.00000	1.00000	1.00000	1.00000	1.00000	1.00000	1.00000	1.00000
2	2.00500	2.01000	2.01500	2.02000	2.02500	2.03000	2.03500	2.04000	2.04500	2.05000
3	3.01502	3.03010	3.04522	3.06040	3.07562	3.09090	3.10622	3.12160	3.13702	3.15250
4	4.03010	4.06040	4.09090	4.12161	4.15252	4.18363	4.21494	4.24646	4.27819	4.31012
5	5.05025	5.10101	5.15227	5.20404	5.25633	5.30914	5.36247	5.41632	5.47071	5.52563
6	6.07550	6.15202	6.22955	6.30812	6.38774	6.46841	6.55015	6.63298	6.71689	6.80191
7	7.10588	7.21354	7.32299	7.43428	7.54743	7.66246	7.77941	7.89829	8.01915	8.14201
8	8.14141	8.28567	8.43284	8.58297	8.73612	8.89234	9.05169	9.21423	9.38001	9.54911
9	9.18212	9.36853	9.55933	9.75463	9.95452	10.15911	10.36850	10.58280	10.80211	11.02656
10	10.22803	10.46221	10.70272	10.94972	11.20338	11.46388	11.73139	12.00611	12.28821	12.57789
11	11.27917	11.56683	11.86326	12.16872	12.48347	12.80780	13.14199	13.48635	13.84118	14.20679
12	12.33556	12.68250	13.04121	13.41209	13.79555	14.19203	14.60196	15.02581	15.46403	15.91713
13	13.39724	13.80933	14.23683	14.68033	15.14044	15.61779	16.11303	16.62684	17.15991	17.71298
14	14.46423	14.94742	15.45038	15.97394	16.51895	17.08632	17.67699	18.29191	18.93211	19.59863
15	15.53655	16.09690	16.68214	17.29342	17.93193	18.59891	19.29568	20.02359	20.78405	21.57856
16	16.61423	17.25786	17.93237	18.63929	19.38022	20.15688	20.97103	21.82453	22.71934	23.65749
17	17.69730	18.43044	19.20136	20.01207	20.86473	21.76159	22.70502	23.69751	24.74171	25.84037
18	18.78579	19.61475	20.48938	21.41231	22.38635	23.41444	24.49969	25.64541	26.85508	28.13238
19	19.87972	20.81090	21.79672	22.84056	23.94601	25.11687	26.35718	27.67123	29.06356	30.53900
20	20.97912	22.01900	23.12367	24.29737	25.54466	26.87037	28.27968	29.77808	31.37142	33.06595
21	22.08401	23.23919	24.47052	25.78332	27.18327	28.67649	30.26947	31.96920	33.78314	35.71925
22	23.19443	24.47159	25.83758	27.29898	28.86286	30.53678	32.32890	34.24797	36.30338	38.50521
23	24.31040	25.71630	27.22514	28.84496	30.58443	32.45288	34.46041	36.61789	38.93703	41.43048
24	25.43196	26.97346	28.63352	30.42186	32.34904	34.42647	36.66653	39.08260	41.68920	44.50200
25	26.55912	28.24320	30.06302	32.03030	34.15776	36.45926	38.94986	41.64591	44.56521	47.72710
26	27.69191	29.52563	31.51397	33.67091	36.01171	38.55304	41.31310	44.31174	47.57064	51.11345
27	28.83037	30.82089	32.98668	35.34432	37.91200	40.70963	43.75906	47.08421	50.71132	54.66913
28	29.97452	32.12910	34.48148	37.05121	39.85980	42.93092	46.29063	49.96758	53.99333	58.40258
29	31.12439	33.45039	35.99870	38.79223	41.85630	45.21885	48.91080	52.96629	57.42303	62.32271
30	32.28002	34.78489	37.53868	40.56808	43.90270	47.57542	51.62268	56.08494	61.00707	66.43885

5.5%	6%	6.5%	7%	7.5%	8%	8.5%	9%	9.5%	10%
1.00000	1.00000	1.00000	1.00000	1.00000	1.00000	1.00000	1.00000	1.00000	1.00000
2.05500	2.06000	2.06500	2.07000	2.07500	2.08000	2.08500	2.09000	2.09500	2.10000
3.16802	3.18360	3.19922	3.21490	3.23062	3.24640	3.26222	3.27810	3.29402	3.31000
4.34227	4.37462	4.40717	4.43994	4.47292	4.50611	4.53951	4.57313	4.60696	4.64100
5.58109	5.63709	5.69364	5.75074	5.80839	5.86660	5.92537	5.98471	6.04462	6.10510
6.88805	6.97532	7.06373	7.15329	7.24402	7.33593	7.42903	7.52333	7.61886	7.71561
8.26689	8.39384	8.52287	8.65402	8.78732	8.92280	9.06050	9.20043	9.34265	9.48717
9.72157	9.89747	10.07686	10.25980	10.44637	10.63663	10.83064	11.02847	11.23020	11.43589
11.25626	11.49132	11.73185	11.97799	12.22985	12.48756	12.75124	13.02104	13.29707	13.57948
12.87535	13.18079	13.49442	13.81645	14.14709	14.48656	14.83510	15.19293	15.56029	15.93742
14.58350	14.97164	15.37156	15.78360	16.20812	16.64549	17.09608	17.56029	18.03852	18.53117
16.38559	16.86994	17.37071	17.88845	18.42373	18.97713	19.54925	20.14072	20.75218	21.38428
18.28680	18.88214	19.49981	20.14064	20.80551	21.49530	22.21094	22.95338	23.72363	24.52271
20.29257	21.01507	21.76730	22.55049	23.36592	24.21492	25.09887	26.01919	26.97738	27.97498
22.40866	23.27597	24.18217	25.12902	26.11836	27.15211	28.23227	29.36092	30.54023	31.77248
24.64114	25.67253	26.75401	27.88805	29.07724	30.32428	31.63201	33.00340	34.44155	35.94973
26.99640	28.21288	29.49302	30.84022	32.25804	33.75023	35.32073	36.97370	38.71350	40.54470
29.48120	30.90565	32.41007	33.99903	35.67739	37.45024	39.32300	41.30134	43.39128	45.59917
32.10267	33.75999	35.51672	37.37896	39.35319	41.44626	43.66545	46.01846	48.51345	51.15909
34.86832	36.78559	38.82531	40.99549	43.30468	45.76196	48.37701	51.16012	54.12223	57.27500
37.78608	39.99273	42.34895	44.86518	47.55253	50.42292	53.48906	56.76453	60.26384	64.00250
40.86431	43.39229	46.10164	49.00574	52.11897	55.45676	59.03563	62.87334	66.98891	71.40275
44.11185	46.99583	50.09824	53.43614	57.02790	60.89330	65.05366	69.53194	74.35286	79.54302
47.53800	50.81558	54.35463	58.17667	62.30499	66.76476	71.58322	76.78981	82.41638	88.49733
51.15259	54.86451	58.88768	63.24904	67.97786	73.10594	78.66779	84.70090	91.24593	98.34706
54.96598	59.15638	63.71538	68.67647	74.07620	79.95442	86.35455	93.32398	100.91430	109.18177
58.98911	63.70577	68.85688	74.48382	80.63192	87.35077	94.69469	102.72313	111.50116	121.09994
63.23351	68.52811	74.33257	80.69769	87.67931	95.33883	103.74374	112.96822	123.09377	134.20994
67.71135	73.63980	80.16419	87.34653	95.25526	103.96594	113.56196	124.13536	135.78767	148.63093
72.43548	79.05819	86.37486	94.46079	103.39940	113.28321	124.21473	136.30754	149.68750	164.49402

Table 2 (*concluded*)
Future Value of an Ordinary Annuity of $1 per Period: 10.5%–20%

Period	10.5%	11%	11.5%	12%	12.5%	13%	13.5%	14%	14.5%	15%
1 ...	1.00000	1.00000	1.00000	1.00000	1.00000	1.00000	1.00000	1.00000	1.00000	1.00000
2 ...	2.10500	2.11000	2.11500	2.12000	2.12500	2.13000	2.13500	2.14000	2.14500	2.15000
3 ...	3.32602	3.34210	3.35822	3.37440	3.39062	3.40690	3.42322	3.43960	3.45602	3.47250
4 ...	4.67526	4.70973	4.74442	4.77933	4.81445	4.84980	4.88536	4.92114	4.95715	4.99337
5 ...	6.16616	6.22780	6.29003	6.35285	6.41626	6.48027	6.54488	6.61010	6.67594	6.74238
6 ...	7.81361	7.91286	8.01338	8.11519	8.21829	8.32271	8.42844	8.53552	8.64395	8.75374
7 ...	9.63404	9.78327	9.93492	10.08901	10.24558	10.40466	10.56628	10.73049	10.89732	11.06680
8 ...	11.64561	11.85943	12.07744	12.29969	12.52628	12.75726	12.99273	13.23276	13.47743	13.72682
9 ...	13.86840	14.16397	14.46634	14.77566	15.09206	15.41571	15.74675	16.08535	16.43166	16.78584
10 ...	16.32458	16.72201	17.12997	17.54874	17.97857	18.41975	18.87256	19.33730	19.81425	20.30372
11 ...	19.03866	19.56143	20.09992	20.65458	21.22589	21.81432	22.42036	23.04452	23.68731	24.34928
12 ...	22.03772	22.71319	23.41141	24.13313	24.87913	25.65018	26.44711	27.27075	28.12197	29.00167
13 ...	25.35168	26.21164	27.10372	28.02911	28.98902	29.98470	31.01746	32.08865	33.19966	34.35192
14 ...	29.01361	30.09492	31.22065	32.39260	33.61264	34.88271	36.20482	37.58107	39.01361	40.50471
15 ...	33.06004	34.40536	35.81102	37.27971	38.81422	40.41746	42.09247	43.84241	45.67058	47.58041
16 ...	37.53134	39.18995	40.92929	42.75328	44.66600	46.67173	48.77496	50.98035	53.29282	55.71747
17 ...	42.47213	44.50084	46.63616	48.88367	51.24925	53.73906	56.35958	59.11760	62.02027	65.07509
18 ...	47.93170	50.39594	52.99932	55.74971	58.65541	61.72514	64.96812	68.39407	72.01321	75.83636
19 ...	53.96453	56.93949	60.09424	63.43968	66.98733	70.74941	74.73882	78.96923	83.45513	88.21181
20 ...	60.63081	64.20283	68.00508	72.05244	76.36075	80.94683	85.82856	91.02493	96.55612	102.44358
21 ...	67.99704	72.26514	76.82566	81.69874	86.90584	92.46992	98.41541	104.76842	111.55676	118.81012
22 ...	76.13673	81.21431	86.66062	92.50258	98.76908	105.49101	112.70149	120.43600	128.73249	137.63164
23 ...	85.13109	91.14788	97.62659	104.60289	112.11521	120.20484	128.91619	138.29704	148.39871	159.27638
24 ...	95.06985	102.17415	109.85364	118.15524	127.12961	136.83147	147.31988	158.65862	170.91652	184.16784
25 ...	106.05219	114.41331	123.48681	133.33387	144.02081	155.61956	168.20806	181.87083	196.69941	212.79302
26 ...	118.18767	127.99877	138.68780	150.33393	163.02341	176.85010	191.91615	208.33274	226.22083	245.71197
27 ...	131.59737	143.07864	155.63689	169.37401	184.40134	200.84061	218.82483	238.49933	260.02285	283.56877
28 ...	146.41510	159.81729	174.53513	190.69889	208.45151	227.94989	249.36618	272.88923	298.72616	327.10408
29 ...	162.78868	178.39719	195.60668	214.58275	235.50795	258.58338	284.03062	312.09373	343.04145	377.16969
30 ...	180.88149	199.02088	219.10144	241.33268	265.94644	293.19922	323.37475	356.78685	393.78246	434.74515

15.5%	16%	16.5%	17%	17.5%	18%	18.5%	19%	19.5%	20%
1.00000	1.00000	1.00000	1.00000	1.00000	1.00000	1.00000	1.00000	1.00000	1.00000
2.15500	2.16000	2.16500	2.17000	2.17500	2.18000	2.18500	2.19000	2.19500	2.20000
3.48902	3.50560	3.52222	3.53890	3.55562	3.57240	3.58922	3.60610	3.62302	3.64000
5.02982	5.06650	5.10339	5.14051	5.17786	5.21543	5.25323	5.29126	5.32951	5.36800
6.80945	6.87714	6.94545	7.01440	7.08398	7.15421	7.22508	7.29660	7.36877	7.44160
8.86491	8.97748	9.09145	9.20685	9.32368	9.44197	9.56172	9.68295	9.80568	9.92992
11.23897	11.41387	11.59154	11.77201	11.95533	12.14152	12.33064	12.52271	12.71779	12.91590
13.98101	14.24009	14.50415	14.77325	15.04751	15.32700	15.61181	15.90203	16.19776	16.49908
17.14807	17.51851	17.89733	18.28471	18.68082	19.08585	19.49999	19.92341	20.35632	20.79890
20.80602	21.32147	21.85039	22.39311	22.94997	23.52131	24.10749	24.70886	25.32580	25.95868
25.03095	25.73290	26.45570	27.19994	27.96621	28.75514	29.56737	30.40355	31.26433	32.15042
29.91075	30.85017	31.82089	32.82393	33.86030	34.93107	36.03734	37.18022	38.36088	39.58050
35.54692	36.78620	38.07134	39.40399	40.78585	42.21866	43.70424	45.24446	46.84125	48.49660
42.05669	43.67199	45.35311	47.10267	48.92337	50.81802	52.78953	54.84091	56.97529	59.19592
49.57548	51.65951	53.83638	56.11013	58.48496	60.96527	63.55559	66.26068	69.08547	72.03511
58.25968	60.92503	63.71938	66.64885	69.71983	72.93901	76.31338	79.85021	83.55714	87.44213
68.28993	71.67303	75.23307	78.97915	82.92080	87.06804	91.43135	96.02175	100.85079	105.93056
79.87486	84.14072	88.64653	93.40561	98.43194	103.74028	109.34615	115.26588	121.51669	128.11667
93.25547	98.60323	104.27321	110.28456	116.65753	123.41353	130.57519	138.16640	146.21244	154.74000
108.71007	115.37975	122.47829	130.03294	138.07260	146.62797	155.73160	165.41802	175.72387	186.68800
126.56013	134.84051	143.68721	153.13854	163.23531	174.02100	185.54194	197.84744	210.99002	225.02560
147.17695	157.41499	168.39560	180.17209	192.80149	206.34479	220.86720	236.43846	253.13308	271.03072
170.98937	183.60138	197.18087	211.80134	227.54175	244.48685	262.72763	282.36176	303.49403	326.23686
198.49272	213.97761	230.71571	248.80757	268.36155	289.49448	312.33225	337.01050	363.67536	392.48424
230.25910	249.21402	269.78381	292.10486	316.32482	342.60349	371.11371	402.04249	435.59206	471.98108
266.94926	290.08827	315.29813	342.76268	372.68167	405.27211	440.76975	479.43056	521.53251	567.37730
309.32639	337.50239	368.32233	402.03234	438.90096	479.22109	523.31215	571.52237	624.23135	681.85276
358.27198	392.50277	430.09551	471.37783	516.70863	566.48089	621.12490	681.11162	746.95647	819.22331
414.80414	456.30322	502.06127	552.51207	608.13264	669.44745	737.03300	811.52283	893.61298	984.06797
480.09878	530.31173	585.90138	647.43912	715.55585	790.94799	874.38411	966.71217	1068.86751	1181.88157

Table 3
Present Value of $1 at Compound Interest: 0.5%–7%

$$P_{i,n} = \frac{1}{(1+i)^n}$$

Period	.5%	1%	1.5%	2%	2.5%	3%	3.5%	4%	4.5%	5%	5.5%	6%	6.5%	7%
1 ...	0.99502	0.99010	0.98522	0.98039	0.97561	0.97087	0.96618	0.96154	0.95694	0.95238	0.94787	0.94340	0.93897	0.93458
2 ...	0.99007	0.98030	0.97066	0.96117	0.95181	0.94260	0.93351	0.92456	0.91573	0.90703	0.89845	0.89000	0.88166	0.87344
3 ...	0.98515	0.97059	0.95632	0.94232	0.92860	0.91514	0.90194	0.88900	0.87630	0.86384	0.85161	0.83962	0.82785	0.81630
4 ...	0.98025	0.96098	0.94218	0.92385	0.90595	0.88849	0.87144	0.85480	0.83856	0.82270	0.80722	0.79209	0.77732	0.76290
5 ...	0.97537	0.95147	0.92826	0.90573	0.88385	0.86261	0.84197	0.82193	0.80245	0.78353	0.76513	0.74726	0.72988	0.71299
6 ...	0.97052	0.94205	0.91454	0.88797	0.86230	0.83748	0.81350	0.79031	0.76790	0.74622	0.72525	0.70496	0.68533	0.66634
7 ...	0.96569	0.93272	0.90103	0.87056	0.84127	0.81309	0.78599	0.75992	0.73483	0.71068	0.68744	0.66506	0.64351	0.62275
8 ...	0.96089	0.92348	0.88771	0.85349	0.82075	0.78941	0.75941	0.73069	0.70319	0.67684	0.65160	0.62741	0.60423	0.58201
9 ...	0.95610	0.91434	0.87459	0.83676	0.80073	0.76642	0.73373	0.70259	0.67290	0.64461	0.61763	0.59190	0.56735	0.54393
10 ...	0.95135	0.90529	0.86167	0.82035	0.78120	0.74409	0.70892	0.67556	0.64393	0.61391	0.58543	0.55839	0.53273	0.50835
11 ...	0.94661	0.89632	0.84893	0.80426	0.76214	0.72242	0.68495	0.64958	0.61620	0.58468	0.55491	0.52679	0.50021	0.47509
12 ...	0.94191	0.88745	0.83639	0.78849	0.74356	0.70138	0.66178	0.62460	0.58966	0.55684	0.52598	0.49697	0.46968	0.44401
13 ...	0.93722	0.87866	0.82403	0.77303	0.72542	0.68095	0.63940	0.60057	0.56427	0.53032	0.49856	0.46884	0.44102	0.41496
14 ...	0.93256	0.86996	0.81185	0.75788	0.70773	0.66112	0.61778	0.57748	0.53997	0.50507	0.47257	0.44230	0.41410	0.38782
15 ...	0.92792	0.86135	0.79985	0.74301	0.69047	0.64186	0.59689	0.55526	0.51672	0.48102	0.44793	0.41727	0.38883	0.36245
16 ...	0.92330	0.85282	0.78803	0.72845	0.67362	0.62317	0.57671	0.53391	0.49447	0.45811	0.42458	0.39365	0.36510	0.33873
17 ...	0.91871	0.84438	0.77639	0.71416	0.65720	0.60502	0.55720	0.51337	0.47318	0.43630	0.40245	0.37136	0.34281	0.31657
18 ...	0.91414	0.83602	0.76491	0.70016	0.64117	0.58739	0.53836	0.49363	0.45280	0.41552	0.38147	0.35034	0.32189	0.29586
19 ...	0.90959	0.82774	0.75361	0.68643	0.62553	0.57029	0.52016	0.47464	0.43330	0.39573	0.36158	0.33051	0.30224	0.27651
20 ...	0.90506	0.81954	0.74247	0.67297	0.61027	0.55368	0.50257	0.45639	0.41464	0.37689	0.34273	0.31180	0.28380	0.25842
21 ...	0.90056	0.81143	0.73150	0.65978	0.59539	0.53755	0.48557	0.43883	0.39679	0.35894	0.32486	0.29416	0.26648	0.24151
22 ...	0.89608	0.80340	0.72069	0.64684	0.58086	0.52189	0.46915	0.42196	0.37970	0.34185	0.30793	0.27751	0.25021	0.22571
23 ...	0.89162	0.79544	0.71004	0.63416	0.56670	0.50669	0.45329	0.40573	0.36335	0.32557	0.29187	0.26180	0.23494	0.21095
24 ...	0.88719	0.78757	0.69954	0.62172	0.55288	0.49193	0.43796	0.39012	0.34770	0.31007	0.27666	0.24698	0.22060	0.19715
25 ...	0.88277	0.77977	0.68921	0.60953	0.53939	0.47761	0.42315	0.37512	0.33273	0.29530	0.26223	0.23300	0.20714	0.18425
26 ...	0.87838	0.77205	0.67902	0.59758	0.52623	0.46369	0.40884	0.36069	0.31840	0.28124	0.24856	0.21981	0.19450	0.17220
27 ...	0.87401	0.76440	0.66899	0.58586	0.51340	0.45019	0.39501	0.34682	0.30469	0.26785	0.23560	0.20737	0.18263	0.16093
28 ...	0.86966	0.75684	0.65910	0.57437	0.50088	0.43708	0.38165	0.33348	0.29157	0.25509	0.22332	0.19563	0.17148	0.15040
29 ...	0.86533	0.74934	0.64936	0.56311	0.48866	0.42435	0.36875	0.32065	0.27902	0.24295	0.21168	0.18456	0.16101	0.14056
30 ...	0.86103	0.74192	0.63976	0.55207	0.47674	0.41199	0.35628	0.30832	0.26700	0.23138	0.20064	0.17411	0.15119	0.13137
31 ...	0.85675	0.73458	0.63031	0.54125	0.46511	0.39999	0.34423	0.29646	0.25550	0.22036	0.19018	0.16425	0.14196	0.12277
32 ...	0.85248	0.72730	0.62099	0.53063	0.45377	0.38834	0.33259	0.28506	0.24450	0.20987	0.18027	0.15496	0.13329	0.11474
33 ...	0.84824	0.72010	0.61182	0.52023	0.44270	0.37703	0.32134	0.27409	0.23397	0.19987	0.17087	0.14619	0.12516	0.10723
34 ...	0.84402	0.71297	0.60277	0.51003	0.43191	0.36604	0.31048	0.26355	0.22390	0.19035	0.16196	0.13791	0.11752	0.10022
35 ...	0.83982	0.70591	0.59387	0.50003	0.42137	0.35538	0.29998	0.25342	0.21425	0.18129	0.15352	0.13011	0.11035	0.09366
36 ...	0.83564	0.69892	0.58509	0.49022	0.41109	0.34503	0.28983	0.24367	0.20503	0.17266	0.14552	0.12274	0.10361	0.08754
37 ...	0.83149	0.69200	0.57644	0.48061	0.40107	0.33498	0.28003	0.23430	0.19620	0.16444	0.13793	0.11579	0.09729	0.08181
38 ...	0.82735	0.68515	0.56792	0.47119	0.39128	0.32523	0.27056	0.22529	0.18775	0.15661	0.13074	0.10924	0.09135	0.07646
39 ...	0.82323	0.67837	0.55953	0.46195	0.38174	0.31575	0.26141	0.21662	0.17967	0.14915	0.12392	0.10306	0.08578	0.07146
40 ...	0.81914	0.67165	0.55126	0.45289	0.37243	0.30656	0.25257	0.20829	0.17193	0.14205	0.11746	0.09722	0.08054	0.06678
41 ...	0.81506	0.66500	0.54312	0.44401	0.36335	0.29763	0.24403	0.20028	0.16453	0.13528	0.11134	0.09172	0.07563	0.06241
42 ...	0.81101	0.65842	0.53509	0.43530	0.35448	0.28896	0.23578	0.19257	0.15744	0.12884	0.10554	0.08653	0.07101	0.05833
43 ...	0.80697	0.65190	0.52718	0.42677	0.34584	0.28054	0.22781	0.18517	0.15066	0.12270	0.10003	0.08163	0.06668	0.05451
44 ...	0.80296	0.64545	0.51939	0.41840	0.33740	0.27237	0.22010	0.17805	0.14417	0.11686	0.09482	0.07701	0.06261	0.05095
45 ...	0.79896	0.63905	0.51171	0.41020	0.32917	0.26444	0.21266	0.17120	0.13796	0.11130	0.08988	0.07265	0.05879	0.04761
46 ...	0.79499	0.63273	0.50415	0.40215	0.32115	0.25674	0.20547	0.16461	0.13202	0.10600	0.08519	0.06854	0.05520	0.04450
47 ...	0.79103	0.62646	0.49670	0.39427	0.31331	0.24926	0.19852*	0.15828	0.12634	0.10095	0.08075	0.06466	0.05183	0.04159
48 ...	0.78710	0.62026	0.48936	0.38654	0.30567	0.24200	0.19181	0.15219	0.12090	0.09614	0.07654	0.06100	0.04867	0.03887
49 ...	0.78318	0.61412	0.48213	0.37896	0.29822	0.23495	0.18532	0.14634	0.11569	0.09156	0.07255	0.05755	0.04570	0.03632
50 ...	0.77929	0.60804	0.47500	0.37153	0.29094	0.22811	0.17905	0.14071	0.11071	0.08720	0.06877	0.05429	0.04291	0.03395
51 ...	0.77541	0.60202	0.46798	0.36424	0.28385	0.22146	0.17300	0.13530	0.10594	0.08305	0.06518	0.05122	0.04029	0.03173
52 ...	0.77155	0.59606	0.46107	0.35710	0.27692	0.21501	0.16715	0.13010	0.10138	0.07910	0.06178	0.04832	0.03783	0.02965
53 ...	0.76771	0.59016	0.45426	0.35010	0.27017	0.20875	0.16150	0.12509	0.09701	0.07533	0.05856	0.04558	0.03552	0.02771
54 ...	0.76389	0.58431	0.44754	0.34323	0.26358	0.20267	0.15603	0.12028	0.09284	0.07174	0.05551	0.04300	0.03335	0.02590
55 ...	0.76009	0.57853	0.44093	0.33650	0.25715	0.19677	0.15076	0.11566	0.08884	0.06833	0.05262	0.04057	0.03132	0.02420
56 ...	0.75631	0.57280	0.43441	0.32991	0.25088	0.19104	0.14566	0.11121	0.08501	0.06507	0.04987	0.03827	0.02941	0.02262
57 ...	0.75255	0.56713	0.42799	0.32344	0.24476	0.18547	0.14073	0.10693	0.08135	0.06197	0.04727	0.03610	0.02761	0.02114
58 ...	0.74880	0.56151	0.42167	0.31710	0.23879	0.18007	0.13598	0.10282	0.07785	0.05902	0.04481	0.03406	0.02593	0.01976
59 ...	0.74508	0.55595	0.41544	0.31088	0.23297	0.17483	0.13138	0.09886	0.07450	0.05621	0.04247	0.03213	0.02434	0.01847
60 ...	0.74137	0.55045	0.40930	0.30478	0.22728	0.16973	0.12693	0.09506	0.07129	0.05354	0.04026	0.03031	0.02286	0.01726

Period	.5%	1%	1.5%	2%	2.5%	3%	3.5%	4%	4.5%	5%	5.5%	6%	6.5%	7%
61 ..	0.73768	0.54500	0.40325	0.29881	0.22174	0.16479	0.12264	0.09140	0.06822	0.05099	0.03816	0.02860	0.02146	0.01613
62 ..	0.73401	0.53960	0.39729	0.29295	0.21633	0.15999	0.11849	0.08789	0.06528	0.04856	0.03617	0.02698	0.02015	0.01507
63 ..	0.73036	0.53426	0.39142	0.28720	0.21106	0.15533	0.11449	0.08451	0.06247	0.04625	0.03428	0.02545	0.01892	0.01409
64 ..	0.72673	0.52897	0.38563	0.28157	0.20591	0.15081	0.11062	0.08126	0.05978	0.04404	0.03250	0.02401	0.01777	0.01317
65 ..	0.72311	0.52373	0.37993	0.27605	0.20089	0.14641	0.10688	0.07813	0.05721	0.04195	0.03080	0.02265	0.01668	0.01230
66 ..	0.71952	0.51855	0.37432	0.27064	0.19599	0.14215	0.10326	0.07513	0.05474	0.03995	0.02920	0.02137	0.01566	0.01150
67 ..	0.71594	0.51341	0.36879	0.26533	0.19121	0.13801	0.09977	0.07224	0.05239	0.03805	0.02767	0.02016	0.01471	0.01075
68 ..	0.71237	0.50833	0.36334	0.26013	0.18654	0.13399	0.09640	0.06946	0.05013	0.03623	0.02623	0.01902	0.01381	0.01004
69 ..	0.70883	0.50330	0.35797	0.25503	0.18199	0.13009	0.09314	0.06679	0.04797	0.03451	0.02486	0.01794	0.01297	0.00939
70 ..	0.70530	0.49831	0.35268	0.25003	0.17755	0.12630	0.08999	0.06422	0.04590	0.03287	0.02357	0.01693	0.01218	0.00877
71 ..	0.70179	0.49338	0.34746	0.24513	0.17322	0.12262	0.08694	0.06175	0.04393	0.03130	0.02234	0.01597	0.01143	0.00820
72 ..	0.69830	0.48850	0.34233	0.24032	0.16900	0.11905	0.08400	0.05937	0.04204	0.02981	0.02117	0.01507	0.01074	0.00766
73 ..	0.69483	0.48366	0.33727	0.23561	0.16488	0.11558	0.08116	0.05709	0.04023	0.02839	0.02007	0.01421	0.01008	0.00716
74 ..	0.69137	0.47887	0.33229	0.23099	0.16085	0.11221	0.07842	0.05490	0.03849	0.02704	0.01902	0.01341	0.00947	0.00669
75 ..	0.68793	0.47413	0.32738	0.22646	0.15693	0.10895	0.07577	0.05278	0.03684	0.02575	0.01803	0.01265	0.00889	0.00625
76 ..	0.68451	0.46944	0.32254	0.22202	0.15310	0.10577	0.07320	0.05075	0.03525	0.02453	0.01709	0.01193	0.00835	0.00585
77 ..	0.68110	0.46479	0.31777	0.21766	0.14937	0.10269	0.07073	0.04880	0.03373	0.02336	0.01620	0.01126	0.00784	0.00546
78 ..	0.67772	0.46019	0.31308	0.21340	0.14573	0.09970	0.06834	0.04692	0.03228	0.02225	0.01536	0.01062	0.00736	0.00511
79 ..	0.67434	0.45563	0.30845	0.20921	0.14217	0.09680	0.06603	0.04512	0.03089	0.02119	0.01456	0.01002	0.00691	0.00477
80 ..	0.67099	0.45112	0.30389	0.20511	0.13870	0.09398	0.06379	0.04338	0.02956	0.02018	0.01380	0.00945	0.00649	0.00446
81 ..	0.66765	0.44665	0.29940	0.20109	0.13532	0.09124	0.06164	0.04172	0.02829	0.01922	0.01308	0.00892	0.00609	0.00417
82 ..	0.66433	0.44223	0.29497	0.19715	0.13202	0.08858	0.05955	0.04011	0.02707	0.01830	0.01240	0.00841	0.00572	0.00390
83 ..	0.66102	0.43785	0.29062	0.19328	0.12880	0.08600	0.05754	0.03857	0.02590	0.01743	0.01175	0.00794	0.00537	0.00364
84 ..	0.65773	0.43352	0.28632	0.18949	0.12566	0.08350	0.05559	0.03709	0.02479	0.01660	0.01114	0.00749	0.00504	0.00340
85 ..	0.65446	0.42922	0.28209	0.18577	0.12259	0.08107	0.05371	0.03566	0.02372	0.01581	0.01056	0.00706	0.00473	0.00318
86 ..	0.65121	0.42497	0.27792	0.18213	0.11960	0.07870	0.05190	0.03429	0.02270	0.01506	0.01001	0.00666	0.00445	0.00297
87 ..	0.64797	0.42077	0.27381	0.17856	0.11669	0.07641	0.05014	0.03297	0.02172	0.01434	0.00948	0.00629	0.00417	0.00278
88 ..	0.64474	0.41660	0.26977	0.17506	0.11384	0.07419	0.04845	0.03170	0.02079	0.01366	0.00899	0.00593	0.00392	0.00260
89 ..	0.64154	0.41248	0.26578	0.17163	0.11106	0.07203	0.04681	0.03048	0.01989	0.01301	0.00852	0.00559	0.00368	0.00243
90 ..	0.63834	0.40839	0.26185	0.16826	0.10836	0.06993	0.04522	0.02931	0.01903	0.01239	0.00808	0.00528	0.00346	0.00227
91 ..	0.63517	0.40435	0.25798	0.16496	0.10571	0.06789	0.04369	0.02818	0.01821	0.01180	0.00766	0.00498	0.00324	0.00212
92 ..	0.63201	0.40034	0.25417	0.16173	0.10313	0.06591	0.04222	0.02710	0.01743	0.01124	0.00726	0.00470	0.00305	0.00198
93 ..	0.62886	0.39638	0.25041	0.15856	0.10062	0.06399	0.04079	0.02606	0.01668	0.01070	0.00688	0.00443	0.00286	0.00185
94 ..	0.62573	0.39246	0.24671	0.15545	0.09816	0.06213	0.03941	0.02505	0.01596	0.01019	0.00652	0.00418	0.00269	0.00173
95 ..	0.62262	0.38857	0.24307	0.15240	0.09577	0.06032	0.03808	0.02409	0.01527	0.00971	0.00618	0.00394	0.00252	0.00162
96 ..	0.61952	0.38472	0.23947	0.14941	0.09343	0.05856	0.03679	0.02316	0.01462	0.00924	0.00586	0.00372	0.00237	0.00151
97 ..	0.61644	0.38091	0.23594	0.14648	0.09116	0.05686	0.03555	0.02227	0.01399	0.00880	0.00555	0.00351	0.00222	0.00141
98 ..	0.61337	0.37714	0.23245	0.14361	0.08893	0.05520	0.03434	0.02142	0.01338	0.00838	0.00526	0.00331	0.00209	0.00132
99 ..	0.61032	0.37341	0.22901	0.14079	0.08676	0.05359	0.03318	0.02059	0.01281	0.00798	0.00499	0.00312	0.00196	0.00123
100 ..	0.60729	0.36971	0.22563	0.13803	0.08465	0.05203	0.03026	0.01980	0.01226	0.00760	0.00473	0.00295	0.00184	0.00115
101 ..	0.60427	0.36605	0.22230	0.13533	0.08258	0.05052	0.03098	0.01904	0.01173	0.00724	0.00448	0.00278	0.00173	0.00108
102 ..	0.60126	0.36243	0.21901	0.13267	0.08057	0.04905	0.02993	0.01831	0.01122	0.00690	0.00425	0.00262	0.00162	0.00101
103 ..	0.59827	0.35884	0.21577	0.13007	0.07860	0.04762	0.02892	0.01760	0.01074	0.00657	0.00403	0.00247	0.00152	0.00094
104 ..	0.59529	0.35529	0.21258	0.12752	0.07669	0.04623	0.02794	0.01693	0.01028	0.00626	0.00382	0.00233	0.00143	0.00088
105 ..	0.59233	0.35177	0.20944	0.12502	0.07482	0.04488	0.02699	0.01627	0.00984	0.00596	0.00362	0.00220	0.00134	0.00082
106 ..	0.58938	0.34828	0.20635	0.12257	0.07299	0.04358	0.02608	0.01565	0.00941	0.00567	0.00343	0.00208	0.00126	0.00077
107 ..	0.58645	0.34484	0.20330	0.12017	0.07121	0.04231	0.02520	0.01505	0.00901	0.00540	0.00325	0.00196	0.00118	0.00072
108 ..	0.58353	0.34142	0.20029	0.11781	0.06947	0.04108	0.02435	0.01447	0.00862	0.00515	0.00308	0.00185	0.00111	0.00067
109 ..	0.58063	0.33804	0.19733	0.11550	0.06778	0.03988	0.02352	0.01391	0.00825	0.00490	0.00292	0.00174	0.00104	0.00063
110 ..	0.57774	0.33469	0.19442	0.11324	0.06613	0.03872	0.02273	0.01338	0.00789	0.00467	0.00277	0.00165	0.00098	0.00059
111 ..	0.57487	0.33138	0.19154	0.11101	0.06451	0.03759	0.02196	0.01286	0.00755	0.00445	0.00262	0.00155	0.00092	0.00055
112 ..	0.57201	0.32810	0.18871	0.10884	0.06294	0.03649	0.02122	0.01237	0.00723	0.00423	0.00249	0.00146	0.00086	0.00051
113 ..	0.56916	0.32485	0.18592	0.10670	0.06140	0.03543	0.02050	0.01189	0.00692	0.00403	0.00236	0.00138	0.00081	0.00048
114 ..	0.56633	0.32164	0.18318	0.10461	0.05991	0.03440	0.01981	0.01143	0.00662	0.00384	0.00223	0.00130	0.00076	0.00045
115 ..	0.56351	0.31845	0.18047	0.10256	0.05845	0.03340	0.01914	0.01099	0.00633	0.00366	0.00212	0.00123	0.00072	0.00042
116 ..	0.56071	0.31530	0.17780	0.10055	0.05702	0.03243	0.01849	0.01057	0.00606	0.00348	0.00201	0.00116	0.00067	0.00039
117 ..	0.55792	0.31218	0.17518	0.09858	0.05563	0.03148	0.01786	0.01016	0.00580	0.00332	0.00190	0.00109	0.00063	0.00036
118 ..	0.55514	0.30908	0.17259	0.09665	0.05427	0.03056	0.01726	0.00977	0.00555	0.00316	0.00180	0.00103	0.00059	0.00034
119 ..	0.55238	0.30602	0.17004	0.09475	0.05295	0.02967	0.01668	0.00940	0.00531	0.00301	0.00171	0.00097	0.00056	0.00032
120 ..	0.54963	0.30299	0.16752	0.09289	0.05166	0.02881	0.01611	0.00904	0.00508	0.00287	0.00162	0.00092	0.00052	0.00030

Table 3 (*continued*)
Present Value of $1 at Compound Interest: 7.5%–14%

Period	7.5%	8%	8.5%	9%	9.5%	10%	10.5%	11%	11.5%	12%	12.5%	13%	13.5%	14%
1 ...	0.93023	0.92593	0.92166	0.91743	0.91324	0.90909	0.90498	0.90090	0.89686	0.89286	0.88889	0.88496	0.88106	0.87719
2 ...	0.86533	0.85734	0.84946	0.84168	0.83401	0.82645	0.81898	0.81162	0.80436	0.79719	0.79012	0.78315	0.77626	0.76947
3 ...	0.80496	0.79383	0.78291	0.77218	0.76165	0.75131	0.74116	0.73119	0.72140	0.71178	0.70233	0.69305	0.68393	0.67497
4 ...	0.74880	0.73503	0.72157	0.70843	0.69557	0.68301	0.67073	0.65873	0.64699	0.63553	0.62430	0.61332	0.60258	0.59208
5 ...	0.69656	0.68058	0.66505	0.64993	0.63523	0.62092	0.60700	0.59345	0.58026	0.56743	0.55493	0.54276	0.53091	0.51937
6 ...	0.64796	0.63017	0.61295	0.59627	0.58012	0.56447	0.54932	0.53464	0.52042	0.50663	0.49327	0.48032	0.46776	0.45559
7 ...	0.60275	0.58349	0.56493	0.54703	0.52979	0.51316	0.49712	0.48166	0.46674	0.45235	0.43846	0.42506	0.41213	0.39964
8 ...	0.56070	0.54027	0.52067	0.50187	0.48382	0.46651	0.44989	0.43393	0.41860	0.40388	0.38974	0.37616	0.36311	0.35056
9 ...	0.52158	0.50025	0.47988	0.46043	0.44185	0.42410	0.40714	0.39092	0.37543	0.36061	0.34644	0.33288	0.31992	0.30751
10 ...	0.48519	0.46319	0.44229	0.42241	0.40351	0.38554	0.36845	0.35218	0.33671	0.32197	0.30795	0.29459	0.28187	0.26974
11 ...	0.45134	0.42888	0.40764	0.38753	0.36851	0.35049	0.33344	0.31728	0.30198	0.28748	0.27373	0.26070	0.24834	0.23662
12 ...	0.41985	0.39711	0.37570	0.35553	0.33654	0.31863	0.30175	0.28584	0.27083	0.25668	0.24332	0.23071	0.21880	0.20756
13 ...	0.39056	0.36770	0.34627	0.32618	0.30734	0.28966	0.27308	0.25751	0.24290	0.22917	0.21628	0.20416	0.19278	0.18207
14 ...	0.36331	0.34046	0.31914	0.29925	0.28067	0.26333	0.24713	0.23199	0.21785	0.20462	0.19225	0.18068	0.16985	0.15971
15 ...	0.33797	0.31524	0.29414	0.27454	0.25632	0.23939	0.22365	0.20900	0.19538	0.18270	0.17089	0.15989	0.14964	0.14010
16 ...	0.31439	0.29189	0.27110	0.25187	0.23409	0.21763	0.20240	0.18829	0.17523	0.16312	0.15190	0.14150	0.13185	0.12289
17 ...	0.29245	0.27027	0.24986	0.23107	0.21378	0.19784	0.18316	0.16963	0.15715	0.14564	0.13502	0.12522	0.11616	0.10780
18 ...	0.27205	0.25025	0.23028	0.21199	0.19523	0.17986	0.16576	0.15282	0.14095	0.13004	0.12002	0.11081	0.10235	0.09456
19 ...	0.25307	0.23171	0.21224	0.19449	0.17829	0.16351	0.15001	0.13768	0.12641	0.11611	0.10668	0.09806	0.09017	0.08295
20 ...	0.23541	0.21455	0.19562	0.17843	0.16282	0.14864	0.13575	0.12403	0.11337	0.10367	0.09483	0.08678	0.07945	0.07276
21 ...	0.21899	0.19866	0.18029	0.16370	0.14870	0.13513	0.12285	0.11174	0.10168	0.09256	0.08429	0.07680	0.07000	0.06383
22 ...	0.20371	0.18394	0.16617	0.15018	0.13580	0.12285	0.11118	0.10067	0.09119	0.08264	0.07493	0.06796	0.06167	0.05599
23 ...	0.18950	0.17032	0.15315	0.13778	0.12402	0.11168	0.10062	0.09069	0.08179	0.07379	0.06660	0.06014	0.05434	0.04911
24 ...	0.17628	0.15770	0.14115	0.12640	0.11326	0.10153	0.09106	0.08170	0.07335	0.06588	0.05920	0.05323	0.04787	0.04308
25 ...	0.16398	0.14602	0.13009	0.11597	0.10343	0.09230	0.08240	0.07361	0.06579	0.05882	0.05262	0.04710	0.04218	0.03779
26 ...	0.15254	0.13520	0.11990	0.10639	0.09446	0.08391	0.07457	0.06631	0.05900	0.05252	0.04678	0.04168	0.03716	0.03315
27 ...	0.14190	0.12519	0.11051	0.09761	0.08626	0.07628	0.06749	0.05974	0.05291	0.04689	0.04158	0.03689	0.03274	0.02908
28 ...	0.13200	0.11591	0.10185	0.08955	0.07878	0.06934	0.06107	0.05382	0.04746	0.04187	0.03696	0.03264	0.02885	0.02551
29 ...	0.12279	0.10733	0.09387	0.08215	0.07194	0.06304	0.05527	0.04849	0.04256	0.03738	0.03285	0.02889	0.02542	0.02237
30 ...	0.11422	0.09938	0.08652	0.07537	0.06570	0.05731	0.05002	0.04368	0.03817	0.03338	0.02920	0.02557	0.02239	0.01963
31 ...	0.10625	0.09202	0.07974	0.06915	0.06000	0.05210	0.04527	0.03935	0.03424	0.02980	0.02596	0.02262	0.01973	0.01722
32 ...	0.09884	0.08520	0.07349	0.06344	0.05480	0.04736	0.04096	0.03545	0.03070	0.02661	0.02307	0.02002	0.01738	0.01510
33 ...	0.09194	0.07889	0.06774	0.05820	0.05004	0.04306	0.03707	0.03194	0.02754	0.02376	0.02051	0.01772	0.01532	0.01325
34 ...	0.08553	0.07305	0.06243	0.05339	0.04570	0.03914	0.03355	0.02878	0.02470	0.02121	0.01823	0.01568	0.01349	0.01162
35 ...	0.07956	0.06763	0.05754	0.04899	0.04174	0.03558	0.03036	0.02592	0.02215	0.01894	0.01621	0.01388	0.01189	0.01019
36 ...	0.07401	0.06262	0.05303	0.04494	0.03811	0.03235	0.02748	0.02335	0.01987	0.01691	0.01440	0.01228	0.01047	0.00894
37 ...	0.06885	0.05799	0.04888	0.04123	0.03481	0.02941	0.02487	0.02104	0.01782	0.01510	0.01280	0.01087	0.00923	0.00784
38 ...	0.06404	0.05369	0.04505	0.03783	0.03179	0.02673	0.02250	0.01896	0.01598	0.01348	0.01138	0.00962	0.00813	0.00688
39 ...	0.05958	0.04971	0.04152	0.03470	0.02903	0.02430	0.02036	0.01708	0.01433	0.01204	0.01012	0.00851	0.00716	0.00604
40 ...	0.05542	0.04603	0.03827	0.03184	0.02651	0.02209	0.01843	0.01538	0.01285	0.01075	0.00899	0.00753	0.00631	0.00529
41 ...	0.05155	0.04262	0.03527	0.02921	0.02421	0.02009	0.01668	0.01386	0.01153	0.00960	0.00799	0.00666	0.00556	0.00464
42 ...	0.04796	0.03946	0.03251	0.02680	0.02211	0.01826	0.01509	0.01249	0.01034	0.00857	0.00711	0.00590	0.00490	0.00407
43 ...	0.04461	0.03654	0.02996	0.02458	0.02019	0.01660	0.01366	0.01125	0.00927	0.00765	0.00632	0.00522	0.00432	0.00357
44 ...	0.04150	0.03383	0.02761	0.02255	0.01844	0.01509	0.01236	0.01013	0.00832	0.00683	0.00561	0.00462	0.00380	0.00313
45 ...	0.03860	0.03133	0.02545	0.02069	0.01684	0.01372	0.01119	0.00913	0.00746	0.00610	0.00499	0.00409	0.00335	0.00275
46 ...	0.03591	0.02901	0.02345	0.01898	0.01538	0.01247	0.01012	0.00823	0.00669	0.00544	0.00444	0.00362	0.00295	0.00241
47 ...	0.03340	0.02686	0.02162	0.01742	0.01405	0.01134	0.00916	0.00741	0.00600	0.00486	0.00394	0.00320	0.00260	0.00212
48 ...	0.03107	0.02487	0.01992	0.01598	0.01283	0.01031	0.00829	0.00668	0.00538	0.00434	0.00350	0.00283	0.00229	0.00186
49 ...	0.02891	0.02303	0.01836	0.01466	0.01171	0.00937	0.00750	0.00601	0.00483	0.00388	0.00312	0.00251	0.00202	0.00163
50 ...	0.02689	0.02132	0.01692	0.01345	0.01070	0.00852	0.00679	0.00542	0.00433	0.00346	0.00277	0.00222	0.00178	0.00143
51 ...	0.02501	0.01974	0.01560	0.01234	0.00977	0.00774	0.00615	0.00488	0.00388	0.00309	0.00246	0.00196	0.00157	0.00125
52 ...	0.02327	0.01828	0.01438	0.01132	0.00892	0.00704	0.00556	0.00440	0.00348	0.00276	0.00219	0.00174	0.00138	0.00110
53 ...	0.02164	0.01693	0.01325	0.01038	0.00815	0.00640	0.00503	0.00396	0.00312	0.00246	0.00194	0.00154	0.00122	0.00096
54 ...	0.02013	0.01567	0.01221	0.00953	0.00744	0.00582	0.00455	0.00357	0.00280	0.00220	0.00173	0.00136	0.00107	0.00085
55 ...	0.01873	0.01451	0.01126	0.00874	0.00680	0.00529	0.00412	0.00322	0.00251	0.00196	0.00154	0.00120	0.00094	0.00074
56 ...	0.01742	0.01344	0.01037	0.00802	0.00621	0.00481	0.00373	0.00290	0.00225	0.00175	0.00137	0.00107	0.00083	0.00065
57 ...	0.01621	0.01244	0.00956	0.00736	0.00567	0.00437	0.00338	0.00261	0.00202	0.00157	0.00121	0.00094	0.00073	0.00057
58 ...	0.01508	0.01152	0.00881	0.00675	0.00518	0.00397	0.00305	0.00235	0.00181	0.00140	0.00108	0.00083	0.00065	0.00050
59 ...	0.01402	0.01067	0.00812	0.00619	0.00473	0.00361	0.00276	0.00212	0.00162	0.00125	0.00096	0.00074	0.00057	0.00044
60 ...	0.01305	0.00988	0.00749	0.00568	0.00432	0.00328	0.00250	0.00191	0.00146	0.00111	0.00085	0.00065	0.00050	0.00039

Period	7.5%	8%	8.5%	9%	9.5%	10%	10.5%	11%	11.5%	12%	12.5%	13%	13.5%	14%
61 ..	0.01214	0.00914	0.00690	0.00521	0.00394	0.00299	0.00226	0.00172	0.00131	0.00099	0.00076	0.00058	0.00044	0.00034
62 ..	0.01129	0.00847	0.00636	0.00478	0.00360	0.00271	0.00205	0.00155	0.00117	0.00089	0.00067	0.00051	0.00039	0.00030
63 ..	0.01050	0.00784	0.00586	0.00439	0.00329	0.00247	0.00185	0.00140	0.00105	0.00079	0.00060	0.00045	0.00034	0.00026
64 ..	0.00977	0.00726	0.00540	0.00402	0.00300	0.00224	0.00168	0.00126	0.00094	0.00071	0.00053	0.00040	0.00030	0.00023
65 ..	0.00909	0.00672	0.00498	0.00369	0.00274	0.00204	0.00152	0.00113	0.00085	0.00063	0.00047	0.00035	0.00027	0.00020
66 ..	0.00845	0.00622	0.00459	0.00339	0.00250	0.00185	0.00137	0.00102	0.00076	0.00056	0.00042	0.00031	0.00023	0.00018
67 ..	0.00786	0.00576	0.00423	0.00311	0.00229	0.00169	0.00124	0.00092	0.00068	0.00050	0.00037	0.00028	0.00021	0.00015
68 ..	0.00732	0.00534	0.00390	0.00285	0.00209	0.00153	0.00113	0.00083	0.00061	0.00045	0.00033	0.00025	0.00018	0.00014
69 ..	0.00680	0.00494	0.00359	0.00262	0.00191	0.00139	0.00102	0.00075	0.00055	0.00040	0.00030	0.00022	0.00016	0.00012
70 ..	0.00633	0.00457	0.00331	0.00240	0.00174	0.00127	0.00092	0.00067	0.00049	0.00036	0.00026	0.00019	0.00014	0.00010
71 ..	0.00589	0.00424	0.00305	0.00220	0.00159	0.00115	0.00083	0.00061	0.00044	0.00032	0.00023	0.00017	0.00012	0.00009
72 ..	0.00548	0.00392	0.00281	0.00202	0.00145	0.00105	0.00075	0.00055	0.00039	0.00029	0.00021	0.00015	0.00011	0.00008
73 ..	0.00510	0.00363	0.00259	0.00185	0.00133	0.00095	0.00068	0.00049	0.00035	0.00026	0.00018	0.00013	0.00010	0.00007
74 ..	0.00474	0.00336	0.00239	0.00170	0.00121	0.00086	0.00062	0.00044	0.00032	0.00023	0.00016	0.00012	0.00009	0.00006
75 ..	0.00441	0.00311	0.00220	0.00156	0.00111	0.00079	0.00056	0.00040	0.00028	0.00020	0.00015	0.00010	0.00008	0.00005
76 ..	0.00410	0.00288	0.00203	0.00143	0.00101	0.00071	0.00051	0.00036	0.00026	0.00018	0.00013	0.00009	0.00007	0.00005
77 ..	0.00382	0.00267	0.00187	0.00131	0.00092	0.00065	0.00046	0.00032	0.00023	0.00016	0.00012	0.00008	0.00006	0.00004
78 ..	0.00355	0.00247	0.00172	0.00120	0.00084	0.00059	0.00041	0.00029	0.00021	0.00014	0.00010	0.00007	0.00005	0.00004
79 ..	0.00330	0.00229	0.00159	0.00110	0.00077	0.00054	0.00038	0.00026	0.00018	0.00013	0.00009	0.00006	0.00005	0.00003
80 ..	0.00307	0.00212	0.00146	0.00101	0.00070	0.00049	0.00034	0.00024	0.00017	0.00012	0.00008	0.00006	0.00004	0.00003
81 ..	0.00286	0.00196	0.00135	0.00093	0.00064	0.00044	0.00031	0.00021	0.00015	0.00010	0.00007	0.00005	0.00004	0.00002
82 ..	0.00266	0.00182	0.00124	0.00085	0.00059	0.00040	0.00028	0.00019	0.00013	0.00009	0.00006	0.00004	0.00003	0.00002
83 ..	0.00247	0.00168	0.00115	0.00078	0.00054	0.00037	0.00025	0.00017	0.00012	0.00008	0.00006	0.00004	0.00003	0.00002
84 ..	0.00230	0.00156	0.00106	0.00072	0.00049	0.00033	0.00023	0.00016	0.00011	0.00007	0.00005	0.00003	0.00002	0.00002
85 ..	0.00214	0.00144	0.00097	0.00066	0.00045	0.00030	0.00021	0.00014	0.00010	0.00007	0.00004	0.00003	0.00002	0.00001
86 ..	0.00199	0.00134	0.00090	0.00060	0.00041	0.00028	0.00019	0.00013	0.00009	0.00006	0.00004	0.00003	0.00002	0.00001
87 ..	0.00185	0.00124	0.00083	0.00055	0.00037	0.00025	0.00017	0.00011	0.00008	0.00005	0.00004	0.00002	0.00002	0.00001
88 ..	0.00172	0.00114	0.00076	0.00051	0.00034	0.00023	0.00015	0.00010	0.00007	0.00005	0.00003	0.00002	0.00001	0.00001
89 ..	0.00160	0.00106	0.00070	0.00047	0.00031	0.00021	0.00014	0.00009	0.00006	0.00004	0.00003	0.00002	0.00001	0.00001
90 ..	0.00149	0.00098	0.00065	0.00043	0.00028	0.00019	0.00013	0.00008	0.00006	0.00004	0.00002	0.00002	0.00001	0.00001
91 ..	0.00139	0.00091	0.00060	0.00039	0.00026	0.00017	0.00011	0.00008	0.00005	0.00003	0.00002	0.00001	0.00001	0.00001
92 ..	0.00129	0.00084	0.00055	0.00036	0.00024	0.00016	0.00010	0.00007	0.00004	0.00003	0.00002	0.00001	0.00001	0.00001
93 ..	0.00120	0.00078	0.00051	0.00033	0.00022	0.00014	0.00009	0.00006	0.00004	0.00003	0.00002	0.00001	0.00001	0.00001
94 ..	0.00112	0.00072	0.00047	0.00030	0.00020	0.00013	0.00008	0.00005	0.00004	0.00002	0.00002	0.00001	0.00001	0.00000
95 ..	0.00104	0.00067	0.00043	0.00028	0.00018	0.00012	0.00008	0.00005	0.00003	0.00002	0.00001	0.00001	0.00001	0.00000
96 ..	0.00097	0.00062	0.00040	0.00026	0.00016	0.00011	0.00007	0.00004	0.00003	0.00002	0.00001	0.00001	0.00001	0.00000
97 ..	0.00090	0.00057	0.00037	0.00023	0.00015	0.00010	0.00006	0.00004	0.00003	0.00002	0.00001	0.00001	0.00000	0.00000
98 ..	0.00084	0.00053	0.00034	0.00021	0.00014	0.00009	0.00006	0.00004	0.00002	0.00002	0.00001	0.00001	0.00000	0.00000
99 ..	0.00078	0.00049	0.00031	0.00020	0.00013	0.00008	0.00005	0.00003	0.00002	0.00001	0.00001	0.00001	0.00000	0.00000
100 ..	0.00072	0.00045	0.00029	0.00018	0.00011	0.00007	0.00005	0.00003	0.00002	0.00001	0.00001	0.00000	0.00000	0.00000
101 ..	0.00067	0.00042	0.00026	0.00017	0.00010	0.00007	0.00004	0.00003	0.00002	0.00001	0.00001	0.00000	0.00000	0.00000
102 ..	0.00063	0.00039	0.00024	0.00015	0.00010	0.00006	0.00004	0.00002	0.00002	0.00001	0.00001	0.00000	0.00000	0.00000
103 ..	0.00058	0.00036	0.00022	0.00014	0.00009	0.00005	0.00003	0.00002	0.00001	0.00001	0.00001	0.00000	0.00000	0.00000
104 ..	0.00054	0.00033	0.00021	0.00013	0.00008	0.00005	0.00003	0.00002	0.00001	0.00001	0.00001	0.00000	0.00000	0.00000
105 ..	0.00050	0.00031	0.00019	0.00012	0.00007	0.00005	0.00003	0.00002	0.00001	0.00001	0.00000	0.00000	0.00000	0.00000
106 ..	0.00047	0.00029	0.00018	0.00011	0.00007	0.00004	0.00003	0.00002	0.00001	0.00001	0.00000	0.00000	0.00000	0.00000
107 ..	0.00044	0.00027	0.00016	0.00010	0.00006	0.00004	0.00002	0.00001	0.00001	0.00001	0.00000	0.00000	0.00000	0.00000
108 ..	0.00041	0.00025	0.00015	0.00009	0.00006	0.00003	0.00002	0.00001	0.00001	0.00000	0.00000	0.00000	0.00000	0.00000
109 ..	0.00038	0.00023	0.00014	0.00008	0.00005	0.00003	0.00002	0.00001	0.00001	0.00000	0.00000	0.00000	0.00000	0.00000
110 ..	0.00035	0.00021	0.00013	0.00008	0.00005	0.00003	0.00002	0.00001	0.00001	0.00000	0.00000	0.00000	0.00000	0.00000
111 ..	0.00033	0.00019	0.00012	0.00007	0.00004	0.00003	0.00002	0.00001	0.00001	0.00000	0.00000	0.00000	0.00000	0.00000
112 ..	0.00030	0.00018	0.00011	0.00006	0.00004	0.00002	0.00001	0.00001	0.00001	0.00000	0.00000	0.00000	0.00000	0.00000
113 ..	0.00028	0.00017	0.00010	0.00006	0.00004	0.00002	0.00001	0.00001	0.00000	0.00000	0.00000	0.00000	0.00000	0.00000
114 ..	0.00026	0.00015	0.00009	0.00005	0.00003	0.00002	0.00001	0.00001	0.00000	0.00000	0.00000	0.00000	0.00000	0.00000
115 ..	0.00024	0.00014	0.00008	0.00005	0.00003	0.00002	0.00001	0.00001	0.00000	0.00000	0.00000	0.00000	0.00000	0.00000
116 ..	0.00023	0.00013	0.00008	0.00005	0.00003	0.00002	0.00001	0.00001	0.00000	0.00000	0.00000	0.00000	0.00000	0.00000
117 ..	0.00021	0.00012	0.00007	0.00004	0.00002	0.00001	0.00001	0.00000	0.00000	0.00000	0.00000	0.00000	0.00000	0.00000
118 ..	0.00020	0.00011	0.00007	0.00004	0.00002	0.00001	0.00001	0.00000	0.00000	0.00000	0.00000	0.00000	0.00000	0.00000
119 ..	0.00018	0.00011	0.00006	0.00004	0.00002	0.00001	0.00001	0.00000	0.00000	0.00000	0.00000	0.00000	0.00000	0.00000
120 ..	0.00017	0.00010	0.00006	0.00003	0.00002	0.00001	0.00001	0.00000	0.00000	0.00000	0.00000	0.00000	0.00000	0.00000

Table 3 (concluded)
Present Value of $1 at Compound Interest: 14.5%–20%

Period	14.5%	15%	15.5%	16%	16.5%	17%	17.5%	18%	18.5%	19%	19.5%	20%
1	0.87336	0.86957	0.86580	0.86207	0.85837	0.85470	0.85106	0.84746	0.84388	0.84034	0.83682	0.83333
2	0.76276	0.75614	0.74961	0.74316	0.73680	0.73051	0.72431	0.71818	0.71214	0.70616	0.70027	0.69444
3	0.66617	0.65752	0.64901	0.64066	0.63244	0.62437	0.61643	0.60863	0.60096	0.59342	0.58600	0.57870
4	0.58181	0.57175	0.56192	0.55229	0.54287	0.53365	0.52462	0.51579	0.50714	0.49867	0.49038	0.48225
5	0.50813	0.49718	0.48651	0.47611	0.46598	0.45611	0.44649	0.43711	0.42796	0.41905	0.41036	0.40188
6	0.44378	0.43233	0.42122	0.41044	0.39999	0.38984	0.37999	0.37043	0.36115	0.35214	0.34339	0.33490
7	0.38758	0.37594	0.36469	0.35383	0.34334	0.33320	0.32340	0.31393	0.30477	0.29592	0.28736	0.27908
8	0.33850	0.32690	0.31575	0.30503	0.29471	0.28478	0.27523	0.26604	0.25719	0.24867	0.24047	0.23257
9	0.29563	0.28426	0.27338	0.26295	0.25297	0.24340	0.23424	0.22546	0.21704	0.20897	0.20123	0.19381
10	0.25819	0.24718	0.23669	0.22668	0.21714	0.20804	0.19935	0.19106	0.18315	0.17560	0.16839	0.16151
11	0.22550	0.21494	0.20493	0.19542	0.18639	0.17781	0.16966	0.16192	0.15456	0.14757	0.14091	0.13459
12	0.19694	0.18691	0.17743	0.16846	0.15999	0.15197	0.14439	0.13722	0.13043	0.12400	0.11792	0.11216
13	0.17200	0.16253	0.15362	0.14523	0.13733	0.12989	0.12289	0.11629	0.11007	0.10421	0.09868	0.09346
14	0.15022	0.14133	0.13300	0.12520	0.11788	0.11102	0.10459	0.09855	0.09288	0.08757	0.08258	0.07789
15	0.13120	0.12289	0.11515	0.10793	0.10118	0.09489	0.08901	0.08352	0.07838	0.07359	0.06910	0.06491
16	0.11458	0.10686	0.09970	0.09304	0.08685	0.08110	0.07575	0.07078	0.06615	0.06184	0.05782	0.05409
17	0.10007	0.09293	0.08632	0.08021	0.07455	0.06932	0.06447	0.05998	0.05582	0.05196	0.04839	0.04507
18	0.08740	0.04081	0.07474	0.06914	0.06399	0.05925	0.05487	0.05083	0.04711	0.04367	0.04049	0.03756
19	0.07633	0.07027	0.06471	0.05961	0.05493	0.05064	0.04670	0.04308	0.03975	0.03670	0.03389	0.03130
20	0.06666	0.06110	0.05602	0.05139	0.04715	0.04328	0.03974	0.03651	0.03355	0.03084	0.02836	0.02608
21	0.05822	0.05313	0.04850	0.04430	0.04047	0.03699	0.03382	0.03094	0.02831	0.02591	0.02373	0.02174
22	0.05085	0.04620	0.04199	0.03819	0.03474	0.03162	0.02879	0.02622	0.02389	0.02178	0.01986	0.01811
23	0.04441	0.04017	0.03636	0.03292	0.02982	0.02702	0.02450	0.02222	0.02016	0.01830	0.01662	0.01509
24	0.03879	0.03493	0.03148	0.02838	0.02560	0.02310	0.02085	0.01883	0.01701	0.01538	0.01390	0.01258
25	0.03387	0.03038	0.02726	0.02447	0.02197	0.01974	0.01774	0.01596	0.01436	0.01292	0.01164	0.01048
26	0.02958	0.02642	0.02360	0.02109	0.01886	0.01687	0.01510	0.01352	0.01211	0.01086	0.00974	0.00874
27	0.02584	0.02297	0.02043	0.01818	0.01619	0.01442	0.01285	0.01146	0.01022	0.00912	0.00815	0.00728
28	0.02257	0.01997	0.01769	0.01567	0.01390	0.01233	0.01094	0.00971	0.00863	0.00767	0.00682	0.00607
29	0.01971	0.01737	0.01532	0.01351	0.01193	0.01053	0.00931	0.00823	0.00728	0.00644	0.00571	0.00506
30	0.01721	0.01510	0.01326	0.01165	0.01024	0.00900	0.00792	0.00697	0.00614	0.00541	0.00477	0.00421
31	0.01503	0.01313	0.01148	0.01004	0.00879	0.00770	0.00674	0.00591	0.00518	0.00455	0.00400	0.00351
32	0.01313	0.01142	0.00994	0.00866	0.00754	0.00658	0.00574	0.00501	0.00438	0.00382	0.00334	0.00293
33	0.01147	0.00993	0.00861	0.00746	0.00648	0.00562	0.00488	0.00425	0.00369	0.00321	0.00280	0.00244
34	0.01001	0.00864	0.00745	0.00643	0.00556	0.00480	0.00416	0.00360	0.00312	0.00270	0.00234	0.00203
35	0.00875	0.00751	0.00645	0.00555	0.00477	0.00411	0.00354	0.00305	0.00263	0.00227	0.00196	0.00169
36	0.00764	0.00653	0.00559	0.00478	0.00410	0.00351	0.00301	0.00258	0.00222	0.00191	0.00164	0.00141
37	0.00667	0.00568	0.00484	0.00412	0.00352	0.00300	0.00256	0.00219	0.00187	0.00160	0.00137	0.00118
38	0.00583	0.00494	0.00419	0.00355	0.00302	0.00256	0.00218	0.00186	0.00158	0.00135	0.00115	0.00098
39	0.00509	0.00429	0.00362	0.00306	0.00259	0.00219	0.00186	0.00157	0.00133	0.00113	0.00096	0.00082
40	0.00444	0.00373	0.00314	0.00264	0.00222	0.00187	0.00158	0.00133	0.00113	0.00095	0.00080	0.00068
41	0.00388	0.00325	0.00272	0.00228	0.00191	0.00160	0.00134	0.00113	0.00095	0.00080	0.00067	0.00057
42	0.00339	0.00282	0.00235	0.00196	0.00164	0.00137	0.00114	0.00096	0.00080	0.00067	0.00056	0.00047
43	0.00296	0.00245	0.00204	0.00169	0.00141	0.00117	0.00097	0.00081	0.00068	0.00056	0.00047	0.00039
44	0.00259	0.00213	0.00176	0.00146	0.00121	0.00100	0.00083	0.00069	0.00057	0.00047	0.00039	0.00033
45	0.00226	0.00186	0.00153	0.00126	0.00104	0.00085	0.00071	0.00058	0.00048	0.00040	0.00033	0.00027
46	0.00197	0.00161	0.00132	0.00108	0.00089	0.00073	0.00060	0.00049	0.00041	0.00033	0.00028	0.00023
47	0.00172	0.00140	0.00114	0.00093	0.00076	0.00062	0.00051	0.00042	0.00034	0.00028	0.00023	0.00019
48	0.00150	0.00122	0.00099	0.00081	0.00066	0.00053	0.00043	0.00035	0.00029	0.00024	0.00019	0.00016
49	0.00131	0.00106	0.00086	0.00069	0.00056	0.00046	0.00037	0.00030	0.00024	0.00020	0.00016	0.00013
50	0.00115	0.00092	0.00074	0.00060	0.00048	0.00039	0.00031	0.00025	0.00021	0.00017	0.00014	0.00011
51	0.00100	0.00080	0.00064	0.00052	0.00041	0.00033	0.00027	0.00022	0.00017	0.00014	0.00011	0.00009
52 .·..	0.00088	0.00070	0.00056	0.00044	0.00036	0.00028	0.00023	0.00018	0.00015	0.00012	0.00009	0.00008
53	0.00076	0.00061	0.00048	0.00038	0.00031	0.00024	0.00019	0.00015	0.00012	0.00010	0.00008	0.00006
54	0.00067	0.00053	0.00042	0.00033	0.00026	0.00021	0.00017	0.00013	0.00010	0.00008	0.00007	0.00005
55	0.00058	0.00046	0.00036	0.00028	0.00022	0.00018	0.00014	0.00011	0.00009	0.00007	0.00006	0.00004
56	0.00051	0.00040	0.00031	0.00025	0.00019	0.00015	0.00012	0.00009	0.00007	0.00006	0.00005	0.00004
57	0.00044	0.00035	0.00027	0.00021	0.00017	0.00013	0.00010	0.00008	0.00006	0.00005	0.00004	0.00003
58	0.00039	0.00030	0.00023	0.00018	0.00014	0.00011	0.00009	0.00007	0.00005	0.00004	0.00003	0.00003
59	0.00034	0.00026	0.00020	0.00016	0.00012	0.00009	0.00007	0.00006	0.00004	0.00003	0.00003	0.00002
60	0.00030	0.00023	0.00018	0.00014	0.00010	0.00008	0.00006	0.00005	0.00004	0.00003	0.00002	0.00002

Period	14.5%	15%	15.5%	16%	16.5%	17%	17.5%	18%	18.5%	19%	19.5%	20%
61	0.00026	0.00020	0.00015	0.00012	0.00009	0.00007	0.00005	0.00004	0.00003	0.00002	0.00002	0.00001
62	0.00023	0.00017	0.00013	0.00010	0.00008	0.00006	0.00005	0.00003	0.00003	0.00002	0.00002	0.00001
63	0.00020	0.00015	0.00011	0.00009	0.00007	0.00005	0.00004	0.00003	0.00002	0.00002	0.00001	0.00001
64	0.00017	0.00013	0.00010	0.00007	0.00006	0.00004	0.00003	0.00003	0.00002	0.00001	0.00001	0.00001
65	0.00015	0.00011	0.00009	0.00006	0.00005	0.00004	0.00003	0.00002	0.00002	0.00001	0.00001	0.00001
66	0.00013	0.00010	0.00007	0.00006	0.00004	0.00003	0.00002	0.00002	0.00001	0.00001	0.00001	0.00001
67	0.00011	0.00009	0.00006	0.00005	0.00004	0.00003	0.00002	0.00002	0.00001	0.00001	0.00001	0.00000
68	0.00010	0.00007	0.00006	0.00004	0.00003	0.00002	0.00002	0.00001	0.00001	0.00001	0.00001	0.00000
69	0.00009	0.00006	0.00005	0.00004	0.00003	0.00002	0.00001	0.00001	0.00001	0.00001	0.00000	0.00000
70	0.00008	0.00006	0.00004	0.00003	0.00002	0.00002	0.00001	0.00001	0.00001	0.00001	0.00000	0.00000
71	0.00007	0.00005	0.00004	0.00003	0.00002	0.00001	0.00001	0.00001	0.00001	0.00000	0.00000	0.00000
72	0.00006	0.00004	0.00003	0.00002	0.00002	0.00001	0.00001	0.00001	0.00000	0.00000	0.00000	0.00000
73	0.00005	0.00004	0.00003	0.00002	0.00001	0.00001	0.00001	0.00001	0.00000	0.00000	0.00000	0.00000
74	0.00004	0.00003	0.00002	0.00002	0.00001	0.00001	0.00001	0.00000	0.00000	0.00000	0.00000	0.00000
75	0.00004	0.00003	0.00002	0.00001	0.00001	0.00001	0.00001	0.00000	0.00000	0.00000	0.00000	0.00000
76	0.00003	0.00002	0.00002	0.00001	0.00001	0.00001	0.00000	0.00000	0.00000	0.00000	0.00000	0.00000
77	0.00003	0.00002	0.00002	0.00001	0.00001	0.00001	0.00000	0.00000	0.00000	0.00000	0.00000	0.00000
78	0.00003	0.00002	0.00001	0.00001	0.00001	0.00000	0.00000	0.00000	0.00000	0.00000	0.00000	0.00000
79	0.00002	0.00002	0.00001	0.00001	0.00001	0.00000	0.00000	0.00000	0.00000	0.00000	0.00000	0.00000
80	0.00002	0.00001	0.00001	0.00001	0.00000	0.00000	0.00000	0.00000	0.00000	0.00000	0.00000	0.00000
81	0.00002	0.00001	0.00001	0.00001	0.00000	0.00000	0.00000	0.00000	0.00000	0.00000	0.00000	0.00000
82	0.00002	0.00001	0.00001	0.00001	0.00000	0.00000	0.00000	0.00000	0.00000	0.00000	0.00000	0.00000
83	0.00001	0.00001	0.00001	0.00000	0.00000	0.00000	0.00000	0.00000	0.00000	0.00000	0.00000	0.00000
84	0.00001	0.00001	0.00001	0.00000	0.00000	0.00000	0.00000	0.00000	0.00000	0.00000	0.00000	0.00000
85	0.00001	0.00001	0.00000	0.00000	0.00000	0.00000	0.00000	0.00000	0.00000	0.00000	0.00000	0.00000
86	0.00001	0.00001	0.00000	0.00000	0.00000	0.00000	0.00000	0.00000	0.00000	0.00000	0.00000	0.00000
87	0.00001	0.00001	0.00000	0.00000	0.00000	0.00000	0.00000	0.00000	0.00000	0.00000	0.00000	0.00000
88	0.00001	0.00000	0.00000	0.00000	0.00000	0.00000	0.00000	0.00000	0.00000	0.00000	0.00000	0.00000
89	0.00001	0.00000	0.00000	0.00000	0.00000	0.00000	0.00000	0.00000	0.00000	0.00000	0.00000	0.00000
90	0.00001	0.00000	0.00000	0.00000	0.00000	0.00000	0.00000	0.00000	0.00000	0.00000	0.00000	0.00000
91	0.00000	0.00000	0.00000	0.00000	0.00000	0.00000	0.00000	0.00000	0.00000	0.00000	0.00000	0.00000
92	0.00000	0.00000	0.00000	0.00000	0.00000	0.00000	0.00000	0.00000	0.00000	0.00000	0.00000	0.00000
93	0.00000	0.00000	0.00000	0.00000	0.00000	0.00000	0.00000	0.00000	0.00000	0.00000	0.00000	0.00000
94	0.00000	0.00000	0.00000	0.00000	0.00000	0.00000	0.00000	0.00000	0.00000	0.00000	0.00000	0.00000
95	0.00000	0.00000	0.00000	0.00000	0.00000	0.00000	0.00000	0.00000	0.00000	0.00000	0.00000	0.00000
96	0.00000	0.00000	0.00000	0.00000	0.00000	0.00000	0.00000	0.00000	0.00000	0.00000	0.00000	0.00000
97	0.00000	0.00000	0.00000	0.00000	0.00000	0.00000	0.00000	0.00000	0.00000	0.00000	0.00000	0.00000
98	0.00000	0.00000	0.00000	0.00000	0.00000	0.00000	0.00000	0.00000	0.00000	0.00000	0.00000	0.00000
99	0.00000	0.00000	0.00000	0.00000	0.00000	0.00000	0.00000	0.00000	0.00000	0.00000	0.00000	0.00000
100	0.00000	0.00000	0.00000	0.00000	0.00000	0.00000	0.00000	0.00000	0.00000	0.00000	0.00000	0.00000
101	0.00000	0.00000	0.00000	0.00000	0.00000	0.00000	0.00000	0.00000	0.00000	0.00000	0.00000	0.00000
102	0.00000	0.00000	0.00000	0.00000	0.00000	0.00000	0.00000	0.00000	0.00000	0.00000	0.00000	0.00000
103	0.00000	0.00000	0.00000	0.00000	0.00000	0.00000	0.00000	0.00000	0.00000	0.00000	0.00000	0.00000
104	0.00000	0.00000	0.00000	0.00000	0.00000	0.00000	0.00000	0.00000	0.00000	0.00000	0.00000	0.00000
105	0.00000	0.00000	0.00000	0.00000	0.00000	0.00000	0.00000	0.00000	0.00000	0.00000	0.00000	0.00000
106	0.00000	0.00000	0.00000	0.00000	0.00000	0.00000	0.00000	0.00000	0.00000	0.00000	0.00000	0.00000
107	0.00000	0.00000	0.00000	0.00000	0.00000	0.00000	0.00000	0.00000	0.00000	0.00000	0.00000	0.00000
108	0.00000	0.00000	0.00000	0.00000	0.00000	0.00000	0.00000	0.00000	0.00000	0.00000	0.00000	0.00000
109	0.00000	0.00000	0.00000	0.00000	0.00000	0.00000	0.00000	0.00000	0.00000	0.00000	0.00000	0.00000
110	0.00000	0.00000	0.00000	0.00000	0.00000	0.00000	0.00000	0.00000	0.00000	0.00000	0.00000	0.00000
111	0.00000	0.00000	0.00000	0.00000	0.00000	0.00000	0.00000	0.00000	0.00000	0.00000	0.00000	0.00000
112	0.00000	0.00000	0.00000	0.00000	0.00000	0.00000	0.00000	0.00000	0.00000	0.00000	0.00000	0.00000
113	0.00000	0.00000	0.00000	0.00000	0.00000	0.00000	0.00000	0.00000	0.00000	0.00000	0.00000	0.00000
114	0.00000	0.00000	0.00000	0.00000	0.00000	0.00000	0.00000	0.00000	0.00000	0.00000	0.00000	0.00000
115	0.00000	0.00000	0.00000	0.00000	0.00000	0.00000	0.00000	0.00000	0.00000	0.00000	0.00000	0.00000
116	0.00000	0.00000	0.00000	0.00000	0.00000	0.00000	0.00000	0.00000	0.00000	0.00000	0.00000	0.00000
117	0.00000	0.00000	0.00000	0.00000	0.00000	0.00000	0.00000	0.00000	0.00000	0.00000	0.00000	0.00000
118	0.00000	0.00000	0.00000	0.00000	0.00000	0.00000	0.00000	0.00000	0.00000	0.00000	0.00000	0.00000
119	0.00000	0.00000	0.00000	0.00000	0.00000	0.00000	0.00000	0.00000	0.00000	0.00000	0.00000	0.00000
120	0.00000	0.00000	0.00000	0.00000	0.00000	0.00000	0.00000	0.00000	0.00000	0.00000	0.00000	0.00000

Table 4
Present Value of an Ordinary Annuity of $1 per Period: 0.5%–7%

$$P_{A_{i,n}} = \frac{1 - \dfrac{1}{(1+i)^n}}{i}$$

Period	.5%	1%	1.5%	2%	2.5%	3%	3.5%	4%	4.5%	5%	5.5%	6%	6.5%	7%
1	0.99502	0.99010	0.98522	0.98039	0.97561	0.97087	0.96618	0.96154	0.95694	0.95238	0.94787	0.94340	0.93897	0.93458
2	1.98510	1.97040	1.95588	1.94156	1.92742	1.91347	1.89969	1.88609	1.87267	1.85941	1.84632	1.83339	1.82063	1.80802
3	2.97025	2.94099	2.91220	2.88388	2.85602	2.82861	2.80164	2.77509	2.74896	2.72325	2.69793	2.67301	2.64848	2.62432
4	3.95050	3.90197	3.85438	3.80773	3.76197	3.71710	3.67308	3.62990	3.58753	3.54595	3.50515	3.46511	3.42580	3.38721
5	4.92587	4.85343	4.78264	4.71346	4.64583	4.57971	4.51505	4.45182	4.38998	4.32948	4.27028	4.21236	4.15568	4.10020
6	5.89638	5.79548	5.69719	5.60143	5.50813	5.41719	5.32855	5.24214	5.15787	5.07569	4.99553	4.91732	4.84101	4.76654
7	6.86207	6.72819	6.59821	6.47199	6.34939	6.23028	6.11454	6.00205	5.89270	5.78637	5.68297	5.58238	5.48452	5.38929
8	7.82296	7.65168	7.48593	7.32548	7.17014	7.01969	6.87396	6.73274	6.59589	6.46321	6.33457	6.20979	6.08875	5.97130
9	8.77906	8.56602	8.36052	8.16224	7.97087	7.78611	7.60769	7.43533	7.26879	7.10782	6.95220	6.80169	6.65610	6.51523
10	9.73041	9.47130	9.22218	8.98259	8.75206	8.53020	8.31661	8.11090	7.91272	7.72173	7.53763	7.36009	7.18883	7.02358
11	10.67703	10.36763	10.07112	9.78685	9.51421	9.25262	9.00155	8.76048	8.52892	8.30641	8.09254	7.88687	7.68904	7.49867
12	11.61893	11.25508	10.90751	10.57534	10.25776	9.95400	9.66333	9 38507	9.11858	8.86325	8.61852	8.38384	8.15873	7.94269
13	12.55615	12.13374	11.73153	11.34837	10.98318	10.63496	10.30274	9.98565	9.68285	9.39357	9.11708	8.85268	8.59974	8.35765
14	13.48871	13.00370	12.54338	12.10625	11.69091	11.29607	10.92052	10.56312	10.22283	9.89864	9.58965	9.29498	9.01384	8.74547
15	14.41662	13.86505	13.34323	12.84926	12.38138	11.93794	11.51741	11.11839	10.73955	10.37966	10.03758	9.71225	9.40267	9.10791
16	15.33993	14.71787	14.13126	13.57771	13.05500	12.56110	12.09412	11.65230	11.23402	10.83777	10.46216	10.10590	9.76776	9.44665
17	16.25863	15.56225	14.90765	14.29187	13.71220	13.16612	12.65132	12.16567	11.70719	11.27407	10.86461	10.47726	10.11058	9.76322
18	17.17277	16.39827	15.67256	14.99203	14.35336	13.75351	13.18968	12.65930	12.15999	11.68959	11.24607	10.82760	10.43247	10.05909
19	18.08236	17.22601	16.42617	15.67846	14.97889	14.32380	13.70984	13.13394	12.59329	12.08532	11.60765	11.15812	10.73471	10.33560
20	18.98742	18.04555	17.16864	16.35143	15.58916	14.87747	14.21240	13.59033	13.00794	12.46221	11.95038	11.46992	11.01851	10.59401
21	19.88798	18.85698	17.90014	17.01121	16.18455	15.41502	14.69797	14.02916	13.40472	12.82115	12.27524	11.76408	11.28498	10.83553
22	20.78406	19.66038	18.62082	17.65805	16.76541	15.93692	15.16712	14.45112	13.78442	13.16300	12.58317	12.04158	11.53520	11.06124
23	21.67568	20.45582	19.33086	18.29220	17.33211	16.44361	15.62041	14.85684	14.14777	13.48857	12.87504	12.30338	11.77014	11.27219
24	22.56287	21.24339	20.03041	18.91393	17.88499	16.93554	16.05837	15.24696	14.49548	13.79864	13.15170	12.55036	11.99074	11.46933
25	23.44564	22.02316	20.71961	19.52346	18.42438	17.41315	16.48151	15.62208	14.82821	14.09394	13.41393	12.78336	12.19788	11.65358
26	24.32402	22.79520	21.39863	20.12104	18.95061	17.87684	16.89035	15.98277	15.14661	14.37519	13.66250	13.00317	12.39237	11.82578
27	25.19803	23.55961	22.06762	20.70690	19.46401	18.32703	17.28536	16.32959	15.45130	14.64303	13.89810	13.21053	12.57500	11.98671
28	26.06769	24.31644	22.72672	21.28127	19.96489	18.76411	17.66702	16.66306	15.74287	14.89813	14.12142	13.40616	12.74648	12.13711
29	26.93302	25.06579	23.37608	21.84438	20.45355	19.18845	18.03577	16.98371	16.02189	15.14107	14.33310	13.59072	12.90749	12.27767
30	27.79405	25.80771	24.01584	22.39646	20.93029	19.60044	18.39205	17.29203	16.28889	15.37245	14.53375	13.76483	13.05868	12.40904
31	28.65080	26.54229	24.64615	22.93770	21.39541	20.00043	18.73628	17.58849	16.54439	15.59281	14.72393	13.92909	13.20063	12.53181
32	29.50328	27.26959	25.26714	23.46833	21.84918	20.38877	19.06887	17.87355	16.78889	15.80268	14.90420	14.08404	13.33393	12.64656
33	30.35153	27.98969	25.87895	23.98856	22.29188	20.76579	19.39021	18.14765	17.02286	16.00255	15.07507	14.23023	13.45909	12.75379
34	31.19555	28.70267	26.48173	24.49859	22.72379	21.13184	19.70068	18.41120	17.24676	16.19290	15.23703	14.36814	13.57661	12.85401
35	32.03537	29.40858	27.07559	24.99862	23.14516	21.48722	20.00066	18.66461	17.46101	16.37419	15.39055	14.49825	13.68696	12.94767
36	32.87102	30.10751	27.66068	25.48884	23.55625	21.83225	20.29049	18.90828	17.66604	16.54685	15.53607	14.62099	13.79057	13.03521
37	33.70250	30.79951	28.23713	25.96945	23.95732	22.16724	20.57053	19.14258	17.86224	16.71129	15.67400	14.73678	13.88786	13.11702
38	34.52985	31.48466	28.80505	26.44064	24.34860	22.49246	20.84109	19.36786	18.04999	16.86789	15.80474	14.84602	13.97921	13.19347
39	35.35309	32.16303	29.36458	26.90259	24.73034	22.80822	21.10250	19.58448	18.22966	17.01704	15.92866	14.94907	14.06499	13.26493
40	36.17223	32.83469	29.91585	27.35548	25.10278	23.11477	21.35507	19.79277	18.40158	17.15909	16.04612	15.04630	14.14553	13.33171
41	36.98729	33.49969	30.45896	27.79949	25.46612	23.41240	21.59910	19.99305	18.56611	17.29437	16.15746	15.13802	14.22115	13.39412
42	37.79830	34.15811	30.99405	28.23479	25.82061	23.70136	21.83488	20.18563	18.72355	17.42321	16.26300	15.22454	14.29216	13.45245
43	38.60527	34.81001	31.52123	28.66156	26.16645	23.98190	22.06269	20.37079	18.87421	17.54591	16.36303	15.30617	14.35884	13.50696
44	39.40823	35.45545	32.04062	29.07996	26.50385	24.25427	22.28279	20.54884	19.01838	17.66277	16.45785	15.38318	14.42144	13.55791
45	40.20720	36.09451	32.55234	29.49016	26.83302	24.51871	22.49545	20.72004	19.15635	17.77407	16.54773	15.45583	14.48023	13.60552
46	41.00219	36.72724	33.05649	29.89231	27.15417	24.77545	22.70092	20.88465	19.28837	17.88007	16.63292	15.52437	14.53543	13.65002
47	41.79322	37.35370	33.55319	30.28658	27.46748	25.02471	22.89944	21.04294	19.41471	17.98102	16.71366	15.58903	14.58725	13.69161
48	42.58032	37.97396	34.04255	30.67312	27.77315	25.26671	23.09124	21.19513	19.53561	18.07716	16.79020	15.65003	14.63592	13.73047
49	43.36350	38.58808	34.52468	31.05208	28.07137	25.50166	23.27656	21.34147	19.65130	18.16872	16.86275	15.70757	14.68161	13.76680
50	44.14279	39.19612	34.99969	31.42361	28.36231	25.72976	23.45562	21.48218	19.76201	18.25593	16.93152	15.76186	14.72452	13.80075
51	44.91820	39.79814	35.46767	31.78785	28.64616	25.95123	23.62862	21.61749	19.86795	18.33898	16.99670	15.81308	14.76481	13.83247
52	45.68975	40.39419	35.92874	32.14495	28.92308	26.16624	23.79576	21.74758	19.96933	18.41807	17.05848	15.86139	14.80264	13.86212
53	46.45746	40.98435	36.38300	32.49505	29.19325	26.37499	23.95726	21.87267	20.06634	18.49340	17.11705	15.90697	14.83816	13.88984
54	47.22135	41.56866	36.83054	32.83828	29.45683	26.57766	24.11330	21.99296	20.15918	18.56515	17.17255	15.94998	14.87151	13.91573
55	47.98145	42.14719	37.27147	33.17479	29.71398	26.77443	24.26405	22.10861	20.24802	18.63347	17.22517	15.99054	14.90282	13.93994
56	48.73776	42.71999	37.70588	33.50469	29.96486	26.96546	24.40971	22.21982	20.33303	18.69854	17.27504	16.02881	14.93223	13.96256
57	49.49031	43.28712	38.13387	33.82813	30.20962	27.15094	24.55045	22.32675	20.41439	18.76052	17.32232	16.06492	14.95984	13.98370
58	50.23911	43.84863	38.55554	34.14523	30.44841	27.33101	24.68642	22.42957	20.49224	18.81954	17.36712	16.09898	14.98577	14.00346
59	50.98419	44.40459	38.97097	34.45610	30.68137	27.50583	24.81780	22.52843	20.56673	18.87575	17.40960	16.13111	15.01011	14.02192
60	51.72556	44.95504	39.38027	34.76089	30.90866	27.67556	24.94473	22.62349	20.63802	18.92929	17.44985	16.16143	15.03297	14.03918

Period	.5%	1%	1.5%	2%	2.5%	3%	3.5%	4%	4.5%	5%	5.5%	6%	6.5%	7%
61 ...	52.46324	45.50004	39.78352	35.05969	31.13040	27.84035	25.06738	22.71489	20.70624	18.98028	17.48801	16.19003	15.05443	14.05531
62 ...	53.19726	46.03964	40.18080	35.35264	31.34673	28.00034	25.18587	22.80278	20.77152	19.02883	17.52418	16.21701	15.07458	14.07038
63 ...	53.92762	46.57390	40.57222	35.63984	31.55778	28.15567	25.30036	22.88729	20.83399	19.07508	17.55847	16.24246	15.09350	14.08447
64 ...	54.65435	47.10287	40.95785	35.92141	31.76369	28.30648	25.41097	22.96855	20.89377	19.11912	17.59096	16.26647	15.11127	14.09764
65 ...	55.37746	47.62661	41.33779	36.19747	31.96458	28.45289	25.51785	23.04668	20.95098	19.16107	17.62177	16.28912	15.12795	14.10994
66 ...	56.09698	48.14516	41.71210	36.46810	32.16056	28.59504	25.62111	23.12181	21.00572	19.20102	17.65096	16.31049	15.14362	14.12144
67 ...	56.81291	48.65857	42.08089	36.73343	32.35177	28.73305	25.72088	23.19405	21.05811	19.23907	17.67864	16.33065	15.15833	14.13219
68 ...	57.52529	49.16690	42.44423	36.99356	32.53831	28.86704	25.81727	23.26351	21.10824	19.27530	17.70487	16.34967	15.17214	14.14223
69 ...	58.23411	49.67020	42.80219	37.24859	32.72030	28.99712	25.91041	23.33030	21.15621	19.30981	17.72974	16.36762	15.18511	14.15162
70 ...	58.93942	50.16851	43.15487	37.49862	32.89786	29.12342	26.00040	23.39451	21.20211	19.34268	17.75330	16.38454	15.19728	14.16039
71 ...	59.64121	50.66190	43.50234	37.74374	33.07108	29.24604	26.08734	23.45626	21.24604	19.37398	17.77564	16.40051	15.20872	14.16859
72 ...	60.33951	51.15039	43.84467	37.98406	33.24008	29.36509	26.17134	23.51564	21.28808	19.40379	17.79682	16.41558	15.21945	14.17625
73 ...	61.03434	51.63405	44.18194	38.21967	33.40495	29.48067	26.25251	23.57273	21.32830	19.43218	17.81689	16.42979	15.22953	14.18341
74 ...	61.72571	52.11292	44.51422	38.45066	33.56581	29.59288	26.33092	23.62762	21.36680	19.45922	17.83591	16.44320	15.23900	14.19010
75 ...	62.41365	52.58705	44.84160	38.67711	33.72274	29.70183	26.40669	23.68041	21.40363	19.48497	17.85395	16.45585	15.24788	14.19636
76 ...	63.09815	53.05649	45.16414	38.89913	33.87584	29.80760	26.47989	23.73116	21.43888	19.50950	17.87104	16.46778	15.25623	14.20220
77 ...	63.77926	53.52127	45.48191	39.11680	34.02521	29.91029	26.55062	23.77996	21.47262	19.53285	17.88724	16.47904	15.26407	14.20767
78 ...	64.45697	53.98146	45.79498	39.33019	34.17094	30.00999	26.61896	23.82689	21.50490	19.55510	17.90260	16.48966	15.27142	14.21277
79 ...	65.13132	54.43709	46.10343	39.53940	34.31311	30.10679	26.68498	23.87201	21.53579	19.57628	17.91716	16.49968	15.27833	14.21755
80 ...	65.80231	54.88821	46.40732	39.74451	34.45182	30.20076	26.74878	23.91539	21.56534	19.59646	17.93095	16.50913	15.28482	14.22201
81 ...	66.46996	55.33486	46.70672	39.94560	34.58714	30.29200	26.81041	23.95711	21.59363	19.61568	17.94403	16.51805	15.29091	14.22617
82 ...	67.13428	55.77709	47.00170	40.14275	34.71916	30.38059	26.86996	23.99722	21.62070	19.63398	17.95643	16.52646	15.29663	14.23007
83 ...	67.79531	56.21494	47.29231	40.33603	34.84796	30.46659	26.92750	24.03579	21.64660	19.65141	17.96818	16.53440	15.30200	14.23371
84 ...	68.45304	56.64845	47.57863	40.52552	34.97362	30.55009	26.98309	24.07287	21.67139	19.66801	17.97932	16.54188	15.30704	14.23711
85 ...	69.10750	57.07768	47.86072	40.71129	35.09621	30.63115	27.03680	24.10853	21.69511	19.68382	17.98987	16.54895	15.31178	14.24029
86 ...	69.75871	57.50265	48.13864	40.89342	35.21582	30.70986	27.08870	24.14282	21.71781	19.69887	17.99988	16.55561	15.31622	14.24326
87 ...	70.40668	57.92342	48.41246	41.07198	35.33251	30.78627	27.13884	24.17579	21.73953	19.71321	18.00936	16.56190	15.32040	14.24604
88 ...	71.05142	58.34002	48.68222	41.24704	35.44635	30.86045	27.18728	24.20749	21.76032	19.72687	18.01835	16.56783	15.32431	14.24864
89 ...	71.69296	58.75249	48.94800	41.41867	35.55741	30.93248	27.23409	24.23797	21.78021	19.73987	18.02688	16.57342	15.32800	14.25106
90 ...	72.33130	59.16088	49.20985	41.58693	35.66577	31.00241	27.27932	24.26728	21.79924	19.75226	18.03495	16.57870	15.33145	14.25333
91 ...	72.96647	59.56523	49.46784	41.75189	35.77148	31.07030	27.32301	24.29546	21.81746	19.76406	18.04261	16.58368	15.33470	14.25545
92 ...	73.59847	59.96557	49.72201	41.91362	35.87462	31.13621	27.36523	24.32256	21.83489	19.77529	18.04987	16.58838	15.33774	14.25743
93 ...	74.22734	60.36195	49.97242	42.07218	35.97524	31.20021	27.40602	24.34861	21.85156	19.78599	18.05675	16.59281	15.34060	14.25928
94 ...	74.85307	60.75441	50.21913	42.22762	36.07340	31.26234	27.44543	24.37367	21.86753	19.79619	18.06327	16.59699	15.34329	14.26101
95 ...	75.47569	61.14298	50.46220	42.38002	36.16917	31.32266	27.48350	24.39776	21.88280	19.80589	18.06945	16.60093	15.34581	14.26262
96 ...	76.09522	61.52770	50.70168	42.52943	36.26261	31.38122	27.52029	24.42092	21.89742	19.81513	18.07531	16.60465	15.34818	14.26413
97 ...	76.71166	61.90862	50.93761	42.67592	36.35376	31.43808	27.55584	24.44319	21.91140	19.82394	18.08086	16.60816	15.35040	14.26555
98 ...	77.32503	62.28576	51.17006	42.81953	36.44269	31.49328	27.59018	24.46461	21.92479	19.83232	18.08612	16.61147	15.35249	14.26687
99 ...	77.93536	62.65917	51.39907	42.96032	36.52946	31.54687	27.62337	24.48520	21.93760	19.84031	18.09111	16.61460	15.35445	14.26810
100 ...	78.54264	63.02888	51.62470	43.09835	36.61411	31.59891	27.65543	24.50500	21.94985	19.84791	18.09584	16.61755	15.35629	14.26925
101 ...	79.14691	63.39493	51.84700	43.23368	36.69669	31.64942	27.68640	24.52404	21.96158	19.85515	18.10032	16.62033	15.35802	14.27033
102 ...	79.74817	63.75736	52.06601	43.36635	36.77726	31.69847	27.71633	24.54234	21.97281	19.86205	18.10457	16.62295	15.35964	14.27133
103 ...	80.34644	64.11619	52.28178	43.49642	36.85586	31.74609	27.74525	24.55995	21.98355	19.86862	18.10860	16.62542	15.36117	14.27228
104 ...	80.94173	64.47148	52.49437	43.62394	36.93255	31.79232	27.77318	24.57687	21.99382	19.87488	18.11241	16.62776	15.36260	14.27315
105 ...	81.53406	64.82325	52.70387	43.74896	37.00736	31.83720	27.80018	24.59315	22.00366	19.88083	18.11603	16.62996	15.36394	14.27398
106 ...	82.12344	65.17153	52.91016	43.87153	37.08035	31.88078	27.82626	24.60879	22.01307	19.88651	18.11946	16.63204	15.36521	14.27474
107 ...	82.70989	65.51637	53.11346	43.99170	37.15156	31.92308	27.85146	24.62384	22.02208	19.89191	18.12271	16.63400	15.36639	14.27546
108 ...	83.29342	65.85779	53.31375	44.10951	37.22104	31.96416	27.87581	24.63831	22.03070	19.89706	18.12579	16.63585	15.36750	14.27613
109 ...	83.87405	66.19583	53.51108	44.22501	37.28882	32.00404	27.89933	24.65222	22.03894	19.90196	18.12872	16.63759	15.36855	14.27676
110 ...	84.45180	66.53053	53.70550	44.33824	37.35494	32.04276	27.92206	24.66560	22.04684	19.90663	18.13148	16.63924	15.36953	14.27735
111 ...	85.02666	66.86191	53.89704	44.44926	37.41946	32.08035	27.94402	24.67846	22.05439	19.91108	18.13411	16.64079	15.37045	14.27789
112 ...	85.59867	67.19001	54.08576	44.55810	37.48240	32.11684	27.96523	24.69082	22.06162	19.91531	18.13659	16.64226	15.37131	14.27840
113 ...	86.16783	67.51486	54.27168	44.66480	37.54380	32.15227	27.98573	24.70272	22.06853	19.91934	18.13895	16.64364	15.37212	14.27888
114 ...	86.73416	67.83649	54.45486	44.76941	37.60371	32.18667	28.00554	24.71415	22.07515	19.92318	18.14119	16.64494	15.37289	14.27933
115 ...	87.29767	68.15494	54.63533	44.87197	37.66216	32.22007	28.02467	24.72514	22.08148	19.92684	18.14331	16.64617	15.37360	14.27975
116 ...	87.85838	68.47024	54.81313	44.97252	37.71918	32.25250	28.04316	24.73571	22.08754	19.93033	18.14531	16.64733	15.37428	14.28014
117 ...	88.41630	68.78242	54.98831	45.07110	37.77481	32.28398	28.06103	24.74588	22.09334	19.93364	18.14722	16.64843	15.37491	14.28050
118 ...	88.97144	69.09150	55.16089	45.16775	37.82908	32.31454	28.07829	24.75565	22.09889	19.93680	18.14902	16.64946	15.37550	14.28084
119 ...	89.52382	69.39753	55.33093	45.26250	37.88203	32.34421	28.09496	24.76505	22.10420	19.93981	18.15073	16.65043	15.37606	14.28116
120 ...	90.07345	69.70052	55.49845	45.35539	37.93369	32.37302	28.11108	24.77409	22.10929	19.94268	18.15235	16.65135	15.37658	14.28146

Table 4 (*continued*)
Present Value of an Ordinary Annuity of $1 per Period: 7.5%–14%

Period	7.5%	8%	8.5%	9%	9.5%	10%	10.5%	11%	11.5%	12%	12.5%	13%	13.5%	14%
1	0.93023	0.92593	0.92166	0.91743	0.91324	0.90909	0.90498	0.90090	0.89686	0.89286	0.88889	0.88496	0.88106	0.87719
2	1.79557	1.78326	1.77111	1.75911	1.74725	1.73554	1.72396	1.71252	1.70122	1.69005	1.67901	1.66810	1.65732	1.64666
3	2.60053	2.57710	2.55402	2.53129	2.50891	2.48685	2.46512	2.44371	2.42262	2.40183	2.38134	2.36115	2.34125	2.32163
4	3.34933	3.31213	3.27560	3.23972	3.20448	3.16987	3.13586	3.10245	3.06961	3.03735	3.00564	2.97447	2.94383	2.91371
5	4.04588	3.99271	3.94064	3.88965	3.83971	3.79079	3.74286	3.69590	3.64988	3.60478	3.56057	3.51723	3.47474	3.43308
6	4.69385	4.62288	4.55359	4.48592	4.41983	4.35526	4.29218	4.23054	4.17029	4.11141	4.05384	3.99755	3.94250	3.88867
7	5.29660	5.20637	5.11851	5.03295	4.94961	4.86842	4.78930	4.71220	4.63704	4.56376	4.49230	4.42261	4.35463	4.28830
8	5.85730	5.74664	5.63918	5.53482	5.43344	5.33493	5.23919	5.14612	5.05564	4.96764	4.88205	4.79877	4.71774	4.63886
9	6.37889	6.24689	6.11906	5.99525	5.87528	5.75902	5.64632	5.53705	5.43106	5.32825	5.22848	5.13166	5.03765	4.94637
10	6.86408	6.71008	6.56135	6.41766	6.27880	6.14457	6.01477	5.88923	5.76777	5.65022	5.53643	5.42624	5.31952	5.21612
11	7.31542	7.13896	6.96898	6.80519	6.64730	6.49506	6.34821	6.20652	6.06975	5.93770	5.81016	5.68694	5.56786	5.45273
12	7.73528	7.53608	7.34469	7.16073	6.98384	6.81369	6.64996	6.49236	6.34058	6.19437	6.05348	5.91765	5.78666	5.66029
13	8.12584	7.90378	7.69095	7.48690	7.29118	7.10336	6.92304	6.74987	6.58348	6.42355	6.26976	6.12181	5.97943	5.84236
14	8.48915	8.24424	8.01010	7.78615	7.57185	7.36669	7.17018	6.98187	6.80133	6.62817	6.46201	6.30249	6.14928	6.00207
15	8.82712	8.55948	8.30424	8.06069	7.82818	7.60608	7.39382	7.19087	6.99671	6.81086	6.63289	6.46238	6.29893	6.14217
16	9.14151	8.85137	8.57533	8.31256	8.06226	7.82371	7.59622	7.37916	7.17194	6.97399	6.78479	6.60388	6.43077	6.26506
17	9.43396	9.12164	8.82519	8.54363	8.27604	8.02155	7.77939	7.54879	7.32909	7.11963	6.91982	6.72909	6.54694	6.37286
18	9.70601	9.37189	9.05548	8.75563	8.47127	8.20141	7.94515	7.70162	7.47004	7.24967	7.03984	6.83991	6.64928	6.46742
19	9.95908	9.60360	9.26772	8.95011	8.64956	8.36492	8.09515	7.83929	7.59644	7.36578	7.14652	6.93797	6.73946	6.55037
20	10.19449	9.81815	9.46334	9.12855	8.81238	8.51356	8.23091	7.96333	7.70982	7.46944	7.24135	7.02475	6.81890	6.62313
21	10.41348	10.01680	9.64363	9.29224	8.96108	8.64869	8.35376	8.07507	7.81149	7.56200	7.32565	7.10155	6.88890	6.68696
22	10.61719	10.20074	9.80980	9.44243	9.09688	8.77154	8.46494	8.17574	7.90269	7.64465	7.40058	7.16951	6.95057	6.74294
23	10.80669	10.37106	9.96295	9.58021	9.22089	8.88322	8.56556	8.26643	7.98447	7.71843	7.46718	7.22966	7.00491	6.79206
24	10.98297	10.52876	10.10410	9.70661	9.33415	8.98474	8.65662	8.34814	8.05782	7.78432	7.52638	7.28288	7.05279	6.83514
25	11.14695	10.67478	10.23419	9.82258	9.43758	9.07704	8.73902	8.42174	8.12361	7.84314	7.57901	7.32998	7.09497	6.87293
26	11.29948	10.80998	10.35409	9.92897	9.53203	9.16095	8.81359	8.48806	8.18261	7.89566	7.62578	7.37167	7.13213	6.90608
27	11.44138	10.93516	10.46460	10.02658	9.61830	9.23722	8.88108	8.54780	8.23552	7.94255	7.66736	7.40856	7.16487	6.93515
28	11.57338	11.05108	10.56645	10.11613	9.69707	9.30657	8.94215	8.60162	8.28298	7.98442	7.70432	7.44120	7.19372	6.96066
29	11.69617	11.15841	10.66033	10.19828	9.76902	9.36961	8.99742	8.65011	8.32554	8.02181	7.73717	7.47009	7.21914	6.98304
30	11.81039	11.25778	10.74684	10.27365	9.83472	9.42691	9.04744	8.69379	8.36371	8.05518	7.76638	7.49565	7.24153	7.00266
31	11.91664	11.34980	10.82658	10.34280	9.89472	9.47901	9.09271	8.73315	8.39795	8.08499	7.79234	7.51828	7.26126	7.01988
32	12.01548	11.43500	10.90008	10.40624	9.94952	9.52638	9.13367	8.76860	8.42866	8.11159	7.81541	7.53830	7.27864	7.03498
33	12.10742	11.51389	10.96781	10.46444	9.99956	9.56943	9.17074	8.80054	8.45619	8.13535	7.83592	7.55602	7.29396	7.04823
34	12.19295	11.58693	11.03024	10.51784	10.04526	9.60857	9.20429	8.82932	8.48089	8.15656	7.85415	7.57170	7.30745	7.05985
35	12.27251	11.65457	11.08778	10.56682	10.08699	9.64416	9.23465	8.85524	8.50304	8.17550	7.87036	7.58557	7.31934	7.07005
36	12.34652	11.71719	11.14081	10.61176	10.12511	9.67651	9.26213	8.87859	8.52291	8.19241	7.88476	7.59785	7.32982	7.07899
37	12.41537	11.77518	11.18969	10.65299	10.15992	9.70592	9.28700	8.89963	8.54072	8.20751	7.89757	7.60872	7.33904	7.08683
38	12.47941	11.82887	11.23474	10.69082	10.19171	9.73265	9.30950	8.91859	8.55670	8.22099	7.90895	7.61833	7.34718	7.09371
39	12.53899	11.87858	11.27625	10.72552	10.22074	9.75696	9.32986	8.93567	8.57103	8.23303	7.91906	7.62684	7.35434	7.09975
40	12.59441	11.92461	11.31452	10.75736	10.24725	9.77905	9.34829	8.95105	8.58389	8.24378	7.92806	7.63438	7.36065	7.10504
41	12.64596	11.96723	11.34979	10.78657	10.27146	9.79914	9.36497	8.96491	8.59541	8.25337	7.93605	7.64104	7.36621	7.10969
42	12.69392	12.00670	11.38229	10.81337	10.29357	9.81740	9.38006	8.97740	8.60575	8.26194	7.94316	7.64694	7.37111	7.11376
43	12.73853	12.04324	11.41225	10.83795	10.31376	9.83400	9.39372	8.98865	8.61502	8.26959	7.94947	7.65216	7.37543	7.11733
44	12.78003	12.07707	11.43986	10.86051	10.33220	9.84909	9.40608	8.99878	8.62334	8.27642	7.95509	7.65678	7.37923	7.12047
45	12.81863	12.10840	11.46531	10.88120	10.34904	9.86281	9.41727	9.00791	8.63080	8.28252	7.96008	7.66086	7.38258	7.12322
46	12.85454	12.13741	11.48877	10.90018	10.36442	9.87528	9.42739	9.01614	8.63749	8.28796	7.96451	7.66448	7.38554	7.12563
47	12.88794	12.16427	11.51038	10.91760	10.37847	9.88662	9.43656	9.02355	8.64349	8.29282	7.96846	7.66768	7.38814	7.12774
48	12.91902	12.18914	11.53031	10.93358	10.39130	9.89693	9.44485	9.03022	8.64887	8.29716	7.97196	7.67052	7.39043	7.12960
49	12.94792	12.21216	11.54867	10.94823	10.40301	9.90630	9.45235	9.03624	8.65369	8.30104	7.97508	7.67302	7.39245	7.13123
50	12.97481	12.23348	11.56560	10.96168	10.41371	9.91481	9.45914	9.04165	8.65802	8.30450	7.97785	7.67524	7.39423	7.13266
51	12.99982	12.25323	11.58119	10.97402	10.42348	9.92256	9.46529	9.04653	8.66190	8.30759	7.98031	7.67720	7.39580	7.13391
52	13.02309	12.27151	11.59557	10.98534	10.43240	9.92960	9.47085	9.05093	8.66538	8.31035	7.98250	7.67894	7.39718	7.13501
53	13.04474	12.28843	11.60882	10.99573	10.44055	9.93600	9.47588	9.05489	8.66850	8.31281	7.98444	7.68048	7.39839	7.13597
54	13.06487	12.30410	11.62103	11.00525	10.44799	9.94182	9.48043	9.05846	8.67130	8.31501	7.98617	7.68184	7.39947	7.13682
55	13.08360	12.31861	11.63229	11.01399	10.45478	9.94711	9.48456	9.06168	8.67382	8.31697	7.98771	7.68304	7.40041	7.13756
56	13.10103	12.33205	11.64266	11.02201	10.46099	9.95191	9.48829	9.06457	8.67607	8.31872	7.98907	7.68411	7.40124	7.13821
57	13.11723	12.34449	11.65222	11.02937	10.46666	9.95629	9.49166	9.06718	8.67809	8.32029	7.99029	7.68505	7.40198	7.13878
58	13.13231	12.35601	11.66104	11.03612	10.47183	9.96026	9.49472	9.06954	8.67991	8.32169	7.99137	7.68589	7.40262	7.13928
59	13.14633	12.36668	11.66916	11.04231	10.47656	9.96387	9.49748	9.07165	8.68152	8.32294	7.99232	7.68663	7.40319	7.13972
60	13.15938	12.37655	11.67664	11.04799	10.48088	9.96716	9.49998	9.07356	8.68298	8.32405	7.99318	7.68728	7.40369	7.14011

Period	7.5%	8%	8.5%	9%	9.5%	10%	10.5%	11%	11.5%	12%	12.5%	13%	13.5%	14%
61	13.17152	12.38570	11.68354	11.05320	10.48482	9.97014	9.50225	9.07528	8.68429	8.32504	7.99394	7.68786	7.40413	7.14044
62	13.18281	12.39416	11.68990	11.05798	10.48842	9.97286	9.50430	9.07683	8.68546	8.32593	7.99461	7.68837	7.40452	7.14074
63	13.19331	12.40200	11.69576	11.06237	10.49171	9.97532	9.50615	9.07822	8.68651	8.32673	7.99521	7.68882	7.40487	7.14100
64	13.20308	12.40926	11.70116	11.06640	10.49471	9.97757	9.50783	9.07948	8.68745	8.32743	7.99574	7.68922	7.40517	7.14123
65	13.21217	12.41598	11.70614	11.07009	10.49745	9.97961	9.50935	9.08061	8.68830	8.32807	7.99621	7.68958	7.40544	7.14143
66	13.22062	12.42221	11.71073	11.07347	10.49996	9.98146	9.51072	9.08163	8.68906	8.32863	7.99663	7.68989	7.40567	7.14160
67	13.22848	12.42797	11.71496	11.07658	10.50224	9.98315	9.51196	9.08255	8.68974	8.32913	7.99701	7.69017	7.40588	7.14176
68	13.23580	12.43330	11.71885	11.07943	10.50433	9.98468	9.51309	9.08338	8.69035	8.32958	7.99734	7.69042	7.40606	7.14189
69	13.24260	12.43825	11.72245	11.08205	10.50624	9.98607	9.51411	9.08413	8.69090	8.32999	7.99764	7.69063	7.40622	7.14201
70	13.24893	12.44282	11.72576	11.08445	10.50798	9.98734	9.51503	9.08480	8.69139	8.33034	7.99790	7.69083	7.40636	7.14211
71	13.25482	12.44706	11.72881	11.08665	10.50957	9.98849	9.51586	9.08541	8.69183	8.33066	7.99813	7.69100	7.40648	7.14221
72	13.26030	12.45098	11.73162	11.08867	10.51102	9.98954	9.51662	9.08595	8.69222	8.33095	7.99834	7.69115	7.40659	7.14229
73	13.26539	12.45461	11.73421	11.09052	10.51235	9.99049	9.51730	9.08644	8.69257	8.33121	7.99852	7.69128	7.40669	7.14236
74	13.27013	12.45797	11.73660	11.09222	10.51356	9.99135	9.51792	9.08688	8.69289	8.33143	7.99869	7.69140	7.40678	7.14242
75	13.27454	12.46108	11.73880	11:09378	10.51467	9.99214	9.51848	9.08728	8.69318	8.33164	7.99883	7.69150	7.40685	7.14247
76	13.27864	12.46397	11.74083	11.09521	10.51568	9.99285	9.51899	9.08764	8.69343	8.33182	7.99896	7.69160	7.40692	7.14252
77	13.28246	12.46664	11.74270	11.09653	10.51660	9.99350	9.51945	9.08797	8.69366	8.33198	7.99908	7.69168	7.40698	7.14256
78	13.28601	12.46911	11.74443	11.09773	10.51744	9.99409	9.51986	9.08826	8.69387	8.33213	7.99918	7.69175	7.40703	7.14260
79	13.28931	12.47140	11.74601	11.09883	10.51821	9.99463	9.52024	9.08852	8.69405	8.33226	7.99927	7.69181	7.40707	7.14263
80	13.29238	12.47351	11.74748	11.09985	10.51892	9.99512	9.52057	9.08876	8.69422	8.33237	7.99935	7.69187	7.40711	7.14266
81	13.29524	12.47548	11.74883	11.10078	10.51956	9.99556	9.52088	9.08897	8.69436	8.33247	7.99942	7.69192	7.40715	7.14268
82	13.29790	12.47729	11.75007	11.10163	10.52015	9.99597	9.52116	9.08916	8.69450	8.33257	7.99949	7.69197	7.40718	7.14270
83	13.30037	12.47897	11.75122	11.10241	10.52068	9.99633	9.52141	9.08934	8.69462	8.33265	7.99955	7.69201	7.40721	7.14272
84	13.30267	12.48053	11.75228	11.10313	10.52117	9.99667	9.52164	9.08949	8.69472	8.33272	7.99960	7.69204	7.40723	7.14274
85	13.30481	12.48197	11.75325	11.10379	10.52162	9.99697	9.52185	9.08963	8.69482	8.33279	7.99964	7.69207	7.40725	7.14275
86	13.30680	12.48331	11.75415	11.10440	10.52202	9.99724	9.52203	9.08976	8.69490	8.33285	7.99968	7.69210	7.40727	7.14277
87	13.30865	12.48455	11.75497	11.10495	10.52240	9.99749	9.52220	9.08987	8.69498	8.33290	7.99972	7.69212	7.40729	7.14278
88	13.31037	12.48569	11.75574	11.10546	10.52274	9.99772	9.52235	9.08998	8.69505	8.33294	7.99975	7.69214	7.40730	7.14279
89	13.31197	12.48675	11.75644	11.10593	10.52305	9.99793	9.52249	9.09007	8.69511	8.33299	7.99977	7.69216	7.40731	7.14280
90	13.31346	12.48773	11.75709	11.10635	10.52333	9.99812	9.52262	9.09015	8.69517	8.33302	7.99980	7.69218	7.40732	7.14280
91	13.31485	12.48864	11.75768	11.10675	10.52359	9.99829	9.52273	9.09023	8.69522	8.33306	7.99982	7.69219	7.40733	7.14281
92	13.31614	12.48948	11.75823	11.10711	10.52383	9.99844	9.52283	9.09029	8.69526	8.33309	7.99983	7.69221	7.40734	7.14282
93	13.31734	12.49026	11.75874	11.10744	10.52404	9.99859	9.52293	9.09036	8.69530	8.33311	7.99986	7.69222	7.40735	7.14282
94	13.31846	12.49098	11.75921	11.10774	10.52424	9.99871	9.52301	9.09041	8.69534	8.33314	7.99988	7.69223	7.40736	7.14283
95	13.31949	12.49165	11.75964	11.10802	10.52442	9.99883	9.52309	9.09046	8.69537	8.33316	7.99989	7.69224	7.40736	7.14283
96	13.32046	12.49227	11.76004	11.10827	10.52458	9.99894	9.52315	9.09050	8.69540	8.33318	7.99990	7.69225	7.40737	7.14283
97	13.32136	12.49284	11.76040	11.10851	10.52473	9.99903	9.52322	9.09054	8.69543	8.33319	7.99991	7.69225	7.40737	7.14284
98	13.32219	12.49337	11.76074	11.10872	10.52487	9.99912	9.52327	9.09058	8.69545	8.33321	7.99992	7.69226	7.40738	7.14284
99	13.32297	12.49386	11.76105	11.10892	10.52500	9.99920	9.52332	9.09061	8.69547	8.33322	7.99993	7.69226	7.40738	7.14284
100	13.32369	12.49432	11.76134	11.10910	10.52511	9.99927	9.52337	9.09064	8.69549	8.33323	7.99994	7.69227	7.40738	7.14284
101	13.32437	12.49474	11.76160	11.10927	10.52522	9.99934	9.52341	9.09067	8.69551	8.33324	7.99995	7.69227	7.40739	7.14284
102	13.32504	12.49513	11.76184	11.10942	10.52531	9.99940	9.52345	9.09069	8.69552	8.33325	7.99995	7.69228	7.40739	7.14285
103	13.32557	12.49549	11.76207	11.10956	10.52540	9.99945	9.52348	9.09071	8.69553	8.33326	7.99996	7.69228	7.40739	7.14285
104	13.32611	12.49582	11.76227	11.10969	10.52548	9.99950	9.52351	9.09073	8.69555	8.33327	7.99996	7.69228	7.40739	7.14285
105	13.32662	12.49613	11.76246	11.10981	10.52555	9.99955	9.52354	9.09075	8.69556	8.33328	7.99997	7.69229	7.40739	7.14285
106	13.32709	12.49642	11.76264	11.10991	10.52562	9.99959	9.52357	9.09077	8.69557	8.33328	7.99997	7.69229	7.40740	7.14285
107	13.32752	12.49668	11.76280	11.11001	10.52568	9.99963	9.52359	9.09078	8.69558	8.33329	7.99997	7.69229	7.40740	7.14285
108	13.32793	12.49693	11.76295	11.11010	10.52573	9.99966	9.52361	9.09079	8.69558	8.33329	7.99998	7.69229	7.40740	7.14285
109	13.32831	12.49716	11.76309	11.11019	10.52578	9.99969	9.52363	9.09080	8.69559	8.33330	7.99998	7.69230	7.40740	7.14285
110	13.32866	12.49737	11.76322	11.11026	10.52583	9.99972	9.52365	9.09082	8.69560	8.33330	7.99998	7.69230	7.40740	7.14285
111	13.32898	12.49756	11.76333	11.11033	10.52587	9.99975	9.52366	9.09082	8.69560	8.33330	7.99998	7.69230	7.40740	7.14285
112	13.32929	12.49774	11.76344	11.11040	10.52591	9.99977	9.52368	9.09083	8.69561	8.33331	7.99999	7.69230	7.40740	7.14285
113	13.32957	12.49791	11.76354	11.11046	10.52595	9.99979	9.52369	9.09084	8.69561	8.33331	7.99999	7.69230	7.40740	7.14285
114	13.32983	12.49807	11.76363	11.11051	10.52598	9.99981	9.52370	9.09085	8.69562	8.33331	7.99999	7.69230	7.40740	7.14285
115	13.33008	12.49821	11.76371	11.11056	10.52601	9.99983	9.52371	9.09085	8.69562	8.33332	7.99999	7.69230	7.40740	7.14286
116	13.33030	12.49834	11.76379	11.11060	10.52603	9.99984	9.52372	9.09086	8.69562	8.33332	7.99999	7.69230	7.40740	7.14286
117	13.33051	12.49846	11.76386	11.11065	10.52606	9.99986	9.52373	9.09086	8.69563	8.33332	7.99999	7.69230	7.40740	7.14286
118	13.33071	12.49858	11.76393	11.11069	10.52608	9.99987	9.52374	9.09087	8.69563	8.33332	7.99999	7.69230	7.40741	7.14286
119	13.33089	12.49868	11.76399	11.11072	10.52610	9.99988	9.52374	9.09087	8.69563	8.33332	7.99999	7.69230	7.40741	7.14286
120	13.33106	12.49878	11.76405	11.11075	10.52612	9.99989	9.52375	9.09088	8.69563	8.33332	7.99999	7.69230	7.40741	7.14286

Table 4 (*concluded*)
Present Value of an Ordinary Annuity of $1 per Period: 14.5%–20%

Period	14.5%	15%	15.5%	16%	16.5%	17%	17.5%	18%	18.5%	19%	19.5%	20%
1	0.87336	0.86957	0.86580	0.86207	0.85837	0.85470	0.85106	0.84746	0.84388	0.84034	0.83682	0.83333
2	1.63612	1.62571	1.61541	1.60523	1.59517	1.58521	1.57537	1.56564	1.55602	1.54650	1.53709	1.52778
3	2.30229	2.28323	2.26443	2.24589	2.22761	2.20958	2.19181	2.17427	2.15698	2.13992	2.12309	2.10648
4	2.88410	2.85498	2.82634	2.79818	2.77048	2.74324	2.71643	2.69006	2.66412	2.63859	2.61346	2.58873
5	3.39223	3.35216	3.31285	3.27429	3.23646	3.19935	3.16292	3.12717	3.09208	3.05763	3.02382	2.99061
6	3.83600	3.78448	3.73407	3.68474	3.63645	3.58918	3.54291	3.49760	3.45323	3.40978	3.36721	3.32551
7	4.22358	4.16042	4.09876	4.03857	3.97979	3.92238	3.86631	3.81153	3.75800	3.70570	3.65457	3.60459
8	4.56208	4.48732	4.41451	4.34359	4.27449	4.20716	4.14154	4.07757	4.01519	3.95437	3.89504	3.83716
9	4.85771	4.77158	4.68789	4.60654	4.52746	4.45057	4.37578	3.30302	4.23223	4.16333	4.09627	4.03097
10	5.11591	5.01877	4.92458	4.83323	4.74460	4.65860	4.57513	4.49409	4.41538	4.33893	4.26466	4.19247
11	5.34140	5.23371	5.12951	5.02864	4.93099	4.83641	4.74479	4.65601	4.56994	4.48650	4.40557	4.32706
12	5.53834	5.42062	5.30693	5.19711	5.09098	4.98839	4.88918	4.79322	4.70037	4.61050	4.52349	4.43922
13	5.71034	5.58315	5.46055	5.34233	5.22831	5.11828	5.01207	4.90951	4.81044	4.71471	4.62217	4.53268
14	5.86056	5.72448	5.59355	5.46753	5.34619	5.22930	5.11666	5.00806	4.90333	4.80228	4.70474	4.61057
15	5.99176	5.84737	5.70870	5.57546	5.44747	5.32419	5.20567	5.09158	4.98171	4.87586	4.77384	4.67547
16	6.10634	5.95423	5.80840	5.66850	5.53422	5.40529	5.28142	5.16235	5.04786	4.93770	4.83167	4.72956
17	6.20641	6.04716	5.89472	5.74870	5.60878	5.47461	5.34589	5.22233	5.10368	4.98966	4.88006	4.77463
18	6.29381	6.12797	5.96945	5.81785	5.67277	5.53385	5.40075	5.27316	5.15078	5.03333	4.92055	4.81219
19	6.37014	6.19823	6.03416	5.87746	5.72770	5.58449	5.44745	5.31624	5.19053	5.07003	4.95443	4.84350
20	6.43680	6.25933	6.09018	5.92884	5.77485	5.62777	5.48719	5.35275	5.22408	5.10086	4.98279	4.86958
21	6.49502	6.31246	6.13868	5.97314	5.81532	5.66476	5.52101	5.38368	5.25239	5.12677	5.00652	4.89132
22	6.54587	6.35866	6.18068	6.01133	5.85006	5.69637	5.54980	5.40990	5.27628	5.14855	5.02638	4.90943
23	6.59028	6.39884	6.21704	6.04425	5.87988	5.72340	5.57430	5.43212	5.29644	5.16685	5.04299	4.92453
24	6.62907	6.43377	6.24852	6.07263	5.90548	5.74649	5.59515	5.45095	5.31345	5.18223	5.05690	4.93710
25	6.66294	6.46415	6.27577	6.09709	5.92745	5.76623	5.61289	5.46691	5.32780	5.19515	5.06853	4.94759
26	6.69252	6.49056	6.29937	6.11818	5.94631	5.78311	5.62799	5.48043	5.33992	5.20601	5.07827	4.95632
27	6.71836	6.51353	6.31980	6.13636	5.96250	5.79753	5.64084	5.49189	5.35014	5.21513	5.08642	4.96360
28	6.74093	6.53351	6.33749	6.15204	5.97639	5.80985	5.65178	5.50160	5.35877	5.22280	5.09324	4.96967
29	6.76064	6.55088	6.35281	6.16555	5.98832	5.82039	5.66109	5.50983	5.36605	5.22924	5.09894	4.97472
30	6.77785	6.56598	6.36607	6.17720	5.99856	5.82939	5.66901	5.51681	5.37219	5.23466	5.10372	4.97894
31	6.79288	6.57911	6.37755	6.18724	6.00734	5.83709	5.67576	5.52272	5.37738	5.23921	5.10771	4.98245
32	6.80601	6.59053	6.38749	6.19590	6.01489	5.84366	5.68150	5.52773	5.38175	5.24303	5.11106	4.98537
33	6.81747	6.60046	6.39609	6.20336	6.02136	5.84928	5.68638	5.53197	5.38545	5.24625	5.11386	4.98781
34	6.82749	6.60910	6.40354	6.20979	6.02692	5.85409	5.69054	5.53557	5.38856	5.24895	5.11620	4.98984
35	6.83623	6.61661	6.40999	6.21534	6.03169	5.85820	5.69407	5.53862	5.39119	5.25122	5.11816	4.99154
36	6.84387	6.62314	6.41558	6.22012	6.03579	5.86171	5.69708	5.54120	5.39341	5.25312	5.11980	4.99295
37	6.85054	6.62881	6.42041	6.22424	6.03930	5.86471	5.69965	5.54339	5.39528	5.25472	5.12117	4.99412
38	6.85637	6.63375	6.42460	6.22779	6.04232	5.86727	5.70183	5.54525	5.39686	5.25607	5.12232	4.99510
39	6.86146	6.63805	6.42823	6.23086	6.04491	5.86946	5.70368	5.54682	5.39820	5.25720	5.12328	4.99592
40	6.86590	6.64178	6.43136	6.23350	6.04713	5.87133	5.70526	5.54815	5.39932	5.25815	5.12408	4.99660
41	6.86978	6.64502	6.43408	6.23577	6.04904	5.87294	5.70660	5.54928	5.40027	5.25895	5.12475	4.99717
42	6.87317	6.64785	6.43643	6.23774	6.05068	5.87430	5.70775	5.55024	5.40107	5.25962	5.12532	4.99764
43	6.87613	6.65030	6.43847	6.23943	6.05208	5.87547	5.70872	5.55105	5.40175	5.26019	5.12579	4.99803
44	6.87872	6.65244	6.44024	6.24089	6.05329	5.87647	5.70955	5.55174	5.40232	5.26066	5.12618	4.99836
45	6.88098	6.65429	6.44176	6.24214	6.05433	5.87733	5.71026	5.55232	5.40280	5.26106	5.12651	4.99863
46	6.88295	6.65591	6.44308	6.24323	6.05522	5.87806	5.71086	5.55281	5.40321	5.26140	5.12679	4.99886
47	6.88467	6.65731	6.44423	6.24416	6.05598	5.87868	5.71137	5.55323	5.40355	5.26168	5.12702	4.99905
48	6.88618	6.65853	6.44522	6.24497	6.05664	5.87922	5.71180	5.55359	5.40384	5.26191	5.12721	4.99921
49	6.88749	6.65959	6.44608	6.24566	6.05720	5.87967	5.71217	5.55389	5.40409	5.26211	5.12738	4.99934
50	6.88864	6.66051	6.44682	6.24626	6.05768	5.88006	5.71249	5.55414	5.40429	5.26228	5.12751	4.99945
51	6.88964	6.66132	6.44746	6.24678	6.05809	5.88039	5.71275	5.55436	5.40447	5.26242	5.12762	4.99954
52	6.89052	6.66201	6.44802	6.24722	6.05845	5.88068	5.71298	5.55454	5.40461	5.26254	5.12772	4.99962
53	6.89128	6.66262	6.44850	6.24760	6.05876	5.88092	5.71318	5.55469	5.40474	5.26264	5.12780	4.99968
54	6.89195	6.66315	6.44892	6.24793	6.05902	5.88113	5.71334	5.55483	5.40484	5.26272	5.12786	4.99974
55	6.89253	6.66361	6.44928	6.24822	6.05924	5.88131	5.71348	5.55494	5.40493	5.26279	5.12792	4.99978
56	6.89304	6.66401	6.44959	6.24846	6.05944	5.88146	5.71360	5.55503	5.40500	5.26285	5.12797	4.99982
57	6.89348	6.66435	6.44987	6.24868	6.05960	5.88159	5.71370	5.55511	5.40507	5.26290	5.12801	4.99985
58	6.89387	6.66466	6.45010	6.24886	6.05974	5.88170	5.71379	5.55518	5.40512	5.26294	5.12804	4.99987
59	6.89421	6.66492	6.45030	6.24902	6.05987	5.88180	5.71386	5.55524	5.40516	5.26297	5.12807	4.99989
60	6.89451	6.66515	6.45048	6.24915	6.05997	5.88188	5.71393	5.55529	5.40520	5.26300	5.12809	4.99991

Period	14.5%	15%	15.5%	16%	16.5%	17%	17.5%	18%	18.5%	19%	19.5%	20%
61	6.89477	6.66534	6.45063	6.24927	6.06006	5.88195	5.71398	5.55533	5.40523	5.26303	5.12811	4.99993
62	6.89499	6.66552	6.45076	6.24937	6.06014	5.88200	5.71403	5.55536	5.40526	5.26305	5.12812	4.99994
63	6.89519	6.66567	6.45088	6.24946	6.06020	5.88206	5.71406	5.55539	5.40528	5.26307	5.12814	4.99995
64	6.89536	6.66580	6.45098	6.24953	6.06026	5.88210	5.71410	5.55542	5.40530	5.26308	5.12815	4.99996
65	6.89551	6.66591	6.45106	6.24960	6.06031	5.88214	5.71413	5.55544	5.40532	5.26309	5.12816	4.99996
66	6.89565	6.66601	6.45114	6.24965	6.06035	5.88217	5.71415	5.55546	5.40533	5.26310	5.12816	4.99997
67	6.89576	6.66609	6.45120	6.24970	6.06039	5.88219	5.71417	5.55547	5.40534	5.26311	5.12817	4.99998
68	6.89586	6.66617	6.45125	6.24974	6.06042	5.88222	5.71419	5.55548	5.40535	5.26312	5.12818	4.99998
69	6.89595	6.66623	6.45130	6.24978	6.06045	5.88224	5.71420	5.55549	5.40536	5.26313	5.12818	4.99998
70	6.89602	6.66629	6.45134	6.24981	6.06047	5.88225	5.71421	5.55550	5.40537	5.26313	5.12819	4.99999
71	6.89609	6.66634	6.45138	6.24983	6.06049	5.88227	5.71422	5.55551	5.40537	5.26314	5.12819	4.99999
72	6.89615	6.66638	6.45141	6.24986	6.06050	5.88228	5.71423	5.55552	5.40538	5.26314	5.12819	4.99999
73	6.89620	6.66642	6.45144	6.24988	6.06052	5.88229	5.71424	5.55552	5.40538	5.26314	5.12819	4.99999
74	6.89624	6.66645	6.45146	6.24989	6.06053	5.88230	5.71425	5.55553	5.40539	5.26314	5.12820	4.99999
75	6.89628	6.66648	6.45148	6.24991	6.06054	5.88231	5.71425	5.55553	5.40539	5.26315	5.12820	4.99999
76	6.89632	6.66650	6.45150	6.24992	6.06055	5.88231	5.71426	5.55554	5.40539	5.26315	5.12820	5.00000
77	6.89635	6.66653	6.45151	6.24993	6.06056	5.88232	5.71426	5.55554	5.40539	5.26315	5.12820	5.00000
78	6.89637	6.66654	6.45153	6.24994	6.06057	5.88232	5.71427	5.55554	5.40540	5.26315	5.12820	5.00000
79	6.89640	6.66656	6.45154	6.24995	6.06057	5.88233	5.71427	5.55554	5.40540	5.26315	5.12820	5.00000
80	6.89642	6.66657	6.45155	6.24996	6.06058	5.88233	5.71427	5.55555	5.40540	5.26315	5.12820	5.00000
81	6.89643	6.66659	6.45156	6.24996	6.06058	5.88234	5.71427	5.55555	5.40540	5.26315	5.12820	5.00000
82	6.89645	6.66660	6.45157	6.24997	6.06058	5.88234	5.71428	5.55555	5.40540	5.26315	5.12820	5.00000
83	6.89646	6.66661	6.45157	6.24997	6.06059	5.88234	5.71428	5.55555	5.40540	5.26316	5.12820	5.00000
84	6.89647	6.66661	6.45158	6.24998	6.06059	5.88234	5.71428	5.55555	5.40540	5.26316	5.12820	5.00000
85	6.89648	6.66662	6.45158	6.24998	6.06059	5.88234	5.71428	5.55555	5.40540	5.26316	5.12820	5.00000
86	6.89649	6.66663	6.45159	6.24998	6.06059	5.88234	5.71428	5.55555	5.40540	5.26316	5.12820	5.00000
87	6.89650	6.66663	6.45159	6.24998	6.06060	5.88235	5.71428	5.55555	5.40540	5.26316	5.12820	5.00000
88	6.89651	6.66664	6.45159	6.24999	6.06060	5.88235	5.71428	5.55555	5.40540	5.26316	5.12820	5.00000
89	6.89651	6.66664	6.45160	6.24999	6.06060	5.88235	5.71428	5.55555	5.40540	5.26316	5.12820	5.00000
90	6.89652	6.66664	6.45160	6.24999	6.06060	5.88235	5.71428	5.55555	5.40540	5.26316	5.12820	5.00000
91	6.89652	6.66665	6.45160	6.24999	6.06060	5.88235	5.71428	5.55555	5.40540	5.26316	5.12820	5.00000
92	6.89652	6.66665	6.45160	6.24999	6.06060	5.88235	5.71428	5.55555	5.40540	5.26316	5.12820	5.00000
93	6.89653	6.66665	6.45160	6.24999	6.06060	5.88235	5.71428	5.55555	5.40540	5.26316	5.12820	5.00000
94	6.89653	6.66665	6.45160	6.24999	6.06060	5.88235	5.71428	5.55555	5.40540	5.26316	5.12820	5.00000
95	6.89653	6.66666	6.45161	6.25000	6.06060	5.88235	5.71428	5.55555	5.40540	5.26316	5.12820	5.00000
96	6.89654	6.66666	6.45161	6.25000	6.06060	5.88235	5.71428	5.55555	5.40540	5.26316	5.12820	5.00000
97	6.89654	6.66666	6.45161	6.25000	6.06060	5.88235	5.71428	5.55555	5.40541	5.26316	5.12820	5.00000
98	6.89654	6.66666	6.45161	6.25000	6.06060	5.88235	5.71428	5.55556	5.40541	5.26316	5.12820	5.00000
99	6.89654	6.66666	6.45161	6.25000	6.06060	5.88235	5.71429	5.55556	5.40541	5.26316	5.12821	5.00000
100	6.89654	6.66666	6.45161	6.25000	6.06060	5.88235	5.71429	5.55556	5.40541	5.26316	5.12821	5.00000
101	6.89654	6.66666	6.45161	6.25000	6.06060	5.88235	5.71429	5.55556	5.40541	5.26316	5.12821	5.00000
102	6.89654	6.66666	6.45161	6.25000	6.06061	5.88235	5.71429	5.55556	5.40541	5.26316	5.12821	5.00000
103	6.89655	6.66666	6.45161	6.25000	6.06061	5.88235	5.71429	5.55556	5.40541	5.26316	5.12821	5.00000
104	6.89655	6.66666	6.45161	6.25000	6.06061	5.88235	5.71429	5.55556	5.40541	5.26316	5.12821	5.00000
105	6.89655	6.66666	6.45161	6.25000	6.06061	5.88235	5.71429	5.55556	5.40541	5.26316	5.12821	5.00000
106	6.89655	6.66666	6.45161	6.25000	6.06061	5.88235	5.71429	5.55556	5.40541	5.26316	5.12821	5.00000
107	6.89655	6.66666	6.45161	6.25000	6.06061	5.88235	5.71429	5.55556	5.40541	5.26316	5.12821	5.00000
108	6.89655	6.66666	6.45161	6.25000	6.06061	5.88235	5.71429	5.55556	5.40541	5.26316	5.12821	5.00000
109	6.89655	6.66667	6.45161	6.25000	6.06061	5.88235	5.71429	5.55556	5.40541	5.26316	5.12821	5.00000
110	6.89655	6.66667	6.45161	6.25000	6.06061	5.88235	5.71429	5.55556	5.40541	5.26316	5.12821	5.00000
111	6.89655	6.66667	6.45161	6.25000	6.06061	5.88235	5.71429	5.55556	5.40541	5.26316	5.12821	5.00000
112	6.89655	6.66667	6.45161	6.25000	6.06061	5.88235	5.71429	5.55556	5.40541	5.26316	5.12821	5.00000
113	6.89655	6.66667	6.45161	6.25000	6.06061	5.88235	5.71429	5.55556	5.40541	5.26316	5.12821	5.00000
114	6.89655	6.66667	6.45161	6.25000	6.06061	5.88235	5.71429	5.55556	5.40541	5.26316	5.12821	5.00000
115	6.89655	6.66667	6.45161	6.25000	6.06061	5.88235	5.71429	5.55556	5.40541	5.26316	5.12821	5.00000
116	6.89655	6.66667	6.45161	6.25000	6.06061	5.88235	5.71429	5.55556	5.40541	5.26316	5.12821	5.00000
117	6.89655	6.66667	6.45161	6.25000	6.06061	5.88235	5.71429	5.55556	5.40541	5.26316	5.12821	5.00000
118	6.89655	6.66667	6.45161	6.25000	6.06061	5.88235	5.71429	5.55556	5.40541	5.26316	5.12821	5.00000
119	6.89655	6.66667	6.45161	6.25000	6.06061	5.88235	5.71429	5.55556	5.40541	5.26316	5.12821	5.00000
120	6.89655	6.66667	6.45161	6.25000	6.06061	5.88235	5.71429	5.55556	5.40541	5.26316	5.12821	5.00000

Index